The Arts of Deception

The Arts of
DECEPTION

PLAYING WITH FRAUD IN THE AGE OF BARNUM

JAMES W. COOK

HARVARD UNIVERSITY PRESS

Cambridge, Massachusetts, and London, England

2001

Library of Congress Cataloging-in-Publication Data
Cook, James W., 1966–
The arts of deception : playing with fraud in the age of Barnum /
James W. Cook.
p.   cm.
Includes bibliographical references and index.
ISBN 0-674-00457-4 (cloth : alk. paper)—
ISBN 0-674-00591-0 (paper : alk. paper)
1. Popular culture—United States—History—19th century.
2. Fraud—Social aspects—United States—History—19th century.
3. Tricksters—United States—History—19th century. 4. Impostors
and imposture—United States—History—19th century. 5. United
States—Social life and customs—19th century. 6. Barnum, P. T.
(Phineas Taylor), 1810–1891. 7. Trompe l'oeil painting—United
States—History—19th century. 8. Magic tricks—United States—
History—19th century. 9. Robots—United States—History—
19th century. I. Title.

E166.C77 2001
973.5—dc21   00-054133

For Rita

Acknowledgments

⊷≡⊙ ⊙≡⊶

Somewhat paradoxically, this book about tricks has grown out of the genuine kindness, sincere generosity, and bona fide criticism of many individuals. It is a great pleasure to thank them all now.

The first outlines of the project emerged in a 1991 seminar paper on *trompe l'oeil* painting that I wrote for Lawrence Levine, who later became my dissertation adviser at the University of California, Berkeley. More than anyone else, Larry taught me how to read, think, and write as a cultural historian. I am enormously grateful for the warm friendship and support that he and Cornelia Levine have given me. Three other Berkeley professors offered expert guidance. Martin Jay suggested many useful sources and helped me sort through a number of tricky theoretical debates. Although Margaretta Lovell was on leave when I began the dissertation, she generously served as an unofficial committee member and welcomed me into her fold of U.S. art historians. At key moments, Don McQuade provided encouragement, inspiration, and ideas. I was also fortunate to have a remarkably talented circle of graduate student friends in Berkeley. Thanks especially to

Acknowledgments

Sam Weinstein, Patrick Rael, Sara Webber, Leif Brown, Marc Davis, Eric Avila, Jill Ginstling, Adam White, Ralph Squillace, Mike Thompson, Derrick Cartwright, Nancy Edwards, Arthur McKee, Brigitte Koenig, Phil Soffer, Paul Reiter, and Ben Reiss.

As the project grew into a book, many colleagues around the country offered citations, encouragement, readings, and advice. John Kasson helped at every stage and in countless ways; his own work on nineteenth-century culture is one of the real inspirations for this book. Bluford Adams was my best Barnum colleague and critic. I am very grateful for the friendship that emerged from all those e-mails, letters, and conversations. Wanda Corn listened to my ideas about *trompe l'oeil* and invited me to great dinners on the other side of the Bay. Jim Green pulled off perhaps the greatest trick of all—finding tickets to see Ricky Jay in New York City. Big thanks also to Waldo Martin, Louise Stevenson, Rosemarie Thomson, Marc Simpson, Mary Witkowski, Fred Pfening, Neil Harris, John Demos, Michael O'Malley, Roy Rosenzweig, Ann Fabian, Bernth Linfors, Faye Dudden, Kenneth Cmiel, Joan Higbee, Janet Davis, Martha Burns, Lisa Lock, Shane White, Jim Gilbert, and Gina Morantz-Sanchez.

The final years of writing and editing were good ones largely because of close friends in Indianapolis and Oberlin. I am especially grateful to Sylvie Vanbaelen, Randy Johnson, Pratima Prasad, Terri Carney, Andy Levy, Hilene Flanzbaum, Steve Perrill, Isaac Miller, Carolyn Fraser, Wendy Kozol, and all of my wonderful colleagues in the Department of History at Butler University. These people taught me much of what I know about the arts of community.

Financial support came from the Jacob Javits Fellowship Program at the U.S. Department of Education; the Mabelle McLeod Lewis Trust; the University of California Heller Fund and Humanities Research Grant Programs; the Library Company of Philadelphia; and the Butler University Faculty Research Grant Program. My research was further aided by the staffs of the Library of Congress Rare Book Division; the Smithsonian Institution Archives; the Historical Society of Pennsylvania; the Library Company of Philadelphia; the New York Public Library Manuscripts Collection; the American Art Study Cen-

Acknowledgments

ter at the De Young Museum; the National Portrait Gallery; the Shelburne Museum; the Hertzberg Circus Collection; the Parkinson Library and Research Center at the Circus World Museum; the Bridgeport Public Library; the Barnum Museum; the Syracuse University Rare Books Division; the University of Pennsylvania Rare Books Division; and the inter-library loan office at Butler University.

At Harvard University Press, Joyce Seltzer provided virtuoso editing; David Lobenstine and Anita Safran gave thoughtful, patient assistance throughout the production process. I am especially grateful to Joyce for her faith and enthusiasm at a very early stage.

Finally, my biggest debts are to my family. My parents, Connie and Jim Cook, have steadfastly supported this book with enthusiasm, kindness, and deep interest. Amy Cook and Dottie Webb provided much-needed diversions and a healthy sense of humor about the whole process. Mari and Lay Chin offered warm encouragement and wonderful visits. Rita Chin's tremendous gifts of love, patience, time, and ideas gave me the strength to write this book. She read every page of every draft, helped me unravel the toughest questions, and kept me going, year after year. Support of such magnitude deserves much more than a few short lines at the end. It's the kind of help that is only adequately repaid by doing the same—for her book.

Portions of Chapters 1 and 3 have appeared in somewhat different form as "From the Age of Reason to the Age of Barnum: the Great Automaton Chess-Player and the Emergence of Victorian Cultural Illusionism," *Winterthur Portfolio*, 30/4 (Winter 1995), pp. 231–257; and "Of Men, Missing Links, and Nondescripts: The Strange Career of P. T. Barnum's 'What Is It?' Exhibition," in *Freakery: Cultural Spectacles of the Extraordinary Body*, ed. Rosemarie Garland Thomson (New York: New York University Press, 1996), pp. 139–157.

Contents

Illustrations

⊷⫧⊜ ⊜⫧⊷

Illustrations

Illustrations

The Arts of Deception

Introduction
Thinking with Tricks

Wonderful, because mysterious.
—P. T. Barnum, 1865

⋯⟹ ⟸⋯

For Phineas Taylor Barnum, show business opportunity came knocking at the door of his grocery store in late July 1835. It arrived in the shape of Mr. Coley Bartram, a fellow Connecticut Yankee with some experience in the show trade, who directed Barnum's attention to an advertisement in the *Pennsylvania Inquirer*. Taking the newspaper from Bartram, the twenty-five-year-old grocer began to read:

> CURIOSITY—The citizens of Philadelphia and its vicinity have an opportunity of witnessing at the Masonic Hall, one of the greatest natural curiosities ever witnessed, viz., JOICE HETH, a negress aged 161 years, who formerly belonged to the father of Gen. Washington. She has been a member of the Baptist Church one hundred and sixteen years, and can rehearse many hymns, and sing them according to former custom. She was born near the old Potomac River in Virginia, and has for ninety or one hundred years lived in Paris, Kentucky, with the Bowling family.

Young Barnum had spent much of the past year searching for a foothold in the exhibition business, so Bartram's news that Heth's current

Portrait commissioned by P. T. Barnum for the 1855 edition of his autobiography. The engraving by E. Teel is from a daguerrotype by Root & Company.

managers were "anxious to sell out" struck a powerful and immediate chord. "The New York newspapers," Barnum later explained, "had already furnished descriptions of this wonderful personage, and becoming considerably excited upon the subject, I proceeded at once to Philadelphia and had an interview . . . at the Masonic Hall."[1]

Traveling exhibitions such as the one Barnum discovered in the *Pennsylvania Inquirer* were not especially rare. Years later Barnum claimed that he had read about dozens of available curiosities for hire in the New York newspapers, but had decided not to pursue them—at least not in the same impulsive, drop-everything-and-go sort of way that Joice Heth inspired.[2] In this short paragraph from Philadelphia, however, Barnum sensed the makings of something remarkable: an exhibition which might appeal to a broad audience of consumers; a potentially lucrative exhibition which might liberate him from a series of dead-end jobs (traveling salesman, boarding house manager, grocer, etc.); an exhibition which, to Barnum's youthful eyes at least, looked so undeniably promising that it warranted the risky prospect of abandoning his partnership in the lower Manhattan grocery, draining his savings, taking out an additional loan, and traveling one hundred miles to cinch the deal. We know now that Barnum's gut instincts about Joice Heth and the American public proved to be right on target—more so, perhaps, than even he realized at the time. Indeed, if we were to pick a single moment to mark the birthdate of modern American popular culture, this just might be the one: on that fateful afternoon in July 1835, when an aspiring impresario from Bethel, Connecticut took off his grocer's apron and began to think seriously about how to market Joice Heth as a popular curiosity in New York City.[3]

By early August, Barnum signed a contract to exhibit Heth for ten months and booked a room in the fashionable entertainment center at Broadway and Prince Streets owned by William Niblo, one of Manhattan's leading cultural entrepreneurs at the time.[4] The particular location of this booking linked Barnum and Heth to a major development in American cultural history: the massive expansion of commercial entertainment that was beginning to take shape on and around lower Broadway.[5] It also connected Barnum to a particular mode of popular culture that would pervade this urban entertainment district (and others around the country like it) throughout the nineteenth century: what might be described, collectively, as *artful deception.* The large space Barnum secured for his 1835 debut, for example, had earlier been developed as a showplace for panorama paintings, a widely popular form of *trompe l'oeil* entertainment, in which material props

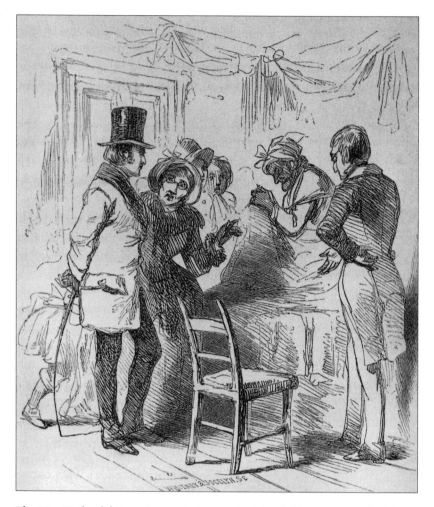

The Joice Heth exhibition at Boston's Concert Hall, 1835. The viewers on the left may be the "ex-congressman and his mother," from the anecdote in Barnum's autobiography. The man gesturing on the right is probably Levi Lyman.

and concealed lighting effects were positioned around minutely detailed murals to produce dazzling feats of verisimilitude. At the nearby American Museum on Broadway and Ann Streets (which Barnum would soon acquire and manage), viewers similarly paid their quarters to witness a "diorama of the dreadful fire in New York."

Introduction

Appearing next door at Niblo's Gardens was the popular Monsieur Adrien, one of the first individuals to perform sleight of hand on a fashionable stage in this country. And at the recently built Masonic Hall a few doors down, there was Signor Antonio Blitz, antebellum America's most successful magician on the urban exhibition circuit, who—like Barnum—was making his New York show business debut at this very same moment.[6]

To compete for viewers within this burgeoning marketplace of playful frauds, Barnum initially chose the tried and true, adhering to the show business formula developed by Heth's former managers: a quintessentially antebellum American mixture of pseudo-scientific analysis, racist gawking, energetic patriotism, and pious musical entertainment. The show began with a brief lecture on Heth's age and physical condition delivered by Barnum's early assistant, Levi Lyman, *physical appearance* during which viewers were encouraged to ask questions and personally examine Heth's diminutive, wrinkled body ("very much like an Egyptian mummy just escaped from the Sarcophagus," according to the *Evening Star*).[7] Viewers also listened to detailed stories about Heth's close relationship to the nation's patriarch. "She was the slave *relation to G.W.* of Augustine Washington (the father of George Washington)," Lyman explained to the crowds, "and was the first person who put clothes on the unconscious infant"—a presentation which sought to establish Heth as the archetypal black "mammy" figure for the white Virginia boy who later became the "father of the country."[8] To reinforce this caricature, Heth entertained viewers with anecdotes of her young *relation to Civil War* master and spoke of the redcoats during the Revolutionary War, noting with proper patriotic fervor that she had not held the British forces in high esteem. And finally, as a kind of musical afterpiece, she sang numerous hymns according to eighteenth-century tradition, a per- *relation to religion* formance that reportedly pleased New York's clergy and seemed to confirm Lyman's claim that Heth had been a member of the Baptist Church for over one hundred years.[9]

Barnum's New York script for the Joice Heth exhibition, in short, relied on a mutually reinforcing trio of promotional seductions: the "strangeness" of Heth's physical appearance in the eyes of Barnum's white audiences; the presumed historical connection between Heth and the infant Washington; and the cultural credibility of Heth as a singer of Baptist hymns. Yet the effectiveness of these interwoven marketing ploys ultimately hinged upon one basic question of authenticity: was this elderly African-American woman sitting on the couch in Niblo's establishment the 161-year-old former slave promised by the showman's firestorm of advertising? Barnum pointed his New York viewers to a framed bill of sale carrying the names of both Heth and Augustine Washington. Each performance began with Lyman reading aloud from the document, to authenticate the age and the biographical details that followed.[10] In his advertisements, Barnum spoke of the bill frequently:

> Original, authentic and indisputable documents prove however astonishing the fact may appear, JOICE HETH is in every respect the person she is represented. The most eminent physicians and intelligent men in Cincinnati, Philadelphia, New York, Boston and many other places have examined this *living skeleton* and the documents accompanying her, and all *invariably* pronounce her to be as represented 161 *years of age!* Indeed it is impossible for any person, however incredulous, to visit her without astonishment and the most perfect satisfaction that she is as old as represented.[11]

Within the next quarter century Barnum would become one the most (in)famous trickster figures in Western cultural history, so it is worth noting his references here to Heth as a form of "representation"—a strangely precocious term which raised the possibility that this exhibition was simply an elaborate hoax. While the showman's advertisements asserted full public confidence in his promotional claims ("all invariably pronounce her to be as represented"), the very fact that they were described as claims (rather than as self-evident facts) suggests that Barnum may have been contemplating the possibility of transforming his debut into an overt game of popular cultural sleuthing. Or, at the very least, he may have been thinking about using the specter of fraud as yet another marketing tease to draw in additional customers.

Introduction

At this very early moment in the exhibition's history, however, both the showman and his audiences seem to have been mostly content—and far more concerned—with Heth's marvelous appearance, stories, and singing. The New York *Courier and Enquirer,* for example, treated Barnum's central promotional claim for the exhibition as fascinating and unproblematic: "This old creature is said to be 161 years of age, and we see no reason to doubt it. Nobody indeed would dispute it if she claimed to be five centuries."[12] The editors at the *Spirit of the Times* seconded this pronouncement of wonder at Heth's ancient appearance, even as they declared the whole enterprise rather amusing: "The dear old lady, after carrying on a desperate flirtation with Death, has finally jilted him. In the future editions, we shall expect to see her represented as the impersonation of Time in the Primer, old Time having given her a season-ticket for life."[13] Such wisecracks suggest a degree of awareness that the still anonymous impresario responsible for this exhibition was probably fudging the details of Heth's biography—at least a little. Most of the early New York press reviews, in fact, have a recurring tongue-in-cheek tone—a steady stream of literary nudges, winks, and nods—all of which seem to indicate that contemporary viewers understood quite well that promotional puffery was an integral part of the showman's craft. Yet no New York reviewer took serious issue with the basic tenets of Heth's biography. No earnest cry of humbug, no pointed accusation of promotional fraud surfaced in close to a dozen newspaper reviews.

Barnum's initial marketing formula—and the reception patterns it provoked—began to change, however, almost as soon as he, Lyman, and Heth hit the road. A couple of weeks later, in Providence, Rhode Island, for example, Barnum developed another facet of his star's biography. Heth, he asserted in a new round of newspaper advertisements and handbills, "has five great-grandchildren, now the slaves of Wm. Bowling, Esq. of Paris, Kentucky, to the purchase of whose freedom the proceeds of this exhibition are to be appropriated."[14] How Providence's abolitionist community responded to this bogus appeal for charity remains uncertain. This was a brief marketing improvisation in a fast-moving tour, and within days Barnum's traveling show was on the move again, heading further north to new venues and new promotional possibilities. After the exhibition had moved out of the Democratic districts of New York City into Whiggish New England and into ideological territory more supportive of manumission efforts, Barnum simply added an abolitionist drawing card to the promotional mix.

The next round of promotional tinkering came a few weeks later, when the show moved to Boston's Concert Hall. Here Lyman and Heth appeared in an exhibition room right next door to the most celebrated popular curiosity of the mid-1830s—Johann Maelzel's automaton chess-player—a wondrous mechanical figure clothed in Turkish attire, whose status as an authentic thinking machine remained a matter of intense public doubt, speculation, and debate. Heth did strong business despite this competition, so strong, in fact, that Maelzel and his automaton were soon induced to give up Concert Hall's large room to their less known rivals from Gotham.[15] But when Heth's audiences finally began to decrease, Barnum decided to cultivate some tantalizing doubts of his own, surreptitiously planting newspaper stories which suggested that Maelzel's chess-playing wonder was not the only piece of mechanical *trompe l'oeil* in Boston. Joice Heth, anonymous press notices suddenly announced, "is not a human being. What purports to be a remarkably old woman is simply a curiously constructed automaton, made up of whalebone, india-rubber, and numberless springs ingeniously put together, and made to move at the slightest touch, according to the will of the operator. The exhibitor is a ventriloquist, and all the conversations apparently held with the ancient lady are purely imaginary."[16]

What made Barnum's new (and seemingly counterproductive) marketing scheme innovative was its clever use of the press to play both sides of the authenticity question. In contrast to his previous assertions of public confidence in Heth, the Boston press notices now deliberately undermined the credibility of Heth's public persona, creating a new tale of managerial deceit to go along with Heth's fascinating tales about raising "dear little George." And as Barnum gleefully explained years later, the nagging uncertainty about Heth's public persona—perhaps the ancient nurse of George Washington, perhaps nothing but an automaton—only added to the public's growing interest in the exhibition:

> On one occasion, an ex-member of Congress, his wife, two children, and his aged mother, attended the exhibition. . . . [H]is old mother was closely scrutinizing Aunt Joice, under the immediate direction of my helpmate, Lyman.
>
> Presently the old lady spoke up in an audible tone, and with much apparent satisfaction,
>
> "There it is alive after all! . . ."
>
> "Why do you think it is alive?" asked Lyman, quietly.
>
> "Because its pulse beats as regularly as mine does," responded the old lady.
>
> "Oh, that is the most simple portion of the machinery," said Lyman. "We make that operate on the principle of a pendulum to a clock."
>
> "Is it possible?" said the old lady, who was now evidently satisfied that Joice was an automaton. Then turning to her son, she said: "George, this thing is not alive at all. It is all a machine."
>
> "Why mother," said the son with evident embarrassment, "what are you talking about?"
>
> A half-suppressed giggle ran through the room and the gentleman and his family soon withdrew.[17]

This passage from the first edition of Barnum's autobiography serves as a kind of primer on the nineteenth-century arts of deception. All of Barnum's early show business tricks are in play here: the deadpan denials from Lyman, which invited as much doubt as they dispelled; the suggestion that the deliberate act of promotional fraud was nothing more than good, clean Yankee fun; and the artful repositioning of the Boston audience from the role of observers to observed, looking and laughing here not only at Heth but at each other. Barnum's signature move, however, was the invitation to the Boston public to push beyond his contradictory claims in the papers, to inspect Heth themselves for evidence of imposture. With each self-directed accusation of fraud in the papers—each coy denial delivered by Lyman to the viewers—Barnum was beginning to transform the Joice Heth exhibition from a plausible work of realism into a far more slippery form of illusionism, one which interwove seemingly straight biographical information with provocative public encouragements to inspect this very same information for evidence of artificial manufacture.

Over the next few months Barnum's exhibition continued in this ambiguous mode, moving through towns and cities in New York, Connecticut, Rhode Island, and Massachusetts, until its elderly star (no doubt weary from such strenuous touring!) became ill and eventually died in February 1836. Even at this juncture, though, the young showman-on-the-make saw further possibilities for "exciting curiosity" and quickly assembled the most morbid spectacle of his entire career: a public autopsy of Heth's corpse to determine her true age before an audience of New York's "physicians, students, and several clergymen and editors"—fifty cents' admission charged at the door. The verdict of the New York doctors, Barnum confessed later, was unequivocal: "there was surely some mistake in regard to the alleged age of Joice; that instead of being 161 years old, she was probably not over eighty."[18]

Yet for months after the public autopsy, the whirlwind of controversy surrounding the Joice Heth exhibition continued to blow; or rather, Barnum, Lyman, and the New York press refused to let it die down. Richard Adams Locke, author of the so-called Moon Hoax (which had falsely celebrated the telescopic discovery of lunar creatures on the front page of the New York *Sun*), initiated the postmortem discussions by describing Barnum's show business debut as "one of the most precious humbugs that ever was imposed upon a credulous community."[19] The Barnum camp, in turn, responded to Locke's accusations by leaking an entirely bogus exposé of the Heth autopsy to the unsuspecting editor of the New York *Herald*, James Gordon Bennett, who took the manufactured bait hook, line, and sinker. "Joice Heth," Bennett excitedly wrote in February 1836,

> *is not dead.* On Wednesday last, as we learn from the best authority, she was living at Hebron, in Connecticut. . . . The subject on which Doctor Rodgers and the Medical Faculty of Barclay street have been exercising

their knife and their ingenuity, is the remains of a respectable old negress called AUNT NELLY, who has lived many years in a small house by herself, in Harlem, belonging to Mr. Clarke. She is, as Dr. Rodgers sagely discovers, and Doctor Locke his colleague accurately records, only eighty years of age. Aunt Nelly before her death complained of old age and infirmity. She was otherwise in good spirits. The recent winter, however, has been very severe, and so she gave up the ghost a few days ago.[20]

This remarkably effective confidence game at the expense of one of the nineteenth century's leading editors marked the end of the Joice Heth exhibition as a topic of current affairs. But it hardly represented the final word on the exhibition's broader historical legacy. Bennett, certainly, never forgave Barnum for his early victimization and took every opportunity to denounce the showman during his long tenure at the *Herald*. Barnum, on the other hand, began to claim that he had not known Heth's true age, even representing himself as an unwitting victim in the deceit. This 180-degree reversal (from virtuoso trickster to unsuspecting dupe) appeared first in the 1855 edition of Barnum's autobiography. "The question naturally arises," Barnum explained, that "if Joice Heth was an imposter, *who* taught her these things? and how happened it that she was so familiar, not only with ancient psalmody, but also with the minute details of the Washington family? To all this, I unhesitatingly answer, *I do not know.* I taught her none of these things. She was perfectly familiar with them all before I ever saw her, and she taught me many facts in relation to the Washington family with which I was not before acquainted."[21]

Whether or not these published claims were themselves promotional tricks designed to distance a middle-aged showman with aspirations for respectability from his youthful indiscretions remains a matter of speculation by Barnum's biographers. The surviving evidence cuts both ways.[22] Joice Heth's role in the deception remains equally tangled, leaving us with a number of unanswered (and, given the paucity of testimony from Heth herself, perhaps unanswerable) questions. Should we read Heth's involvement in the humbug as a self-conscious choice made by a tough, elderly woman with shrewd business instincts, one who, given the shortage of opportunities open to former slaves in the antebellum North, willingly allowed herself to become a "living curiosity" for the small economic advantages such a career offered? Or should we read the entire tour as a troubling case of popular cultural exploitation quite typical for its era, one in which white northern urbanites spent a great deal more time gazing at caricatures of blackness on stage than interacting with African Americans outside the exhibition hall?[23]

Aesthetic Blueprints

The answer to both of these complex questions is probably "yes." And regardless of how we untangle the problems of human agency, show business exploitation, and social significance at stake in this story, one larger conclusion seems clear: there is perhaps no other exhibition which anticipated more of the main currents of nineteenth-century American popular culture. From the minstrel show to the magic show, from the freaks of the Midway Plaisance to the ethnographic displays of the White City—in all of these entertainments (and many others) we can see lingering traces of what Barnum was concocting in 1835. For better or worse, this was what Barnum did more effectively than anybody else. Even as a show business neophyte who knew more about groceries than exhibition halls, he seems to have had an almost instinctive sense of what America's very first mass audiences would find especially curious and pay to see.

Barnum's debut thus serves as a kind of prologue to the much broader history of nineteenth-century American popular culture. But it also serves as a useful starting point for analyzing one of the most pervasive currents within this culture—the countless forms of artful deception that so thoroughly excited, dazzled, teased, and even angered the crowds. As long as there have been books on Barnum, writers have pointed to deception as a fundamental component of the showman's cultural production: it is the single skill (along with circus management) for which he is best remembered today. And Barnum was hardly alone in producing playful frauds for public deliberation.

Introduction

As we shall see, artful deception was one of the main currents in American popular culture during the Age of Barnum, both inside and outside of the Great Yankee Showman's exhibition rooms. Minstrelsy and melodrama are the only other nonliterary cultural currents even comparable in scale, durability, and diversity during the same time period.[24]

Simply to point out the popularity of artful deception, however, is also to beg a number of aesthetic and historical questions. Much like the reaction of a perplexed viewer standing before one of Barnum's dubious curiosities, our first impulse is to place this current in some kind of familiar, fixed category, but it is a remarkably elusive subject. It flows easily through a wide variety of urban venues: rented rooms, museums, theaters, industrial expositions, art galleries, and middle-class parlors. It resists consistent placement in any of the aesthetic categories conventionally employed to describe such things (such as realism, illusionism, *trompe l'oeil*—or even popular culture, for that matter). And it does not simply begin and end during Barnum's six-decade career, although this period seems to represent a kind of high-water mark. For the most part, these cultural deceits have been treated by historians as uncomplicated aesthetic phenomena—as if every dubious museum curiosity, stage magic performance, and *trompe l'oeil* painting tricked its audience in roughly the same way. Yet, as Barnum's debut demonstrates, even particular nineteenth-century exhibitions often relied on multiple, overlapping modes of trickery—modes for which we lack clear aesthetic blueprints and consistent names. We would probably do well, then, to think a bit more carefully about those first months of Barnum's career and ask what, exactly, he was doing in the fall of 1835.

Was this exhibition merely an exercise in fooling the public—a *trick* in the purely surreptitious sense, one whose representational status went largely undetected by the showman's audiences? If the first New York newspaper reports on the Heth exhibition are our measuring stick, the answer would seem to be a resounding yes: certainly, many of the elements of Barnum's elaborate fiction (Heth's wildly exaggerated age, bogus background, and trumped-up stories about the past) were accepted, discussed, and applauded as plausible facts. Plausibility, however, is not the same thing as certainty, and it seems clear from the steady stream of sarcasm running through these reports that many contemporaries suspected that they were witnessing something less than what the showman promised in his ads. This distinction is a subtle but crucial one: while it is perfectly reasonable to conclude that Barnum's first audiences were fooled to one degree or another, they were hardly the unsuspecting suckers of show business folklore.

Even these careful qualifications, however, only get us about as far as the Boston stop on the Joice Heth tour. At that point, when Barnum deliberately poked holes in his own fictional claims with new, competing fictional claims ("what purports to be a remarkably old woman is simply a curiously constructed automaton"), the exhibition began to take on features of a perceptual contest played out between showman and viewer, in which the curiosity on display was approached by the public as dubious and evaluated according to competing claims of authenticity set out by the showman's advertisements.[25] This more self-conscious mode of sleuthing soon became one of the exhibition's primary draws: many Boston patrons were well aware of the possibility of fraud in the showman's promotional puffs—and they evaluated them as puffs. That was what made the Heth exhibition so provocative; so enticing as a potential source of public exposé; so intensely curious.

But Barnum usually remained one step ahead of his viewers in exposing his deceits. Indeed, while his self-directed exposés deliberately drew attention to the artificiality of Heth's public persona, they also served as a calculated act of misdirection, a kind of red herring leading viewers down a road of inquiry that eventually proved to be a dead end (Joice Heth was not an automaton; that much, at least, we know with certainty). It is far more accurate, then, to say that Barnum often created the appearance of behind-the-scenes secrets and promotional deceits for public evaluation, rather than simply disclosing the secrets/deceits themselves. This final act of unmasking—the crucial moment when the trickster exposes his own fictional exposés—Barnum usually saved for his autobiographies, years or decades later, and even then he rarely told the entire behind-the-scenes story. Following the practices of his colleagues in the prestidigitatorial arts, Barnum pulled back one representational curtain after another, drawing the audience deeper and deeper into the trick, but his most secret working methods remained hidden. Whether Barnum was truly aware of Heth's correct age during the fall of 1835, we will never know. That secret he probably told only to his closest co-conspirators, or perhaps to no one at all.

It is important to remember that Barnum's cultivation of public suspicion in Boston did not eclipse or cancel out public interest in the image of the 161-year-old nursemaid that he had cultivated in New York. In the conversation quoted above between the Boston ex-Congressman and his mother, for example, belief and skepticism intermingle from one line to the next, without any clear resolution. As the episode comes to a close, both of the showman's competing representations—Joice Heth as ancient house slave and Joice Heth as automaton—remain actively in play. One might argue, in fact, that it was this lingering perceptual uncertainty which lay at the heart of the "half-suppressed giggles." While the viewers projected their anxious laughter onto the ex-Congressman and his family, they were really laughing at themselves, too. At the core of the joke was a giddy rush of self-awareness—a collective recognition that the exhibition hall debates were producing plenty of contradictory theories, but very few convincing solutions.

This somewhat paradoxical reception pattern—a curiosity seen by contemporary viewers as both representation and substance, counterfeit and currency—brings us to what was perhaps Barnum's most important early observation about cultural fraud. We are all familiar, of course, with the apocryphal dictum attributed to Barnum at the end of his career: that "there is a sucker born every minute."[26] What Barnum did say (in his 1855 autobiography) about the public's responses to his early efforts as trickster was actually far more interesting. Between reminiscences of the Joice Heth tour and a bogus rivalry staged between two of his jugglers, Barnum paused to offer a broader conclusion (a "trick of the trade," as he put it) about the

behavioral patterns of his viewers in the context of half-exposed humbuggery. "The public," he noted after two decades in the business,
"appears disposed to be amused even when they are conscious of
being deceived."[27]

What makes this observation so intriguing is its suggestion that artful deception was never a hard and fast choice between complete
detection and total bewilderment, honest promotion and shifty misrepresentation, innocent amusement and social transgression. Rather,
Barnum suggests, it was precisely the blurring of these aesthetic and
moral categories that defined his brand of cultural fraud and generated much of its remarkable power to excite curiosity. This observation applies equally well to any of the other forms of deception with
which Barnum came into contact in 1835. Maelzel's "automaton
chess-player" also relied on multiple (if not logically consistent) public
identities: it was admired as a worthy chess competitor as well as a possible hoax; a work of remarkable mechanical skill as well as an ingenious form of clandestine manipulation by a hidden assistant inside the
cabinet. Its enormous popularity grew directly out of this capacity to
be both things at once, an ambiguity that was never fully solved. It was
just this sort of built-in perceptual fuzziness, too, that lay at the heart
of the sleight-of-hand performances and *trompe l'oeil* paintings that
pervaded lower Broadway at the time. Whether in the theater or the
panorama building, what antebellum audiences witnessed was a deliberate juxtaposition of relatively obvious forms of representation (a
stage magician producing doves out of thin air, or a panoramic depiction of an urban fire) with feats and images whose illusions were
momentarily plausible—or even undetectable.

This is not to suggest that artful deception represented a specific
nineteenth-century period style (such as Romanticism), nor even a
historically distinct, cohesive movement (such as Impressionism).
Like the much older Western traditions of carnivalesque entertainment and still life painting whose aesthetic roots it shares, artful
deception is a cultural current far too eclectic and long-running to fit
neatly within any one of the nineteenth century's many categorical
boxes. Nevertheless, between about 1830 and 1900 this diverse collec-

tion of exhibitory tricks followed a number of relatively consistent, observable patterns.

First, it seems clear that artful deception in the Age of Barnum routinely involved a calculated intermixing of the genuine and the fake, enchantment and disenchantment, energetic public exposé and momentary suspension of disbelief. Merely offering one or another of these things was not simply bad form; it also usually lowered the door receipts. Second, as Barnum often noted in his own self-defense, no producers of such entertainment who wanted to stay in business for long simply fooled their viewers without also drawing attention to the act of fooling—or at least the possibility thereof. There is little question that most contemporary consumers of artful deception entered the exhibition hall looking for fraud. And third, none of the tricksters in Barnum's milieu simply peddled deception as an end in itself. Whether presented in the context of Joice Heth's anecdotes about dear little George, the automaton chess-player's Turkish clothes, Signor Blitz's stage patter, or the landscape imagery in a panorama painting, the deception always involved at least a modicum of narrative—an entertaining story that delivered the trick.

Another useful way to bring coherence to this diverse assortment of popular deceits is to consider them in relation to W. J. T. Mitchell's recent definition of "illusionism": the activity of "playing with illusions, the self-conscious exploitation of illusion as a cultural practice." As Mitchell reminds us, this subtle distinction between "illusion" and "illusion*ism*" is crucial, but it is frequently collapsed in our conventional speech. "Illusion," as we generally use the term, refers to a "natural, universal phenomenon" built into the "very conditions of sentience" and conventionally associated with "error, delusion, or false belief." "Illusionism," by contrast, describes a recurring style or aesthetic mode in Western culture, one that inhabits a "dialectical realm . . . on the boundary between fact and fiction." Part of what makes the arts of deception so categorically slippery is the fact that illusion is almost always a product of illusionism. While illusionism describes what Barnum was selling in 1835 (a kind of popular cultural play, on the very boundary between fact and fiction), the latter—

illusion—refers to the moment of misperception experienced by many of the showman's patrons.[28]

Artful deception in the Age of Barnum, however, routinely intermixed illusionism with a second distinctive aesthetic mode—realism. Once again, the Joice Heth exhibition is useful as an example. In the Boston audience's "half-suppressed giggle" at the indeterminacy of Barnum's representation, we have a first-hand account of the capacity Mitchell attributes to illusionistic images: their power "to deceive, delight, astonish, amaze, or otherwise take power over a beholder."[29] Yet to the extent that Boston viewers continued to maintain a "conviction in the extreme longevity of Joice"—and thus engaged the representation as plausible fact—illusionism merged seamlessly with what Mitchell describes as realism: a category of image which "doesn't take power over the observer's eye so much as . . . stands in for it, offering a transparent window onto reality, an embodiment of a socially authorized and credible 'eyewitness' perspective."[30]

It is not very difficult to discern what sort of perspective Barnum was attempting to embody in 1835. His evolving promotions during this six-month campaign operated much like a magic lantern show of the racialist stereotypes common in the particular social milieu where Joice Heth performed. She was an African-American woman "pictured" by Barnum as physically strange, curious, and exotic; a faithful slave who spoke no ill of her former masters; a nurturing black nursemaid who helped raise a white Virginia patriarch; a deeply pious Christian, steadfast in her faith for over a century; and a gifted folk singer who pleased audiences with her ancient musical talents. Each one of these images of "blackness" had a broad circulation in the antebellum North.[31] What made Barnum's caricature exceptional, then, was not so much its constituent parts as its comprehensiveness and flexibility. If this was realism, it was realism of a particularly omnivorous strain, a realism that ingested and re-presented the racialist assumptions of its public almost continuously, from week to week and place to place. And quite unlike the many other showmen in this milieu, Barnum was perhaps the only disseminator of racialist stereotypes who deliberately tried to convince his audiences that the images they were viewing might be just that—artful deception rather than the real thing.

In the grand sweep of Barnum's career, this initial fusion of illusionism and realism served as the prototype for both of his most conventional exhibition modes over the next six decades. Whereas the showman's infamous "humbugs" (for example, the Feejee Mermaid) emphasized the illusionistic skills Barnum first developed with Heth in Boston, his diverse parade of "living curiosities" (for example, General Tom Thumb) relied on the same sort of caricatured realism he employed in Heth's New York debut. But this distinction in aesthetic modes was never absolute, never mutually exclusive. On the contrary, these two aesthetic impulses continued to work—as they had during the later months of the Joice Heth tour—in a mutually reinforcing, even synergistic way throughout the showman's career.

The effectiveness of his "humbugs" as targets of public exposé always required the opposite possibility: that they might in fact be genuine curiosities. Otherwise, why even bother to enter the exhibition room and join the public debates? Conversely, the possibility of deception that perpetually hovered over Barnum's entire exhibition catalog only fueled public excitement for discussing the perceived strangeness of his "living curiosities," represented as mostly authentic in the showman's promotional materials. Because viewers suspected that Barnum might have embellished the physical and cultural anomalies of these curiosities, they rarely hesitated in picking and choosing which of the advertised features to accept, reject, or amend. The precise combination of illusionism and realism varied from curiosity to curiosity as well as from audience to audience; and it was not uncommon for illusionism and realism to co-mingle in the comments of a single viewer. In the nineteenth-century arts of deception, then, illusionism and realism were always interconnected—at least as aesthetic antipodes.[32] That was the discovery that first made Barnum famous. There was no need to *choose* between illusionism and realism. The public was amused even when it was conscious of being deceived.[33]

The Arts of Deception

Historical Rhythms

To speak of discoveries here, however, is to raise a new and different set of historical questions—questions which force us to account for cultural lineages that begin well before 1835. While the Joice Heth exhibition may have launched Barnum's career as a maker of artful deceptions, the more basic model of "curiosity" on which it was based (racialized exoticism fused with questions of authenticity) had roots in a much older lineage of pre-industrial exhibitions, one which extends backward through centuries of fairs, taverns, museums, and curiosity cabinets. Much the same can be said about the lineages of the other artful deceptions with which Barnum came into contact in 1835. Maelzel's automaton chess-player was actually built in 1769 for a European empress, and made its public debut in the royal court of the Hapsburgs. Similarly, the feats of theatrical magic performed by Monsieur Adrien and Signor Blitz grew out of a broad, transatlantic tradition of disenchanted sleight of hand dating from the earliest years of the Enlightenment. And the *trompe l'oeil* effects of the panorama paintings on lower Broadway were in many ways merely oversized versions of one of the oldest traditions in Western painting, a tradition that stretches all the way back to the classical contest of mimetic skill waged between Zeuxis and Parrhasius, who "painted so naturally" that they "deceived the birds."[34]

The question here, then, seems to be not whether the nineteenth-century arts of deception grew out of longstanding lineages in Western culture, but *how?* In formulating an answer, it is useful to consider the related history of still life painting, another very old current in Western culture which, as Norman Bryson has observed, resurfaces regularly but unpredictably. While painted images of table-top objects have appeared in numerous eras and locations—forming an ongoing series—this series is not strictly linear or consistent in its historical intervals. Rather, it often seems to jump from one country to another; and it sometimes skips entire decades or centuries.[35] Such admissions, however, should not lead us to conclude that still life painting is simply time*less*, or that it is immune to historical analysis. "No less than wars or revolutions," Bryson suggests, the culture of the table is the product of "historical pressure" that manifests itself in two distinctive ways. On the one hand, the fundamental forms of still life painting demonstrate very little innovation over time: the bowls, jugs, and fruit appear again and again, over hundreds of years. On the other hand, each particular canvas demonstrates a certain "receptivity" to its immediate historical context by "inflecting" these fundamental forms as culturally unique images.[36]

The history of artful deception follows a similarly complex pattern. The fundamental forms of artful deception—curious objects of wonder, sleight-of-hand tricks, *trompe l'oeil* pictures—are all hundreds of years old, and change only at a glacial pace. At this level, their history operates according to the *longue durée*—so long, in fact, that it requires a periodization of at least three or four centuries to become visible. Yet the nineteenth-century inflections of these forms—Barnum's exhibition of Joice Heth, Blitz's sleight-of-hand shows, Niblo's panorama paintings—were positively evanescent in their historical variations, evolving into something new with each performance, playbill, venue, and audience. The remarkable durability of artful deception thus forces us to think historically on multiple levels: observing changes in these cultural forms locally, and across continents; from day to day, and over centuries. It also requires a somewhat broader evidentiary net than is usually the case, one which sweeps through the fairgrounds, cabinets, theaters, and galleries of pre-industrial Europe, as well as the daily advertising columns, newspaper notices, and editorial reviews of nineteenth-century America.

There is no other way to make historical sense of these cultural forms. Just as the promotional innovations Barnum developed in 1835 remain largely unrecognizable when separated from the much older transatlantic history of carnival exhibitions, simply describing the Joice Heth exhibition as one more "carnivalesque" attraction in a centuries-old cycle tells us almost nothing.[37] But what of Mitchell's suggestion that illusionism itself is "a specific cultural practice, valued only at certain special historical moments"?[38] The preliminary evidence, certainly, seems to suggest that the Age of Barnum represented one of those moments—a period in which artful deception rose to especial prominence in American cultural history. The mere fact that the nineteenth century's most successful show business figure, P. T. Barnum, referred to himself as "the Prince of Humbug" speaks volumes about the extent to which artful deception was valued at the time. Also telling are the larger patterns of consumer demand for such entertainment during the showman's lifetime. As Barnum himself meticulously documented, it was a particular hoax—the infamous Feejee Mermaid—which almost single-handedly built the financial foundation for his cultural empire during the 1840s. During the months immediately following the Mermaid's debut in New York City, door receipts for his fledgling American Museum increased by almost 300%.[39]

And Barnum was not the only nineteenth-century trickster whose career was taking off. By the early 1840s, newspaper reports described Maelzel's automaton chess-player as "seen by more eyes than any terrestrial object ever exhibited"—a self-consciously hyperbolic claim to be sure, but one that was not far from being literally true.[40] Similarly, by the 1860s, the fashionable sleight of hand introduced to Americans by Signor Blitz was much more than just a mainstay of theatrical entertainment. It grew into one of the Gilded Age's leading cultural crazes, a multifaceted industry which spawned hundreds of new books, magazines, and pamphlets, a number of international celebrities, and a broad middle-class fad for performing tricks at home (parlor magic). Although disdained by the emerging fine arts academies in this country, *trompe l'oeil* painting flourished throughout the Age of Barnum, too, from the panoramas and dioramas of the 1820s and 1830s to the more modestly scaled canvases of William M. Harnett, who became one of the country's most commercially successful oil painters after 1875. What particularly upset Harnett's critical detractors, in fact, was their sense that his *trompe l'oeil* paintings deliberately subverted "true art" by catering to (and profiting from) the popular taste of the day.

As this highbrow resistance to Harnett's work demonstrates, commercial success did not equal universal or unambiguous social acceptance. On the contrary, these were some of the most controversial and energetically contested cultural forms in all of nineteenth-century America. Barnum, in particular, spent much of his long career testing the moral limits of what constituted artful deception—a category which always carried at least a whiff of its opposite: criminal fraud. As the showman himself observed, the term he chose for his princely alias was deeply loaded. While humbug came to be associated (largely through Barnum's relentless promotional energy) with a socially acceptable form of amusement, this term was also used frequently to condemn any form of economic, social, or political deception that was deemed morally reprehensible.[41]

This close rhetorical proximity between forms of popular entertainment and social deviance points to a considerable challenge of historical interpretation. What needs to be explained here is how Barnum and his fellow practitioners of artful deception were able to walk the fine line between illusion and illusionism, to refashion potentially upsetting and immoral acts of fraud into more manageable and acceptable forms of amusement. Yet the very fact that they were so successful at this sort of refashioning opens up a wealth of opportunities for exploring some of the most widely discussed ideological thresholds in nineteenth-century America: the boundaries separating clever promotional ingenuity and devious commercial fraud; respectable selves in the audience and freakish others on stage; supernatural agency and scientific simulation; artistic imitation and criminal counterfeiting. Even more than is usually the case, aesthetic evaluation and social judgment are hopelessly entangled here: any effort to construct an aesthetic taxonomy of artful deception leads quickly and inescapably to a social taxonomy of the value system in which it was produced. It is simply impossible to discuss one without the other.

But whose values are we talking about, exactly? And why such intense public interest in artful deception at this particular historical moment? The first question forces us to wrestle with the problem of applying concrete social categories to early forms of urban mass consumption.[42] No one, after all, kept careful, systematic records about who actually went to see these exhibitions. The surviving evidence consists of brief newspaper items: a story about a man in the audience who played chess against Maelzel's automaton; the price of an admission ticket to one of Signor Blitz's magic shows; a Barnum advertisement boasting that his humbuggery represented legitimate family entertainment fit for women and children. Such evidence merely serves as a rough indicator of whose values and opinions were at stake. And in many cases, the exceptions are just as important as the rules. Modest ticket prices, for example, tell us something about the social status of a particular entertainment, but they do not preclude occasional visits by patrons from above or below that status group. Likewise, advertised pronouncements about the respectability of a particular exhibition often serve more as an indicator of whom the manager hoped to attract than a perfectly reliable record of audience demographics in the exhibition hall.

Nevertheless, it is possible to say something meaningful and relatively precise about the sorts of consumers who made artful deception one of the mainstays of nineteenth-century popular culture. We know, for example, that these audiences were almost entirely white, since most forms of big-city popular entertainment—even in the North— remained rigidly segregated throughout the century (in the case of the American Museum, Barnum did not regularly welcome African Americans until the Civil War, and even then the number of black patrons seems to have been very small). We also know that these audiences routinely included men, women, and children, and that the shows generally clustered in predominantly middle-class commercial districts such as lower Broadway—a location which situated the entertainments, both geographically and symbolically, just above the more exclusively masculine and risqué minstrel shows and concert saloons associated with working-class districts such as the Bowery and Five Points. The audiences for artful deception were religiously, politically, and ethnically diverse, as well as mostly Northern and urban in their origins. But these big-city audiences also included large numbers of transient traders and tourists from all over the country.[43]

Much like the mass audiences that patronize the Disney empire today, in other words, the nineteenth-century patrons of artful deception were neither rigidly homogeneous nor without a recognizable core constituency.[44] And in the latter case, this constituency seems to have been roughly equivalent to what historians have defined as "the new middle class," a rapidly expanding segment of the population that emerged at approximately the same time as Barnum's show business career (the 1830s and 1840s) and in the same sorts of places (the urban-industrial centers of the antebellum North). In acknowledging this larger consumption pattern, it is important not to discount the highly constructed character of the socioeconomic identities at work here. Middle class, in this context, had as a much to do with outlooks, aspirations, and tastes as with levels of income, places of residence, and types of work.[45] Yet when we turn to the more nebulous issues of cultural marketing and consumer self-definition, artful deception likewise appears to have been very much a middle-class phenomenon.

Barnum, for example, was eager to bring almost anyone who could afford the twenty-five-cent price of a ticket into his American Museum: urban merchants and country traders; Democrats, Whigs, and Republicans; new immigrants and old Knickerbockers; even the sometimes volatile "b'hoys" and "g'hals" of the Bowery, who were more commonly associated with lower Manhattan's East Side venues. Barnum, however, welcomed this popular patronage with an increasingly rigid proviso that they check their Bowery behavior (public shouting, drinking, prostitution, labor radicalism) at the door. Barnum's brand of "democratic amusement," in other words, was not just a code word for low prices, lots of exhibitory choices, and demographic inclusivity. It was defined, too, by the viewer's willingness to expose him/herself to a barrage of middlebrow social values and consumption conventions, to participate in an enterprise which projected the new middle class's dominant concerns (temperance, domesticity, Christianity, self-control) into the metropolitan sites of public entertainment and play.[46]

The patterns are similar with the other major forms of artful deception. In the late 1820s and 1830s, Maelzel (in many ways the prototype for Barnum's middlebrow entertainment empire) made every effort to stage his illusionistic roadshow as family entertainment, offering sweetmeats for the children in his audience, holding charity benefits for orphans and widows, marketing his shows to gentlemen's chess clubs, and generally conducting himself, in the words of one contemporary biographer, as "the perfection of politeness and amiability."[47] The leading stage magicians of the Gilded Age, too, sought to adorn their performances with the clearly recognizable accoutrements of new middle-class refinement. Presenting themselves as more respectable alternatives to earlier "occultists" and "carnival jugglers," these self-described magical "modernists" adopted a distinctly bourgeois form of dress (the tuxedo), stage design (much in the style of a Victorian parlor), and public rhetoric (they referred to their performances as scientific exercises, designed to instruct rather than deceive). Likewise, William Harnett achieved his success within an urban nexus of solidly middle-class venues: his *trompe l'oeil* paintings hung in fashionable retail stores and hotel lobbies, the art galleries of the annual industrial expositions, and most famously, Theodore Stewart's Warren Street Saloon, a luxurious New York City watering hole catering to brokers and downtown businessmen as well as their "ladies," who came to view Harnett's aesthetic trickery at special times in the morning, when the alcohol was not flowing.[48]

Artful deception, then, was a major part of the urban entertainment landscape dominated by the new middle class and its values between 1830 and 1900. But this should strike us as somewhat peculiar, for the new middle class maintains a well-deserved scholarly reputation for having been deeply concerned—even downright anxious—about questions of fraud in almost every facet of its historical development. These nineteenth-century urbanites worried frequently, for example, about how to represent themselves—and identify each other—as genuinely respectable. They fretted about how to distinguish the public behavior of their central mythic hero (the self-made man) from that of the era's most notorious white-collar criminal (the confidence man). They even worried about deception in the spirit world, mounting public investigations to differentiate between authentic mediums and a distressingly large assortment of parlor charlatans. Worries about deception, in short, were positively endemic to the culture of the new middle class. They surfaced at home and in the streets, at work and at play, in this world and in the afterlife.

New Middle-Class Tricksters

Over the past two decades, much of the best scholarship on new middle-class culture has focused on these widespread concerns.[49] And these studies have pointed to a recurring historical pattern, one in which social anxieties about fraud and imposture fueled a wide range of popular cultural antidotes: the burgeoning industry of etiquette manuals, for example, which defined itself as an authority for differentiating authentic respectability from social impostures of various sorts, or the similarly ubiquitous genre of the urban guidebook, which provided an imaginative tool for navigating the tricks and traps of the new metropolis.[50] In each case, these cultural forms were marketed quite explicitly as defense mechanisms against deception, as mass-distributed means by which anxious middle-class urbanites might restore some sense of social, moral, and semiotic order amidst the rapid upheaval and flux of modernization.[51]

There was, however, a fundamental paradox at the heart of the cultural defenses. Simply put, the etiquette manuals, advice columns, and city guides seem to have promoted precisely the same anxieties they claimed to alleviate. The cultural work of guarding against social impersonation was never done. And reading about the deceptive dangers of the metropolis involved almost as many voyeuristic thrills as self-defense lessons. The paradoxes become even more pronounced when we think of Barnum's over-the-top promotional claims and bogus newspaper exposés as some sort of solution to the fears about imposture. These quasi-deviant forms of artful deception were, quite clearly, part of the problem—another source of the growing conviction that the urban-industrial world was becoming distressingly illegible, a place in which human eyes, spoken words, and written texts could not be trusted in the traditional ways. But to the extent that Barnum and his colleagues positioned their tricks as public forums for problem-solving, they also served virtually the opposite function.

They suggested in principle (if not always in practice) that the older Enlightenment ideals of reasoned analysis, exposé, and perceptual mastery were still possible; that somewhere—buried beneath all the playful misrepresentations and promotional teases—there still was a truth to be uncovered.

These striking ambiguities in the arts of deception cry out for historical verdicts. They encourage us to state our judgment in clear, unequivocal terms: either to view them as a gross imposition on the public (the trickster as show business manipulator), or as an egalitarian exercise in cultural sleuthing (the trickster as a maker of useful puzzles, cheerfully debated and solved by eager audiences). Yet this lingering impulse to take sides may in fact be Barnum's final ruse, for it encourages us to replicate much the same analytical mode as the nineteenth-century viewer: namely, debating the level of disingenuousness and moral propriety of the entire enterprise!

Perhaps there is another way. Perhaps, that is to say, these artful deceptions need to be understood not so much in terms of zero sum choices (truth-making versus unmaking, fraud versus exposé), but as a more slippery mode of new middle-class play—a play whose moral ambiguity and epistemological flexibility were always built into the larger process.[52] One major appeal of this play, certainly, was the opportunity it afforded for public debate and judgment in the exhibition room—Barnum's trademark offer to "let the public decide" for itself.[53] But like any tricksters worth their cultural salt, Barnum and his colleagues created as many problems as they solved. They marked the conventional thresholds of immorality and deviance in their society, but they also provided a means of crossing those thresholds. Their puzzles held out the promise of truth, but they also helped socialize their audiences to a brave new world in which the very boundaries of truth were becoming more and more puzzling.[54]

Barnum's brand of deception, in other words, was always multifunctional, always ambivalent, always dialectical in its relationship to the social, political, and economic changes taking place in nineteenth-century America. More than a mere reflection of—or antidote for—new middle-class anxieties about modernization, these exhibitory tricks alternatively defined, buttressed, skirted, and violated the values of their consumers, often in the very same show. They also violated many of our conventional assumptions about how trickster cultures operate.

These, after all, were tricksters who frequently exposed their own tricks, accused themselves of fraud, and publicly defined their cultural labors as honest amusement. They did so, moreover, for upstanding middle-class audiences which were largely aware of their own victimization, yet continued to embrace the trickster's seductive cycle of fraud, controversy, and exposé. Perhaps most surprising of all, these mass-consumed tricks had a startling propensity to move back and forth across the mimetic threshold separating representation from real life. Indeed, quite unlike the purely allegorical trickster tales which have fascinated historians in the past, one of the most widely discussed facets of tricksterism in the nineteenth-century exhibition room was its representational indeterminacy, the lingering possibility that it was not really *art* at all.[55]

Thus what begins as an analysis of Barnum's early promotional puffery ultimately becomes an examination of the much larger value system he, his fellow tricksters, and their audiences helped to create, as well as the emergence of a new way of thinking about popular culture—one in which deception (artful and otherwise) came to be understood as an intrinsic component of the commercial entertainment industry.[56] If we are to make much sense of when and how this particular strain of trickery got started, though, we will need to spend some time exploring the long-forgotten career of an old German showman named Maelzel, who helped teach Barnum the arts of deception in 1835. And we will need to become better acquainted with the even older mechanical puzzle from Vienna that served as young Phineas' object lesson.

1

The Death and Rebirth of the
Automaton Chess-Player

⊷⇒⊙ ⊙⇐⊶

In 1857, respected Philadelphia physician John Kearsley Mitchell sat down to write an obituary for a recently deceased entertainer with whom he had become intimately acquainted in recent years. It was an admiring biography, full of wild metaphors and winking puns, of a remarkable transatlantic figure—and it was (mostly) true.

> The subject of our sketch was born of reputable parentage, about the close of the year 1769, in the city of Pressburg, in Hungary. If he ever had a mother, history has failed to record her name. His paternal relative was a Hungarian official of good birth and fair character. Although himself a Christian, he had the singular caprice of clothing his child in oriental attire, and even obliged him to wear, during his whole life, the outward emblems of the creed of Mahomet. From his earliest years the lamented departed wore a look of solemn gravity. He never smiled, and was rarely heard to speak. Though compelled, by circumstances of primitive forma- tion, to remain seated during many long years, and though gifted by illib- eral Nature with the use of but one arm, he exhibited signs of a clear and precocious intellect.

It is, however, but little to his credit, that he beat his father before he was six months old, and not long after, waged successful war against his legitimate sovereign, the Empress Maria Theresa. Later in life, he was the friend of [Benjamin] Franklin, the opponent of George the Third, and Louis XV—the slave of Eugène de Beauharnais—the conqueror of Napoleon—the favorite of Frederick the Great, and the Grand Turk—to-day a pet of aristocratic circles—to-morrow the denizen of a garret. . . . As a republican, he must undoubtedly claim our respect, since, perhaps, no other man has ever checked the march of so many kings as he.[1]

Few readers today will recognize the unnamed protagonist in this odd, star-crossed tale. Yet Mitchell's enigmatic subject—the legendary automaton chess-player—was perhaps the preeminent entertainer of the late eighteenth and early nineteenth centuries, a genuine international celebrity seen and admired by more audiences than any performer of its time.[2] This automaton was also the subject of a surprisingly large body of contemporary literature, including a successful play by Heinrich Beck, a well-known scientific treatise by Sir David Brewster, and a short story by E. T. A. Hoffmann.[3] Its most famous chronicler in the United States was none other than Edgar Allan Poe, who in 1836 wrote an essay both extolling its virtues as a "curiosity" and denouncing the performance as fraud against an overly credulous public. Poe had become convinced that the automaton's remarkable achievements at the chess board were—by all rational criteria of interpretation—impossible. The most celebrated mechanical wonder from the Age of Enlightenment simply had to be something more than springs, wood, gears, and plaster.[4]

But how was it done? Was this life-sized mannequin actually an expression of mechanical genius, the long-sought-after thinking machine, as many continued to believe year after year? Or were the automaton's strategic decisions and elaborate dexterity actually the result of hidden manipulations by its American exhibitor, Johann Nepomuk Maelzel, who only appeared to watch from a distance? Or could it be that Maelzel had an accomplice, someone inside the automaton—a dwarf or a child, perhaps—who somehow managed to

The first portrait of the great automaton chess-player. The eighteenth-century engraving is by P. G. Pintz.

remain undetected during the meticulous public demonstrations of the device's gear-filled interior. Remarkably, the complete answer remained elusive throughout the exhibition's long history, appearing in print only after the automaton had gone through four owners, toured two continents, and withstood the scrutiny of seventy years' worth of guessing. And even then, the automaton's ambiguous status, on the very boundary between ingenious machine and clever imposture, remained thoroughly uncertain. After decades of false theories and competing speculations, early nineteenth-century audiences treated any answer—even THE answer—as provisional, always suspect and probably destined for further refinement.

The Automaton Chess-Player

Over the past century and a half, published writings on this artifact have done little more than sift through the many layers of truth and falsity, searching for some kind of closure to one of the greatest cultural conundrums of the modern era.[5] What follows here, however, is a different kind of history: not simply another guess about the automaton's operational principles, but an examination of past modes of guessing. It is also an effort to convey something of the experience of witnessing the automaton at first hand. Thus the reader should proceed forewarned. There will be plenty of clues about Maelzel's secret, but no quick-and-easy solutions—none, that is, before working through the same wonderfully excruciating analytical process undertaken by thousands of earlier, curious viewers. This remarkable power to excite curiosity needs to be re-experienced even as it is understood as something historically contingent, an ever-changing dynamic of puzzle-making and unmaking shaped by a wide variety of cultural variables: the automaton's operators and the various performances they assembled; the evolving demographics of the crowds and their diverse patterns of play; and, above all, the public's impassioned attempts to define this object, the cacophony of clashing verdicts reverberating from the exhibition halls. "Machine!" "Man in a machine!" "Ingenious mechanism!" "Ingenious deception!" "Philosophical amusement, designed for public edification!" "Elaborate hoax, designed for fleecing honest republicans!"

Here, in short, was an entire historical catalog of strategies for making sense of the visually mysterious, the perceptually uncertain, the intensely curious—all embodied in one astonishing mechanical figure. Because of its longevity and cultural plasticity, the automaton resists our conventional pigeonholes for dividing up the period. It was at once an Enlightenment and a post-Enlightenment object, a leading representative of eighteenth-century Europe's curiosity cabinets, royal amusements, and fairs, as well as nineteenth-century America's emerging urban-industrial landscape of theaters, exhibition halls, and popular museums.[6] While revolutions brought down the Old Regime, Maelzel's chess-playing wonder survived and moved west, triumphing once again in the new commercial culture dominated by America's emerging middle class.

This may have been part of what Dr. Mitchell had in mind when he referred to the automaton's eighty-five-year career as "paradoxical" earlier in his biography. While the workings of the mechanism itself remained virtually unchanged from the model first exhibited in 1769 Vienna, its broader cultural meanings as a form of artful deception went through numerous, often dramatic transformations before coming to a fiery end in 1854 Philadelphia. Above all, it outlived both its creator and his late eighteenth-century understanding of the moral boundaries separating visual education and frivolous fraud. Once hailed as the most impressive of the Enlightenment's many philosophical amusements, the automaton chess-player died as something quite different. As Barnum himself noted with great admiration, this was the very first exhibition in the history of American show business to make dubious authenticity a perpetual—and profitable—source of popular entertainment.

Baron von Kempelen's Bagatelle

The automaton chess-player came into being three years before Maelzel himself was born, about thirty miles from Vienna in the Slovakian city of Bratislava (or Pressburg as it was known at the time). Its builder was the Baron Wolfgang von Kempelen (1734–1804), a moderately distinguished Hungarian official and member of the Royal Chamber of Domains serving Empress Maria Theresa.[7] How Kempelen came by his considerable mechanical expertise and decided to launch a career as an inventor of automata remains somewhat unclear. Following legal training in Vienna, he worked a series of unexceptional bureaucratic jobs, first as *Hofkammerrat* (court counselor) and later as a supervisor of the royal salt industry. Contemporary accounts simply describe Kempelen as naturally gifted, his tinkering in the workshop as a hobby. Karl Gottlieb von Windisch, the automaton's first published chronicler, provides the only surviving glimpse of the place where Kempelen exercised this passion, a creative sanctuary on the second story of the family residence in Pressburg: "in passing through the work-shop, which serves as an anti-chamber to the study, you see naught but joiners, smiths, and clockmakers tools, laying in heaps, in that confusion, so characteristic of the abode of a mechanical genius. The walls of the study are, in part, hid by large presses, some containing books, others antiques, and the remainder, a small collection of natural history; the intermediate spaces are decorated with paintings or prints, the performances of the master of the house."[8]

To our eyes, this eclectic assortment of mechanical tools, reference books, rare objects, and paintings seems a bit strange—especially in the home of a government official who appears to have had no formal training in the arts or sciences. Yet during the late seventeenth and eighteenth centuries these activities served to define a relatively common social type—the "virtuoso"—a category of scientific amateurs which intersected the ranks of the leading university faculty and provided an enthusiastic market for their ideas.[9] These part-time investigators popularized the Scientific Revolution in myriad ways: as members of the emerging coffee-house culture where scientific enthusiasts of all stripes met and traded ideas; as a segment of the book-buying public which fueled demand for subscription series and inexpensive editions; even as producers themselves of books, scientific apparatus, and cabinets of curiosities.[10] While the virtuoso came under attack during the 1760s by scientific professionals who placed accuracy above wonder and formal training above amateur knowledge, most contemporary observers who witnessed the automaton chess-player—even those who doubted it was all machine—hailed Kempelen's tinkering as a triumph of intellect.[11] Charles Hutton's *Mathematical and Philosophical Dictionary* (1795), for example, described it as nothing less than "the greatest master-piece in mechanics that ever appeared in the world."[12]

Building automata, however, was not simply an expression of Baconian idealism—it was also the basis for an expanding entertainment industry. And in this particular line of entertainment, no figure was better known than Jacques de Vaucanson (1709–1782), a French virtuoso who, according to contemporary writers, probably provided the model for Kempelen's ambitions as an amusement entrepreneur.[13] Like Kempelen, Vaucanson was employed as a middle-rank government official. The rest of his time and most of his energy, however, went into the production of such wonders as *le canard artificiel* (the automaton duck), an ingenious contraption which quacked, ate, drank, splashed in the water, and finally, as a kind of encore, defecated a small pellet. Vaucanson wore such mechanical pursuits as a badge of learning and social distinction, ultimately riding the popularity of his automata into the leading courts and aristocratic circles of Europe. For Kempelen, the message of Vaucanson's wonders must have been clear: building automata offered the possibility of rapid upward mobility for the scientific amateur. And no subject was more fascinating in an age seeking to demystify the workings of the mind and body than machines which closely duplicated the animated functions of living things.

Opportunity presented itself for Kempelen in 1769, when he was invited by the Hapsburg Empress Maria Theresa to witness a series of experiments of magnetism by a French performer named Pelletier. Such performances before royalty were quite common in late eighteenth-century Vienna; it was at this very same court where a young Mozart enchanted the Hapsburg crown with his marvelous musical skills. On this occasion, however, the subject was mechanical wizardry, and Kempelen found himself fortuitously "honoured with the familiar conversation of the Empress," who wished to learn how Pelletier produced such astonishing effects. Before long, the royal discussion turned away from the Frenchman: "M. de Kempelen . . . dropped a hint that he thought himself competent to construct a piece of mechanism, which should produce effects far more surprising and unaccountable than those which she then witnessed. The curiosity of the Empress being strongly raised, she expressed a lively desire to see his idea carried into execution, and drew from him a promise that he would gratify her wishes without delay."[14]

Six months later, Kempelen's automaton chess-player was finished and "brought to Vienna, where it excited the admiration and surprise of her Majesty, and her august family, of the court, of foreign ministers, of the learned, of artists, in short of every one, who either saw the Automaton play, or played with it."[15] Whereas Vaucanson's wonders had merely imitated the physical movements and actions of living beings, here was a machine whose performative talents seemed to transcend the most elaborate clockworks and pre-programming, a man-made creation that could think on its feet, strategize, and respond to its audience: in short, a "thinking machine" that could play chess, an inherently unpredictable game requiring the one skill which had for so long marked the final boundary between men and machines—*reason*. As Windisch explained, this seeming ability to strategize, adjust, and compete with human beings made Kempelen's device unique among Enlightenment automata.[16]

Following its auspicious debut at Schoenbrun Palace, the automaton chess-player began the first major phase of its long career, a series of public demonstrations spanning almost two decades as well as most of the major cities of Europe. The initial exhibitions took place at Kempelen's home in Pressburg, where a company of curious viewers and chess enthusiasts would assemble in the lower apartment and then proceed upstairs for a match.[17] Accounts from these years suggest a standard pattern of demonstration. First, Kempelen wheeled the automaton around the room, a ritual which allowed the public to gaze more closely at the mannequin itself. This life-sized figure was distinguished by its downcast eyes, mustache, and gloved hands, as well as a collection of elaborate accessories: a white turban, a fur-trimmed jacket, a striped shirt, and a prominent smoking apparatus. Next, the cabinet drawers below the mannequin were opened and closed to reveal the internal structure, a space which appeared so full of "levers and wheelwork" that there was "not room to hide a kitten." Kempelen then lit a candle behind the cabinet to illuminate the interior and placed a small wooden "case" on a table near the machine. Finally, a cushion was placed under the right elbow of the automaton, after which Kempelen rolled the entire apparatus "behind a balustrade," where it remained during the rest of the show.

The chess contests then began in earnest. After "winding up" a clockwork mechanism, Kempelen presented one viewer with a choice of six "end-games" (that is, abridged matches, with only a few pieces for each contestant), which were played on a separate table on the audience's side of the barrier. While the challenger could choose between the red or white pieces, the automaton always got the first move. Once play started, Kempelen functioned as an intermediary, repeating the challenger's move on the chess board of the automaton, and vice-versa. The automaton, however, was responsible for directing its own pieces, a process described in detail by Windisch:

> The Automaton when he is to move, lifts up his arm leisurely, and directs it to that side of the chess-board where the piece is, which he wants to move; he carries his hand to it, opens his fingers to lay hold of it, takes it, removes, and places it on the spot intended for it, withdraws his arm, and rests it again on the cushion. . . . Every move he makes, a small noise of the wheelwork is heard, somewhat resembling that of a repeater [i.e. a spring-driven clock mechanism]. This noise ceases as soon as the move is made, and the Automaton's arm replaced on the cushion.[18]

Games typically went on like this for about thirty minutes, usually ending in a win for the automaton, who signified checkmate with two self-satisfied nods of his head.

In Pressburg, Kempelen occasionally allowed challengers to play on the automaton's board, although Windisch, who saw a number of matches there, claimed the audience was more often separated from the automaton to prevent them from "shaking the machine." Contemporary accounts also noted that an assistant named Anton was sometimes responsible for moving the pieces, a deviation from the regular routine which seemed to remove suspicion that Kempelen's mediation was critical for a successful performance. During almost every match, Kempelen mysteriously opened the "small case" on the adjoining table and "examined its contents"—which of course raised all sorts of questions about the role of this object in the automaton's operation.

It was this show that Kempelen presented at Schoenbrun Palace for the visiting Grand Duke Paul of Russia in September 1781, a spectacularly successful event which prompted Maria Theresa's son, Emperor Joseph II, to send Kempelen and his mechanical prodigy on a lengthy European tour. Records of the automaton's exploits during this period come to us from a truly remarkable cast of observers: the French Duc de Croy, who watched the chess-player conquer a succession of royal adversaries at Versailles Palace and confessed in his diary that he had no idea how it worked; Baron Friedrich Melchior Grimm, who wrote in a letter to Diderot that the automaton must "be under the continuous influence of an intelligent being"; the son of Europe's greatest contemporary chess champion, François André Philidor, who reported that his father played and beat the automaton at the Académie des Sciences in Paris; Benjamin Franklin, who, after losing to the automaton in the same city, provided Kempelen with a glowing letter of introduction to the Parisian chess-playing elite; and the eminent German mathematician, Johann Jacob Ebert, who carefully observed a series of games in Leipzig and exclaimed, "I am fully convinced that the movements of the machine are not produced by any concealed person."[19] Still mystified a year later, when he sat down to write a pamphlet essay on the automaton, Ebert pronounced Kempelen's exhibition one of the most remarkable "curiosities of the last Michaelmas Fair."[20]

Even this brief catalog of responses demonstrates that the automaton chess-player was a particularly contradictory and complex kind of cultural object, which its late eighteenth-century audiences interpreted in a variety of ways. Let us begin with what seems to be the most straightforward and least contentious of these responses— Ebert's claim that the automaton represented a remarkable curiosity. In one sense, this categorization simply served as a generic endorsement, hardly different than describing the automaton as popular or interesting.[21] Yet it also says a number of important things about the specific cultural category and milieu in which the automaton operated. First, it linked Kempelen's creation to the long exhibitory tradition of the curiosity cabinet, since the late Renaissance the primary European site for collecting and looking at "marvelous objects," whether natural or artificial (man-made).[22] The famous curiosity cabinet of Rudolf II in Prague, for example, included numerous similar automata and mechanical wonders among its wealth of fossils, shells, animal skins, bones, antlers, coins, silverware, sculptures, paintings, and cultural artifacts from the New World.[23] The automaton chess-player, however, never spent much time in any one exhibition room, building, or city. Right from the start, it traded duty as both a royal commission and an object of the marketplace, appearing before a wide range of wonder-seekers, in fairs and private halls as well as the courts of foreign dignitaries. Although closely tied to the collecting traditions of the virtuoso and initially supported by royal patronage, the automaton quickly became a free-floating entertainment industry, a curiosity independent of any particular court, cabinet, museum, or fair.[24]

Ebert's choice of the label "curiosity" says something, too, about the kind of visual engagement practiced by Kempelen's audiences, regardless of whether they viewed his creation as a machine or some kind of visual trick. More than a function of the places it appeared or the kinds of objects with which it kept company, this categorization underscored the device's ability to *excite curiosity* among those who witnessed Kempelen's exhibitions: viewers such as Empress Maria Theresa, whose royal "curiosity," we are told, "was strongly raised" during the automaton's debut; or Windisch, who wrote, "you are sure, I was not the least eager to gratify my curiosity; I examined even the minutest corner of it, without being able to find anything."[25] Windisch, in fact, described the machine's curiosity-raising powers as virtually boundless, cautioning his readers that he could not possibly quench their desire to solve its mysteries: "Do not expect, my dear friend, that I should answer every question you put to me, relative to M. de Kempelen's famous chess-player. The Ozanams, the Guyots, and other writers of that class, would be as unsuccessful as myself, in their attempts to satisfy your curiosity."[26]

This second sense of curiosity—a kind of voracious intellectual desire, provoked by some remarkable object or entertainment— seems to have been an invention of the Enlightenment, stimulated by the era's new understanding of the goal and function of knowledge. As the German philosopher Hans Blumenberg has demonstrated, the very notion of "this-worldly" curiosity was viewed throughout the

Middle Ages with deep suspicion, as a dangerous distraction from the more serious business of acquiring divine knowledge.[27] Not until such forms of intellectual pretension were disassociated from the goal of personal salvation and placed within "the logic of the methodical process of scientific cognition" did curiosity finally shed its stigma of vice.[28] One sees this shift taking place in the many *Oxford English Dictionary* definitions of curiosity under the heading "as a personal attribute."[29] Early entries describe curiosity as a "desire to know or learn," but only "in a blamable sense," as "the disposition to inquire too minutely into anything." By the first decades of the seventeenth century, however, other, more positive senses of the term begin to appear as well, including a whole new subcategory which equated curiosity with a "scientific or artistic interest; the quality of a curioso or virtuoso."[30]

It was precisely this quality—this strenuous activity of puzzling over and trying to penetrate the unknown or unseeable—that Kempelen packaged and sold in half-hour bundles to his audiences. Windisch's 1783 description of one of the automaton chess-player's shows demonstrates this process in action. He begins by pointing out the extent of Kempelen's mechanical accomplishment, focusing on the mental processes of the virtuoso: "The boldest idea that ever entered the brain of a mechanic was, doubtless, that of constructing a machine to imitate man, the masterpiece of creation, in something more than figure and motion."[31] Over the next few pages, however, Windisch shifts his attention to the intellectual activities of Kempelen's viewers, who now have taken over the role of investigator: "Far from believing all that you have heard related, or read of this machine, you say, your reflections on it have only increased your doubts of the possibility of a thing so incredible. . . . You will place no trust either in my eyes, or those of so many others, not even with the assistance of spectacles! You doubt we did not see clearly, and heap IFS upon BUTS."[32] E. T. A. Hoffmann, too, placed the intellectual struggles of the viewer at the center of his automaton tale. "People," he notes, "wearied themselves with conjectures concerning the source and agent of this marvelous intelligence. The walls, the adjoining room, the furniture, everything connected with the exhibition, were carefully examined and scrutinized."[33]

On a very basic level, then, Kempelen's exhibitions of the automaton functioned as an egalitarian celebration of science, a popularization of the Enlightenment through visual entertainment, allowing non-virtuosi to try on the persona and intellectual machinations of the machine's inventor.[34] Even if the viewer could not solve the puzzle and match Kempelen's cognitive prowess, he or she could take pride in having participated in the struggle and constructed a theory. As Windisch noted, the remarkable opacity of the automaton was at once absolutist and democratic: absolutist in the sense that Kempelen alone held the secret to the chess-player's "cognition"; and democratic in the sense that virtually all of the automaton's challengers—from the Empress herself to her most humble citizens—ultimately could do little more than offer inconclusive guesses. "I myself," Windisch confessed, "who [has] so often seen it, who has examined it, and has played with it, am obliged to make the humiliating avowal, that it is incomprehensible to me, as it can be to you. This, however, serves to keep me in countenance, that others, endowed with much superior knowledge, and quicker penetration, have not been more successful than myself. Among the many thousands, of all ranks, who have seen it, not one has been able to develop the mystery."[35]

Yet to describe the automaton simply as an exercise in popular science is to say very little about its particular aesthetic form. What about the rather intriguing fact that this Hapsburg bureaucrat chose to clothe his thinking machine in "the outward emblems of a Mahomet"? Why not dress him instead in the more respectable garments of a *philosophe*, or perhaps those of a French chess champion such as Philidor? Sadly, no record of Kempelen's thoughts on these matters has survived. But we do have those of Joseph Friedrich Freiherr zu Racknitz, who first saw the automaton on tour in Dresden in late 1784 and asked a similar set of questions in a published pamphlet. For Racknitz, the automaton's "Turkish" appearance made sense on two levels: first, because the "Middle East" (here broadly defined as the non-Christian lands east of Europe) was thought to be the birthplace of chess; and second, because this region, more than any other, signi-fied exoticism and irrational wonder in the Western European popular imagination.[36] It was a place, Racknitz tells us, commonly "associated with mysterious and magical powers."[37]

Such cross-cultural attitudes, fantasies, and associations were quite common during the late eighteenth century; indeed, they were part of a much larger process of Western mental projection in which "the Orient" was transformed into a "living tableau of queerness," and anything marked as "Oriental" came to be "synonymous with the exotic, the mysterious, the profound, the seminal."[38] Kempelen's deci-sion to make his automaton Turkish thus cut two ways, on the one hand legitimating the figure's public persona as a chess master, on the other serving to transform him into an exotic Eastern other—a sym-bolic adversary existing outside of, and in opposition to, the dominant Christian-scientific ethos of the Enlightenment. For the Viennese court, in particular, this symbolic adversary carried very real historical baggage. Twice before—in 1529 and 1683—the city had experienced major attacks at the hands of Turkish armies, first by Sultan Suleiman I, the Magnificent, who conquered Hungary and brought 120,000 sol-diers to the city's gates, and then by Sultan Mohammed IV, who blasted Vienna with 300 cannons. And even as Kempelen brought his more playful Turk to Maria Theresa's court during the 1760s and 1770s, skirmishes between Hapsburg and Ottoman forces continued sporadically along the Eastern frontier.[39]

E. T. A. Hoffmann, who must have grown up hearing such stories, quite deliberately played on public fears of the Eastern other in his automaton story, noting that "there was no denying . . . the Turk had an unmistakable air of Oriental *grandezza*."[40] Lewis, his protagonist, in fact becomes so nervous at the very idea of a thinking machine clothed in Turkish attire that he begins to question the wisdom of attending the exhibition. "I feel sure," he exclaims, that "this wonderful, ingen-ious Turk will haunt me with his rolling eyes, his turning head, and his waving arm, like some necromantic goblin, when I lay awake nights; so, the truth is I should very much prefer not going to see him. I should be quite satisfied with other people's accounts of his wit and wisdom."[41] Here Kempelen's automaton served not merely as an Enlightenment wonder, but also as an early Romantic image of exoticized techno-horror. It was at once an Eastern vehicle for powerful spiritual communication and a potentially dangerous expression of Western mechanical genius out of control—an amusement-hall Frankenstein appearing in Turkish robes and turban four years before Mary Shelley's less culturally specific monster sprang to fictional life.[42]

The automaton's Turkishness, however, was never simply a one-dimensional metaphor for the uncanny and uncivilized, the inexplicable and demonic. These qualities could also be turned around and used as part of a popular cultural exercise in which "enlightened" Westerners triumphed over dangerous "foreign" irrationalism. West European viewers could take comfort, after all, that it was a university-educated, Hapsburg man who had built this formidable non-Western figure and who, alone, fully understood its operational principles. While the Turk seemed to possess enormous mental powers, there was always at least one individual looming above it in the culturally constructed cognitive pecking order—its master, the Hungarian Baron. To the extent that Kempelen conceived of the plan, penetrated the Turk's mysteries, and controlled its movements, he also demonstrated for his European audiences the power of Western civilization's intellectual accomplishments and its ability to dominate and contain that which lay outside it—geographically, mentally, and culturally.

On certain occasions, this mastery over the Turk extended to the actual games with European opponents. During the spring of 1783—in the middle of its first international tour—the automaton lost two matches in Paris at the Café de la Régence, as well as a third, highly anticipated match at the Académie des Sciences with the Café's greatest player, Philidor. These defeats, of course, may have had something to do with the enormous skill of the automaton's French opponents, who at the time were considered the finest players on the Continent. It is hard to imagine, however, that Kempelen was unaware of the larger cultural and political issues surrounding these games, or the outpouring of public excitement that would result from allowing the Turk to lose a few matches in the one place synonymous with

European chess greatness—especially after public reports that the automaton initially "declined" offers to play Philidor because "he was not worthy."[43] Whether Kempelen somehow threw the games or chose his Parisian opponents precisely because he knew they would win, these were the Turk's only eighteenth-century defeats.[44]

Less decisive victories over the automaton occurred at the hands of his numerous would-be exposers. For them, the very act of exposing the automaton in print—of laying its secrets bare—produced a kind of provisional, localized intellectual authority. Racknitz, a citizen of Dresden, went to extraordinary lengths to claim relatively modest victories. Unlike most of the other exposé writers, Racknitz built two scale models of the automaton in an effort to test his ideas. He also repeatedly badgered Kempelen with technical questions, even sending him a complete theory of operation on one occasion. Racknitz's published essay from 1789 is a testament to hours of tortuous mental struggle, offering four different hypotheses—the machine is pre-programmed and self-sufficient; it is started and stopped by an outside force rather than a predetermined pattern; it is controlled by external magnetism; and it is controlled by invisible wires—each of which the author himself dismissed as untenable. Ultimately, Racknitz decided on a fifth hypothesis: that the machine must be controlled by a hidden dwarf/child, who hid behind false panels during Kempelen's meticulous demonstrations of the cabinet's interior.

If we dismiss this exposé as a mere exercise in inductive logic (and a faulty one at that!), we miss what it tells us indirectly about the status system that was taking shape in the automaton's early reception. By going to such great lengths to decipher the automaton, Racknitz fashioned himself an expert within his milieu, a member of an intellectual middle rank positioned somewhere between the absolutism of the automaton's creator and the democracy of the baffled. Although Kempelen rightly denied that this explanation was fully correct, it was, without question, the best one the citizens of Dresden had. And when the English encyclopedia writer Thomas Collinson journeyed to the city on a research trip, there was only one man to consult about his own lingering automaton questions—"a gentleman of rank and

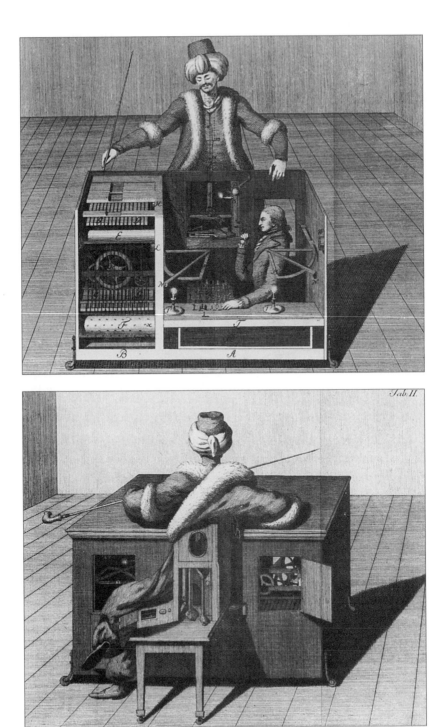

Joseph Friedrich Racknitz's explanations of the automaton's functioning, 1789.

talents, named Joseph Freidrick Freyhere [Racknitz], who seems completely to have discovered the *Vitality* and soul of the chess-playing figure." Racknitz could not erase the "seems" in Collinson's description. But he had become an intellectual authority among Dresden's virtuosi, one whose speculations were deemed worthy of publication by a prominent writer from abroad.

Perhaps the most significant event of all during the automaton's early career, however, occurred only after the final stop on its European odyssey: upon returning to Vienna around 1790, Kempelen took his remarkable machine apart, loaded the components in boxes, and stashed them away in the bowels of Schoenbrun Palace. Although he lived until 1804, Kempelen never demonstrated the automaton again.[45] Perhaps he felt overburdened by his growing stardom as an itinerant showman. Or he may simply have wanted to spend more time with his family, whom he had partially abandoned for almost seven years. Or perhaps he feared that Racknitz and the other exposé writers were slowly but surely working their way toward a complete solution, something which might later diminish the automaton's drawing power. Why not get out of the philosophical amusement business on top, with the thinking machine's secret still largely intact?[46]

The limited evidence we have from Kempelen himself suggests that his motives for retirement were actually far more complex, and, in fact, grew out of what he saw as a basic flaw in the automaton. Vaucanson, it is important to remember, had constructed life-like automata that were pure machine; even the automaton duck's celebrated defecation finale was the result of an ingenious mechanical sphincter. In promotional pamphlets the Frenchman emphasized this fact, boasting of his ability to imitate "by art everything human kind is compelled to make."[47] Kempelen, however, never made such lofty claims about the automaton chess-player, insisting instead that his mechanical creation was actually just a "happy deception."[48] It was, he often emphasized to viewers, "a *bagatelle*" [a trifle], not without "merit in point of mechanism, but the effects of it appear so marvelous only from the boldness of the conception, and the fortunate choice of the methods adopted for promoting the illusion."[49] At least initially,

Kempelen fully encouraged and profited from such promotions. The small case that he regularly placed on a separate table and examined during the early stages of the show, for example, had nothing at all to do with the automaton's operation: it was a bluff, a Barnumesque gesture of misdirection, designed to invite suspicion and convert the automaton's public identity from that of a one-dimensional machine into a multi-dimensional machine-puzzle.[50]

Ultimately, however, these bluffs seem to have weighed heavily on Kempelen's conscience, especially to the extent that they served to transgress and undermine his reputation as an honest mechanic. This, after all, was a man who really did possess a degree of mechanical genius—a genius which had not only garnered him an invitation to Maria Theresa's court but also produced a large *oeuvre* of more honest machines (an Arkwright cotton mill, for example, and an improved circulation system for the Schoenbrun Palace fountain).[51] On tour, Kempelen paired the chess-player with a mechanical speaking machine that was unequivocally identified as being "entirely the effect of art."[52] And according to Windisch, it was this second, more authentic category of invention that gave Kempelen the most pride: "He went so far as totally to neglect the [chess-player], in order to give himself up to new researches, and mechanical inventions of a more serious nature, and more calculated for public utility."[53] Although the chess-player was far and away his most popular creation, Kempelen often kept it hidden even before the European tour began, sometimes lying to friends that it could not be seen because it was "broken." Had it not been for the Emperor's royal directives, Windisch explains, the chess-player would have probably remained but one of many curious objects in Kempelen's upstairs workshop, an object of occasional interest, brought out now and again for a fellow virtuoso.[54]

This, then, was the moral threshold separating artful deception from deviance at the end of the Enlightenment, the publicly defined limit to which playful fraud could be self-consciously pursued in the name of honest amusement. As an inventor of considerable mechanical skills and hopes for upward mobility, one might build a mechanical trick, identify it as such, and even embellish the trick with a few clever feats of promotional misdirection. Ultimately, however, such an act could not stand on its own. It had to be paired with some less dishonest marvel such as the unambiguous (and far less intriguing) speaking machine, or downplayed through public gestures of self-effacement. It had to be described, that is, as a trifle—as a momentary diversion from more practical matters such as fixing the royal fountain.

In the moral hierarchy of Enlightenment careers, one simply could not build a professional identity based entirely on public misinformation and ingenious fraud. To do so was to give up the more solid titles of virtuoso, bureaucrat, scientist, and mechanic in favor of a public persona as charlatan or con man.[55] Faced with the danger of creating a reputation for himself as a maker of hoaxes rather than machines, Kempelen chose to disassemble his illusionistic celebrity and put him in a box in the basement, leaving such marketing innovations (and notoriety) for the less scrupulous showmen of the next century.

Enter Maelzel

For the next thirty-five years (from about 1790 to 1825), the automaton's career was turbulent, lacking the stability and management of a single owner/operator. Initially, the device remained in Schoenbrun Palace—ignored by Kempelen, who had moved on to more pedestrian pursuits, and misunderstood by the other members of Joseph II's royal entourage. If the automaton did play any additional matches before Kempelen's death in 1804, no one seems to have seen or made the effort to write about them. The automaton's fortunes began to pick up again, however, in 1805, when Kempelen's family sold the machine to Johann Nepomuk Maelzel (1772–1838), a German university student and frequent visitor to the Viennese court.

Previously, Maelzel had supported himself both by giving piano lessons and building a wide range of mechanical devices: musical instruments, metronomes, music boxes, even an ear trumpet for the increasingly hard-of-hearing Ludwig van Beethoven.[56] His most impressive early inventions were two self-standing musical machines—

the life-sized automaton Trumpeter, and the Panharmonicon, a kind of spring-driven military band, both of which he exhibited at Schoenbrun Palace and took on tour.[57] Such marvelous imitations of nature garnered enormous praise for their mastermind, who was promptly promoted by the Emperor to *Hof-Mechanikus,* the new court mechanic of the Hapsburg throne. With his prestige and income on the rise, Maelzel purchased the automaton chess-player and opened a curiosity cabinet in Vienna to display his expanding collection of philosophical toys.

After this promising start, the automaton's early nineteenth-century career hit a few bumps. The first of these was Napoleon's invasion, which transformed Schoenbrun Palace into a military garrison. Although Maelzel managed to engineer a match with the French Emperor in 1809 (a match that the Turk reportedly won, thus avenging its early losses to the Parisian chess aristocracy!), the ensuing political chaos slowed the automaton's touring schedule considerably. Another disturbance came around 1811, when Napoleon's nephew, Eugène de Beauharnais, Viceroy of Italy, decided to purchase the automaton for 30,000 francs.[58] For the next five years, the automaton languished in Beauharnais' Milanese estate with little attention from its new owner, who became considerably less "curious" about his expensive toy after peeking inside the cabinet.[59]

By 1818, however, Maelzel and the automaton were out on tour again, with a number of improvements in the show, and at least part of the money filtering back to Beauharnais.[60] It was at this point that Maelzel gave the automaton the power of speech, so that now, instead of simply nodding its head to signal a victory, the automaton actually spoke to its human antagonists in French. With each winning move, it declared, *"échec et mat* [checkmate]."[61] Maelzel also enhanced the exhibition with the "Conflagration of Moscow," a large panorama painting of Napoleon's invasion of the Russian capital.[62] In contrast to Kempelen, who had exhibited his invention alone or with one other attraction (the speaking machine) and had limited his shows to a couple of dozen viewers at a time, Maelzel now presented the chess-player as part of a multi-media extravaganza including the Panorama, the Panharmonicon, and his Trumpeter. He also sought out larger urban venues such as 29 St. James Street in London, which, according to William Lewis (one of Maelzel's London "directors"), held about one hundred spectators and had a stage large enough to hold the Conflagration.[63] For the first time in its career, the automaton chess-player was fully independent of royal patronage, functioning now as part of a budding urban middle-class leisure market, one located downtown rather than in a court or country fair, supported by ticket sales at the doors of rented halls, and engineered by a full-time, show business entrepreneur.

The fact that we even know these things about Maelzel's London exhibitions—that this information is available now as historical evidence—is itself an important development. Compare this early nineteenth-century information, for example, to that which we have about Anton, Kempelen's late eighteenth-century protégé. Although one early pamphlet writer mentioned that Anton assisted Kempelen during his Leipzig exhibitions, we are left with numerous, unresolved questions. Who was this shadowy figure? How did Kempelen enter into business with him? Was he ever responsible for the automaton's play? Of William Lewis, on the other hand, we know many things. We know that he did indeed produce the automaton's thoughts and movements in London, and that he was London's best chess-player at the time. We also know that Maelzel recruited him privately, paid him a salary, and entrusted him with the secret of the automaton, and that he was actually one of two Londoners employed by Maelzel (the other was a French chess champion named Mouret).

These facts about the London exhibitions are available for one obvious, but easily forgotten, reason: Lewis and Mouret *told them* to others. This does not mean, of course, that they simply broadcasted Maelzel's secrets to an eager public—to do so would have been economically disadvantageous for all parties, at least in the long term. Rather, these facts began to surface through a series of leaks, bits of information haphazardly released and absorbed into the larger body of public knowledge about the automaton. They appeared through Lewis, years later, telling a friend that he had been one of Maelzel's directors; or Mouret letting an important fact slip here and there to an acquaintance while drinking.[64] While neither source was decisive or complete, the circle of insider knowledge about the automaton—as well as the volume of evidence and possible theories in public circulation—was slowly expanding with each new director hired by Maelzel.[65]

We also have more facts about Maelzel's London exhibitions because the very nature of public information was changing during these years. Whereas Kempelen's eighteenth-century career comes down to us through a relatively limited body of published information—eight pamphlets written by those who could afford to print their ideas, a couple of letters between Kempelen and Franklin, and a short story by Hoffmann—Maelzel's subsequent exploits are preserved in two additional and more widely circulated public media: urban newspapers and mass-produced handbills. When Kempelen first took his exhibition to Paris, he contacted Franklin through a personal letter; Franklin, in turn, provided Kempelen with a letter of introduction to a few of his French chess-playing friends, a relatively small and elite group defined by personal ties and long-held relationships. Maelzel, by contrast, made his introduction to Londoners in public, through frequent advertisements in the London *Times* and scores of handbills posted on the city's walls.

Although the automaton still received little or no unpaid coverage in newspapers—something which would not take place for about another decade, with the rapid expansion of the urban popular press—a much broader group of Londoners now had access to information about the device. They knew where and when it was showing (a hall in St. James Street, every afternoon and evening). They knew how much a glimpse would cost (a shilling). And they knew what kind of entertainment this was (a "popular" exhibition, offered not just to aristocratic elites but to the general public).[66] "Mr. Maelzel," noted one *Times* paragraph from May 12, 1819, "begs to express his very grateful acknowledgements for the very distinguished and liberal patronage with which he has been honoured. During an active campaign of 6 months, the most celebrated chess players in England have entered the lists against the Automaton without once defeating it, and the principle of its action still remains as before, a problem involved in mystery."[67]

This mysterious problem arrived in New York City on February 3, 1826.[68] By April, Maelzel had set up his headquarters in a hotel and once again made his introduction to "the public" through newspaper advertisements:

> Automaton Chess-Player.
> Mr. Maelzel, Proprietor of the celebrated and only Automaton Chess-player in the world, informs the public that the first exhibition will take place on Thursday, the 13th insa., in the assembly room at the National Hotel, No. 112 Broadway, opposite the City Hotel. The order of exhibition will be as follows:
> 1st. The Automaton Chess-player, who will play a number of ends of games, giving the choice of pieces to any antagonist that offers. These ends of games are played in preference to whole games, as they exhibit the powers of the machine equally well, and do not fatigue the attention of the company.
> 2d. The Automaton Trumpeter, invented by Mr. Maelzel. He will play a number of marches composed expressly for him by the first masters.
> 3d. The Automaton Slack Rope Dancers, also invented by Mr. Maelzel, and the only ones ever exhibited on a slack rope.
> The exhibition to continue daily, commencing precisely at 12 at noon, and at 8 in the evening.
> N.B. Amateurs wishing to engage the Chess-player at whole games, can be accommodated with private meetings on application to the proprietor. Admittance 50 cents. Children under 12 years half price.[69]

Both Maelzel's admission price (twice as much as a ticket to Barnum's American Museum twenty years later) and the discount offered to children help to refine our understanding of the automaton's egalitarianism. This was a form of *popular* culture, to be sure, but it did not fall within an affordable price range for many manual workers, nor did it operate according to the rowdy consumption practices of many New York amusements.[70] Maelzel's initial American audiences probably included property owners, merchants, and master craftsmen, but it is unlikely that many New Yorkers lower down in the artisan workshop's increasingly differentiated class system saw the automaton chess-player at first hand.[71] It is also worth noting that the address given in the advertisement places Maelzel's exhibition within about a block of New York's other established collections of curiosities in 1826: John Scudder's American Museum and Rubens Peale's New York Museum. Given the fact that both of these collections contained numerous automata of their own, Maelzel's claims to originality and authenticity in the first sentence make perfect sense.[72]

It was up to viewers, of course, to decide whether the automaton chess-player was a remarkable machine or some sort of hoax. But Maelzel wanted to make clear, right from the start, that this was the original machine/hoax Americans had heard about for so long, the one automaton in New York worth the price of admission. Also significant are Maelzel's obvious attempts to define a public persona for himself as an inventor of automata. As most Americans knew, it was another European who had actually built the chess player; Maelzel was simply responsible for bringing it across the Atlantic. Yet he defines himself here publicly as something more than an impresario: he is also the brains and hands behind the Trumpeter, a device known to be purely mechanical, as well as an original group of automata never exhibited before—the Slack Rope Dancers. This self-definition proved critical not only in leaving open the possibility that the chess-player was all, or at least part, machine, but also in assuaging public concerns about paying to see something they knew—at least in their more clear-headed moments—to be an elaborate deception. As one contemporary noted, Americans saw Maelzel first and foremost in terms of his mechanical skill and gentility, even as they devoted enormous amounts of time, money, and energy to the activity of proving his best-known entertainment a hoax:

> He stood before the visitors of his room, by no means as a showman, but as a great inventor. Such he had proved himself to be by his Panharmonicon, and his Rope-dancers; such he appeared to be, where he was less original, in his Metronome and his Trumpeter; and a genius that could do so much was *half-believed* to be capable of inventing a machine that could calculate the combinations of Chess. And not his talents alone—his

appearance and manners attracted the applause of his visitors. He was the perfection of politeness and amiability; he was passionately fond of children, and invariably reserved for them his front seats and distributed sweetmeats among them; and he occasionally gave a benefit to orphans, or widows, or some other charity, in a way that evinced real benevolence of disposition.[73]

Maelzel, in other words, seemed to play little role in fostering the "half-belief" of his spectators: he was a well-mannered and honest mechanic; his inventions spoke for themselves. Yet, as Poe pointed out in his 1836 essay, this popular cultural enterprise was actually far more complicated. Indeed, precisely because of his mechanical talent, Maelzel could have refined Kempelen's design by making the chess-player more "realistic"—like his Rope-Dancers, for example—a group of automata which demonstrated a "full ability to copy the notions and peculiarities of life with the most wonderful exactitude."[74] The fact that he did not suggests that Maelzel was quite content to confuse the line between reality and illusion. "Were the Automaton life-like in its motions," noted Poe, "the spectator would be more apt to attribute its operations to their true cause (that is, to human agency within), than he is now, when the awkward and rectangular maneuvers convey the idea of pure and unaided mechanism."[75] Also telling were Maelzel's deliberately ambiguous responses to the questions of his American audiences. Whereas Kempelen had admitted to practicing deception, Maelzel left it to viewers to decide for themselves: "When the question is demanded explicitly of Maelzel: 'Is the Automaton a pure machine or not?' his reply is invariably the same: 'I will say nothing about it.'"[76]

The American response to these aesthetic and verbal equivocations was more rewarding than Maelzel could have anticipated. "Last evening," gushed the *Evening Post,* "the first exhibition of Mr. Maelzel's automatons took place before a company of upwards of a hundred persons, and we believe we speak the opinion of every individual present, in saying, that nothing of a similar nature has ever been seen in this city, that will bear the smallest comparison with it."[77] A week later the paper noted that "the Chess-player continues to attract full and fashionable houses: upwards of a hundred persons have been every evening disappointed in getting seats, and obliged to leave the door."[78] "We may appear to permit the automaton to occupy too much of our columns," wrote the *Post's* editor, "but persons at a distance can form no idea how much the attention of our citizens is engrossed by it at this present writing."[79]

While the automaton had been lauded in print before, these reports from Maelzel's American debut marked a new form and level of press coverage. Suddenly, the show had become newsworthy: an event of sufficient importance to receive frequent editorial attention, even without payments from Maelzel. Unprecedented, too, was the level of cross-referencing among newspaper reports on the automaton. The author of the first *Evening Post* review, for example, based his claim that the automaton was operated by a dwarf or child on an exposé by Sir David Brewster in the *Edinburgh Journal of Arts and Sciences*.[80] As other writers followed suit, each one referring to other recent articles on the automaton, the urban newspaper quickly became the public's best interlocutor of circulating theories. A second audience outside of the exhibition hall—one much larger, more amorphous, and even international in scope, something closer to what we might now describe as a mass audience—was beginning to take shape.

Yet, right from the start, this media-driven public discourse was provisional and highly unstable. It could boldly claim to have "solved" the mystery and then quickly change theories in as little as a week, or even a few days later. Only seven days after its first review, the *Evening Post* put forth a new explanation based on Maelzel's secret manipulation—the source this time was a writer in the New York *National Advocate* known as "the Old Chess Player"—and referred to Brewster's dwarf/child theory merely as a possible explanation discredited "several years" ago.[81] Six days later, the *Evening Post* began denouncing the writer from the *Advocate,* noting that "the automaton has twice publicly finished games in the presence of upwards of three hundred persons, without Mr. Maelzel's touching the board or box at all; which would seem enough to convince a person of the futility of the Old Chess Player's theory."[82] The day after that, the paper voiced a frustration no doubt shared by readers who had been following this dizzying string of reversals and counter-theories:

> The chess automaton is most alarming! . . . the secret has been discovered in this city, on a moderate calculation, about one dozen times during the last week. A young gentleman called on the proprietor, a day or two since, and after telling him that he had found out his secret, modestly offered, for a proper consideration, to conceal the discovery from the world. Another contends that a sort of piano is played upon; a third insists that a full grown gentleman plays the game through the waistcoat of the figure; while a fourth supports the more *rational* conjecture that a learned dwarf or dog or pig is concealed—a poor compliment to the great players who have unsuccessfully opposed the figure.[83]

Here was much the same catalog of "cognition" theories offered by viewers of the automaton's first European tour. But whereas Kempelen's viewers had been separated from one another by geography and limited print sources, Maelzel's fans had access to a single textual intermediary through which to negotiate and consume this information maelstrom—their daily newspaper.

As the summer season began, Maelzel moved to Boston, and almost immediately the automaton began to transcend its previous promotional schemes. In New York, Maelzel had advertised a series of end-games; complete matches with the automaton were available by appointment only. In Boston, however, Maelzel offered full games during every performance—a difference in format which led one writer to the New York *American* to complain of a double standard. Maelzel's clever reply soon appeared in two Boston newspapers:

> Sir: A writer in the New York American of Sept. 30th having endeavored to make it appear that my Automaton was not able to cope with some of the New York players in whole games, and as I think the players of Boston are at least equal to those of New York, and being under obligations to them for their patronage and courtesy, I propose during the ensuing week to entertain them with entire games. It has never been made a pretension of mine that the Automaton was invincible; and it is only my wish to defend his character so far as to show he is entitled to the fame he acquired during his visits to London and Paris [where] many of

the most respectable [players] and some from this place witnessed his performances.

If this defense of the automaton's character produced profitable inter-city rivalries with Gotham, so much the better. Maelzel "therefore invited" all Boston "gentlemen desirous of playing full games to favor me with their names that I may make the necessary arrangements."[84]

Once again, the automaton was becoming a focal point for re-gional contests and cross-cultural rivalries, yet this was a very different species of symbolic conflict than the earlier matches played out between the Turk and its West European adversaries. The most obvi-ous difference involved the particular historical contexts for these rivalries: while both sets of matches were understood as forms of pub-lic amusement, only the first contest took place with real Ottoman armies and cannons positioned along the nation's borders. The spe-cific meanings and functions of the automaton's Orientalism seem to have been transformed in the United States, too. Whereas Philidor had once defended the honor of the Enlightenment against the Ori-ent's "mysterious and magical powers" (powers that kept Hoffmann's characters up at night with worry), the gentlemen of Boston now lined up to vanquish a popular cultural other that was somewhat less threat-ening and immediate, both in the name of their own republican inge-nuity, and as a means of publicly trumping their New York rivals.[85]

This is not to suggest that American audiences were less prone to Orientalist fantasy and caricature than their European predecessors. In fact, during the automaton's very first American season, New York theater patrons paid their quarters to see a variety of extravagantly Orientalist productions (for example, "The Sultan," "Bluebeard," and "Aladdin"), often with Near Eastern settings and Turkish slaves as characters.[86] One might even argue that the core imagery at the heart of Maelzel's show—a prosperous European man flanked by his obedi-ent Turkish servant—recapitulated the dominant mode of U.S. Orien-talism during the antebellum years, in which fictional representations of "Islamic" civilizations served as a coded cultural mechanism for dis-cussing the problem of slavery in this country.[87] Yet it is also true that most American writers did not go very far in casting Maelzel's automaton as a non-Western exotic or slave. Poe, significantly, said virtually nothing about the automaton's Turkish appearance in 1836, choosing instead to focus on its means of operation (a decision which seems especially surprising given Poe's usual fondness for exoticism and horror).[88] And in 1856, as we have seen, Mitchell portrayed the Turk as a sympathetic friend and colleague, a "republican" worthy of "our respect, since, perhaps, no other man has ever checked the march of so many kings as he."

These new wrinkles in the automaton's reception, however, only begin to describe the full scope of its early nineteenth-century evolution—a fact well-illustrated by the diverse social positions of the players who actually defeated Maelzel's prodigy in the United States. In New York, Boston, Philadelphia, and Baltimore, the automaton was beaten by a small number of "gentlemen" opponents, many of whom had some kind of affiliation to a local lyceum or chess organization.[89] Dr. Joshua Cohen, a member of the Baltimore Chess Club, was typical of this milieu:

> Altho' a constant visitor to the Exhibition, I never took part in play—but on [one] occasion, with the room full of company, there was no one who would come forward to play; and at last I yielded to the request of Maelzel, as well as of several friends who were amongst the company. The Game set was a very complicated one—I could not of course see at the moment the relative bearings of the pieces, and on being asked, "which side I would take," I seeing that one side had a Queen, and the other had not I selected at random the side *without* the queen. The game began, and I thought, after playing ten or fifteen minutes, that my side was the stronger, and then feeling some interest in it (for I sat down under the full expectation of being checkmated in a few moves) I took some care in my moves—as we reopened the spectators evinced great interest in the game, and after contending an hour the Automaton yielded. I was sorry at the moment, knowing my real relative strength . . . and still more worried was I the next morning on seeing in the Papers, *"The Chess Player Beaten."* [90]

As Cohen later explained, he actually knew the true identity of his opponent, an Alsatian chess master whom Maelzel hired as his primary assistant after 1826. Thus, in Cohen's mind, this match represented not so much an encounter with mechanical genius—or a battle for the honor of Baltimore's gentlemen—but a rare opportunity to play a "masked" European champion in public, one so thrilling that Cohen still remembered many of his own moves a quarter-century after the fact. Having watched and admired the play of his true opponent on numerous previous occasions, Cohen was almost apologetic about the result, knowing in his heart of hearts that his victory was not a real indication of superior skill ("I was sorry at the moment, knowing my real relative strength").

Cohen and the other club-affiliated "gentlemen" who defeated the automaton during the late 1820s resembled Kempelen's infrequent late eighteenth-century "conquerors." All were part of an urban chess-playing elite that was entirely male, and all were unusually talented players with a detailed knowledge of the game. Other American winners, however, deviated from this mold in significant ways. In Philadelphia, for example, the automaton lost a full game over the course of two exhibitions to a Mrs. Fisher, described in the front-page headlines as a "lady" of the city. Although the Philadelphia press explained very little about who this woman was or how she conducted herself during the course of the long match, the reporters were careful to record her intellectual achievement, even going so far as to transcribe the entire series of moves by which she had checkmated the automaton.[91] And this was not the only instance of an American woman successfully battling the automaton in public. In New York, the *Evening Post* hailed "a most scientific and masterly attack" by an "antagonist" of the automaton, "who was a lady."[92] This particular match ended in a draw. But the editors nevertheless saw the event as remarkable precisely because of the gender and formidable play of Maelzel's volunteer: "We believe we express the sentiments of the company in regretting that this portion of the exhibition is limited to so short a period, more particularly that it was so on the present occasion, when so much skill had been exhibited by the fair antagonist of the imperturbable Turk."[93]

Another celebrated performance came eight years later, when Samuel Smyth, a "handsome youth" of eighteen, defeated the automaton in a full game at Philadelphia's Masonic Hall.[94] According to one frequent spectator at Maelzel's Philadelphia exhibitions during the early 1830s, Smyth's victory was "unusually exciting" because of the "interesting appearance of the youthful champion." Shocked at the prospect of seeing someone so young—and from outside the chess-playing elite—actually defeat the automaton, "a gentleman, among the spectators, was so far beside himself, that he rushed out of the room, and ran up Chestnut street, without his hat, to publish the rare phenomenon of a victory over the invincible Turk."[95]

These surprising losses at the hands of the fair and youthful fit none of the patterns we have encountered previously. They were neither the product of great historical rivalries between East and West, nor in the service of the usual promotional themes (Enlightenment science, republican ingenuity, or even Maelzel's profit-driven attempts to flatter the members of American chess clubs). Rather, these losses were exciting largely because their protagonists were "ordinary citizens," people one was not used to seeing on stage or on the front page of the newspaper. But were they rigged? Perhaps not. Perhaps the newspaper writers were correct. Perhaps Maelzel and the automaton were simply outmaneuvered by the "scientific and masterly attacks" of these amateurs. If the automaton could lose a careless match to a chess expert like Cohen, it could certainly lose once in a while to an exceptional amateur like Mrs. Fisher or Samuel Smyth. Yet the surviving evidence suggests that Maelzel was obsessive about quality control during these years, hiring as far as possible only international champions as the automaton's hidden directors. And during these particular losses the automaton was directed by one of the world's finest chess players—the Alsatian champion William Schlumberger—a man who, playing as himself, *never* lost a match in the United States.[96] Thus it only seems reasonable to ask what sort of tricks Maelzel might have had up his sleeve. What might he have been selling to his American audiences with this wave of losses after 1826?

One possible answer involves the rapidly changing relation of machines to socioeconomic identity during these years. Maelzel's arrival in the United States coincided with a fundamental reorganization of the craft professions in the Northeast's urban centers, a reorganization which subdivided and de-skilled many traditional artisanal careers in the name of increased production.[97] For those who could afford to attend Maelzel's shows, the new division of labor was not an immediate threat; it was not the jobs of master craftsmen, merchants, and salaried office workers being lost to the new industrial system of production. Still, it was a subject of concern, and given the fact that industrial workers did complain loudly during the late 1820s and 1830s, both on the shop floor and, increasingly, in the streets, the automaton's wordless, buzzing, ruthlessly efficient displays must have offered a reassuring image: one of complete and total subservience, both to Maelzel (a *master* mechanic, in both senses of the term), and, by extension, to his new legions of bourgeois fans. For members of this audience to defeat the automaton in public was not simply mindless fun. It was also to recapitulate—as symbolic play and public ritual—the early nineteenth-century metropolis's emerging socioeconomic and professional hierarchies.

These public defeats of the automaton can also be connected to a major change within the show trade itself: the emergence of what Barnum later described as family entertainment. Indeed, by extending the circle of victory to the "fair" and "youthful" members of his urban middle-class audiences, Maelzel helped to create this cultural category: at least for a moment, Mrs. Fisher and Smyth could become like Maelzel, a figure possessed of "extraordinary faculties," and demonstrate their "powers of intellect" on stage, an activity more conventionally reserved for older male elites like Dr. Cohen. Of course, there were limits to this sort of egalitarianism. In addition to the obvious racial and class boundaries they enforced, Maelzel's American exhibitions maintained one major gendered distinction from the Age of Enlightenment: it was always an enlightened male persona who ultimately controlled the rules of the game. While middle-class women increasingly shared center stage with Maelzel's automaton, they did so as consumers of its wonders. Even as artful deception moved into the more heterosocial confines of middlebrow commercial entertainment, playing the role of trickster continued to be a (mostly) male cultural prerogative.[98]

But what about the more pressing matter of solving the automaton's operational mysteries, a cultural conundrum described by one New York newspaper in 1826 as "the greatest puzzle ever seen"?[99] Significantly, there was no published American counterpart to Johann Ebert, the Leipzig mathematician who had confidently argued that the automaton was indeed an ingenious machine. By the 1820s and 1830s, viewers focused on determining not whether, but how this thinking machine was a form of artful deception. And they did so in novel ways, again and again fashioning this debate so as to leave its decisive question open-ended. This is not to suggest that they lacked theories; from published exposé writers like Poe down to the nameless shouting "individuals" mentioned in the daily newspaper stories, American viewers offered countless opinions on how an assistant might have been concealed in the automaton's cabinet, escaped detection during the preliminary inspections, and guided the automaton's movements.

Yet they also increasingly treated these operational ideas *as theories*—possible, to be sure, but certainly not the only possible explanations. "We take pleasure," noted the *Evening Post* after two months of New York automaton shows, "in saying this wonderful effort of human genius still retains his original popularity in all its freshness, and that not the least approach has been yet made towards discovering the wonderful secret that for more than 50 years has puzzled the world."[100] This was patently untrue: hundreds if not thousands of approaches had been made toward discovering the secret, many of which were actually very close to *the* answer. But to acknowledge them as such, to admit a kind of closure in this process, was to end the game and unnecessarily disenchant the machine. Why quell such endlessly interesting play and debate when both the machine itself, and its remarkably provisional new chronicler—the urban newspaper—provided opportunities for perpetual life and controversy?

Such willful, collective suspension of disbelief is difficult to prove. Certainly, no viewer ever claimed to be working against—or deliberately impeding—the solution of the automaton's operational mysteries. Still, there is some unmistakable evidence that Maelzel's American audiences often resisted the possibility of bringing the puzzle to closure, particularly during the automaton's 1827 tour stop in Baltimore. This exhibition began like all the others: Maelzel set up shop at a local hotel, took out advertisements in the daily newspapers, and welcomed large crowds of excited viewers eager to speculate on the automaton's operational principles. Due to particularly high summer temperatures, however, the unthinkable happened: during one of the automaton's mid-day shows, Schlumberger, dizzy from heat exhaustion inside the cabinet, began signaling to Maelzel to end the match in progress. Before the showman could fashion a plausible excuse for the audience—and wheel the machine completely into their backstage dressing room—a sweaty Schlumberger burst out of the cabinet, gasping for air. The audience before the stage, we are told, witnessed the event simply as a "problem with the machine." But two teenage boys, who happened to be standing on an adjacent rooftop, saw all of the backstage activity through a dressing room window. Predictably, they rushed home and told the story of Schlumberger's emergency evacuation to their parents, who promptly called the Baltimore *Gazette*.[101]

Less predictable, however, are the events which transpired next. First, the *Gazette* ran a front-page article exposing the automaton's "internal organs" to the community:

This ingenious contrivance of M. Kempelen, which has occasioned so much curious conjecture, and excited so much interest in the principal cities of Europe, and in various parts of the United States, after a period of nearly sixty years of doubt as to the mode of its operation, has at length been discovered by accident to be merely the case in which a human agent has always been concealed, when exhibited to an audience. This discovery, as we learn, was made by a person who had not formed any plan or design for that purpose; an accidental circumstance exposed to his view the concealed agent as he emerged from the case, just after the conclusion of an exhibition of the Automaton.[102]

Maelzel, in turn, removed the chess-player from his exhibitions, announcing to the public that it was broken. For the next couple of months, the Conflagration and Trumpetplayer performed without their more famous headliner. Yet by almost all contemporary accounts, the *Gazette* exposé did relatively little damage to Maelzel's enterprise. George Allen, a frequent patron, described the temporary hiatus as completely unnecessary: "nobody credited the pretended discovery. The world had set its heart upon believing that the secret, which had puzzled mechanicians, mathematicians, and monarchs, for more than half a century, was something quite too deep to be penetrated by a couple of boys."[103]

Three days after the Baltimore exposé, the venerable Washington, D.C. *National Intelligencer* suggested a case of naiveté on the part of its journalistic rival, noting that "the proprietor" of the exhibition "may have played off a *ruse* to mislead the public."[104] According to Allen, the *Gazette* never printed a word about the Baltimore boys' story again: "the smaller fry of editors, after being put on their guard by the 'Newspapers' Mother,' were far too cautious to make fools of themselves by repeating the shallow story; and thus it was that a revelation, which might have been expected to spread all over the country like wild-fire, did nothing but raise a slight smoke in one city, and even there, as if fairly ashamed of itself it soon vanished into air."[105]

It would be left to Barnum to plant false stories and self-directed accusations in the newspapers; Maelzel, as far as we can tell, merely invited suspicion through his silence. Yet it is clear that even in 1827 Barnum's popular cultural universe has begun to emerge: one in which dubious authenticity *defined* the object on display—made it curious—and in which cheap daily print sources served as the primary tool for big-city showmen to construct and manipulate such suspicions. It is a strategy Barnum later confessed to have learned, at least in part, from Maelzel. While on the Boston stop of his tour with Joice

Heth in 1835, Barnum discussed the "value of the press" with the old European showman next door:

> The celebrated Maelzel was exhibiting his equally celebrated "automaton chess-player" in the large ball-room of Concert Hall. . . . I had frequent interviews and long conversations with Mr. Maelzel. I looked upon him as the great father of caterers for public amusement, and was pleased with his assurances that I would certainly make a successful showman. "I see," said he, in broken English, "that you understand the value of the press, and that is the great thing. Nothing helps the showmans like the types and inks."[106]

This was one of Barnum's crucial early lessons in the trickster trade, for it demonstrated the importance of keeping one's artful deceptions in the spotlight through a relentless barrage of printed advertising. Even more important for the young impresario, however, was the example Maelzel provided in how to deploy the press as part of the show: not simply to notify the public about one's popular cultural tricks, but to keep the public guessing at all times, to destabilize and perpetuate the process of public solution.

"Echec! Echec!"

Two years after Maelzel's conversations with Barnum, the Philadelphia *National Gazette Literary Register* published a particularly detailed front-page exposé of the automaton chess-player.[107] Racknitz, it explained, had been exactly right about the existence of a concealed "director" working inside the cabinet. What he had not fully comprehended was the method of concealment and operation. During the preliminary demonstration of the interior, the director would shift his position behind a series of false panels; as Maelzel closed one door and opened the next, the director slid back and forth on a rolling seat. Thus there was no need to employ a child or dwarf to operate the automaton, as Racknitz, Brewster, Poe, and so many other previous published exposé writers had argued. This method of concealment allowed even a very tall man such as Schlumberger, who was over six feet, to direct the automaton's moves.

Once the cabinet was locked, the director pushed all the panels to one side, stretched out his legs, lit a candle, and followed the automaton's game from inside the cabinet, viewing magnet-activated markers under the chess pieces. To keep track of which piece value (knight, pawn, etc.) was on which square—which, of course, was easy to forget over the course of a thirty or sixty minute match—the director played simultaneously on another, smaller chess board inside the cabinet. As thousands of viewers had long suspected, then, the automaton's *thoughts* were actually those of a human mind. The automaton's *movements*, however, were the result of machinery. To control the automaton's arm and fingers, the director maneuvered an ingenious pentagraph device carefully synchronized with the two chess boards. As the director touched a pointer to a square inside the cabinet, the automaton's hand moved to the appropriate square above. Maelzel's only role in these games was to mediate between the chess boards of the volunteer and the automaton.

This was indeed *the answer*—the endlessly sought after explanation of the most perplexing cultural conundrum of the late eighteenth and early nineteenth centuries.[108] What made this exposé particularly worrisome for Maelzel, however, was not so much its accuracy as its vehicle and source. Unlike many of the newspapers and journals which had already published exposés of the automaton, the *National Gazette* was one of Philadelphia's oldest and most respected news organs. And the source behind the article was none other than Mouret, one of the automaton's hidden directors in London, who, in his old age, sold his insider's story to a French newspaper in 1834.[109] Two years later, the world's first professional chess journal, *Le Palamède*, republished the story, along with a certificate of authenticity signed by the journal's publisher. Thus it is hardly surprising to learn that Maelzel packed up the automaton and headed to Cuba within weeks of the first American re-publication of the Mouret/ *Palamède* article. The problem with this particular exposé was not only that it was correct, but that it was certified publicly by the most powerful and respected chess authority in Maelzel's and Schlumberger's milieu. It seemed to destroy any ambiguity that still adhered to the automaton.[110]

Maelzel and Schlumberger both died of yellow fever during the Cuban tour, so we will never know what sorts of spin control they might have engineered to cope with the *National Gazette* story. In retrospect, however, it appears that any concerns about public humiliation or lost profits were probably unnecessary. In 1840, Dr. John Kearsley Mitchell (the author of the automaton's "obituary") bought the device at auction with a number of chess-playing friends precisely because he could not accept the reports from Europe as conclusive. "The newspaper translations," Allen explained, "could not work perfect conviction in [Mitchell's] mind. Who could tell whether Mouret had not earned his money, and preserved his honor (in some sort), by telling what only looked like, but in fact was not, the real secret? There could obviously be no satisfactory, final test, but that of the actual inspection of the mechanism itself."[111] The Philadelphia *North American and Daily Advertiser* echoed this sentiment in 1840, concluding that despite years of theorizing, the city's audiences were still no further along in solving the puzzle than the automaton's very first viewers in 1769:

> Whether the secret, which is now in the possession of a few gentlemen of this city, will be exposed, is uncertain; but whether it shall turn out to be a mere machine directed by springs and wheels, set in motion by the exhibitor, or an assistant at a greater distance; or a mere puppet, moved by a player within, who has, for over half a century, eluded the observations of thousands of eagerly watchful spectators, it must be admitted to be one of the most ingenious, and completely successful contrivances, which has ever been offered to the public. Instead of satisfying, it seems continually to excite curiosity, and the more one goes to see it, the more desirous he becomes to visit it again.[112]

What this account pointed to was not simply a replication of the virtuoso's experience, but a new, media-driven form of curiosity—perpetually excited, yet never fully satisfied. It also described an equally unprecedented curious object, one which offered no single answer, no fundamental truth. For those who continued to think of truth—particularly visual truth—as universal, objective, and absolute, as something revealed through human powers of perceptual and cognitive penetration, these changes in the forms and meanings of the automaton were troubling. Kempelen, clearly, had found it difficult to give up on the older Enlightenment ideals. To manufacture deceiving appearances, and to leave these deceptions ambiguously defined in the public's mind, was not simply a transgression of the boundary between honesty and fraud. To his mind it also began to undermine or devalue his more solid achievements as a mechanic.

Maelzel, on the other hand, seems to have been far less disturbed by the automaton's challenge to visual transparency and utilitarian production. Indeed, his steadfast, calculated equivocation in the face of public questioning served to push this exhibition beyond even the broadest late eighteenth-century conceptions of philosophical amusement, and towards a new category of curiosity—one whose illusionism lay not in its ability simply to imitate nature in the form of a machine, but to render the process of imitation itself an open question. Kempelen, to be sure, had engineered his fair share of bluffs around the automaton. But now Maelzel was self-consciously and aggressively making the bluff the center of the show, the entertainment form itself.

In redefining philosophical amusement, Maelzel transformed his own public persona as well. Although a mechanic of considerable skill, he had become something quite different when Barnum met him during the mid-1830s: he was now a showman, a maker of ingenious hoaxes rather than ingenious machines, a brilliant manipulator of the press and public opinion to whom young Barnum turned for advice and examples. This is not to suggest that Maelzel's identity as master craftsman became superfluous. Again and again, American audiences commented on the fact that Maelzel's mechanical skills were crucial to the effectiveness of the entertainment. Without these skills, the possibility that the automaton might be a thinking machine—a possibility essential to the device's effectiveness as a popular cultural puzzle—seemed far less likely.

Yet this was hardly the same kind of craftsman that Vaucanson, or even Kempelen personified. Maelzel's public reputation as a mechanic now functioned primarily as a calculated pose—a marketing trick—one engineered to leave the question of the automaton's authenticity deliberately confused. Was this man a brilliant inventor or a cunning trickster? The fact that American audiences never quite answered this bottom-line question and did not seem to mind—that such unresolved theorizing was generally considered fun and entertaining—made Maelzel the one and only show business mentor Barnum mentioned in his 1855 autobiography.

The role of the media in these historical developments was pivotal. Clearly, the rapid expansion of the urban press in the 1820s and 1830s had a great deal to do with the automaton's increasingly provisional status as an object of continuous public inquiry—solved one day, only to be *re*-solved the next, always according to a new and improved theory. By the late 1820s, much of what made the automaton unusual and exciting was the fact that its puzzle never seemed fully solved and produced different debates from week to week. As the volume of articles, readers, and theories increased, so too did the size of the "middle rank" of automaton experts.

Blumenberg makes special note of these historical changes in the form and context of "theoretical curiosity," pointing to Alexander von Humboldt's landmark astronomical work, *Kosmos* (1849), and its enthusiastic reception by the popular press in Germany, as his central example. As a champion of the Enlightenment and a promoter of "theoretical activity," Humboldt faced a dilemma. On the one hand, the popular success of *Kosmos* ("*Kosmos* mania," as he called it) seemed to gratify and fulfill its author's Enlightenment idealism. The work's popular appeal provoked citizens "from the court, through the society of the capitol, all the way to the countryside and the parsonages" to try their hand at "speculative manuscripts on constellations, planetary disturbances, and general world views." On the other hand, the level on which this "popular curiosity" took place deeply troubled Humboldt. It was, as Blumenberg explains, "journalistically stimulated and then satisfied by unsupervised means," especially through

the inexpensive and often inaccurate *Leipzig Illustrated News*. Much
to Humboldt's dismay, the Leipzig editors even went so far as to offer
a "false table of geographical altitudes" for public consumption. "This
newspaper," Humboldt complained to a colleague, aims only at "the
momentary satisfaction of curiosity, not of the appetite for knowledge,
and of course deeper learning is entirely out of the question."[113]

It is easy to sympathize with Humboldt's predicament. After working so hard to make Enlightenment science accessible to the urban
middle-class masses, he now found his careful researches transformed
into a kind of popular amusement. His work was read and talked about
by a new, much larger audience, but often at the cost of precision
and rigor. Still, it seems important to question—or at least qualify—
Humboldt's appraisal of popular curiosity as an intellectual mode
quite separate, even opposed to "knowledge" and "learning." Were the
automaton chess-player's international audiences simply participating
in a seventy-year fit of self-delusion? Were their unsupervised attempts
to replicate the investigatory experience of the virtuoso ultimately hol-
low, nothing more than a scientific posture lacking theoretical substance? If our sole criterion is the correct explanation, then the answer
is certainly yes: even brilliant intellectuals such as Franklin, Brewster,
and Poe got Kempelen's puzzle wrong with astounding regularity.

But it should also be clear that the automaton's meanings and
functions as a form of artful deception were never limited to a single,
narrowly defined analytical problem. On the contrary, viewers used
this popular cultural puzzle to think about and offer opinions on an
astounding assortment of late eighteenth- and early nineteenth-
century issues: the increasingly fuzzy moral threshold separating artful imitation and criminal deception; a wide variety of geo-cultural
rivalries symbolized and contested through a caricatured non-Western
other; the socioeconomic and gendered implications of playing, beat-
ing, and controlling Maelzel's diligent laborer; and the increasingly
provisional and unstable status of printed information in the emerging
urban-industrial society.

This was Maelzel's real legacy for the Age of Barnum: not simply
an ambiguous, media-driven mode of artful deception, but one whose

uncanny resistance to solution made it a powerful catalyst for the public discussion—and construction—of new middle-class tastes, values, and concerns. On July 5, 1854, however, this legacy became a mere memory, as the automaton itself perished by fire along with most of the contents of the Chinese Museum in Philadelphia. Dr. Mitchell, the automaton's principal owner during the early 1850s, provides a final glimpse of the international champion in the moments before his destruction, peacefully resigned to a fiery fate, yet still able—even in death—to spark the imagination of his admirers:

> At the Eastern end of this building, nearest to the fire, our friend had dwelt for many years. Struggling through the dense crowd, we entered the lower hall, and passing to the far end, reached the foot of a small back stair-case. . . . To ascend was impossible. Already the fire was about him. Death found him tranquil. He who had seen Moscow perish knew no fear of fire. We listened with painful anxiety. It might have been a sound from the crackling wood-work or the breaking window-panes, but, certain it is, that we thought we heard, through the struggling flames, and above the din of outside thousands, the last words of our departed friend, the sternly whispered, oft repeated syllables, *"échec! échec!"*[114]

2

The Feejee Mermaid and the
Market Revolution

⸭⸺◉ ◉⸺⸭

In March 1868, just a few days after P. T. Barnum's American Museum
burned to the ground, the New York *Times* editorial staff decided to
offer a few strong words about the city's exhibition trade. Their article
began with a question: "Why cannot we now have a great popular
Museum in New York, without any 'humbug' about it? Mr. Barnum
does not propose to attempt to get up his Museum again, and it is his
intention to retire . . . from that line of business." It was the perfect
moment, the *Times* editors reasoned, to execute a kind of ritual
cleansing of the city's cultural life—to start from scratch—to rethink
the proper goals, functions, and forms of New York's "popular museums." "In no department of natural history or scientific study" they
concluded, "is there anything open to the public worthy of notice. Yet
we believe our people would be vastly interested in a well gotten-up
museum embracing such matters as these, and we are sure it might
be made as attractive even to country folks and youngsters as a paltry
collection of preposterous things which Mr. Barnum so justly styles
humbugs."[1]

This editorial anticipated what one leading historian has described as "the sacralization of American culture," a sweeping late nineteenth-century reform program which divided the nation's cultural landscape according to an increasingly wide fault line of highbrow and lowbrow institutions.[2] Yet in calling for such reforms, the *Times* editors also looked backward, towards the start of Barnum's career as a museum manager during the early 1840s and the emergence of his "preposterous" exhibition program. While this editorial insisted that humbug was merely a passing style rather than an intrinsic component of the exhibition trade—and thus could be replaced by another, more worthy style—it also underscored Barnum's pivotal role in shaping the city's museum trade prior to 1868. In the eyes of the *Times* editorial staff, it would take nothing less than the final retirement of the Prince of Humbug, and the total conflagration of his vast collections, to eradicate fully New York's epidemic of exhibitory imposture.

How had the exhibition trade come to this? What, exactly, did it mean to say that New York's museums were full of humbug and preposterous things? How, in the span of about three decades, had Barnum's artful deceptions become so completely associated with popular exhibitionism in America's urban centers? These are central questions in nineteenth-century cultural history and have been addressed before, most notably by Neil Harris, whose pioneering 1973 biography of Barnum continues to shape our view of them today. The showman's exhibitory "art," Harris argued, was an "aesthetic of the operational, a delight in observing process and examining for literal truth. In place of intensive spiritual absorption, Barnum's exhibitions concentrated on information and the problem of deception."[3] The great strength of this interpretation is its emphasis on the interactive nature of Barnum's humbuggery (which Harris described as a kind of perceptual "combat" between showman and viewer), as well as its willingness to treat this interaction as a popular cultural phenomenon worthy of serious historical consideration.[4] Whereas most previous writers had simply cataloged Barnum's hoaxes and obliquely noted his viewers' fondness for "being fooled," Harris placed the showman's deceits in a more concrete context and demonstrated the presence of "operational" tendencies in a wide range of antebellum cultural forms: Richard Adams Locke's Moon Hoax, how-to manuals, political exposés, detective fiction, even Transcendentalist thought.[5]

Over the past quarter century, historians of nineteenth-century American culture have only added to the list.[6] In the process, however, there has been surprisingly little effort to build upon this notion of an "operational aesthetic," and thus deepen our understanding of the origins, forms, and popularity of Barnum's humbuggery. That such reevaluation is now overdue becomes clear as soon as we consider the very basic question of innovation. For the most part, scholars have treated Barnum's trickery as something distinctive to antebellum America, as one of the period's defining cultural traits. Yet virtually all eighteenth- and early nineteenth-century cabinets, fairs, museums, and traveling shows contained at least a few similar tricks of their own, each one soliciting the careful scrutiny of its audiences. Maelzel's automaton chess-player is one major case in point. So, too, is the Philadelphia Museum of Charles Willson Peale—America's foremost producer of exhibitions during the Early National period—who liberally sprinkled his collections with a wide range of illusionistic exhibits: distorting mirrors; moving picture displays; a *trompe l'oeil* portrait of Peale's sons; phantasmagoria; a bogus perpetual motion machine; automaton birds and flowers; even a life-sized wax figure of Peale himself, stationed by the entrance to produce double-takes from incoming viewers.

Peale, however, was never accused of humbuggery—not in his entertainments, not in his marketing strategies, and above all not in his public persona. More than any other early American cultural figure, in fact, he is often described as Barnum's moral and artistic opposite, a popular museum proprietor whose "honest" persona and "scientific" program eventually withered away in the face of the Great Yankee Showman's hyperbolic marketing schemes and less serious mode of exhibitionism.[7] The fact that Barnum actually purchased many of his own museums' collections directly from the Peale family during the 1840s only complicates the picture further.[8]

One thing which set Barnum's trickery apart from these earlier cultural forms was his enormous skill at scripting his promotions according to the egalitarian ideals and rhetorics of the 1830s and 1840s. Harris describes this brand of promotion as a "democratic" mode of cultural discourse (in the Northern Jacksonian sense of the term), one which respectfully courted close scrutiny from New York's "average citizens" and thus encouraged their oft-noted propensity to celebrate new discoveries in natural history and technology—without interference from condescending social elites or scientific experts. "Technological progress and egalitarian self-confidence," Harris concludes, "combined to make many Americans certain of their opinions—and so, easy prey for the hoaxers."[9] In her recent study of the antebellum penny press, Andie Tucher echoes this conclusion, adding that Barnum's humbugs indulged a Jacksonian fondness for energetic, vocal participation in the urban public sphere, regardless of whether the puzzle in question involved a dubious exhibitory object, a crime of passion, or a political conspiracy. "Working through and solving a hoax," she argues, became a kind of "republican right," for it "demanded from every citizen the democratic duty of judgment. It offered to every citizen the democratic delight of choice. It allowed to every citizen the democratic satisfaction of participating in public life."[10]

This line of analysis helps explain the specific rhetoric articulated by Barnum and his American Museum patrons in the act of hoaxing. Yet it also seems important not to confuse a *style* of public discourse—democratic, Jacksonian, republican, or whatever term we choose to apply here—with the specific "problems" at the center of the discourse. Simply describing these problems as hoaxes does not say very much at all. If the Joice Heth and automaton chess-player exhibitions demonstrate nothing else, it is that hoaxes came in a wide variety of forms and often changed dramatically over time. So while it is useful to think of Barnum's trickery as a popular cultural exercise based on "observing process" and "examining for literal truth," we also need to ask, more specifically, what kinds of social, economic, and moral concerns were at stake in the showman's exhibitions, as humbuggery

P. T. Barnum's American Museum on lower Broadway, around mid-nineteenth century.

became one of America's most pervasive forms of urban amusement. How was literal truth defined—and differentiated from other forms of truth—in these battles of wits between showman and audience? What larger processes were these viewers observing during the early years of Barnum's career as museum manager, as they gazed intently at his dubious cultural goods on lower Broadway?

To answer these questions, Barnum's humbuggery needs to be considered in an additional context: not merely the democratic rhetoric of see-for-yourself problem-solving employed by Barnum and his customers, but also the larger urban market forces which fueled the problems themselves. The complex system of urban market exchange that emerged during the first half of the nineteenth century looked to many contemporary observers like a kind of humbug, too: a novel and perceptually confusing system driven by unpredictable fluctuations of supply and demand, transmitted through mass-circulated printed instruments, and mediated by urban strangers.[11] What needs to be explained here is how Barnum's advertised riddles about the authenticity of his cultural goods were part of these socioeconomic transformations. How did Barnum's deceits play on more general anxieties about commercial imposture practiced in the city's streets, newspapers, or shops? By what criteria did antebellum Americans explain the crucial distinction between humbug-as-amusement and humbug-as-crime, and why did this distinction dissolve on certain occasions during the 1840s?

At the heart of these questions is the fact that all of the heated public conversations that took place in and around Barnum's exhibitions ultimately turned on a financially driven question of authenticity: a payment at the door to see something promised in advance by the showman. To be sure, Barnum's tricksterism generated debate on plenty of topics other than money: the questions of Joice Heth's age, appearance, and background, for example; or the necessity of freeing her great-grandchildren. But even these debates retained the emerging market economy as subtext, for they focused on publicly traded curiosities and bold, advertised claims which were always understood as (at least) potentially untrue—each one looked at, read about, and evaluated by wary urban viewers in much the same way they might evaluate a heavily promoted patent medicine, or cut-rate goods at a Chatham Street auction. As Barnum explained in his 1865 work, *Humbugs of the World,* no good or service in the contemporary metropolis was completely free from suspicion. Suspicions about fraud were rife everywhere in this brave new economic world, part of what made it feel so new and different. It was thus up to each and every consumer, he concluded, to "transact . . . business to the best of your ability" and "on your own judgment."[12]

The subject of this chapter is the first piece of business to make Barnum and the American Museum nationally famous, a commercial enterprise which quickly became synonymous with the showman's tricksterism, perhaps the one object most responsible for his title as Prince of Humbug—the notorious Feejee Mermaid. Precisely

The Feejee Mermaid in all its hideous glory. According to
Barnum, this was an accurate likeness of the "crittur" as it
appeared in 1842.

because it was so notorious, the Mermaid has special advantages as a historical tool for measuring Barnum's evolution as a nineteenth-century trickster figure. From its New York debut in the summer of 1842 right up until Barnum's death, neither the showman nor the press ever really grew tired of discussing this perplexing "crittur." Also advantageous is the fact that mermaids comprised a standard category of popular curiosity decades and even centuries before Barnum got his start, a pattern which allows us to isolate subtle forms of promotional innovation employed by the young showman, as well as within the early nineteenth-century curiosity trade as a whole.

As was the case with the automaton chess-player, the novelty of the Feejee Mermaid was a function of the object itself, what the showman did to the object, and the kinds of questions and concerns its audiences brought to the exhibition room. In many ways, though, this is a very different sort of history than the automaton's, one that might have caused Maelzel to blush a bit, had he lived to see it unfold. It is about a practitioner of artful deception without a morally solid alter ego (such as virtuoso, government bureaucrat, or mechanic); a scruffy little half fish/half monkey concoction with no utilitarian or productive associations (such as ingenious machine); a promotional campaign unconcerned with engaging in acts of flattery towards social elites (such as Maelzel's practice of holding private exhibitions at gentlemen's chess clubs). Although Barnum certainly claimed to provide a useful public service (inexpensive family entertainments for labor-weary republicans), he was far better known, especially during the late 1830s and 1840s, for serving up something else: big fat lies.

But they were lies which raised fundamental questions about the workings of the emerging market economy and the more fluid system of urban social relations it was producing.[13] Questions about what it meant—both morally and legally—to get one's money's worth in antebellum America. About how to reconceptualize truth in a society that increasingly allowed urban merchants to exaggerate claims about themselves and the products they traded. About the acceptable limits of such embellishment in the context of mass-distributed newspapers and printed advertisements. And how to distinguish entrepreneurial ingenuity from unscrupulous acts of criminal misrepresentation. In each of these important respects, Barnum's Mermaid exhibition did more than simply reflect the novel forms of urban commerce and socioeconomic values produced by America's market revolution. It helped define those values. It was those forms.[14] This was one of the most important breakthroughs of Barnum entire career. Why confine public speculation about one's new curiosity to the conventional questions of natural history when this curiosity might also serve as a public litmus test for debating the conventional deviance of market capitalism?

Mermaids Enter the Market

Histories of the Feejee Mermaid generally begin in early 1842, when Moses Kimball, a leading Boston museum operator and Barnum's close confidant, purchased this "creature" from the son of a local sailor.[15] Barnum described the Mermaid's features in some detail:

> The monkey and the fish were so nicely conjoined that no human eye could detect the point where the junction was formed. The spine of the fish proceeded in a straight and apparently unbroken line to the base of the skull—the hair of the animal was found growing several inches down on the shoulders of the fish, and the application of a microscope absolutely revealed what seemed to be minute fish scales lying in myriads amidst the hair. The teeth and formation of the fingers and hands differed materially from those of any monkey or orang-outang ever discovered, while the location of the fins was different from those of any species of the fish tribe known to naturalists. The animal was an ugly, dried-up, black-looking diminutive specimen, about three feet long. Its mouth was wide open, its tail turned over, and its arms thrown up, giving it the appearance of having died in great agony.[16]

In mid-June Barnum and Kimball signed a time-share agreement and hired Barnum's old partner in deception, Levi Lyman, as the primary exhibitor.[17] The Mermaid's first American tour began with

Lyman posing as an English naturalist—"Dr. Griffin, agent of the Lyceum of Natural History in London, recently from Pernambuco"—and mailing notices about his exploits (some real, some entirely fabricated) to the New York press from a variety of locations. Initially, at least, many newspaper editors hailed the creature as evidence of one of the world's oldest mythic beings. Others immediately suspected some kind of fraud and began to speculate on how this Griffin fellow might have orchestrated the deception. But virtually all encouraged their readers to visit Dr. Griffin's curiosity and decide for themselves.

In late July, the Mermaid stopped in Philadelphia, prompting extensive reviews, as well as a budding controversy regarding the authenticity of the exhibition. As Barnum gleefully put it, "the mermaid fever was now getting pretty well up."[18] The creature then spent a couple profitable weeks at New York's "spacious saloon known as Concert Hall," a venue just up the street from the American Museum at 404 Broadway, where Lyman first exhibited the Mermaid to the general public, with no mention whatsoever of Barnum's involvement. Meanwhile, Barnum planted histories of mermaid sightings in a number of New York newspapers (complete with outrageously untrue, bare-breasted illustrations) and printed 10,000 Mermaid pamphlets, to be "sold at a penny each, (half the cost), in all the principal hotels, stores, etc., etc."[19] With Gotham's curiosity now on "tip toe," and Barnum's newspaper advertisements graciously announcing that he had purchased the Mermaid from Dr. Griffin ("to be seen at no extra cost"), door receipts for the American Museum almost tripled during the first month of the exhibition's debut, a success the showman later used as a retroactive justification for any morally dubious activities in connection with the exhibit.[20]

A few months later the Mermaid headed south to Charleston, South Carolina, with Barnum's uncle, Alanson Taylor, who became embroiled in a nasty controversy between local clergymen, naturalists, and newspaper editors. Some of these Southern critics immediately denounced the Mermaid as a biological impossibility—a mixture of species and physical characteristics that simply could not exist or survive in nature—while others lashed out at the naysayers for daring to define the biologically possible, something only "the Creator" could do. Barnum, predictably, welcomed all this public attention and even fanned the controversy himself by sending feigned letters of outrage to the Charleston newspapers. But he later canceled the tour when physical harm to Taylor and prosecution for criminal fraud became serious possibilities. In later years the Mermaid appeared regularly in Barnum's exhibition venues in Boston, New York, and Philadelphia, and was prominently featured in his best-selling autobiographies. It also accompanied Barnum on a transatlantic speaking tour, serving as a prop for the showman's trademark lecture, "The Art of Money-Getting." And like the automaton chess-player before it, the Mermaid came to a fiery end (probably in the same 1868 American Museum fire cited by the New York *Times* as a good way to eradicate Gotham's epidemic of exhibitory imposture).

Much of this brief overview of the Feejee Mermaid's career will be familiar to those acquainted with Barnum's own writings. Less well known is the much older tradition of mermaid exhibitions which preceded—and may even have produced—the "curious crittur" that took New York by storm in 1842.[21] As Barnum discovered during the late 1850s, his early star was probably none other than the St. James Mermaid, a curiosity exhibited over three decades earlier at Watson's Turf Coffeehouse in London.[22] Whether or not the St. James Mermaid had even earlier names and incarnations is harder to determine. English newspaper reports from the 1820s mentioned only that this Mermaid had been purchased by a sea captain named Eades in Batavia, Dutch East Indies—the same geographic information Barnum later provided for the Feejee Mermaid in public forums.[23] The St. James Mermaid's leading contemporary rival, the Strand Mermaid, was shown extensively during the late eighteenth century.[24] And the Strand model was not alone. In fact, the further back one searches in the archives of Western popular culture, the more mermaids one finds on display.[25]

Aesthetically, at least, these early modern mermaids have a lot in common with Barnum's model. All of them have vaguely human breasts, yet many also replace the European facial features and long, flowing tresses of Western folklore with some kind of non-Western (or even nonhuman) head. And as eighteenth-century engravings show, some of the leading European mermaids were dead ringers for the Feejee Mermaid—with wide noses, high foreheads, five-fingered hands, muscled arms, tufts of hair above the back of the neck, and distinctive split fin appendages marking the line between torso and tail.[26] In a purely physical sense, then, Barnum's 1842 celebrity was a relatively conventional sort of curious object, one consistent with a much older tradition of cabinet, carnival, and museum display.

But we also need to remember that the problems of authenticity posed by these curiosities changed dramatically over time. Consider, for example, a typical mid-eighteenth-century handbill promoting a mermaid exhibition in London: "A surprising young Mermaid, taken on the coast of Aquapulca, which, though the generality of mankind think there is no such thing, has been seen by the curious, who express their utmost satisfaction at so uncommon a creature, being half like a woman, and half like a fish, and is allowed to be the greatest curiosity ever exposed to the public view."[27]

Now compare this with a Barnum notice from 1843, a fiendishly slippery paragraph that captures the young showman at the height of his promotional powers:

> Engaged for a short time the animal (regarding which there has been so much dispute in the scientific world) called the
> *FEEJEE MERMAID!*
> positively asserted by its owner to have been taken alive [in] the Feejee Islands, and implicitly believed by many scientific persons, while it is pronounced by other scientific persons to be an *artificial* production, and its natural existence claimed to be an utter impossibility. The manager can only say that it [h]as such *appearance of reality* as any fish lying [in] the stalls of our fish markets—but [who] is to decide when *doctors* disagree. At all events whether this production is the work of *nature or art* it is decidedly the most stupendous curiosity ever submitted to the public for inspection. If it is artificial the senses [of] sight and touch are useless for *art* has rendered them totally ineffectual—if it is natural then all concur in declaring it
> *the greatest Curiosity in the World.*[28]

Both notices place the origins of their mermaids in exotic locations, point to swelling public excitement, and pronounce their offerings to be truly exceptional curiosities. The earlier ad, however, largely resolves the question of authenticity for the reader. While "the generality of mankind think there is no such thing," this uncommon creature has actually been "seen" and "exposed" by the curious, an assertion which seems to prove the larger category of mermaids—at least for the time being. Here one goes to mermaid exhibitions looking for material proof, for a sense of closure to the mostly unsubstantiated public speculation regarding the existence of the mythic creature. The mermaid on display in London was a great curiosity because it showed contemporary audiences something in material form that they had previously only experienced as scientific hypotheses and the often unreliable reports of sea captains.

In Barnum's ad, by contrast, seeing is definitely not believing, and the words coming from the showman only contribute to the viewer's nagging sense of uncertainty. Again and again, Barnum's text undermines the reader's attempts to resolve the authenticity question. Scientists, we are told, do not know what to make of this mermaid and are split in their opinions. The manager (the one person who should know about the authenticity of his own cultural goods) twice qualifies his claim of presenting a mermaid, saying only that it has the appearance of reality. These qualifications all push towards the next and most crucial line, which cheerfully invites the public to enter the controversy— and decide for themselves. The question Barnum's 1843 patrons are asked to decide, however, is not whether mermaids exist as a species in nature, but whether this particular exhibitory commodity—the one reclining grotesquely in Barnum's glass case, the one metaphorically tied to New York's disorienting markets—is in fact what the promoter claims it to be.

Further evidence of this epistemological divide lies in what the nineteenth-century writer, Thomas Frost, could not find in his oft-cited history of the early modern fair trade—a book written, it is important to note, in 1874, at the tail end of Barnum's career. On page after page Frost reproduces newspaper ads, handbills, and diary accounts of a wide range of London curiosities from the seventeenth and eighteenth centuries: a strange calf with five legs, a huge lobster with six claws, a girl about sixteen years of age, born in Cheshire, and not much above eighteen inches long, and so forth.[29] These exhibitions, Frost observes, "show that the passion for monstrosities was as strongly developed in the later half of the 17th century as the present day." Yet, as he surveys his sources, Frost's perspective as a citizen from the late nineteenth century forces him into a rather surprising conclusion: "How many of these show creatures were impostures, and how many eccentricities of human nature, is impossible to say. Barnum's revelations have made us skeptical."[30]

Frost's conclusion is entirely accurate. Using these early modern sources as our guide, we cannot tell with much certainty whether the curiosities on display were real (undoubtedly some were not), nor whether contemporary viewers even contemplated such matters (undoubtedly some did). But that is also what makes Frost's conclusion so intriguing: we cannot tell because, for the most part, early modern handbills simply did not dwell on the truthfulness of the showmen's promotional claims—at least not in the same self-conscious and deliberately ambiguous manner that we find in Barnum's notices. To explain the origins of Barnum's tricks, then, Frost's question needs to be reformulated. We need to ask, that is, not simply whether, but when audiences started focusing on the promotional truthfulness of the curiosities they paid to see—and why?

One important answer seems to lie in the methods by which early modern curiosities were conventionally collected and distributed and assembled into collections. For most of this period, curiosities were personal and mostly noncommercial objects, with backgrounds of some certainty. They were amazing machines built by a virtuoso, or a member of one's family or village who was unusual in some way, or an exotic object brought back from a colonial expedition.

Over the course of the eighteenth century, however, this network of curiosity distribution became much more anonymous, complex, and commercial, particularly with the emergence of the so-called curiosity shop, an institution which first appeared around 1700.

Richard Altick has hinted at these changes, noting that the disposal of private collections "became a thriving business in the course of a century. Virtuosi died, or tired of their toys, or suddenly needed ready cash . . . to the profit of both brokers or auctioneers."[31] Curiosities, in other words, were slowly but surely becoming commodities, objects of fluctuating value, bought and sold through middlemen on the open market. We have seen some of the effects of these market mechanisms before—during the late 1820s, for example, when Maelzel assured his New York viewers that what they were paying to see was the "real" automaton chess-player of legend, as opposed to some poor, falsely advertised imitation. We have also seen their effects on the Joice Heth exhibition, which had at least three different managers/promoters during the 1830s, none of whom seems to have been long acquainted with his forerunner or with Heth's history. By necessity, the information that they provided to one another was of the sort that is traded among strangers and taken on faith. Whether or not we believe Barnum's retrospective claim about not knowing Heth's true age in 1835, one thing seems relatively clear about the larger enterprise. By the time Barnum took over the exhibition, it was a business, and an increasingly complex, unreliable sort of business at that.

Of course, what looks complicated and unreliable in one marketplace may seem like business as usual in another. It is particularly fortunate, therefore, that Barnum left us with a detailed, first-hand account of New York's curiosity trade during the mid-1830s, when he was first contemplating a career in the show trade. It is an account, moreover, written by a young man who had just moved there from Bethel, Connecticut, and was acutely aware of the differences between New York's market system and the trading practices he had experienced at home. "Every morning at sunrise," he explains of his early travails in Gotham,

> my eyes were running over the columns of "Wants" in the New York "Sun," hoping to hit upon something that would suit me. Many is the wild-goose chase which I had in pursuit of a situation so beautifully and temptingly set forth among those "wants." Fortunes equaling that of Croesus, and as plenty as blackberries, were dangling from many an

advertisement which mysteriously invited the reader to apply at Room No. 16 in the fifth story of a house in some retired and uninviting local-ity. . . . I remember that, on one occasion, an advertisement was headed, "IMMENSE SPECULATION on a small capital!—$10,000 easily made in one year! Apply to Professor, at Scudder's American Museum." I had long fancied that I could succeed if I could only get hold of a public exhi-bition, and I hastened with all dispatch to call on the kind Professor who held forth such flattering promises at the Museum.[32]

Barnum's use of the word "promises" here is revealing. In this context, a curiosity's value no longer hinged upon the labor of its creator or its placement in a royal collection. Instead, it was based on a claim of value made by a salesman who probably did not produce the good. It was thus up to the neophyte showman to evaluate the situation, hypothesize a potential profit, and decide whether or not the seller's claim was worth the gamble. And as Barnum discovered when he called upon the author of this particular speculation (a Hydro-oxygen microscope), it would cost him $1,000 cash in advance, paid to a stranger, to take his chances.[33] As Barnum noted, too, speculating on profits was but one of many perceptual challenges initiated by the antebellum marketplace. A few years later, Barnum placed his own ad in a newspaper, offering venture capital for the right kind of business opportunity. The people who soon came calling read like a catalog of the era's most familiar swindlers: patent medicine men and pawnbro-kers; a counterfeiter in need of new paper and dyes; an oat salesman, dressed in a Quaker costume, who confessed to regularly cheating his customers; and the owner of a perpetual motion machine, which, as Barnum noted, contained a "main-spring slyly deposited under one of the hollow posts, and so connected as to make the motion perpetual—until it ran down!"[34]

Upon careful consideration of these dubious prospects, Barnum decided to throw his money in with a German manufacturer of "leather treatments" named Proler, and initially their partnership gen-erated some income. But within a year this business venture proved perilous, too. After selling his share of the company on credit, Proler absconded with Barnum's cash, leaving the young showman with piles of unsold leather treatments and a sizable unpaid loan.[35]

It would be easy to read these episodes from Barnum's early career simply as the first, unsuccessful chapters in a conventional rags-to-riches story—certainly, that is what the showman seems to have intended when he included them in his autobiography. But there are other important lessons here as well, lessons which say as much about the specific impacts of America's market revolution as they do about Barnum's precarious place therein. First and foremost, Barnum experienced the transformation of the market from a specific place to a more abstract process, one which lacked the agrarian village's bonds of mutualism, face-to-face negotiations, and personal reputations behind finished products. Barnum also experienced the rapid expansion of credit, a process which fueled the young showman's entrepreneurial schemes, but also enabled the sort of unscrupulous business practices executed by Proler. In his earlier pursuit of the Hydro-oxygen microscope, Barnum experienced some of the speculation fundamental to urban commodity exchange, a system in which value itself was becoming increasingly nebulous and unstable. And through it all, Barnum experienced the rise of mass-circulated advertising, which provided a powerful but easily corruptible network of disembodied economic information through new penny dailies like the New York *Sun*.[36]

This is not to suggest that Barnum's market education simply began when he moved from rural Connecticut to lower Manhattan. Indeed, as historians have increasingly noted, it was actually in the New England countryside where America's market revolution first took root during the 1780s and 1790s—in places just like Bethel, where Barnum and his sharp-trading Yankee relatives had long run a small freight enterprise, worked as lottery agents, entertained various peddling schemes, and proudly celebrated the business acumen of local merchants, who were never above "shaving" a customer here and there to get ahead.[37] One of the most remarkable features of this story, then, is the extent to which—despite almost two decades of intensive Yankee training—Barnum found himself woefully unprepared to forge a career as a Manhattan speculator. While he had brokered his fair share of sharp deals in Bethel, he had never experienced market capitalism on such a grand urban scale, in such a rapidly changing and complex environment.

Barnum also learned a significant lesson about the place of the curiosity trade within the expanding market economy: namely, that acquiring a microscope or a perpetual motion machine was often just as perplexing an enterprise—and just as open to potential fraud—as investing in patent medicines or leather treatments. Each type of speculation required capital up front to get the enterprise rolling. Each involved a close acquaintance with complex credit networks. Each forced the gathering of information from unreliable media sources. And each required the entrepreneur to trade in goods he/she did not produce, many of which often proved to be falsified, overvalued, or inauthentic in some way.

Two Museums, Two Mermaids

How, then, did these growing concerns about authenticity and value begin to creep into the antebellum show trade, not just at the level of distribution and exchange, but also in terms of the cultural problems that showmen like Barnum constructed in, around, and through their exhibitions? There are no quick-and-easy, deterministic answers here. Each early American showman reacted to the expanding market economy in his/her own distinctive ways—ways that were often radically different from Barnum's. Consider, for example, the late eighteenth-century exhibition model developed by Charles Willson Peale, a man frequently described as too busy with the work of natural science and the arts to worry much about market economics. Peale built his Philadelphia Museum as a "Encyclopedia of God's wondrous Creation," in which the natural world was divided into a carefully delineated system of species and subspecies, and represented as faithfully as possible in material form. This enlightened vision was clearly represented in the museum's first newspaper advertisement from July 7, 1786: "Mr. Peale, ever desirous to please and entertain the Public, will make a part of his House a Repository for Natural Curiosities. . . . The several Articles will be classed and arranged according to their several species; and for the greater ease to the Curious, on each piece will be inscribed the place from whence it came, and the name of the Donor, unless forbid, with such other information as may be necessary."[38]

This approach to museum management was not simply an unmediated, objective expression of Enlightenment ideals. It also expressed deliberate choices by Peale about how to guarantee the authenticity of each and every one of the curiosities for which he sold tickets. Peale could have been much less clear, for instance, about the origins and presentation of his curious objects. Both Kempelen and Maelzel had achieved commercial success and royal applause by constructing curiosities of uncertain authenticity. So, too, had countless other, lesser known contemporary exhibitors such as the individual showing "The Celebrated Windsor Fairy," an English dwarf exhibit from the 1790s, whose advertisements expressed the first public comments about imposture to be found in Frost's catalog of early modern curiosities. "In this and many other parts of the Kingdom," one handbill for the Fairy noted, "it is too common to show deformed persons, with various arts and deceptions, under denominations of persons in miniature to impose upon the public."[39]

At much the same moment, then, when uncertainty about the commercial authenticity of curiosities was becoming the norm (both in their purchase and in their promotion), Peale moved squarely in the opposite direction, towards a rigorous taxonomic orthodoxy intended to dispel any public uncertainty about the contents of his popular museum. He set out, that is, to exhibit the most authentic and the most representative curiosities he could find, and to inscribe these qualities as prominent parts of his exhibition program. As Peale explained in an 1804 letter to Thomas Jefferson, "Linnaeus' classification of animals is framed in the [Museum's] Rooms. The names of each genus and the various specimens are numbered, and the Latin, English and French names placed over each case, so that no visitor ought to expect any attendant to accompany them through the Rooms."[40] The principles of clarity and legibility were also written into the by-laws of the museum, which stated that "all articles admitted to the Museum shall be, as far as practicable, methodically arranged, and distinctly exhibited. Each article shall be accompanied by a label, giving its scientific and its vulgar name, and the locality from which it was obtained, when these are known, and, if presented to the Museum, the name of the donor."[41] Peale left nothing to chance: not the typicality of the stuffed animal or its habitat; not how it was understood or classified by naturalists; not even where he, as museum director, had obtained the skin to be stuffed.

Collectively, these decisions articulated what Jonathan Crary has described as the Enlightenment's "camera obscura" model of visuality: a clear and unambiguous perceptual relationship between viewer and object, in which "observation leads to truthful inferences about the world."[42] This perceptual relationship was only possible, however, because Peale had already enacted a kind of mediation himself, most notably in his painstaking choices about which particular objects he would elevate to the status of exhibition specimens. As the Philadelphia Museum's Record Book makes abundantly clear, not every curiosity that was offered to Peale or made its way into his possession became part of his public displays.[43] Some objects replicated species or artifacts already represented in the Long Room. Others were viewed as imperfect in some way and were therefore rejected in favor of more typical specimens. And still others turned out to be frauds crafted by shady salesmen, such as the remarkable "Tubularia" with "104 heads," which was offered to Peale for the sum of $6,000 by a Kentucky dealer promising "easy" profits of "500 per Annum."[44]

Just how far Peale was willing to go in the pursuit of truth and clarity is illustrated in the record book entry from May 6, 1806, which recorded the acquisition of some "black bugs, worms, and flies collected from the stomach [vomit]" of a Mrs. P. R. from Maryland. It is unclear whether these curiosities were simply donated by her doctor, Clement Stafford, or were actually purchased for the Philadelphia Museum. Peale, however, was not going to put them on display without carefully documenting the find. To finalize the transaction, he required specific dates and locations of the vomit collection, as well as a note of certification from Dr. John Redman Coxe, director of Philadelphia's Medical Museum. Both Coxe and Stafford, in fact, were ordered to return to Mrs. P. R.'s residence to procure a second specimen, just to make sure there was no mistake. Peale described the trip in detail: "A few days ago she consented to take a vomit to see if there were any more of those bugs remaining, (in presence of her family, and a gentleman of respectability, whom I purposefully took with me, and myself), when we procured from the contents of the stomach, one of the bugs of a smaller size; which upon examination, was found to have wings. . . . I have sent you several for your inspection."[45] Strange as it may seem, such gastrointestinal wonders were relatively common in the era's display cases (Barnum, too, would later offer his fair share of regurgitated wonders for public deliberation). What made this one unique in the history of early American exhibitions was the rigorous method by which Peale collected and displayed the stomach contents of Mrs. P. R. While early nineteenth-century audiences had witnessed a wide assortment of parasites and hairballs before, they had never seen any presented with such a careful scientific pedigree.

This meticulous approach to authentication extended, as well, to the occasional "deceptions" Peale put on display among his specimens. In 1813, when Charles Redheffer arrived in Philadelphia with a wondrous Perpetual Motion Machine, Peale commissioned a copy of the machine for his galleries and labeled it a hoax, suggesting (much as Kempelen had years before) that viewers attempt to deduce the method behind a publicly acknowledged trick. As Peale's son, Rubens, noted in one of his official memoranda as manager, the Philadelphia Museum was not above exhibiting such things, provided they were clearly and unambiguously labeled: "It was proposed to me by some members of the [American Philosophical] Society that this model should be left in the museum for the gratification of its visitors, I consented to receive it *but not as the perpetual motion.* I therefore exhibited it as a model with a concealed apparatus to show that a machine could be constructed that no one could discover the moving power."[46] Significantly, Rubens placed the device in a section specially designated for "optical illusions," rather than among the museum's many other artificial curiosities (for example, paintings, steam engines, Native American artifacts), which needed no such disclaimers about their representational status.[47]

To confuse or obscure the authenticity of the Philadelphia Museum's curious contents simply made no sense within this Enlightenment model of exhibitions. Even during the 1830s and 1840s, as the Philadelphia Museum began offering less scientific entertainments such as minstrel shows in an attempt to avoid financial ruin, its strict policies about certifying each of its curiosities as completely genuine or completely counterfeit never wavered. Desperate for capital in 1842, Peale's sons went so far as to show a copy of Barnum's Mermaid. But true to the founder's Enlightenment principles, they presented their oddity clearly and unambiguously—as a "clever deception" manufactured by "Japanese artists."[48]

Charles Coleman Sellers features this episode in the final chapters of his history of the Philadelphia Museum, suggesting in somewhat tragic tones that the "light entertainment and honest science" of the Peales proved, finally, to be "no match for Barnum's fake demonstrations, which never disappointed an audience."[49] "Hard times in the flashy, unstable 1830's," Sellers concludes, "had taken their toll of museums. Only Barnum in New York and Kimball in Boston continued to thrive. Kimball was finding stability in legitimate drama, and Barnum in the sheer weight of gaudy and tawdry fantastics. Kimball was cautious; Barnum, combative, expanding, eager to outsmart and outlive all rivals. He watched the decline at Philadelphia, ready to move in."[50] This vignette of Barnum's predatory instincts makes for great moral drama, but it does not tell us why his "gaudy" promotions proved so much more compelling than those of the Peales. Was the difference between success and failure in the antebellum exhibition trade merely a function of promotional "tawdriness" and "combativeness"—or the mere absence of labels on an exhibition case? Why did one fake mermaid rocket Barnum to stardom in New York, while another in Philadelphia hardly made a ripple in the public's consciousness?

The best place to start answering these questions is the June 18, 1842, business contract Barnum signed with Moses Kimball to show the Feejee Mermaid:

> . . . the said Kimball has possession and control of a curiosity supposed to be a mermaid, which he hereby agrees to hire to the said Barnum for four eight or twelve weeks for the sum of twelve dollars and fifty cents per week, it being optional with the said Barnum to have the said curiosity whichever term of time above named he pleases. . . .
>
> And the said Barnum in consideration of the above agreement of Mr. Kimball hereby agrees to take all proper and possible care of said curiosity and not allow it to be handled or in manner injured or abused. He also agrees to exert himself to the utmost without regard to trouble or expense to bring it before the public in such a manner as to make it a highly popular and profitable exhibition. . . . [51]

At first glance, this text appears rather unexceptional. In comparing it to Peale's dealings, however, a number of crucial distinctions begin to emerge. Most obvious is the document's status as a contract, the very terms and form of which presupposed a wholly different kind of relationship between exhibitor and curiosity than one finds anywhere in the documentary records of the Philadelphia Museum. Whereas Peale's Record Book demonstrates the naturalist's rigorous note-taking (with detailed margin comments about the "black spots" on the head of a stomach bug), the Mermaid contract features the logistical concerns of dedicated salesmen (financial terms, tour schedules, and promotional strategies), all of which lead directly to the pecuniary bottom line—to make this curiosity a "highly popular and profitable exhibition." Significantly, the Barnum-Kimball contract says nothing at all about the Mermaid itself: nothing about its looks, nothing about its origins, nothing even about who might have originally produced it.

This is not to suggest that Peale was simply unconcerned with the profitability and logistics of his exhibitions, or that Barnum's Mermaid exhibition lacked substance or forethought. Indeed, if one looks closely, it is possible to see the contours of an extraordinary new exhibition model taking shape in the Barnum-Kimball contract. The commodity in question is described as a "curiosity *supposed* to be a mermaid," a remarkably loose definition which might lead us to pronounce Barnum (as Peale undoubtedly would have) rather sloppy in his classification efforts. Yet the contract's language also suggests another interpretation: namely, that Barnum tolerated, and perhaps even delighted in the fact that the authenticity of his new curiosity was somewhat fuzzy. This fuzziness was precisely what Barnum was about to sell.

Barnum simply had no interest in documenting the authenticity of Kimball's Mermaid—at least not according to the strict standards of natural history championed by the Peales. Rather, what Barnum seems to have desired was a curiosity of the sort he had first encountered with Maelzel in 1835: one both plausible enough to be taken seriously and dubious enough to inspire uncertainty. Like Maelzel, too, Barnum was concerned, right from the start, with preserving this ambiguity. In fact, Barnum made such preservation a specific contract point, agreeing "to take all proper and possible care of said curiosity and not allow it to be handled or in any manner injured or abused." More than a pragmatic pledge to maintain the shared property in good condition, this provision seems to have reflected careful decisions about the specific form of exhibition Barnum and Kimball planned to offer. Viewers would be allowed to look long and hard for a connecting seam between the monkey body and the fish tail. And Barnum would "exert himself in the utmost" to encourage look after profitable look. But viewers would not be allowed to "handle" the object, an activity which might remove the crucial ingredient of "supposition" from the audience's mind.

There remained, however, a significant promotional challenge: how to mold the ambiguous wording of the Mermaid contract into a mass-marketed exhibition program—one which, through its very ambiguity, might excite public curiosity well beyond the levels generated by Peale's exhibitions and his own Joice Heth campaign of 1835. These two exhibitory precedents were in fact crucial for Barnum's 1842 Mermaid program, for they had established a competing set of possibilities—legitimate wonders versus fascinating frauds—in the public mind. During the first week of the Mermaid campaign, the Philadelphia *Public Ledger* oscillated back and forth between these possibilities. Following their initial glimpse of Dr. Griffin's Mermaid, the *Ledger* editors welcomed the exhibition as an important and genuine scientific "discovery"—much as they had hailed Peale's numerous natural history wonders over the years. The very next day, Barnum began running reprints of the *Public Ledger* testimonial as a paid advertisement of his own in the New York papers.[52]

Almost immediately, the editors at the *Public Ledger* became suspicious. Perhaps they wondered how and why their front-page article celebrating Dr. Griffin's Mermaid had found its way into the advertising sections of the New York press so quickly. Or perhaps they started to question first impressions when their principal Philadelphia rival, the *Spirit of the Times,* openly mocked this great discovery: "The Mermaid which we noticed a day or so ago, and which our friends of the *Ledger* wrote half a column about in the way of a eulogy, turns out to be—the head of a monkey fastened to the tail of a fish!! That was too shabby."[53] By the end of the next week, the *Public Ledger* had made an abrupt about face, now pronouncing the exhibition—with equal confidence and on the front page once again—nothing more than a "fabrication." "We trust," the editor concluded, "that the people of this country will be wise enough to discourage this impudent fraud, by *letting it alone.* If they pay their money for such a sight, they will deserve to be imposed upon by every pretender who comes along. . . . It is said to be the property of an 'English gentleman'; and he is probably some *cute* Yankee, intent on a 'Joice Heth' scheme."[54]

This early rhetorical gesture deserves some amplification. As most Northeastern newspaper readers knew by 1842, the original "Joice Heth scheme" from 1835 had relied on a variety of public misrepresentations: Barnum's publicly touted autopsy of Heth's corpse had made this clear, even if some of the details of the scheme remained uncertain. And "cute Yankee" referred to a familiar social type—usually a Northeastern entrepreneur renowned for his "sharp" trading practices.[55] The meanings of these labels become far more complex, however, when we consider the fact that Barnum himself authored an outrageous satire of his own Yankee behavior in connection with Heth in a serialized novella for the New York *Atlas* only a few months before the start of the Mermaid exhibition. Entitled *The Adventures of an Adventurer, Being Some Passages in the Life of Barnaby Diddleum,* this semi-autobiographical tale incorporated a number of unmistakable details from 1835.[56] As the story begins, "money making schemes" present themselves to Barnaby's view like an "air drawn dagger," many of them inspiring moral uncertainty in the young man from the countryside: "I confess the soft impeachment, I was a young beginner in humbug, and this did appear to me to be such a downright and damnable swindling, that hang me if I didn't turn away from it in right down earnest disgust." This initial "squeamishness" about speculations begins to evaporate when he comes upon an "old superannuated negro woman" by the name of "Joyce Heth," whom he quickly contracts and promotes as "the nurse of the immortal George Washington."[57] "My good genius hovered over her," Barnaby boasts, "and showed countless wealth to be made out of her. But how? Her great age was a great thing, but after all, an old woman, how old so ever she may be, is but an old woman. . . . It is associations that draw in the gaping and admiring crowd, and cause them to pour their cash into the longing hands of Barnaby Diddleum."[58]

At this point in the story, there was relatively little to offend Barnum's target audience of white New York readers. Barnaby's "genius" at trickery, the real Barnum made clear, was Northeastern in its origins—a distinction demonstrated with gusto in one riverboat scene, during which Barnaby bested a Southern gentleman in a battle of practical jokes. By and by, however, Barnaby begins to target some of the very same Yankees whose honor he had pledged to defend: a "greenhorn" from his home state of Connecticut; the "editors of the emporium city" (one of whom was running Barnum's novella!); even "the good people of New York," who attend Barnaby's exhibitions.[59] Barnaby admits to all of these indiscretions in a crescendo of megalomania: "Crown me with fame—create a monument to my memory—decree me a Roman triumph—I deserve all—I stand alone—I have no equal, no rival—I am the king of Humbugs—the king among princes. O, it is great, it is glorious—I chuckle now at the might of my sovereignty, the extent of my works, and laugh in ecstasy!"[60]

Like most effective trickster tales, *Adventures of an Adventurer* is a deeply ambivalent and morally ambiguous story, one which championed some of the proudest achievements of Barnum's antebellum milieu (the proverbial "cunning" of the self-made Northeastern entrepreneur) and exposed its deepest fears (cunning taken to the point of criminal treachery).[61] Yet what makes this particular trickster tale from 1841 especially interesting was that only about six months later, Barnum began to stage some of the morally ambiguous questions raised by Barnaby Diddleum in the form of a new exhibition, using Kimball's recycled bundle of fur and scales as the nonliterary center of attraction. This shift from literary tricksterism back to the exhibition room involved a kind of calculated cross-referencing between his public persona as P. T. Barnum (the showman) and Barnaby Diddleum (his literary alter ego). Whereas Barnum's real-life exploits with Joice Heth had provided the raw material for a satirical comedy of Yankee excess, Barnaby Diddleum now provided a useful literary subtext for his next round of transgressions in the exhibition hall.

And transgress he did in 1842, far exceeding in scope and complexity all of his previous efforts as professional trickster. Following Dr. Griffin's triumph in Philadelphia, Barnum pushed his clandestine promotional campaign a step further in New York, opting now to generate his own parallel press coverage. Most frequently, this took the form of short newspaper paragraphs about the Mermaid, which looked a great deal like ordinary exhibition reviews, but were in fact paid advertisements, anonymously authored by Barnum. During the Mermaid's first week in Gotham, readers of the *Herald* encountered the following unsigned endorsement of the exhibition:

> The exhibition of Mr. Griffin's Mermaid opened yesterday morning at Concert Hall, Broadway, for six days. The Hall was crowded throughout the day and evening. More than a thousand persons must have visited

here yesterday, among whom we noticed a number of our most prominent naturalists. . . . The excitement in the city in relation to this curious
Feejee beauty is tremendous, and we doubt that the hall will contain all
that apply for admission this week.[62]

By the end of the week, Barnum's *Herald* notices presented the public's verdict about the authenticity of the Mermaid as a *fait accompli:*
"There is no mistake about this being the greatest curiosity we ever
saw, and the most curious thing of all is that naturalists, who before
disputed the existence of such an animal, now have all skepticism
removed on the subject."[63]

Particularly clever in these passages was Barnum's subtle manipulation of a ventriloquistic literary voice, one confidently articulated
through the plural first-person pronoun. While the real editors of the
Herald had yet to utter more than a few words of their own about
the exhibition, Barnum's rapid-fire advertisements suggested official
media endorsements of a number of claims: that "we" (meaning the
press) had witnessed an enormous crowd of visitors, unprecedented in
the history of New York exhibitions; that "we" had pronounced the
Feejee beauty to be the most extraordinary curiosity ever seen; and
that "we" had noticed a number of our most prominent naturalists in
attendance, many of whom were now throwing skepticism to the
wind. Similarly, the Mermaid pamphlet which Barnum sold on the
streets of New York included an unsigned "letter from an eminent
Professor of Natural History," which vouched for the creature's full
authenticity.[64] "That the animal has lived, moved, and had its being, *as
it is*," this "letter" exclaimed, "ADMITS NOT THE SHADOW OF A
DOUBT, as all must acknowledge who see it; and that it is the animal
heretofore described as the MERMAID, and hitherto considered as a
fabulous creature, is equally certain."[65]

Had Barnum stopped here, the Mermaid campaign of 1842 might
have amounted to nothing more than a relatively conventional antebellum hoax—one which bilked a few hundred Gothamites before
being exposed and forgotten. Barnum, however, rarely relied on others to expose his own hoaxes. Even before the New York press had

found time to articulate its own doubts, the showman himself raised public suspicions about the authenticity of the Mermaid, as in the following *Herald* notice, which appeared simultaneously with the anonymous naturalist endorsements: "Mr. Griffin, the proprietor of this curious animal, informs us that some persons have the impression that he is getting certain editors to call it a 'humbug', for the purpose of drawing public attention to it, but he assures us positively that this is not the fact, no such clap-trap being necessary."[66]

On the one hand, this text served as a kind of preemptive strike against accusations of fraud. Speaking once again through the editorial voice of "we" (which, in turn, referred to bogus conversations with the bogus Doctor Griffin), Barnum assured readers that the Mermaid was so remarkable as to require no planted newspaper stories ("such clap-trap"). On the other hand, given the fact that no New York paper had yet made such an accusation, Barnum's defensive posturing also served as a subtle act of misdirection, one which generated and defined its own forms of public controversy: could it be that the Mermaid was indeed a piece of humbug, as "some persons" were now suggesting? In many respects, this was the Barnaby Diddleum effect now put into exhibitory practice. Just as in 1841, Barnum was actively and publicly accusing himself of promotional indiscretions through a disembodied literary mouthpiece. This time, though, he also fought back against the attacks, complaining that his own planted accusations were entirely baseless!

The calculated double talk became even more complex a few months later, when Barnum hired a competitor, Henry Bennett, to exhibit a poor imitation of the Feejee Mermaid at the nearby New York Museum (a venue recently vacated by Rubens Peale).[67] Behind the scenes, Barnum retained complete control of the competition and pocketed profits from both institutions. But in the press he presented Bennett as an independent and increasingly bitter rival, one eager to demonstrate just how easy it was to defraud the public with bogus curiosities. While American Museum advertisements continued to promote the Real Mermaid with glowing endorsements from naturalists, Barnum now paired these promotions with New York Museum ads—often side by side—announcing that: "Mr. H. Bennett, Manager, begs leave to state that . . . he has manufactured a FUDGE MER-MAID! which he willingly leaves to the public to pronounce whether it is not infinitely superior to the one now exhibiting."[68]

In his unsigned press notices for the New York Museum, Barnum also prodded readers to consider the possibility that Bennett's frauds were part of a much larger wave of imposture plaguing Manhattan's show trade. "People," he playfully groused, "will not believe the [Fudge] Mermaid is manufactured. They say they are told at . . . [Bar-num's] Museum that their [Feejee] Mermaid is a real one, and they feel quite confident the one is as genuine as the other.—Pretty correct in their conclusion."[69] This last line was the clincher, for it correctly suggested that neither Mermaid was real, despite all the huffing and puffing in the papers. Yet to describe this as an exposé in any conven-tional sense is to miss much of Barnum's virtuosity as trickster. What the showman was exposing here was not the truth, but another layer of his own elaborate con. Even when he admitted his own frauds, the goal was to produce suspicion rather than closure, to raise interpretive possibilities rather than solve the case.

There may be no more ironic moment in the history of nineteenth-century American museums than these mermaid wars from late 1842. As Barnum was well aware, the Fudge Mermaid was appearing in a building formerly used by the Peales to promote genuine wonders of nature, the power of human reason, and the virtues of a clearly organ-ized collection. Barnum, by contrast, quite deliberately promoted these virtues' opposites: a dubious representation of a natural wonder, a mass exercise in perceptual confusion, and perhaps the most unsci-entific collection of curiosities in the history of Western culture. Meanwhile, back in Philadelphia, the Peales were attempting to avoid financial ruin with an artificial mermaid of their own, one presented explicitly as a product of "native Japanese" craftsmen, who "are very expert in manufacturing such great natural curiosities from fish bones, properly shaped and cemented with some adhesive composition." Despite their considerable skill as taxidermists, the Peales did nothing to hide a visible blemish in this "composition," leaving the "tail" of their curiosity "broken off, showing a stick which supports the frame." There could only be one conclusion about the Peale exhibition. "As to our Mermaid," the Philadelphia *North American and Daily Advertiser* observed, "there is not a particle of humbug about it. It is precisely what it professes to be, a capital *effigy* of amphibious piscine humanity."[70]

Barnum offered plenty of confessions, too, even going so far as to describe the Fudge Mermaid as "the head of a monkey and the tail of a fish, so admirably fitted together as to deceive the most experienced person."[71] But he deliberately left the details of this ruse unclear, explaining only that the exhibition had "arrived from HUMBUG Island."[72] Moreover, by simultaneously arguing for and against the authenticity of both of his mermaids (often in adjacent advertisements), Barnum called into question the validity of all of his promotional claims. And by staging this rivalry as a contest between two big-city businessmen—each of whom publicly accused the other of fraud and of giving a low return for the customer's entertainment dollar—Barnum redefined the kinds of questions a popular museum exhibition stimulated in its viewers.

Whereas Peale's curiosities encouraged his viewers to pursue the questions of an Enlightenment naturalist (where does it live? how was it captured? what does it eat?), the Feejee Mermaid encouraged viewers to think like an antebellum speculator: to recreate, in a sense, the young showman's own somewhat perilous economic education at the hands of shifty curiosity traders and unscrupulous business partners. The questions excited by Barnum's Mermaid were much the same questions he had asked himself almost a decade earlier, as he entered New York's curiosity trade. Is this advertised commodity genuine? How much should I pay to find out? Are the remarkable claims in the papers to be trusted? or is this merely another overrated fraud in a vast sea of dubious commodities? This promotional campaign, then, was built on a pack of lies, but also on a new kind of lying: lying which reconstructed the daily dramas of urban market exchange as a form of popular cultural play; lying which encouraged its consumers to bring the distinctive epistemological dilemmas of antebellum capitalism into the exhibition hall with them.

Barnum was not the first figure in Western cultural history to address the perceptual challenges of market relations on stage. Market-driven questions of authenticity, value, and truth had surfaced in the dramas of Elizabethan theater, for example, with great regularity.[73] And as we have seen, Maelzel was also flirting with this market-driven mode of artful deception a decade earlier. Barnum, however, pushed the boundaries of market culture in dramatically new directions during the 1840s. The Feejee Mermaid did not merely represent antebellum market relations in a cultural setting—it was a publicly scrutinized form of those relations. Whereas early modern theater audiences had looked on from the pit, boxes, and galleries, Barnum's American Museum audiences broke down the fourth wall and entered the drama. Or rather, their attempts to sort out Barnum's dubious claims about his cultural goods was the drama. These viewers were both subject and object in a grand passion play of antebellum commodity exchange authored by the Great Yankee Showman. And by the time the audience was fully cognizant of its role in Barnum's drama, the curtain was already starting to come down.

The Social Meanings
of Barnum's Mermaid

How, then, did contemporary viewers make sense of this elaborate, mass-circulated trickery? On the basis of the American Museum's skyrocketing ticket sales during the fall of 1842, it is hard to argue that Barnum was anything other than successful in his efforts to collapse the distinction between curiosity-viewing and curiosity-trading. Yet it is also important to acknowledge that the commercial success of Barnum's Mermaid was always a contested, morally problematic sort of success—and not merely in the South. In Philadelphia, the *Public Ledger* editors (feeling sore, perhaps, that they had been taken in at first) called for a Mermaid boycott, strongly encouraging "the people

American Museum viewers attempt to make sense of Barnum's Feejee Mermaid.

of this country" to "let it alone." In New York, too, some of the early press coverage suggested that Barnum might have gone too far in this particular case, perhaps even transgressed a fundamental moral threshold. The first and only real review of Barnum's exhibition in the *Herald,* for example, curtly dismissed the Mermaid on the grounds that it pushed the editors' tolerance for promotional puffery beyond acceptable limits: "Humbug—the Mermaid—and no mistake. We can swallow a reasonable dose, but we can't swallow this."[74]

Other Northern commentators were less dismissive. "That Mermaid," noted the New York *Tribune* in its first review,

> has arrived in this City on its way to the British Museum, and we were yesterday gratified with a private view of it. We tried hard to detect where

and how some cute Yankee had joined a monkey's head to a fish's body, but had to give up, though our incredulity still lingers. If such an animal ever *did* exist, it is surely the most extraordinary fact in Natural History. Believe it we can hardly; but how to account otherwise for what our eyes have seen staggers us. We should like to hear the opinion of better judges, after a rigid scrutiny.[75]

Written a few days before Barnum's self-made accusations of fraud had begun, this review continued to hold out the possibility of truth in Dr. Griffin's remarkable claims—a possibility which, at least for a fleeting moment, followed in the tradition of early modern mermaid exhibitions. The *Tribune's* willingness to consider that a real mermaid might be on display in lower Manhattan serves as a reminder, too, that during the first half of the nineteenth century such a discovery was not entirely unimaginable for many Americans. While the American scientific community was becoming increasingly skeptical of "sea serpent sightings," such sightings did continue with some regularity, often provoking at least passing interest in the urban press.[76]

Yet the *Tribune* review also speaks volumes about Barnum's— and the market revolution's—impact on the antebellum exhibition trade as a whole. Right from the start, the *Tribune* editors entered Dr. Griffin's exhibition looking not so much for an authentic sea monster as for evidence of the handiwork of some cute Yankee. After giving up the hunt themselves, they encouraged other, better judges to continue looking for evidence. And perhaps most significant, despite their lingering incredulity, they did not launch into public accusations of impudence or unreasonable doses on the part of Dr. Griffin. On the contrary, the *Tribune* seemed to find the good Doctor's apparent counterfeit relatively inoffensive, even intellectually stimulating—so much so that they recommend the experience to other New Yorkers.

Of course, the gratification described here remained carefully circumscribed and provisional. What the *Tribune* editors were tentatively endorsing was not the misrepresentation itself, but the excitement of looking for, and possibly exposing, such a thing. In other Northeastern reviews, though, one finds a few tentative celebrations of the Mermaid as a fully acknowledged act of imposture—an act which might be appreciated purely for the representational trickery of its promoter. The *Spirit of the Times,* for example, applauded whoever had put one over on their Philadelphia rivals: "speaking of the Mermaid . . . the N.Y. *Union* observes that the Japanese were clever in manufacturing these articles by attaching the head and shoulders of a she monkey to the tail of a fish. Very clever indeed, as our neighbor of the *Ledger* must admit."[77] In this formulation, clever marketing has become virtually equivalent to, and indistinguishable from, clever taxidermy. Indeed, it is hard to determine exactly who is responsible here for manufacturing the *Ledger*'s public meal of crow: both the Japanese producers of the article and the unnamed figure promoting it seem to play a part.

The deeply sarcastic voice employed by the *Spirit* editors signals that we are entering murky ethical territory. But there is also an unmistakable hint of respect here for the clever promoter who could pull off such a bold publicity stunt. And upon learning that the Mermaid had found its way to paying customers in New York rather than the display cases of the British Museum (as Dr. Griffin had originally promised), the *Spirit of the Times* editors could only tip their figurative hats: "*That* Mermaid which 'couldn't be seen' no how in this country by the public because it was sent for from London, is now being exhibited at Concert Hall, New York. We thought that 'the ship wouldn't be ready' and that the Yankees would get a peek at the monkeyfied *mer-baby.*"[78]

Collectively, then, the Northeastern urban press placed the showman's promotional deceits within a broad spectrum of interpretive categories: from bewilderment, indignation, and public calls for a Mermaid boycott, to fascination, amusement, and grudging respect for anyone who could actually turn a profit this way. But this spectrum had limits. No audience in New York, Philadelphia, or Boston physically attacked the Mermaid or staged noisy protests outside the exhibition hall (as happened in response to the showman's high ticket prices for Jenny Lind in the early 1850s). And even the most disgruntled commentators never suggested that Barnum be run out of town or

thrown in jail for his deceits. While the Northeastern press greeted
the Mermaid with moral reservations, even their most heated public
complaints usually acknowledged that the exhibition's commercial via-
bility was a *fait accompli*—an acknowledgment which gave these complaints a tone of grudging impotence, as if Barnum could be scolded
for his cultural sins, but certainly not stopped altogether.

Only a few weeks later, however, Barnum found himself confronted with a Southern controversy unlike any of the Northern ones
he had so skillfully managed thus far. It all began quite unexpectedly
in Charleston, South Carolina, during the final days of January 1843,
as Alanson Taylor, the showman's uncle, got to work as the Mermaid's
new road manager. Taylor's Southern entertainment program largely
followed Barnum's Northern precedents. In his first newspaper ads,
Taylor promised a "Grand Exhibition!!!" and "Wonders of Nature!!!"
at Charleston's Masonic Hall. He then regaled Charlestonians with
descriptions of "the real Mermaid, taken near the Feejee Islands, and
whose recent exhibition in New York, Boston, Baltimore, Washington,
&c., &c., has utterly dispelled the doubts of thousands and thousands
of naturalists." He even threw in two authentic natural wonders (a
duck-billed platypus and an orangoutang), as well as a glass blower
(Belzoni Davidson), an automaton exhibit, and some sleight-of-hand
tricks by one of the era's leading magicians (John Wyman). All in all, it
was standard fare from Barnum's antebellum handbook of variety
entertainment and hyperbolic advertising.[79]

The respected Charleston minister and naturalist, John Bachman,
was not amused, however. He immediately sent off angry letters to
the newspapers with the signature "No Humbug," denouncing the
Mermaid as nothing more than a "clumsy affair" created by our "Yankee neighbors." He argued that the seams connecting the body
and tail were not "sufficiently covered to conceal the point of union
even through a glass case." He also demanded that a group of
Charleston naturalists be allowed to examine the Mermaid outside of
its exhibition case, even offering to sign a certificate of authenticity
himself if the examinations proved the dubious creature to be real.

And perhaps worst of all from Barnum's perspective, Bachman pronounced the true value of Taylor's 50-cent road show to be about "6 and ½ cents."[80]

Over the next few weeks, this one-man assault on Taylor's Grand Exhibition gained a number of local allies, with J. Edwards Holbrook, E. Geddings, and Lewis Gibbes—all credentialed members of local academic institutions—joining the fray. The Mermaid debates also became somewhat nastier as Bachman turned his attack directly against a local foe, Richard Yeadon, a lawyer and editor of the Charleston *Courier*. Fueling his rancor was Bachman's perception that his honor had been insulted by Yeadon, who rejected Bachman's original anti-Mermaid letter for publication because he found it too "severe."[81] "We refused the first article of 'No Humbug'," Yeadon explained in an editorial, "because we thought it written in bad taste, and under excited feeling, using language we did not feel at liberty to admit into our columns—and when told who was the author, we expressed our surprise that he should be so far carried away by excitement to have penned it."[82]

To make matters worse, Yeadon published his own Mermaid testimonial in the *Courier*, suggesting that "we *lean* to the opinion that the Feejee Lady may be real and not counterfeit"—a pronouncement that infuriated Bachman and his fellow "certifiers," who wondered how Yeadon's "untrained eyes" could judge more accurately than their own.[83] Yeadon, in turn, insisted that the Mermaid was merely "plausible" (rather than self-evidently real or fake) and complained that Bachman refused to publicly sign his articles with his real name, as a Southern gentleman should. The matter became so delicate "that it required the intervention of a 'mutual friend' to prevent the dispute from ending in an exchange of pistol shots."[84]

Barnum and Taylor, meanwhile, did their very best to keep the controversy moving in profitable directions. Responding to Bachman's call for an out-of-case inspection, Taylor protested that to do so would damage the Mermaid irreparably. Using some of Barnum's well-oiled egalitarian rhetoric, Taylor also suggested that the untrained eyes of

Charleston were perfectly capable of detecting a seam on the creature's exterior:

> Gentlemen, with all your real and *boasted learning* and *wisdom,* and talents, *we* can see *as far* into a millstone as *any of you.* We ask not of you to teach us *that* about this "Mermaid," which, from the very nature and circumstances of the [display] case, *you cannot possibly know yourselves.* This, sir, we think will be the way, and the *proper way,* too, in which the people of Charleston—the unlettered people—the *poor plebeians in knowledge,* will treat this grand and majestic certificate.[85]

Just as Barnum had promoted the rights of average New Yorkers to judge for themselves, Taylor now sounded the rallying cry for Charleston's "poor plebeians" to enter the debate with their admission fees in hand.

Unlike Dr. Griffin, however, the "eminent naturalists" of Charleston were all too real, and they were becoming angrier and more aggressive with each of Taylor's new promotional teases. Bachman exclaimed that Taylor's "wonder of nature" was nothing but a "contemptible hoax" that ought to be immediately "thrown into the fire." He also recommended rather ominously that Taylor "clear himself from the city as fast as his heels can carry him."[86] These threats, Yeadon observed in one editorial, were not idle; he even urged the people of Charleston to refrain from mob violence.[87] For Barnum, the message from Charleston was clear: it was time to cut losses and retreat. Less than a month after the Southern tour had begun, the Mermaid was on its way North in an unmarked box—an unexpected denouement which Barnum related to Kimball in a frantic letter: "I believe the *maid* would have [been] *mince meat* ere this, had Taylor persisted in attempting to [stem] the tide which set so strong against him through the papers."[88]

This was one of the greatest defeats of Barnum's entire career. Yet, precisely because it came right on the heels of one of his greatest triumphs, it serves as an especially useful barometer of regional responses to Barnum's exhibitory innovations during the early 1840s. One possible explanation for the Southern debacle lies with the man who was running things in Charleston: perhaps Taylor simply was not as skilled a trickster as his nephew. Whereas Barnum had poked fun at the findings of fictional, unnamed naturalists conjured by his own pen, Taylor made these provocations personal. He named names and took sides—two rather crude marketing moves Barnum rarely executed. Taylor also doubled the admission price of the Mermaid in the South, a decision which no doubt made it more difficult for the poor ple-beians of Charleston to *see* the Mermaid, let alone defend their republican right to judge the creature. Although Taylor continued to pitch a debate between "plebeians" and "gentlemen" in the papers, one suspects his exhibition hall was mostly full of the latter. And at any rate, it was a group of Charleston gentlemen who ran the Mermaid show out of town.

This evacuation might not have been necessary, however, if the specific form of controversy promoted by Taylor and Barnum—a pub-lic discourse based on bold accusations, flaming exposés, and ambigu-ous public appearances—had not clashed so strongly with the strict code of honor maintained by Southern gentlemen. For Bachman and Yeadon to accuse each other of false Mermaid verdicts in the newspa-pers was tantamount to public accusations of lying. And among honor-able gentlemen in the antebellum South, such accusations usually led to calls for a duel—or even death.[89] The contrast here with the Mer-maid's Northern reception is particularly striking. While the pride of the *Public Ledger* editors was clearly bruised by the public teasing from the *Spirit of the Times,* they defended themselves according to the market-driven logic of the Philadelphia economy. That is, rather than physically threaten Dr. Griffin or challenge their journalistic rivals to a meeting on the field of honor, the *Ledger* editors simply panned Barnum's exhibition as an unworthy commercial product.

These distinctions in sanctions begin to articulate a second, very different Southern species of antebellum reception for Barnum's Mermaid tricks. Whereas most Northerners responded to Barnum's dubious commodity using the conventional terms of praise or dis-praise from the marketplace (arguing, for example, that the Mermaid was worth a look, regardless of its authenticity; or conversely, that it was not worth the price of admission and should be boycotted),

Bachman and his Southern allies steadfastly refused to allow the mechanisms of commodity exchange to operate. On both scientific and moral grounds, they pronounced Taylor's exhibition unworthy of entry into Charleston's marketplace—they did not want this Yankee production to compete for the quarters of Charlestonians, not even for a few weeks. What makes this strict prohibition especially note-worthy is the fact that it took place in one of the antebellum South's most highly developed market systems. Indeed, by 1843, the gentle-men of Charleston knew a great deal about market economics. They were keenly aware of, and largely dependent upon shifting inter-national crop prices to keep the Charleston economy afloat. They routinely borrowed money on interest to compensate for the interna-tional market's rapid fluctuations. And of course, they bought slaves on the principle of speculation, assessing the potential productivity of each worker in relation to the market price.[90]

Yet these gentlemen also created a set of public rituals that simply would not accommodate the ambiguities of representation on which Barnum's brand of artful deception depended. As Kenneth Green-berg has skillfully demonstrated, the rituals of Southern male honor— no less than those practiced by Yankee traders—were themselves representations. But the broader function of representation was understood in radically different ways in these two antebellum cul-tures.[91] Whereas Barnum viewed words and actions as the malleable instruments of economic and cultural contest, to Bachman words and actions conveyed unequivocal meanings about the morals and status of the speaker. In fact, it was precisely the refusal of Southern gentle-men to search beneath the surface meanings they manipulated— refusing, for example, to focus on the inner beings of their slaves rather than on the social status ascribed to skin color—which helped define and solidify their power *as* Southern gentlemen.[92]

No wonder, then, that the Charleston certifiers responded to the Mermaid quite literally and took each spokesman in the public contro-versy fully at his word. When Barnum promised a natural wonder for fifty cents, they expected the wonder to be natural. When Taylor ques-tioned the eyes and opinions of the Charleston gentlemen in his advertisements, they took these questions as an insult and threatened to run him out of town. And when one of their peers publicly suggested they might be wrong about the meaning of a seam on the surface of the Mermaid's torso (as Northern viewers did quite frequently, with little hostility), they understood this suggestion as a deliberate attempt at public humiliation. The same basic forms of trickery, in other words, that Barnum successfully promoted as "curious" throughout the urban North, the Charleston gentlemen defined as self-evidently immoral and worthy of quick and aggressive sanction. Bachman and his friends did not find Barnum's brand of teasing funny at all.[93]

The Mermaid's antebellum travels thus marked a series of sharp ideological fault lines between Northern and Southern conceptions of authenticity, value, and representation. But where, exactly, are we to place Richard Yeadon, a Southern gentleman whose actions and statements during much of the controversy hardly seem honorable at all in the sense delineated by Greenberg? What did Yeadon mean, for example, when he described himself as "not at liberty to admit" Bachman's hostile letter for publication in the *Courier*? This very same letter was in fact published by a rival Charleston paper, so why not here? And why did Yeadon emphasize again and again that he was especially concerned not to rush to judgment on the questions of authenticity raised by Taylor's dubious promotional claims?[94] "Dr. B is much in the wrong," Yeadon wrote after his public reconciliation with Bachman, "in saying that I speak less confidently now, on the subject of Mermaids, than I did at first—I never did speak confidently—on the contrary I always spoke *doubtingly*."[95]

Perhaps most intriguing of all is the fact this Southern gentleman was also secretly sending Barnum and Kimball advice about the possibility of suing Bachman for libel during the latter stages of the Mermaid controversy. In response to Barnum's suggestion that a legal battle with Bachman might renew public interest in the Mermaid ("*such* a suit would I think stir up the biggest kind of an excitement"), Yeadon urged caution, warning the Northern showmen that he was "*not* [by] any manner of means" confident of a win in a Charleston court.[96] He also pointed out to his Northern clients that they might have a case against Bachman, but only "provided it [the Mermaid] be a *genuine* specimen."[97] This last point gave Barnum cause for serious reflection: "Now my dear [Moses], every devil among the scientifics would *swear* that its existence is a *natural impossibility*—and would they not raise suspicions too strong in the minds of the *canaille* [rabble] for us to use *them* to advantage?"[98]

That Barnum still understood the question of the Mermaid's authenticity purely as a marketing matter—even at this critical juncture, as he was contemplating a lawsuit against his Southern accuser— is instructive. What concerned the showman was what the "scientific devils" would say about his exhibition in public. As Barnum knew, if these devils publicly resolved the matter with expert testimony or a dissecting knife, his days of reaping expansive profits were numbered. It is also instructive that Yeadon advised Barnum against taking his fight into a Charleston courtroom, a bit of Southern advice on the question that stands in sharp contrast to Bachman's moral tirades. In fact, all of Yeadon's 1843 concerns were articulated in the more provisional language of liability, not in terms of scientific and moral absolutes. Yeadon, in other words, was a Southern lawyer as well as a Southern gentleman. And as such, he had been trained to think about authenticity in ways that transcended the ideological chasm separating Barnum's cunning and Bachman's honor.

As Charles Sellers has demonstrated, it was Yeadon's professional colleagues (at least in other parts of the country) who often spearheaded the market revolution: "lawyers were the shock troops of capitalism. . . . During the commercial boom, merchants abandoned informal arbitration and relied increasingly on lawyers and courts to settle more disputes over ever larger sums. Even the criminal courts shifted from enforcing communal morality to enforcing the market's property relationships."[99] Whereas the common law passed down through the eighteenth century had "enforced equity and fair value in contracts," the increasingly market-friendly law in most of antebellum America came to favor a strict enforcement of *caveat emptor*. Three years before the Feejee Mermaid controversy, for example, a Pennsylvania state court judge scoffed at the notion that the buyer of a horse could claim an implied warranty when the horse was found to have glanders: he who is so simple as to contract without a specification of the terms, "is not a fit subject for legal guardianship."[100]

This prevailing pattern of antebellum lawyers and judges greasing the wheels of market capitalism carried over to the more specific legal definition of misrepresentation they developed. "In the era's fraud doctrine," Morton Horwitz explains, "the postulates of a market economy required the sharp distinction between 'facts' on the one hand and 'estimates' and 'opinions' on the other, whose effect was to sharply limit the finding of fraud."[101] Significantly, even those promotional claims known by a seller to be exaggerated or false fell into the category of nonactionable opinion at the time that Barnum was testing the waters of public tolerance with his bogus Mermaid. Ruling on an 1843 real estate case in Massachusetts, the judge treated "false affirmations" about the value of a piece of land as nothing more than the conventional seductions employed in the world of business.[102]

Until his troubles began in Charleston, Barnum never mentioned the possibility of legal difficulties with his Mermaid. One suspects that he came to understand the thresholds of antebellum criminal fraud simply by pushing too far. More certain is the fact that Yeadon's lingering concerns about the authenticity of the Mermaid placed him outside the main currents of contemporary legal practice. As Yeadon no doubt knew, his was the only state in the country whose courts had a well-documented track record of resisting a strict principle of "buyer beware" in market transactions. In 1818, for example, when barrels of blubber were sold as "oil" and later disputed in court, the South Carolina judge ruled strongly for the buyer, publicly denouncing *caveat emptor* as a "disgrace to the law."[103] Thus legal precedent dictated that the Mermaid was not a "sound commodity," and Charleston's consumers were not expected to beware the misrepresentations of sellers—especially when they were Yankee salesmen. Although Barnum whined to Kimball about Yeadon's fees ("I think that the *very* richest part"), his legal counsels may have saved Alanson Taylor from serving jail time. And the very fact that Yeadon urged such caution suggests that the American market revolution was still unfinished in 1843.

After "sleeping" on Yeadon's advice for a couple weeks, Barnum described a new plan of action to Kimball in a letter:

> [W]e had better keep up the excitement as much as we [can] and *not* go to law—but open the mermaid *here* soon on the strength of the anticipated or *pretended* law suit. *I* would [do] right well to open her here in a week or two—first preparing her way by means of *our papers* stating that the scientifics were to be prosecuted etc. . . . Exhibiting the critter *here* just now *might not* draw and *might* some . . . my wife and all the old maids in town think . . . it would *ruin* me but *I will try it* if you think it will help establish elsewhere, or in other words if you *don't* think I ought to *pay* much for the *privilege* of trying it.[104]

This was antebellum humbuggery of the most sophisticated sort: rather than let the Southern certifiers and courts have the last word on his Mermaid, Barnum would make them part of the show, adding a pretended law suit to rekindle the flames of public curiosity in friendlier Northern markets. It is worth noting, however, that at least a few of the Southern gentlemen seem to have been keenly aware of Barnum's maneuvers. As an anonymous writer in the Charleston *Mercury* observed:

> I have strong suspicions that these [public threats of a lawsuit] are only false fires to aid a retreating army . . . there is a chain of circumstantial evidence, that those men [Barnum and Taylor] had some misgivings in regard to their speculations on the credulity of the South. . . . If their letter of instructions could be laid hold of, it would probably be found that their orders were—"Show the manufactured handbills and pictures— puff away—collect as much money as you can. When here and there a Naturalist expresses doubts, threaten and abuse, but don't stay—fight as you run."[105]

Few antebellum documents more clearly articulate the legal, economic, and moral fault lines carved out by the American market revolution than these two late soundings from Barnum's traveling Mermaid show. For the Charleston scientifics, such deliberate misrepresentation of a publicly consumed exhibitory commodity was a dishonorable and potentially punishable criminal offense. For Barnum, a leading Northern entrepreneur, this sort of speculation was nothing more than a conventional business practice, something to be proposed matter-of-factly to one's partner and put into action—provided it did not offend any particular market segment too strongly. And for Charity Barnum, the showman's less reckless, bourgeois wife, these Mermaid tricks boiled down to a transgression worthy of moral reform, rather than criminal sanction.[106] While Charity knew from experience that the showman could probably get away with his promotional trickery in New York, she nevertheless cautioned that such overt duplicity might lead in morally dangerous directions.

Humbug Universal

Who ultimately prevailed in these ideological struggles over the meanings of Barnum's Mermaid? In one sense, we might say that the showman did in fact take Charity's advice. Rather than risk ruin by flouting the values of the new middle class, Barnum modified his amusement program after the 1843 setback, adding a new assortment of "moral and reformatory entertainments."[107] The temperance and biblical dramas that began to appear on Barnum's stage around 1850 were one prominent example. So, too, were his new, more rigidly enforced rules about drinking, gambling, and prostitution in the American Museum at about the same time. And perhaps most dramatically, there was the Jenny Lind Enterprise of 1850: Barnum's year-long promotional celebration of the artistic genius and moral virtues of the era's leading European opera singer, which he undertook quite deliberately to refashion his old image as the purveyor of "a stuffed monkey skin" and "a dead mermaid."[108]

Yet these mid-century attempts at show business respectability hardly signaled the end of Barnum's career as trickster. There simply is too much evidence to the contrary: the long behind-the-scenes chronicle of the Mermaid in his 1855 autobiography, for example, which transformed the original exhibitory humbug into a best-selling literary trickster tale; the reemergence of the Mermaid a few years later as a prop for his "Art of Money-Getting" lecture, a public performance he repeated hundreds of times throughout the 1860s; and the publication of his 1865 treatise, *Humbugs of the World,* which analyzed deception in all of its contemporary forms (electoral politics, spiritualism, patent medicines, etc.). Rather than simply abandoning his Mermaid tricks, then, it is probably more accurate to say that Barnum brought them up the socioeconomic ladder with him. To do so, however, he subtly redefined the parameters of his Prince of Humbug identity: from a maker of ingenious hoaxes to a professional expert on the topic, a recognized public authority on the arts of deception, both harmless and otherwise.

Barnum also began to argue that the deceptions involved in his Mermaid campaign were harmless precisely because they were now so pervasive in the urban market economy. "Business," he wrote in the opening chapter to *Humbugs,*

> is the ordinary means of living for all of us. And in what business is there not humbug? "There's cheating in all trades but ours," is the prompt reply from the boot-maker with his brown paper soles, the grocer with his floury sugar and chicoried coffee, the butcher with his mysterious sausages and queer veal, the dry-goods man with his "damaged goods wet at the great fire," and his "selling at a ruinous loss," the stock-broker with his brazen assurance that your company is bankrupt and your stock not worth a cent (if he wants to buy it) . . . all and every one protest their innocence, and warn you against the rest. My inexperienced friend, take it for granted that they tell the truth—about each other![109]

What Barnum was proposing here was something far more ambitious than a pardon for his youthful sins. He also wanted to convince readers that his early tricks were nothing less than a microcosm of Gilded Age market principles—or at least a *modus operandi* for living in the complex market economy that had grown up with him. What had started as a playful cultural scheme grounded in the "sharp trading" and "speculations" of his youth, Barnum redefined in 1865 as the conventional way of doing modern business. And in a sense, that was his greatest trick of all: to convince many of his new middle-class peers that humbug in the exhibition room was merely market capitalism by another name.

3

Describing the Nondescript

The Feejee Mermaid made Barnum the most famous trickster of the nineteenth century. But there was another mode of trickery in his repertoire: not so much Barnum in the role of Prince of Humbug—the winking puffer behind half-exposed deceits—but Barnum as the straight-faced producer of seamless deceptions. This second aesthetic mode was especially common in his living curiosity exhibitions—General Tom Thumb, for example, whose name, age, history, and appearance Barnum embellished with great success—and in many respects represented a strategic reversal of the aesthetic priorities and marketing methods employed in the Mermaid campaign. Rather than focusing public attention on the boundaries between authenticity and fraud, Barnum's living curiosities depended on a presumption of at least partial authenticity, as well as the perception that the showman was largely uninvolved in *creating* their curious features.

Either way, the wonders sold to audiences were nothing more than elaborate representations: fictional identities worn by an inanimate object (a stuffed monkey corpse fused to a fish tail) or a human actor

(Charles S. Stratton, the Connecticut boy behind the General persona). Built into these exhibition models, however, were two very different modes of viewership. The Mermaid's viewers focused on the act of representation itself (how might this monkey-fish concoction have been manufactured?), as well as on its moral and legal legitimacy (is this representational act worthy of the admission price?). Viewers of the living curiosity exhibitions, by contrast, focused on the content of Barnum's representations (how does the General look and behave, dance and sing, dress and talk?), as well as the representation's larger social implications (what sort of public persona is being articulated through this remarkable man-child?).

Surprisingly, it is only very recently that historians have begun to grapple with the showman's living curiosities, despite the fact that it was Barnum who essentially invented the freak show as a "formally organized institution" during the early 1840s.[1] One reason for this lack of attention may be that the freakish portion of the showman's repertoire cuts so squarely against the grain of current notions of decency. While it is still easy to laugh with Barnum at his half monkey/half fish scam—and to some extent, admire his promotional audacity—his living curiosity exhibitions appear in retrospect to have encouraged the very worst kinds of prejudices, stereotyping, and human exploitation. What has thus emerged in most histories of Barnum's amusement empire is a somewhat misleading pattern of neglect and omission. Although living curiosities were one of the cornerstones of Barnum's cultural production (and nineteenth-century American popular culture, more generally), they have been greatly overshadowed by Barnumesque amusements that strike us as less offensive: the Feejee Mermaid, the moral dramas, the Jenny Lind opera tour, and the circus.

Furthermore, Barnum's living curiosity images do not mesh particularly well with the extensive historical literature on nineteenth-century American stereotyping—a literature which has done a far better job of cataloging contradictory attitudes and images (for example, the common pattern of stereotyping African-American slaves as both happy laborers and prone to violence) than explaining the historically specific ideologies that could accommodate such inconsistencies.[2] In Barnum's exhibition rooms, boundary-blurring images of difference were not simply a common occurrence; they were the very basis of the entertainment form itself. Every single one of Barnum's living curiosities was a liminal figure of some sort, a caricatured disruption of the normative boundaries between black and white (albino Negroes), male and female (bearded ladies), young and old (General Tom Thumb), man and animal (dog-faced boys), one self or two (Siamese twins).[3]

Given the vast mainstream popularity of these exhibitions, it seems safe to say that the contemporaneous emergence of the new middle class and Barnum's living curiosities was hardly coincidental. Indeed, it is difficult to find another cultural institution that so fully articulated the new middle class's tangle of attitudes toward race, class, gender, nationality, sexuality, and disability: they are all there, in various combinations, among the parade of living curiosities standing on Barnum's platforms after 1842. Yet, as liminal figures that, by their very design, blurred the conventional physiological and cultural boundaries on which difference depends, Barnum's living curiosities resist any dull interpretive tools we might try to apply. Sweeping retroactive assertions of prejudice or vague ahistorical generalizations about exoticized others on stage hardly even begin to explain the cacophony of voices and competing theories of difference set in motion by the showman's open-ended promotional maneuvers. Just as the public discourse surrounding the Feejee Mermaid was never limited to a simple choice between natural wonder and clever counterfeit, the caricatured liminality of Barnum's living curiosities was much more than a straightforward representation of authentic freakishness. If this was realism, it was a form of realism understood as thoroughly flexible, provisional, and uncertain—a realism whose specific outlines emerged only through relentless public speculation and equivocation.

Consider, for example, the living curiosity known as What Is It?, a wildly popular American Museum exhibition which made its debut in February, 1860. This exhibition has been described by one recent group of Barnum biographers as the most famous freak of its era.[4]

Certainly, it was one of the showman's most audacious and complex efforts within the genre. Following the publication of Charles Darwin's *Origin of Species* by only three months, Barnum promoted the dark-skinned performer playing What Is It? as a possible missing link between man and beast—an obvious attempt to capitalize on Darwin's evolutionary hypothesis, which also risked public accusations of sacrilege. Sacrilege, however, was merely the first and most obvious potential flashpoint for the exhibition. As Barnum and his customers knew all too well, the "scientific" questions raised by What Is It? were inextricably linked to issues of racial definition, social order, and political partisanship. And by February 1860, none of these subjects was to be broached lightly in public.

It was at this very moment that the long-simmering sectionalist controversies of the 1850s were coming to their dramatic climax. Only three years earlier, Supreme Court Chief Justice Roger Taney had issued his notorious *Dred Scott* decision, which suggested that race alone—rather than place of residence—condemned those of African descent to a constitutional status somewhere below full humanity (let alone full citizenship). And side by side with Barnum's daily advertisements for What Is It?, the New York newspapers chronicled the progress of the 1860 presidential election—a watershed decision that would be won or lost largely on the question of how each candidate defined the status of people of African descent in American society. The appearance of What Is It? at this volatile moment raises tricky questions about the larger ideological implications of Barnum's amusement program. Did the African figure who appeared in Barnum's exhibition rooms during the early 1860s fit any particular partisan agenda? Was the public excitement about African acculturation on lower Broadway a subtle threat or a popular cultural boon to the racialized logic of the *Dred Scott* decision?

Precisely because of its close ideological proximity to these scientific, political, and legal debates, What Is It? carried the potential for generating lucrative public excitement, or, if handled recklessly, intense public outrage. Barnum thus chose his terms carefully. The

A Currier and Ives lithograph of Barnum's What Is It? exhibition from the early 1860s.

figure appearing at the American Museum, he explained to his audiences, was simply indescribable—neither man nor monkey, a creature demonstrating characteristics animal as well as human, civilized as well as brutish. It was, as his vast stream of promotional materials insisted, a *nondescript:* a remarkable, previously undiscovered being in need of more precise classification, yet one remarkably resistant to the management's best efforts to do so. While Barnum had banked on such deliberately equivocal forms of promotion before, this 1860 exhibition raised the bar of the showman's puffery to new heights of imprecision. In both its name (What Is It?) and its remarkably evasive categorization (nondescript), Barnum's most successful exhibition of the Civil War years literally and figuratively begged the public to fill in the blanks.

It is just this calculated ideological imprecision that needs to be contextualized and explained. Three contemporary contexts, in particular, seem especially relevant: the ongoing public debates about the political status of free African Americans in the North; the so-called scientific theories of racial distinction with which such political judgments were often made; and the intricate codes of white social respectability Barnum's viewers brought with them into the exhibition room. By tracing the reception of What Is It? through this range of interconnected issues, I hope to explain more fully the enormous appeal of the exhibition for its American Museum audiences—an appeal which is often hard for us to understand, much less appreciate, in retrospect. But this difference in audience appreciation is precisely what makes the exhibition so illuminating as a cultural artifact. What it demonstrates is a culturally and historically specific set of images, attitudes, and bigotries, some of which fit easily within our conventional assumptions about how white northern urbanites wielded racial prejudice during the 1860s (the frequent comparisons of What Is It? to "savages" and "apes"), and others which seem, initially at least, to undermine these very same forms of ridicule (Barnum's frequent assurances that there was "nothing at all repulsive about the creature").

Also valuable are the various ways that Barnum's exhibition helps us to understand how race itself was constructed as a cultural category during this period.[5] While viewers often remarked upon the bodily features of What Is It? (his skin color, facial structure, hair, etc.), and used these features to make claims about his status as an African or Negro, their comments also suggest an ideology of racial distinction that transcended surface impressions, one in which corporeal evidence was but a single type of signifier marking distance between the figure on stage and those who went to see him. Equally important in their eyes were the performer's manners or lack thereof, his level of intelligence, his countenance, even the clothes he wore and the foods he ate. During the 1860s, in other words, the cultural boundaries of blackness and whiteness were built (just as they are today) upon a wide range of remarkably subjective, inconsistent, and often nonphysiological variables. And Barnum's patrons enthusiastically debated these variables, not merely to ridicule the caricatured figure standing before them, but also to make reciprocal claims about their own identities, to define themselves in contrast to what they were not.

Yet the nagging imprecision of their racialist claims says something, too, about the transgressive possibilities of the nondescript, a kind of anticategorical category whose novelty lay precisely in rendering the classification process itself equivocal, perpetual, subject to endless discussion and revision. While Barnum's audiences clearly understood What Is It? as their physical and cultural other, they also just as clearly reveled in the flexibility and open-endedness of their judgments, a somewhat paradoxical pattern which suggests that these viewers may have been up to something more than merely drawing fixed lines of racial distinction in the popular cultural sand. Within the playful confines of the American Museum's exhibition rooms, Barnum's audiences cast What Is It? in endless and endlessly contradictory ways: as man and monkey, child and adult, self-evidently brutish and self-evidently delightful, reformable citizen and unredeemable savage, even a possible hoax (which, of course, it was).

What seems to be missing here, then, is not so much an interpretive way out of the contradictions and tangled qualifications, but a way into the culturally and historically specific thinking that made them possible. Why, in other words, did this particular set of contradictions and qualifications emerge here, in Barnum's American Museum, a venue catering to a more broadly heterogeneous assortment of white Northern viewers than any other popular cultural institution of its time? And perhaps more important, why did this particular caricature emerge during the early 1860s, as the country as a whole was coming apart so violently at the seams?

The Actors, Barnum's Character, and Its Slippery Categorization

Perhaps the most troubling aspect of this exhibition's long and ugly history is that we do not know who was standing on Barnum's platform in February 1860, or what this person might have thought or said about his performances as a nondescript. It is Barnum's racist caricature that emerges most clearly from the surviving source materials: a representation called What Is It? and its meanings in the eyes of contemporary white viewers, rather than the very real African-American man who performed Barnum's caricature. We do know the names of two other men who performed the role before and after the 1860s: Hervey Leech, a disabled New York actor who played the character briefly in Barnum's employ in London in 1846; and William Henry Johnson, a young man from New Jersey, who seems to have been pushed into Barnum's service by family members sometime during the late 1870s.

Leech, according to most accounts, was born in Westchester County, New York, in 1804 and worked a number of show business jobs under the *nom de théâtre,* Signor Hervio Nano. Both this Italianate title and contemporary portraits suggest that Leech was probably white. According to a newspaper article from 1847, his only "remarkable" physical feature was the size of his legs, which were unusually small in proportion to the rest of his powerful body:

> This extraordinary cripple . . . exhibits the very rare combinations of perfect symmetry, strength, and beauty, with a great amount of deformity. The head is remarkably fine in form, and the expression intelligent and

benign; the chest, shoulders, and arms form a perfect model of strength and beauty; the arms are exceedingly muscular, and the hands very well and strongly formed . . . in the place of legs there are two limbs, the left about 18 inches from the hip to the point of the toes, the right about 24 inches from the same points. The feet are natural.[6]

Such an "arrangement," the writer suggested, gave Leech double power between his feet and hands, and allowed him to demonstrate extraordinary feats of leaping.

It also allowed him to play numerous monkey characters on the antebellum American stage: "Jocko, the Brazilian Ape" at the Chatham Theater in New York; "Bibbo, the Patagonian Ape" at Palmo's; and an "Ape" of unspecified origin at the Bowery Theater. His most successful and enduring role, however, was the "Gnome Fly," a kind of dramatic triptych which debuted at the Bowery in January 1840 and required Leech to transform himself from the gnome "Sapajou" into a baboon, and then (through a "wonderful flight, in magnificent costume . . . from the ceiling, back of the gallery, to the back of the stage, a distance of 250 feet") into a blue-bottle fly.[7] Barnum, who was working as a New York theatrical manager during these years, must have heard a great deal about the new production. Indeed, one imagines the young impresario seated in the pit of the Bowery Theater, fully mesmerized by the strangeness of Leech's performance, his mind racing with ideas about future schemes for the diminutive star.[8] Whatever the precise circumstances, by August 1846 a deal had been struck between Barnum and Leech for the showman's second European tour. Leech acquired a "hair dress" from a New York wigmaker and "stained" his hands and face.[9] Barnum rented a room in London's Egyptian Hall.[10] And Londoners began reading advertisements about a new American curiosity with an unlikely name: What Is It?[11]

The first version of the exhibition—which consisted of Leech standing in a cage, grunting, and eating raw meat—lasted less than a half hour before being exposed by a rival showman, who, despite Leech's elaborate disguise, immediately recognized the American actor and entered the cage to greet him. According to one perhaps exaggerated account, Barnum's rival quickly proceeded to tear the fur suit off of Leech's body and then publicly offered to buy him a broiled steak at a restaurant down the street.[12] In the broad span of Barnum's career, it was a minor failure—this time with relatively little financial damage. Over the next fourteen years, he kept the unrealized scheme filed away in the back of his mind, perhaps to be used again when the right moment presented itself. Meanwhile, he openly laughed about the escapade in the 1855 edition of his autobiography and professed total ignorance about who might have been responsible for the scam.[13]

The details of William Henry Johnson's tenure as What Is It? are even harder to nail down. Numerous publicity photographs suggest that he was a short, African-American man with a sharply sloping brow line, although as one writer observed at Johnson's funeral in 1926, out of costume—and removed from the circus platform—there was nothing particularly exceptional about his famous head.[14] We know, too, that Johnson played the character for decades before his death and that many early twentieth-century observers, including a few long-term Barnum employees, described him as the original What Is It?[15] But more reliable evidence suggests that Johnson was actually the third man to play the role. Sarah Van Duyne, Johnson's sister, told reporters in 1926 that her brother did not work for Barnum until 1877, when he left his home in Bound Brook, New Jersey, to join the circus. And federal census records support these dates. When Barnum reinvented his What Is It? exhibition for New York audiences in 1860, William Henry Johnson was listed as a resident of Bound Brook, New Jersey—only three years old.[16]

The scant testimony left behind by Barnum is not much help in sorting out the identity of Johnson's predecessor. The only surviving clue appears in an early 1860 letter from the showman, which simply noted: "A certain museum proprietor in St. Louis—I don't know his name—saw a queer little crittur exhibiting in Phila. a few months since. I have since secured it, and we call it 'What is It?' "[17] This distressingly vague note represents the extent of what is known about the professional background of the young man who looks out at us in a pair of Mathew Brady publicity photographs from the early 1860s.[18] We can, however, establish some rough parameters for gauging his agency in Barnum's enterprise. It seems relatively safe to assume, for example, that he, like Johnson, did not have complete control over his early show business career. (According to his sister, William Henry Johnson was pushed into Barnum's employ by his parents and neighbors during the 1870s, the same sort of show business entrée by which a young Charles Stratton became General Tom Thumb in 1842.)[19] The person playing What Is It? during the early 1860s, moreover, was young, African American at a time when Northern blacks enjoyed few if any legal protections, and may have suffered from microcephaly, a physiological condition that often produces mental retardation—all of which would suggest that his ability to resist the show business advice from his family and Barnum was probably limited.[20]

Yet it also seems clear that the person in the Mathew Brady photographs was not simply a passive victim in his show business labors. Although later accounts differ widely about his mental competence—and in many cases seem to tell us more about the prejudices of the commentators than anything substantive about the actor—the man who played What Is It? during the early 1860s had the language and logic skills necessary to follow a carefully choreographed American Museum routine: as Barnum's manager described the limited ambulatory abilities of What Is It?, the actor walked across the stage in an appropriately awkward manner; as the character's "African" diet was listed, this actor ate the appropriate meat and nuts; as viewers were told of the character's limited speech capabilities, he grunted on cue; and so on and so forth, month after month, often two or three times per day. The so-called brutishness of What Is It?, in other words, was an ongoing theatrical production—an act of "enfreakment"—with an intricately detailed script.[21] And at the very least, the man who played the character had a steady command of these details, offering much the same performance for thousands of shows, over a number of years.

For the most part, the New York performances (quite unlike the 1846 debacle in London) went off without a hitch. In fact, throughout dozens of exhibition reviews from the early 1860s, one finds very few

Mathew Brady's photographic portraits of What Is It? taken during the 1860s. Note the various efforts (fur suit, shaved head, walking stick, exotic backdrops) to reinforce Barnum's racialist caricature.

public hints that this was simply an African-American man performing in racialist drag—a reception pattern which says as much about the agency of the actor on stage as the deep prejudices or gullibility of the people in the audience. The most notable exception was a March 1860 article in the New York *Clipper*, which observed "many sly manoeuvers" that let "in the light of the humbug terribly."[22] What these maneuvers actually signified, however, is unclear. One can speculate, for example, that they represented a momentary act of subterfuge from a disgruntled employee, or perhaps even a man expressing some initial uneasiness about the sort of popular cultural work he was beginning to perform. Or they may have simply reflected the newspaperman's eagerness for yet another game of overt humbuggery—an eagerness which may have led the *Clipper* correspondent to see things on the American Museum stage that most other contemporary observers did not. Or it may be that Barnum, aided by a willing collaborator on stage, sought to raise the specter of humbug as an additional drawing card for the exhibition (a promotional trick which, as we have seen, Barnum routinely employed during the 1830s and 1840s).

The *Clipper* article's quite accurate perception of fraud, however, was the exception rather than the rule during the early 1860s. New York audiences, that is to say, had little doubt that some of Barnum's hyperbolic claims were exaggerations or misrepresentations. Yet these doubts ultimately pushed more in the direction of realism than illusionism: in this case, the core issue was not so much whether the exhibition was authentic or inauthentic, but how, exactly, it was curious. That the man on stage was indeed a curiosity of some sort held the status of self-evident fact for most American Museum viewers. Again and again, they treated Barnum's transparent racialist fiction as if it were something more, something at least partially genuine.

But what kind of racialist fiction was this, really? Here, there is a far more detailed history and clearly recognizable set of Western cultural precedents. Much as Shakespeare did with Caliban, Barnum located the origins of his *Homo Ferus* caricature in an exotic, vaguely aboriginal setting somewhere in "the interior of Africa," where it was said to have been "living in a tree."[23] The elaborate costume in one of the early 1860s Mathew Brady photographs—a suit of black hair, covering most of the performer's body—followed squarely in the tradition of eighteenth-century European carnival "savages" (such as The Black Hairy Pigmy from Araby), in which fur served as a multidimensional signifier for non-Western origin, as well as a physiological connection to anthropoid animals.[24] Even the promotional slogans Barnum used were partially borrowed from earlier cultural forms. Whereas Charles Willson Peale had presented an orangoutang as The Wild Man of the Woods at his Philadelphia Museum in 1799, Barnum offered Hervey Leech to Londoners in 1846 as The Wild Man of the Prairies.[25]

But Barnum never completely recycled the promotional wares of his competitors, never limited himself to permanently fixed, or one-dimensional character molds. For What Is It? he developed three separate inflections. The short-lived London character was said to have been discovered in "the wilds of California," where "for the last 10 months it has been with a tribe of Indians." In New York, Barnum shifted the habitat to the African jungle and gave his character an additional moniker—the Man-Monkey. Around the turn-of-the-century, this persona, too, was modified. Although the actor, costume, and older missing-link rhetoric remained largely consistent, promotional materials added a less geographically specific title (Zip), as well as a more fantastic place of origin ("the land beyond the moon").

This flexibility in the construction of Barnum's caricature, one suspects, followed the tides of public taste. In London, for example, Barnum seems to have designed his Wild Man of the Prairies production with the hope of capitalizing on the same English enthusiasm for the American West that had carried George Catlin's traveling Indian exhibit to enormous success at the Egyptian Hall only a year before. Yet it is important not to overemphasize this kind of popular cultural borrowing in Barnum's production schemes. Writing to Moses Kimball two weeks before the London opening, Barnum was mostly uninterested in his new character's geographic or racial details. These he threw off quickly and carelessly, focusing instead on the character's hybrid status, somewhere between man and animal, as well as his desire to pitch the exhibition in such a way as to encourage public debate about this hybridity:

> The *animal* that I spoke to you & Hale about comes out at Egyptian Hall, London, next Monday, and I half fear that I will not only be exposed, but that *I* shall be *found out* in the matter. However, I go it, live or die. The thing is not to be called *anything* by the exhibitor. We know not & therefore do not assert whether it is human or animal. We leave that all to the sagacious public to decide.
>
> The bills & advertisements will be headed as follows:
>
> "WHAT IS IT?" Now exhibiting at the Egyptian Hall etc. etc. Found in the forests of California, etc. etc.[26]

Whether his hybrid creature came from the forest or the prairie, California or Araby, seems to have been a secondary concern. At the core of the new caricature was Barnum's desire to create a fundamentally liminal creature, onto which numerous geographic, racial, and cultural templates could be applied.

The boundary-blurring hybridity of What Is It? provided Barnum with a flexible promotional tool—a tool the showman repeatedly adapted for a wide range of market segments over time. Ambiguity was also a subject that Barnum grew increasingly adept at describing over the course of his career. The best example is his development of the category "nondescript" to describe What Is It? Significantly, it was at this very moment—as Barnum was searching for the right words to promote his new character—that the term "nondescript" first appears in the English language as a noun for "a person or thing that is not easily described, or is of no particular class or kind."[27] Prior to this time, it had been used as an adjective for something not yet described. This sense too was useful for Barnum's character-in-the-making: it was precisely the kind of new, previously unseen animal or species Barnum was trying to represent. By mid-century, however, the word also took on a distinct, secondary meaning: the more liminal sense of resisting classification, or straddling descriptive boundaries.[28] So while the older definition provided Barnum with a means of capturing the nov-

elty of What Is It?—his pristine status as the aboriginal inhabitant of
some far-off land—the term's newer meaning offered a subtle linguistic tool for talking about this aborigine's physical and behavioral ambiguities: a being intersecting the existing scientific categories.

Barnum began to use the term "nondescript" in 1849 to describe
new animal attractions such as the Woolly Horse (Col. Freemont's
Nondescript, the "ambiguous quadruped"), which debuted under an
assistant's charge in Philadelphia. He also employed the term to spec-
ify a particular category of museum display, as in the lengthy title of a
guidebook from the same year: *Sights and Wonders in New York;
including a description of the mysteries, marvels, phenomena, curiosities, and nondescripts, contained in that great congress of wonders,
Barnum's Museum.*[29] In this instance, the term "nondescript" may
have referred to any number of wonders in the American Museum's
vast exhibition halls—his orangoutang, for example, or perhaps the
duck-billed platypus—both of which had been described by naturalists as possible intermixtures of species for years.[30] What Barnum was
actually inaugurating was the precision of language necessary to differentiate the curious hybrid from thousands of less categorically
ambiguous artifacts (stuffed eagles, fossils, models of Niagara Falls,
etc.) in his American Museum display cases.

To move from nondescript horses and platypuses to nondescript
caricatures of human beings represented a major conceptual shift,
however, one Barnum appears not to have undertaken in earnest until
the American debut of What Is It? in 1860. Above all, it required far
more attention to manners and behaviors than Barnum had attempted
in any of his previous nondescript productions. In the case of the
Woolly Horse, for example, the categorical imprecision remained
mostly a function of ambiguous surfaces and complicated physical
markings. "This most astounding of all flesh is," Barnum explained, "in
size, like the ordinary Horse; but exhibits portions of the Buffalo,
Camel, Deer, Elephant, and [is] covered with FINE CURLY MATTED
SILK of the colour of camel's hair. He has not the mane or the tail of
the horse, but *the tail of the Elephant!*"[31] Regarding the conventional
behavior of this astounding creature, Barnum noted only that it

"bounds twelve or fifteen feet high." How exactly "old Woolly" ate, ran, or slept—or which animal in his "ambiguous composition" had produced such remarkable bounding skills—audiences were left to ponder for themselves.[32]

By contrast, the What Is It? campaign of 1860 wove ambiguous physical descriptions into a far more complex package. "The curious creature is two thirds [the] size of Man. Laughs, but can't speak," noted one of Barnum's ads in the New York papers.[33] Exclaimed another: "Looks like a Man! Acts Like a Monkey!"[34] Despite the fact that his "natural position" was "on all fours," the creature could, with effort and the careful guidance of his trainer, slowly assume the natural, bipedal position of man—an important distinction from the rest of "brute creation." In other behaviors, however, What Is It? seemed to follow some atavistic urge, distancing him from the rest of mankind. "When he first came," noted Barnum's exhibition program, "his only food was raw meat, sweet apples, oranges, nuts, &c., of all of which he was very fond; but he will now eat bread, cake, and similar things, though he is fonder of raw meat, or that which, when cooked, is rare."[35] Confronted with that pivotal anthropological distinction between the raw and the cooked (and by implication, nature versus civilization), Barnum's nondescript steadfastly maintained his liminal persona—and opted for both.[36]

In similar fashion, Barnum's elaborate descriptions attempted to place his character's physiognomy somewhere between humanity and brute creation, often identifying evidence of both categories in the same anatomical regions:

> The formation of the head and face combines both that of the native African and of the Ourang Outang. The upper part of the head, and the forehead in particular, instead of being four or five inches broad, *as it should be, to resemble that of a human being,* is Less Than Two Inches! The Head of the What Is It is very small. The ears are set back about an inch *too far for humanity,* and about three fourths of an inch too high up. They should form a line with the ridge of the nose *to be like that of a human being.* As they are now placed they constitute the perfect head and skull of the Ourang Outang, while the lower part of the face is that of the native African.[37]

Barnum provides no answers to the questions he raises in this promotional puff, no guidance at all about what final conclusions to draw. Is the racialized message here to focus on forehead size and define What Is It? as simian in his "formation"? Or is Barnum suggesting that this caricatured apishness is incomplete by his own admission, with enough recognizably human attributes to require close measurements and comparisons? The answer, of course, is that Barnum was suggesting neither—or rather, both—of these positions. For every human feature and behavior ascribed to this character, Barnum counterpoised a bestial trait, each one deliberately designed to both link and mark distance between What Is It? and his audience of armchair physiologists.

It is tempting to dismiss this categorical flip-flopping as nothing more than the bluster of a fast-talking carney. Even beyond the racist assumptions running through the entire discourse, these physiological analyses often seem more like exhibitory nonsense ("ears set back too far for humanity") than careful descriptions of the human being who appears in the Mathew Brady photographs. But the evidence pushes towards a different conclusion: namely, that there was a quite deliberate promotional scheme at the heart of Barnum's double-talk. At the very least, it seems clear that Barnum's endless equivocations about the physiognomy of What Is It? represented a significant departure from the more conventional racialist entertainments promoted on other Northern stages during these years. Compare it, for example, with this newspaper ad from Philadelphia, which promised "The Bush Negro, or *Wild Man of the Woods* . . . the connecting link between the brute and human species, and it is difficult [to determine] to which race it belongs."[38] Barnum's caricature was at once more detailed and more ambiguous. Although What Is It? naturally walked on all fours, it could be trained to stand on two. The top half of its head was clearly too small for humanity, yet the lower part of its face was just as clearly "that of the native African."

And Barnum, quite unlike the antebellum competition, never used the word "Negro"—not even a somewhat displaced or modified variation on the term, like "Bush Negro"—to describe his wild man exhibition. Rather, he offered a kind of categorical stand-in: a racially undefined figure (at least by the showman) which was positively loaded with physical signifiers of blackness, but which also allowed for discussions of this phenomenon as a "singular" being of "uncertain" categorization and origin. By promoting his wild man exhibition as a nondescript rather than a Negro, Barnum provided his white viewers with a public forum to talk openly and confidently about the boundaries of racial distinction, often in brutally dehumanizing ways—to glide back and forth between straightforward physical description and gross cultural caricature—without even acknowledging who, exactly, they were talking about.

Yet this begs a far trickier historical question: why was such pseudo-scientific equivocation and racial double-talk even necessary? Why not simply come out and attach these stereotypes and classifications to their usual minority targets, as was so commonly practiced in every other corner of American popular culture during these years? Certainly, no antebellum minstrel show troop attempted to identify the conventional caricatures of blackface as anything other than authentically Negro, African, or Ethiopian. Nor did their audiences ever hesitate to suggest that the "brutishness" of Sambo, Jim Crow, and Zip Coon was, at base, African in origin. Such equivocation about racial origins and identity would have been largely antithetical to the ideological work of the minstrel show, one of whose primary functions was to essentialize certain physical and cultural attributes as Negro through and through.[39]

Barnum, then, appears to have been offering something a bit different—and a bit riskier, perhaps—in early 1860: a program in many ways more dehumanizing than the minstrel show's conventional brand of racial ridicule (instead of blackface on white, what might be termed bruteface on black), as well as a new mode of aesthetic misdirection (not simply white men performing as caricatured Negroes, but an African-American man performing as a caricatured nondescript). Much like his earlier enterprises with Joice Heth and the Feejee Mermaid, Barnum's What Is It? scheme was designed to absolve the showman of any definitional agency in the matter, or at least to place the final act of definition in the hands of his audience. Rather than say what this exhibition was, Barnum offered only a range of possibilities. But in so doing, he also initiated something else: a series of public conversations in which the potentially divisive issues of sectional politics, racial science, and social respectability began to serve as topics of popular amusement, the more playful stuff of exhibition hall debate.

The Politics of Nondescription

Among the first Gothamites to visit Barnum's new attraction was George Templeton Strong—one of the city's leading lawyers, socialites, and patrons of the fine arts. In between his musings on John Brown's trial and last night's dinner party, Strong put down a few words about What Is It? in his famous mid-century diary:

> Stopped at Barnum's on my way downtown to see the much advertised nondescript. Some say it's an advanced chimpanzee, others that it's a cross between nigger and baboon. But it seems to me clearly an idiotic negro dwarf, raised, perhaps, in Alabama or Virginia. The showman's story of its capture (with three other specimens that died) by a party in pursuit of the gorilla on the western coast of Africa is probably bosh. The creature's look and action when playing with his keeper are those of a nigger boy. But his anatomical details are fearfully simian, and he's a great fact for Darwin.[40]

This diary passage challenges our expectations about Barnum's exhibition and its audiences in a number of ways. The mere presence of someone like Strong, for example, says something improbable about the New York viewership for freakery in the 1860s: namely, that these exhibitions were patronized by an audience of surprising socioeconomic breadth, from manual laborers with a bit of disposable income to the city's social elite—even a few non-New Yorkers came, such as the visiting Prince of Wales, who made What Is It? his first stop on an October 1860 tour of the city's cultural attractions.[41] What needs to be explained here is precisely what makes Strong's and the Prince's attendance somewhat surprising: the fact that, unlike today (or even a few

decades later), respectable urbanites went to see living curiosities
such as What is It? all the time, often hailing them, like one New York
Times reviewer of Barnum's exhibition, as "a profitable addition to the
many excellent items provided by the liberal management." While this
sort of exhibition would later be confined to more carefully segregated
lowbrow venues (the carnival midway, or the seaside amusement
park), during the 1860s What Is It? was still considered solid family
entertainment, an exhibition worthy of visits by the upper crust as well
as respectable workers, women and children as well as men, serious
naturalists as well as fun-seekers.[42]

Strong's diary passage also reflects the remarkable range of interconnected social meanings and aesthetic impulses at work in Barnum's production. Confident claims about racial superiority and
intelligence ("clearly an idiotic negro dwarf") slip easily into more
nebulous notions of proper behavior ("the creature's look and action
when playing"); self-consciously scientific points about body type ("his
anatomical details are fearfully simian") quickly merge with Strong's
regional prejudices about the effects of slavery on its human victims
("raised, perhaps, in Alabama or Virginia"). This passage also demonstrates a subtle shifting between illusionistic and realistic modes of
viewership. While Strong enters the exhibition aware of Barnum's
widespread reputation for humbuggery and remains largely uncon-
vinced by the manager's biographical bluster ("probably bosh"), he has
little difficulty, only a sentence or two later, in concluding with an
endorsement line straight out of the showman's promotional materials
("he's a great fact for Darwin").

There seems to be little or no consistency of mind in this passage:
certainly not between Strong's anti-slavery leanings during these years
and the surprisingly nasty racist epithets he put down in his diary;
nor between his interpretations of What Is It? as both an obvious hoax
and a legitimate piece of Darwinian evidence; nor even between his
own motives for writing, which seem to waver, almost line by line,
from condescension towards Barnum's brand of popular amusement
on the one hand, to earnest scientific curiosity on the other. What
has become increasingly clear from recent scholarship, however, is

that such inconsistencies were actually part of a fundamental and recurring ideological pattern in nineteenth-century America—especially where matters of race were involved.[43] As Barbara J. Fields first noted of this pattern, "we cannot resolve the problem quantitatively, by the addition of example or counterexample. We can resolve it only by posing the question 'What kind of social reality is reflected—or refracted—in an ideology built on a unity of . . . particular opposites?' "[44]

Barnum was in fact a major cultural player in the sectional controversies of the 1850s, especially with his deliberately provocative decision to run H. J. Conway's version of *Uncle Tom's Cabin* in direct competition with the more famous (and more faithful) George Aiken adaptation of the novel.[45] Only a few decades earlier (following the Missouri Compromise of 1820), no New York theatrical productions would put on stage the subject of slavery's moral legitimacy. While the melodramas of the 1830s and 1840s had plenty to say about race in the North, they usually observed the same constraints as those upheld by most contemporary politicians: they did not specifically address the potentially volatile political repercussions of African Americans' legal status in the South and West.[46]

As this evasion began to unravel in Congress during the late 1840s, New York theatrical managers followed suit, using different adaptations of Harriet Beecher Stowe's controversial novel as public vehicles for endorsing or opposing abolitionist ideas. Whereas Aiken's National Theater production offered *Uncle Tom* primarily as a sentimental tragedy, designed to provoke sympathy for its Christ-like protagonist and his unjust plight, Barnum's version of the play highlighted slaves singing blackface choruses and had a more comic, ridiculing tone (what Eric Lott has described as the conventional "racial meanness" of antebellum blackface).[47] Of the latter production, William Lloyd Garrison's *Liberator* vehemently complained: "Barnum has offered the slave-drivers the incense of an expurgated form of Uncle Tom. He has been playing a version of that great story at his Museum, which omits all that strikes at the slave system, and has so shaped his drama as to make it quite an agreeable thing to be a slave."[48]

Such abolitionist complaints—with their steadfast rejection of racialist humor—still represented a minority position in New York during the mid-1850s. Other Northern press commentators were far less critical of Barnum's intermixing of abolitionist themes with black-face entertainment, and defended the Conway production as appropriately even-handed. But that is precisely what made this theatrical rivalry so engaging. Unlike his earlier theatrical successes (*The Drunkard*, for instance, a popular melodrama promoting temperance), Barnum was now constructing public entertainments which aggressively courted political controversy; indeed, they made this kind of controversy their principal drawing card. As Lott concludes, "the *Uncle Tom's Cabin* plays institutionalized the social divisions they narrated. Sectional debate henceforth became theatrical ritual, part of the experience of *Uncle Tom*."[49]

Barnum's new willingness to bring contemporary politics into his cultural productions did not end with *Uncle Tom's Cabin*. By the time What Is It? made its 1860 American Museum debut, Barnum was offering two equally provocative entertainments upon which New Yorkers could express sectionalist opinions: a collection of artifacts from John Brown's 1859 raid on Harper's Ferry (including a wax statue of the radical abolitionist himself); and a theatrical production of Dion Boucicault's *The Octoroon*, which told the tragic story of a mixed-blood Louisiana free woman, courted by the son of a wealthy white judge, but ultimately sold into slavery to save her family from financial ruin.[50] According to a New York *Tribune* review, a number of "touchy students from the South" initially tried to block the play's opening in Philadelphia; the "excitement," explained the reviewer, "fully parallels the enthusiasm that was excited here by the same play, and the best seats are all taken a week in advance." Joseph Jefferson, star of *The Octoroon*, noted that this combination of heated debate and packed houses seemed to grow out of the play's ability to provoke public support for both sides of the controversy: "When Zoe, the loving octoroon, is offered to the highest bidder, and a warm-hearted Southern girl offers all her fortune to buy Zoe, and release her from threatened bondage . . . the audience cheered for the South; but when again the action revealed that she could be bartered for, and was bought and sold, they cheered for the North, as plainly as though they had said, 'Down with slavery.' "[51]

Within this combustible mix of sectionalist politics, moral debate, and racialist entertainment, What Is It? served a number of different functions. In some cases, Barnum presented the exhibition as an entracte during American Museum performances of *The Octoroon.* And in this context, What Is It? seems to have operated as a kind of "reactionary" counterweight to Zoe, one which reestablished the "racial hierarchy shaken by Boucicault's play."[52] Yet this sort of "cross-reading" with *The Octoroon* is but one of many ways to explain Barnum's 1860 entertainment program. It is also possible, for example, to read What Is It? as a kind of exhibitory analog to one of sectionalism's defining events: the landmark Supreme Court case, *Dred Scott vs. Sanford* (1857), in which Scott, a former Missouri slave, became the focus of a national dialogue on the legal subtleties of African-Americans' basic human rights.[53] The chronology of Barnum's exhibition parallels Scott's long-running court battle almost exactly. Both began rather quietly in 1846—the same year as the Wilmot Proviso, an early piece of sectionalist legislation which helped usher in the political crises of the 1850s—and drifted out of public consciousness for over a decade, returning with a bang just before the Civil War. Both returns, moreover, were played out within the context of bitterly contested national elections (*Dred Scott* in 1856, What Is It? in 1860) in which the question of how to define the legal status of African Americans in the Western territories emerged as a central point of partisan contention.

Whereas Scott's lawyers described their client as a quasi-citizen, born a slave but seemingly emancipated by his temporary residence in two free states, Barnum offered What Is It? as a newly discovered quasi-man, born a "brute" in the African jungle, but beginning to take on various human features during his stay in New York. In both ideological arenas, the theoretical problem confronting self-appointed white jurors boiled down to one of innate qualities versus environmental impact. Was the brutishness of Barnum's nondescript simply intrinsic, or did it somehow fade away when removed from its original context? Was Scott's identity as slave defined forever by his African ancestry, or did it fluctuate according to the jurisdictions of different states? Not surprisingly, the actual African-American men at the center of these debates quickly became secondary to the larger categorical groups they were perceived to represent. In much the same way that Chief Justice Taney engaged Scott's personal appeal for freedom as an opportunity to hold forth on the racial parameters of the Constitution, Barnum's audiences responded to his actor's performance as a test case through which to speculate on the biological and cultural development of Africans in general.

In both cases, though, the rhetorical route to judgment was lined with sharp equivocations. Just as historians now still argue over the implications of the Taney Court's stinging rejection of Scott's full humanity—perhaps a general ruling on "Negro citizenship," perhaps a recision of the Missouri Compromise, perhaps nothing more than the reversal of an earlier state court decision freeing Scott—so it is often hard to tell exactly what the New York press ruled on What Is It?, except perhaps that he, like Scott, was of a "lower order" than those passing judgment.[54] In its first review of Barnum's exhibition, the *Herald* described What Is It? as "a most extraordinary freak of nature," which has "all the appearance of a human being," only to assert a few lines below that "the formation of its hands, arms, and head are those of an ourang outang." "A cloud of doubt and uncertainty," the article concluded, "hangs about the exhibition room." A reporter from the *Sun* moved in the opposite direction, pointing out the physical difference between What Is It? and a "typical" African-American man: "The ears are far too high and too much back for a negro; the arms are several inches too long in proportion, and the jaws and teeth are entirely animal." Yet the review concluded by suggesting that "Dan Rice in his palmiest days never could produce a heartier Jim Crow laugh than this creature gets out on the slightest occasion."[55] (The subtle irony in this reviewer's use of a minstrel performer, T. D. Rice, as his benchmark for defining the Negro laugh of What Is It? seems to have been purely unintentional, although perhaps what it really acknowledged was that both the minstrel show and Barnum's exhibit were all about masking!)

Other 1860 New York commentators duplicated and expanded this "cloud of uncertainty" ad nauseam, providing one lengthy description after another of the performer's hybridized grin (deemed both "idiotic" and "friendly"), posture ("exceedingly awkward" yet nonetheless "erect"), precarious bipedal walk (sometimes "elderly" or "animal," on other occasions "child-like" or "sportive"), and temperament ("not at all vicious," but also "enjoying a distinguished reputation for ferocity").[56] All of which suggests that the New York press treated What Is It? much like any other contemporary free person of color in 1860: as a kind of liminal being whose *true* social status depended upon the circumstances and contexts of conversation, as well as the patronizing judgments of white critics.[57] What Is It? was docile enough to demonstrate the complete control of his trainer, as well as ferocious enough to demonstrate the need for such control; savage enough to imply genetic inferiority, but civilized enough to inspire evolutionary hope for the future; strange enough to become a museum curiosity, yet familiar enough to be routinely compared to ordinary black New Yorkers.

Here, in a sense, was W. E. B. Du Bois's 1903 theory of "double consciousness" staged as popular cultural spectacle: a "dark body" whose "twoness" was created and imposed "through the eyes of others"; a "soul" measured "by the tape of a world that looks on in amused contempt and pity."[58] The precise ratio of contempt to pity was, however, far from fixed or predetermined. Indeed, in the larger spectrum of Northern racialist tropes, the nondescript was a remarkably flexible instrument of white supremacism. At certain moments, Barnum's caricature seems like nothing more than the reinvention of a much older brand of European stereotyping from the earliest days of the African slave trade, one which equated "blackness" with the "savage," the "low," the "ape-like"—and then used these distinctions as the basis for condemning blacks to a permanent position of social inferiority.[59] The *Courier and Inquirer,* for example, confidently claimed to recognize Negro features and gestures in Barnum's nondescript and then pointed to its subhuman status: "The head is shaped like that of a monkey, but the face is more like that of an African negro of the lower order. The creature moves along with a shuffling gait very much like an elderly negro. . . . It has been pronounced by naturalists as a specimen of the connecting link between man and monkey."[60]

Yet, on other occasions, Barnum's caricature served as the basis for arguing that even the lowest African contained and was capable of basic, universally shared human qualities. In this vein, a writer from the *Tribune* lauded "the brightness of its eye, and intelligent response to the words and motions of the person in charge," which "at once relieve it of the imputation of imbecility."[61] Other commentators similarly focused on the propensity of What Is It? for rapid physical and cultural development—"like a child just learning," according to the *Express*—which, for a moment at least, seemed to undermine or at least temper the very same racialist hierarchies constructed by American Museum viewers to establish the subhuman status of What Is It? in the first place.[62]

To be sure, both inflections of What Is It? involved some assumption of a racially defined social order: either a dispassionate evaluation of degradation within an immutable racial hierarchy, or a somewhat less rigid verdict of partial degradation that allowed for small degrees of paternalistic reform and uplift. But what kind of social order was really at stake here? Given the timing of this exhibition—right in the midst of heated presidential election debates about the morality and scope of slavery—as well as the performance, right next door, of a controversial slavery melodrama, it seems at least a little surprising to find no overt references to the "peculiar institution" surrounding What Is It? at all. Although quite consistent in their efforts to use this caricature as an instrument for establishing racial distinctions, Barnum and his viewers also consistently avoided at least one of the most common weapons of antebellum white supremacism: the notion of a basic "negro predisposition" for agrarian labor.[63] Whereas Southern "fire-eaters" like George Fitzhugh and John C. Calhoun went to great lengths to promote images of African Americans as natural, productive, and even happy field workers requiring the paternalistic control of a slave system, Barnum's Northern brand of racial paternalism made little if any reference to physical ability or productive capability. On the contrary, both the showman and his audiences were quite insistent that What Is It? could barely walk or even stand up on his own, let alone perform exhausting manual work. As the *Times* noted of this performance, "the little creature is sadly attenuated in body."[64]

What, then, was the ideological utility of this popular cultural enterprise: a mode of public debate clearly shaped by the sectional controversies of the 1850s, yet also lacking any clear references to slavery; a liminal caricature of blackness which easily absorbed both hard-line (immutable) and reformist (evolutionary) visions of a racially determined social hierarchy, yet also remained staunchly uncommitted to either position? Did such forms of equivocation somehow make What Is It? less political than *The Octoroon*, which offered a readily identifiable social problem and context? Ultimately, I would suggest that the answer (with no equivocation intended) is both yes and no. What Is It? was less overtly political than *The Octoroon* because it allowed for spirited public discussions about the racial boundaries of humanity without reference to any of the volatile political issues normally fundamental to such discussions (in particular, the morality of slavery in a Christian society). But this process of building public consensus around caricatured, racialist abstractions was itself deeply political in its larger social implications, for it promoted a kind of bipartisan, racially determined caste system.

What Barnum seems to have been particularly adept at representing and promoting was a kind of convergence of contemporary racialist assumptions.[65] From Northern Whigs and Republicans he took the moderate or "soft racist" notion of paternalistic reform, which posited that Africans would benefit from the ameliorative influence of Anglo-Saxon culture (evidenced here by the shift from a quadrupedal to bipedal stance, and raw to cooked food); as well as the Whig/Republican presumption of a fixed social order which allowed for charitable guidance from on high (symbolized here by Barnum's white trainer— always above his black student, yet aiding his gradual uplift). From Northern Democrats Barnum took the "hard racist" notion of biological

competition, which posited the existence of intrinsic physiological differences between blacks and whites (demonstrated here by measurements of facial angles and the character's lack of speech); as well as the
Democrats' insistence on a more fluid social order within which Africans should be confined to the lowest rungs (a position articulated here
through the "ventriloquist" voice of unnamed naturalists, who were
said to have "pronounced" upon the subhuman status of What Is It?).[66]

What Is It?, in other words, expressed—or more specifically,
embodied—virtually all of the disparate strands of white racialist
thinking common in the North during the 1860s. But he also embodied something else: the deep contradictions within white Northern
racialism, as well as the oft-noted tendency of Northern Whig, Republican, and Democratic attitudes towards African Americans to blur
together, especially when the related issues of slavery and the Western
territories were left out of the equation.[67] Horace Greeley's *Tribune*, a
Whig-supported paper with antislavery leanings, railed against other
newspaper reviewers' attempts to condemn What Is It? to "imbecility," but also routinely described the African-American man standing
on Barnum's stage as an "animal."[68] Benjamin Day's *Sun,* a Democratic vehicle openly hostile to abolitionism, predictably emphasized the
"small brain," "exceedingly awkward walk," and "Jim Crow laugh" of
What Is It?, but also noted—like Greeley's *Tribune* reporter—the figure's "bright and intelligent eyes."[69] None of these tangled webs of
conventionally distinct racial attitudes and political positions can compare, however, to the ideological incongruity which emerged during a
benefit for the U.S. Sanitary Commission and the National Freed-
man's Association at the Cooper Institute in 1864. To this event, in
principle designed to raise money for recently emancipated slaves and
presumably attended by at least a few orthodox abolitionists, Barnum
offered What Is It? as part of the evening's entertainment—a contri-
bution which, according to the *Tribune,* left the Cooper Institute audience in an almost continual roar of laughter and "much gratified."[70]

That such an exhibition could elicit laughter and gratification from
this particular audience only reinforces a troubling paradox long noted
by historians of abolitionism: even those white Northerners most

deeply involved in the crusade to dismantle slavery often questioned the full humanity—not to mention the full equality—of their political beneficiaries.[71] The contrast here with Barnum's earlier *Uncle Tom's Cabin* production and its mixed public reception is striking. Instead of noting abolitionist outrage at the Cooper Institute, the New York press now commented only on the audience's unqualified amusement.

This shift had less to do with any major changes in white abolitionism than with Barnum's increasing skill at weaving together the common threads of white prejudice. By 1860 a new model of racialized entertainment was emerging in the American Museum. First, develop a thoroughly flexible, indeterminate African being in which each of the North's normally antagonistic political constituencies could see its own racialist assumptions embodied. Second, describe the actual African-American man at the center of public attention as something else—a nondescript—so as not to offend the sensibilities of white abolitionists. And, finally, use this caricature as the basis for generating energetic public debate about the terms—rather than the existence—of the North's deeply entrenched racial hierarchy, a debate which allowed for vigorous controversy over the degree, causes, and mutability of African brutishness, yet (precisely because of the highly circumscribed questions being posed) appealed to struggling Democratic artisans as well as affluent Republican elites.[72]

Having built a bipartisan mass audience around his What Is It? exhibition during the early 1860s, Barnum decided in 1865 to enter electoral politics, running—with success here, too—for a seat in the Connecticut General Assembly on the Union ticket. Along the way, Barnum began to express a novel sympathy and regret about the subjugation of African Americans—or at least to approach civil rights matters at the end of the Civil War with a new, somewhat softer vision of racial paternalism, one which more decisively attributed the "downtrodden condition of the Negro" to the social institutions engineered by white Southerners. Speaking before the Connecticut legislature in May of 1865, he even went so far as to promote a universal manhood suffrage amendment for the state constitution.[73] Two years later, during an unsuccessful run for the U.S. Congress as a Republican,

Barnum publicly acknowledged this dramatic reversal in his racial politics, confessing a (now) embarrassing Southern episode from his early show business travels. As he explained in a campaign speech just before the election: "I lived [in the South] myself and owned slaves. I did more. I whipped my slaves. I ought to have been whipped a thousand times for this myself. But then I was a Democrat—one of those *nondescript* Democrats, who are Northern men with Southern principles."[74]

This stunning rhetorical gesture brought Barnum's earlier uses of the nondescript full circle: with the Civil War over and a new, more solidly Republican spirit of reconstruction seizing his conscience, Barnum projected the image of the nondescript onto his own youthful misdeeds and asked the voters of Connecticut to forgive much the same sort of ideological slipperiness he had worked so hard to promote in his American Museum just a few years earlier. Yet even as Barnum's political affiliations and ideas about slavery were changing, his enthusiasm about presenting racialist entertainments for "scientific" evaluation remained largely unmitigated. This apparent inconsistency can be understood in terms of the wide ideological gap that existed more generally between civil rights reform and full racial egalitarianism in the postwar years. What seems to have changed in Barnum's thinking during the 1860s was not his typical bourgeois confidence in white racial superiority, but his growing distaste for racial bondage in a free society. Thus, much like the federal government's own tentative initiatives to legislate a new balance of racial power during and after the war, Barnum's personal reconstruction seems to have been a decidedly unfinished revolution.

A Nondescript Racial Science

There is a certain insidious logic in Barnum's decision to continue promoting scientific exhibitions of African inferiority during the volatile 1860s—an era in which the traditional political, social, and economic structures of power were so dramatically in flux. And here again, Barnum was not alone. Indeed, the broader historical career of "scientific racism" in the United States seems to have followed a kind of inverted trajectory in relation to the history of abolitionism, first taking shape during the late eighteenth and early nineteenth centuries (at precisely the same time that the Northern states were passing emancipation laws) and reaching its high-water mark late in the century (when a new, postemancipatory social order was taking shape). Without the institution of slavery to explain the position of African Americans at the bottom of the social hierarchy, other novel (and in many ways just as damaging) scientific justifications for America's ongoing racial caste system were sought out and promoted.[75]

Barnum's "biography" for What Is It? followed this general trend. Instead of focusing on slave traders, his narrative featured "a party of adventurers . . . in search of the gorilla," who haphazardly "fell in" with What Is It? and his aboriginal cohort. This search, moreover, took place as part of a "natural history" expedition in a vaguely sketched African habitat, rather than any particular African culture—about as far away from Barnum's exhibition room as his audiences might imagine. Once "forwarded to this country" and the American Museum (the "middle passage" was entirely eliminated from the story now), What Is It? became not a Southern field hand or domestic servant, but a Northern piece of evidence—"the latest of nature's mysteries," to be "examined by some of the most scientific men we have."[76]

But if Barnum helped forge the scientific first principles of racial difference in the wake of emancipation, he also—like any shrewd impresario—encouraged his viewers to make the final decisions about how to formulate and interpret these principles.[77] For one of them, George Templeton Strong, this interpretive process was sparked by a provocative new book he had just finished reading—Darwin's *Origin of Species*—and led to careful natural history discussions with his old Columbia College friend and intellectual playmate, George Anthon. As Strong noted in his diary, what particularly intrigued these two members of the New York bourgeoisie was Darwin's novel proposition that "the original creative act was on the smallest scale and produced only some one organism of the humblest rank but capable of development into the flora and fauna of the earth, from moss to oak and from monad to man, under . . . [the] law of progress and natural selection."[78]

Did What Is It? provide evidence of such evolutionary progress? Ultimately, Strong seems not to have been entirely sure—or more specifically, he seems to have had some trouble squaring the "fearfully simian anatomical details" of the caricature with his traditional theological convictions about the mechanics of creation. After "looking further" into Darwin's writing, Strong remained unsatisfied with what he perceived to be the English naturalist's efforts to minimize "the original agency of supernatural power," a fault which led Strong to denounce the Origin of Species, finally, as "a shallow book, though laboriously and honestly written."[79]

Yet Strong did call What Is It? a Darwinian "fact." Whatever the creature's true history—whether "raised in Alabama or Virginia" or "on the western coast of Africa"—Strong drew two relatively confident conclusions from the exhibition: first, that an evolutionary link between man and beast was, in fact, possible; and second, that this nondescript was, without question, a Negro.[80] By insisting on this racial categorization (even as he expressed doubts about so much else), Strong was not simply commenting on the performer's skin color or calling Barnum's bluff about African expeditions. This was perhaps the very first of countless late nineteenth-century efforts to use Darwin's treatise (a book which actually had little to say about the origin of man directly) as a scientific tool for explaining and justifying America's long-standing racial hierarchy.[81] In a sense, Barnum and Strong were ahead of their time. Well before most American Social Darwinists had started thinking about a new biological model of human progress, the first outlines of a theory of Anglo-American superiority derived from evolutionary science were beginning to take shape in Barnum's exhibition rooms.[82]

The word "beginning" is key here, because Strong and Anthon seem to have been mostly alone in their attempt to make sense of What Is It? using the Origin of Species as guide. In fact, among all of this exhibition's numerous published commentators during the early 1860s, Strong was the only one to mention Darwin specifically. Most

other American Museum viewers used another set of ideas to interpret Barnum's "possible missing link": the much older and more theo-
logically palatable doctrine of *Scala Naturae* (also known as the Great
Chain of Being)—a kind of ranking system by species, thought to have
been born fully formed through a single, original creative act.[83] This
pre-Darwinian approach to biological classification appears in the
exhibition's very first American press coverage, a New York *Sunday
Times* article which described What Is It? as "an animal which would
seem to supply the link supposed by philosophers to exist between the
human race and brutes. . . . all the species of fish, fowl, and beast are
connected by links—as, for instance, fish and fowl by the flying fish:
fish and animals by the warm blood whale which suckles its young like
a cow: and so throughout the whole range of animated nature."[84]

In this conservative blueprint for an orderly and ultimately static
earthly taxonomy, each of God's creatures naturally occupied its
appropriate station—fish below fowl, whales below cows, and brutes
below the human race. Chain-of-Being theorists could thus celebrate
remarkable hybrids such as the flying fish, warm-blooded whale,
or even Barnum's "man-monkey" without much trepidation: these
boundary-blurring creatures were understood as curious anomalies
rather than evidence of some evolutionary trend and thus posed little
threat of seriously encroaching on the natural levels above them.[85]
Unlike Strong, the *Sunday Times* writer made no effort to classify
What Is It? by race, describing Barnum's dark-skinned celebrity
instead as a one-of-a-kind "freak of nature" from "the interior of
Africa—a land still full of unknown wonders."[86]

In another sense, though, this was the freakish exception that
proved the racialist rule for many white viewers of What Is It?, a *lusus
naturae* which seemed to demonstrate both the human qualities of
African apes (and thus the upper threshold of the animal kingdom)
and the brutish qualities of African people. This mode of association
also surfaced in the New York *Times*'s first review: "The proprietors of
[the American Museum], it seems, have secured . . . a bipedal creature, with traits of animalism that seem to confound it with the brutes,
and hence, seeking knowledge—they demand from the philosophical

'What is It?' We are not, of course, vain enough to reply, but may state briefly and superficially that, to the eye, the nondescript bears a striking resemblance to a malformed African and a curious approximation to an ourang-outang."[87] In this formulation, What Is It? functions as a racialist common denominator. While the *Times* reporter feels much too modest to speculate on the precise species of What Is It?, she or he has few qualms about using the exhibition as a vehicle with which to assert the resemblance between a "malformed African" and an orangoutang.

This was nineteenth-century scientific racism at its most discrete: a tentative yet still subjugating picture of African brutishness articulated through confounding traits, striking resemblances, and curious approximations. In this particular review, the description was literally superficial: that is, it referred to the reviewer's perceptions of physical features. Other reviewers' attempts at scientific analysis moved directly from physical description to detailed pronouncements about behavior. One *Evening Post* reviewer applied the theories of Orson S. Fowler— nineteenth-century America's most popular practitioner of the phrenological arts—to the "cerebral organization" of What Is It? "You see," the *Post* reporter noted, "a head which if subjected to the professional manipulations of Professor Fowler, would be pronounced to have very small perceptive and intellectual faculties, without ideality, reverence or conscientiousness; with large animal propensities, and with a bump of combativeness and destructiveness which would render it unnecessary to explain the command of Peter, 'Rise, kill, and eat,' nor would he have the scruples of Peter against eating things common and unclean."[88]

Today these categorizations read like a series of racialist hieroglyphs. While the words are familiar, their culturally specific meanings seem almost unintelligible. For nineteenth-century New Yorkers familiar with Fowler's best-selling books, lectures, and nearby Phrenological Museum on Nassau Street, however, such categorizations served as a kind of cranial code for recording character.[89] Individuals exhibiting small intellectual and perceptive faculties, explained the professor's *New Illustrated Self-Instructor in Phrenology and Physiology* (1859), "are naturally idiotic" and "know almost nothing about the external world, its qualities, and relations," whereas large "bumps" of "combativeness" and "destructiveness" demonstrated a disposition towards "perversion" and, in extreme cases, "fighting" or even "murder." A paucity of cranial markings for ideality corresponded to a "marked deficiency in whatever appertains to taste and style, also to beauty and sentiment." Those without the "organ of conscientiousness" were deemed sorely lacking in "moral principle; integrity, perception and love of right." Perhaps worst of all, such a skull demonstrated little "sense of guilt" or "desire to reform."[90]

These phrenological evaluations illustrate just how closely the racial attitudes of Barnum's audiences were bound up with contemporary ideas about refinement, character, and taste. Like nineteenth-century scientific racism more generally, this *Evening Post* review understood white superiority as a first principle, one to which Barnum's mysterious discovery merely added new data for elaboration and articulation. More distinctive, however, were the reviewer's rhetorical means: not merely cranial measurements and essentialist claims, but a set of claims that easily merged with the standard social advice offered by new middle-class etiquette books.[91] What this figure on Barnum's stage needed to cultivate, in the view of the *Evening Post,* was more guilt and sentiment, a greater appreciation of beauty and style, a better developed sense of integrity. His potential phrenological downfall, by contrast, was an innate propensity for perversion—an inability to control his passions—as well as a lack of skill at perceiving intricate social relations. Read through the decoding prism of Fowler's *Self-Instructor,* this review suggested a clear subtext. Barnum's nondescript might resemble many things—perhaps even humanity—but of one basic distinction *Evening Post* readers could rest assured: What Is It? was the very antithesis of a New York gentleman.

In "Every Way Pleasing, Interesting, and Amusing"

Thus far, much of the reception for What Is It? squares easily with our conventional understanding of the scope and intensity of racial prejudice in the 1860s. Certainly, it is not surprising that a middlebrow audience of white New Yorkers embraced a dehumanizing caricature of blackness during these years, nor that American Museum viewers utilized pseudo-scientific theories to bolster their claims of white supremacism, nor even that Barnum, resourceful cultural entrepreneur that he was, made his racial caricature flexible enough to appeal to a broad audience of politically, economically, and geographically diverse consumers. What was particularly innovative was the way this caricature endorsed and helped define a broad range of racialist ideas: confidently, publicly, inclusively—with little *divisive* controversy of any kind.

Harder to explain, however, are the various ways that both Barnum and his audiences expressed attraction towards the very same caricatured figure they went to such enormous lengths to define as racially, socially, and biologically lower than themselves (a pattern of racialist ambivalence equaled only by the blackface minstrel show, with its deeply conflicted celebration/ridicule of slave culture). A great deal of ambivalent evidence has emerged already in this sea of racialist testimony, most obviously in the descriptions of the half human/half animal head and body of What Is It?, as well as in the frequent references to the creature's alternating propensities for civilized and brutish behavior. Ambivalence was also central to the Mathew Brady portraits, which were produced in the cheap carte-de-visite format, for sale as souvenirs to be collected, taken home, and saved in parlor photograph albums. As photography historians have noted, such portraits of living curiosities comprised a standard entry in new middle-class photo albums, often appearing in the same section with other celebrities from the stage, literary life, and government.

It is an enormously strange cultural phenomenon to contemplate: What Is It?, the very antithesis of bourgeois respectability, commemorated on film by the era's leading portrait photographer, purchased as a keepsake by his white critics, brought into the very center of the domestic sphere, and placed among other prized photographic images of family, friends, and illustrious Americans.[92] Barnum's written promotional materials gave expression to this odd attraction, too, noting that What Is It?—despite his "brutish" demeanor—was quite pleasant

LITH. BY CURRIER & IVES.

WHAT IS IT?—OR "MAN MONKEY".
ON EXHIBITION AT BARNUM'S MUSEUM, NEW YORK.

This is a most singular animal, with many of the features and other characteristics of both the HUMAN and BRUTE species. It was found in Africa, in a perfectly nude state, and with two others captured.—The others died on their passage to this country. At first it ran on all fours, and was with difficulty learned to stand as nearly erect as here represented. It is the opinion of most scientific men that he is a connecting link between the WILD NATIVE AFRICAN, AND THE ORANG OUTANG.

He is playful as a kitten and every way pleasing interesting and amusing.
TO BE SEEN AT ALL HOURS.

What Is It? as middle-class entertainment. Unlike twentieth-century freak shows, this exhibition was considered perfectly appropriate for family viewing by well-dressed New Yorkers such as the people shown in this Currier and Ives lithograph.

to visit. "There is nothing repulsive to his appearance," promised one New York *Times* advertisement from the showman. "On the contrary, all who see him are captivated, astonished and delighted."[93]

This delight was most clearly and elaborately represented in an early 1860s Currier and Ives lithograph. Surrounding What Is It? is a well-dressed group of white viewers, clearly marked by the artist as solidly bourgeois consumers. On one level, the relationship between viewers and performer is defined purely in terms of difference: they are light-skinned where he is dark; elaborately dressed where he is only partially clothed; confidently erect where he is holding a support-ive stick; mannered in expression where he is grinning carelessly; numerous where he is alone. This image also places Barnum's "wild African" at the same level as the white child (a point of comparison often employed by race theorists during these years). Racial hierarchy is even built into the lithograph's image of viewership, displaying what Pierre Bourdieu has termed "the pure gaze," a distinctly bourgeois attitude that "constitutes itself as respectable and superior by substi-tuting observation for participation."[94] Whereas conventional social discourse might require some form of interaction, conversation, or at least a meeting of eyes, What Is It? looks away blankly, surrounded by viewers who treat him purely as an object of visual evaluation.

Yet in spite (or perhaps because) of these rigidly hierarchical rela-tionships, What Is It? maintains a strong hold on his audience, one which can hardly be described as straightforward repulsion or fear. The women and child in the lithograph—the two social groups fre-quently assigned the role of litmus test for an urban entertainment's respectability—stand closest to What Is It?, even smiling a bit. The men, too, look intrigued, their bodies and attention fixed squarely on What Is It? rather than on their vulnerable loved ones. In contrast to the segregated society in which these cultural interactions were taking place, the viewers in the lithograph make no effort to separate them-selves from their racial other; indeed, they seem to be delighted by the opportunity to spend some extended, intimate time with this particu-lar "African." The text at the bottom of the lithograph ends on a note of unqualified attraction: *"He is* playful *as a Kitten and in every way* pleasing, interesting, *and* amusing."

But delighted about what, exactly? Pleasing how? One relatively straightforward answer involves the analogy which appears just before these assurances. Perhaps there was nothing repulsive to his appearance precisely because he was playful *as* a kitten—and therefore quite unlike the noncaricatured men and women of African descent who resided outside of Barnum's Museum. As recent historians have demonstrated with great detail, the small population of free African Americans living in the North fought hard to challenge such conventional white-produced images of "black degradation"—issuing lectures, writing editorials, and even refashioning their own public personas through visual media such as lithographs, photographs, and parades.[95] Sojourner Truth's famous photographic self-portraits from this very same time period constitute only the best known examples of such visual cultural resistance.[96] Part of the "pleasure" of Barnum's exhibition, then, seems to have stemmed from its calculated elisions— elisions which replaced the proud and militant images constructed by Truth and other black leaders with a brutish figure who smiled a lot, remained under the steady control of his white manager, and appeared perfectly content with a career as a racialized spectacle.

It is also possible to make a case here for the presence of what George Frederickson first identified as romantic racialism, a distinctly mid-century ideological tendency, usually propagated by white abolitionists, which celebrated the "innocence" and "good nature" of black people. Proponents of this ideology never disputed the conventional racialist wisdom that African Americans were essentially different from European Americans, but they also merged these claims with a romanticized notion of white paternalism and uplift. One can see traces of Barnum's What Is It? promotions, for example, in the writings of Orville Dewey, a New York minister who praised "the singularly childlike, affectionate, docile, and patient" qualities of "the Negro," noting that these qualities were precisely those supposed to be found in good Christians.[97]

Yet to describe the appeal of Barnum's caricature exclusively in terms of its nonthreatening, child-like qualities leaves a number of basic questions unanswered. Above all, this line of analysis ignores what was most distinctive about Barnum's 1860 exhibition: the image of the nondescript itself, a liminal being with no fixed or final boundaries, no single or easily legible identity—which, as we have seen, served as the focus of attention for contemporary audiences more than any of its constituent parts or personas. It is also worth considering why Currier and Ives chose a group of well-dressed, white, middle-class urbanites to observe and interact with Barnum's boundary-blurring nondescript—and more astonishing still, pronounce its categorical indeterminacy pleasing in every way.

The viewers in this lithograph are just the sort of New Yorkers one might expect to be put off, disturbed, or even frightened by such a figure—at least judging on the basis of the larger codes of respectability crafted by the new middle class during the 1830s and 1840s. It was precisely in opposition to the liminal self that new middle-class urbanites initially defined their own social status, character, and virtue. Whether in the context of phrenological lectures, fashion advice, etiquette books, or guides to the new metropolis, the antebellum cultural messages about crafting a respectable public persona were roughly the same: a categorically precise, easy-to-read self was generally moral, upstanding, and trustworthy, whereas a formless, illegible, or variable self was at the very least rude—and potentially criminal.[98]

It all boiled down to a set of bedrock tensions in the new middle class's patterns of historical development. Because it was so difficult to determine who was genuinely respectable in the increasingly anonymous environment of the antebellum metropolis, the emerging middle class created elaborate new systems of signification and distinction (their heads, wardrobes, gestures, homes, and urban landscapes served as the raw materials), all with the same basic impulse: to fix one's social status rigidly and unambiguously. The historical rub, however, was that these concerns about social formlessness and misreading were born from the same developments that had produced the new middle class in the first place: a market economy, in which the transmutation of the individual across broad categories of income and status was defined as a fundamental objective; a sprawling urban environment, in which rapid mobility, social anonymity, and an ever greater reliance on visual codes of interpersonal identification became standard facets of modern life; and an expanding consumer culture, which made the markers of respectability accessible to almost anyone.

Initially at least, the new middle class attempted to resolve these tensions by making sincerity one of its highest ideals: if respectability was defined and articulated through appearance, those in search of respectability set out to construct their public selves as unambiguously as possible (with plain speech and clothing, for example) and treated the very idea of appearance as if it were a reflection of something deeper, more fundamental, and fixed (an unwavering character).[99] By the time of the Civil War, however, there was growing evidence of a new, more playful middle-class tolerance of "liminal men and women" and "theatricality for its own sake." Whereas the 1830s and 1840s were dominated by long black dresses, pale complexions, and anxious warnings about duplicitous strangers, the succeeding decades witnessed middle-class fads for parlor theatricals, cosmetics, and role-playing.[100]

Barnum's nondescript stood right on the cusp of this watershed in middle-class identity formation. On the one hand, the showman's emphasis on the unresolved liminality of What Is It? served to further mark the figure as a low other; the very idea of a hard-to-read being situated between the existing categories violated almost every impulse and rule essential to antebellum respectability. On the other hand, the fact that such a liminal being could be described as alternatively brutish *and* pleasing during the early 1860s suggests that Barnum and his viewers were doing more here than merely reinforcing the older strictures. By openly celebrating What Is It? as delightful—even as they went to such great lengths to establish its racialized vulgarity— these viewers at least tentatively flirted with the idea of social formlessness as an attractive end in itself. Indeed, it may have been only because of its well-established vulgarity that What Is It? enabled such flirtations in a public forum.

The temptation here is to try to resolve this ambiguity one way or the other: to insist that Barnum's nondescript represented either an instrument of racialist ridicule or an object of sublimated desire, but not both. As Peter Stallybrass and Allon White have demonstrated, however, it is precisely this "conflictual fusion of power, fear, and desire" which has routinely accompanied such imagery in the transgressive cultural spaces of carnivals, fairs, popular museums, and amusement parks. The pattern, in fact, seems to be as old as modernity itself, extending from the carnivalesque rituals that emerged after the Renaissance until well into our own time.[101] The real challenge, then, is to give Barnum's nondescript and its ambivalent reception historical specificity, to offer some concrete idea of why this mid-nineteenth-century American brand of cultural equivocation was so useful and appealing for its particular constituency of urban consumers.

This exhibition was about power because it treated any attempt by the low other to participate in the social world of its viewers as absurd—curious and amusing, to be sure, but also ultimately ridiculous. What Is It? might wear velvet pants, eat cake, and mingle with members of the New York social elite, but these deliberately farcical performances only emphasized that such refined activities were not the proper or natural choices of "wild Africans." It was about fear because the social boundaries at the heart of these "amusing" performances were never truly natural, nor even particularly stable. Indeed, they were so entirely unnatural that they needed to be constructed and reinforced constantly—especially during the early 1860s, as the country's social, political, and racial orders seemed to be falling apart. And finally, this exhibition was about desire because it articulated—in one ambivalent statement after another—precisely what the new middle class had denied itself so aggressively in the process of self-creation: the somewhat frightening notion of social formlessness at the very core of one's identity, a fully liminal self of *one's own.*

4

Modern Magic

⋯⟞⟝⋯

More than any of the arts of deception we have considered to this point, magic resists neat historical periodization. And in many ways, this resistance stems from a certain vagueness in the term itself. If we follow the current edition of *Webster's Dictionary* and use the term to describe techniques "believed to have supernatural power over natural forces," magic virtually transcends periodization.[1] The problem, at least for the cultural historian, is the wording "believed to have"—and the vast range of meanings and practices such a qualification signifies. *Webster's* definition includes almost anything and everything: premodern rituals and practices that were once understood as supernatural acts but have since been disenchanted or superseded by new systems of belief; more recent faiths in supernatural agency that continue to hold meaning for some, yet are understood as mere superstition or delusion by others; even explicitly natural forms of magic such as card tricks or levitations on stage, which only seem supernatural in the theatrical sense. Today the term "magic" encompasses a vast assortment of cultural and historical meanings. And in actual practice, the distinctions between these meanings are not always entirely clear, as anyone who has witnessed a spoon-bending spiritualist on late-night television knows all too well.

Not surprisingly, historians of magic have expressed some concern about their subject's resistance to categorization, especially those who have attempted to make the case for a major shift in the meanings and conventions of magic. Consider, for example, Keith Thomas' classic study of the magical beliefs of early modern England, *Religion and the Decline of Magic* (1971), still the most important work on the subject by an academic historian. Following more than 600 pages of painstaking analysis of cunning men, village wizards, astrology, and witchcraft, Thomas steps back to assess the legacy of these figures and practices, offering a wide range of historically specific developments associated with the decline of traditional magic after the late seventeenth century: the Protestant Reformation, with its insistence on self-help and individual stoicism (rather than necromantic forms of assistance); the scientific and philosophical revolutions, which suggested that the universe was subject to immutable natural laws; new technical aids such as fire-fighting and property insurance, which helped one guard against life's unexpected misfortunes; the impact of urbanization, which undercut the intimate personal relationships on which accusations of sorcery had formerly depended; and theoretical innovations in mathematics, psychology, and sociology, which provided victims with novel intellectual tools for explaining the causes of the disasters in their lives.[2]

Yet Thomas never presents this story of decline as a completed process, opting instead to problematize the notion that traditional magic quickly and easily withered away in the face of modernity. In technology and medicine, he points out, Enlightenment did not simply conquer traditional magic; rather, "supernatural theories went out" before effective replacements "came in."[3] Nor "has the place of the village wizard ever been fully taken by the police force and the advertisement columns of the newspapers: today's agencies for detecting thieves and recovering missing property are only moderately successful." "The wonder," Thomas observes, "is not that older systems of divination should have lasted so long, but that we should now feel it possible to do without them."[4]

These conclusions have obvious relevance for the artful deceptions we have examined thus far. The antebellum curiosities engineered by Maelzel and Barnum, after all, would not have been possible if the decline of traditional magic had effectively quelled all sense of mystery and enchantment in the world. For viewers to find these riddles about thinking machines, mermaids, and nondescripts intriguing, a modicum of public uncertainty about their impossibility was essential. Thomas's suggestion that daily newspapers were only "moderately successful" as a substitute for traditional magic helps us make sense of Barnum's world, too. In fact, this argument could be pushed a bit further here: as both Maelzel's and Barnum's careers demonstrate quite dramatically, the bold pronouncements of the penny press routinely created as much confusion as they alleviated. And while property insurance and professional police forces may have replaced divination as the conventional means of guarding against loss, these transitions hardly signaled the end of socioeconomic anxiety. Indeed, as Thomas notes in the final lines of his study, "if magic is to be defined as the employment of ineffective techniques to allay anxiety when effective ones are not available, then we must recognize that no society will ever be free from it."[5]

These lingering questions about what happens to magic in a post-Enlightenment, urban-industrial context form the subtext of this chapter. But I want to address this complex historical problem by focusing on a figure that is strangely absent in Thomas's conclusion: the magician himself. Given its central importance throughout the rest of the book, one might expect that some reflections on the Western magician's historical evolution from village wizard to theatrical performer would be essential to explaining the status of magic in the modern world. Thomas, however, abandons the magician as a historical subject somewhere in the late seventeenth century—and he is hardly alone. While academic historians have often looked to occult rituals, witchcraft, and magical beliefs as important cultural sources for exploring the lives and concerns of pre-industrial peoples, few have attached much significance to the more profane magical practices of the urban exhibition hall.[6] It is almost as if academic historians have taken Max Weber's classic theory about the "disenchantment of the world" as a guide for assessing the social significance of the magician during the nineteenth and twentieth centuries.[7] With the rise of what Weber called rationalization, the magician no longer seems to "signify anything" of social or cultural importance.[8] His magic wand becomes a mere prop; his tricks nothing more than frivolous amusements; his larger social function simply that of a professional actor putting on entertaining shows.

Most late nineteenth-century observers, however, would have been baffled by such suggestions. In their eyes, the very fact that magic had become mere entertainment only increased its fascination, social relevance, and historical importance. Dr. Paul Carus, a passionate contemporary devotee of stage magic and a published historian of its evolution, expressed a typical view: "It is true that magic in the old sense is gone; but that need not be lamented. The coarseness of Cagliostro's frauds has given way to the elegant display of scientific inventiveness and an adroit use of the human wit. . . . We believe that the spread of modern magic and its proper comprehension are an important sign of progress, and in this sense the feats of our Kellars and Herrmanns are a work of religious significance."[9] The two performers he mentions—Alexander Herrmann and Harry Kellar—will be familiar to very few readers today. But during the final decades of the nineteenth century, these men were the celebrated stars of something called "modern magic," a proud and enormously successful "reform" program in stage conjuring that emerged around the same time as Barnum's show business empire and quickly became one of the era's most pervasive cultural phenomena.

Magical modernism included a colorful cast of celebrities from both sides of the Atlantic: Signor Antonio Blitz, an English magician who sailed to New York from Liverpool in 1835, appeared at almost every exhibition hall, museum, and theater in the United States over the next four decades, and introduced countless Americans to the novel concept of magic as an explicitly disenchanted form of fashionable theatrical entertainment; Jean-Eugène Robert-Houdin of France, the most famous stage magician of the century, who never actually made it to the United States but nevertheless did much to establish, codify, and promote the conventions of modern magic in this country through his extensive publications of the late 1850s and 1860s; Robert Heller, the classically trained English pianist/magician, whose *Salon Diabolique* on lower Broadway during the mid-1860s became one of the longest-running one man shows in New York theater history; and Compars Herrmann (the older brother of Alexander), who performed primarily in Vienna and London, but during three major American tours (1861, 1865, and 1869) introduced New Yorkers to a brand of stage magic fashionable enough even for the venerable Academy of Music. And of course there was the young man from Appleton, Wisconsin—Ehrich Weiss, the last of nineteenth-century America's modern magicians—who named himself after Robert-Houdin during the 1890s (by adding an i), only to renounce his professional role model in print a few years later.

Before Houdini's early twentieth-century act of literary patricide, these late nineteenth-century practitioners of modern magic developed many of the rituals and images central to our inherited notion of what a stage magician is and does. First and foremost, they brought the magician fully into the more respectable confines of the urban middle-class theater. They also refashioned the public persona of the magician, overhauling his professional nomenclature, wardrobe, stage props, patter, and marketing techniques, a reform program that placed the modern magician squarely within the new middle-class culture of professionalism taking shape during the second half of the century. Through their myriad publishing efforts (something else stage magicians had rarely undertaken before) these modernists virtually invented parlor magic as one of the Gilded Age's most popular bourgeois hobbies. And much like the avant-garde painters and writers of their era, modern magicians championed a vast assortment of bold new aesthetic techniques, many of which have become stereotypes in our time. Pulling objects out of a hat, levitating an assistant on stage, mind reading and spirit communication, lifting jewelry from an

A typical promotional image of the "modern magician."

unsuspecting audience volunteer: what these performers defined and promoted as modern magic during the second half of the century reads now much like a syllabus for Stage Conjuring 101.[10]

The real issue here, however, is what these rituals, tricks, and personas signified to their consumers—especially *after* the figures on stage began admitting that their performances were nothing but simulations of the supernatural. For Carus, these performances represented nothing less than works "of religious significance"—strong words, indeed, from a late nineteenth-century gentleman, and hardly the sorts of words we might expect to be directed at stage tricks. H. J. Burlingame, another of the era's leading writers on magic, went so far as to place the modern magician within the same eminent social milieu as "the successful physician, the able lawyer, the brilliant writer, the clear statesman, the bright inventor, and all others who attain high places in any respectful and helpful calling."[11]

Clearly, these magicians signified something of importance to their audiences. But what, exactly? And how? What might their audiences have seen in these sleight-of-hand performances that we just do not see anymore? Why do we merely see well-dressed men with quick hands, plying their trade on stage? The great paradox here is that no modern magician would have disputed our perceptions at all: it was precisely their status as "actors, merely playing the part of a magician" that they routinely emphasized and celebrated.[12] What emerges here, then, is a very different sort of problem than the one emphasized by previous scholars: not so much that of explaining the waning status and efficacy of the village wizard, but the emergence of the theatrical magician as a powerful symbol of progress.

The Old and the New Magic

As is often true with modern cultural industries (rock n' roll, for example), modern magic gave rise to endless debates among its late nineteenth-century devotees about who was responsible for its origins and early development. Arguing about this cultural phenomenon's seminal figures was part of the fun, part of being a fan. Yet virtually every producer and consumer of modern magic agreed on one thing: that beginning in the eighteenth century something truly remarkable had happened to magic, something fundamental, something of epistemic importance. H. J. Burlingame offered a typical summary of these changes: "Enlightenment fought constantly against the more notorious productions of this fictitious world. The practice of magic as a business had to be abandoned, and its practice threw off more and more of its garb of deceit. The magicians of the first half of our century . . . all took the modern point of view, and labored to make magic appear as entertainment only."[13] Henry Ridgely Evans's 1898 essay, "The Mysteries of Modern Magic," suggested a similar shift, citing the career of Count Cagliostro (the notorious mesmerist who duped Marie Antoinette in Paris during the 1780s) to make his case that magic had been radically transformed at the end of the Enlightenment: "With Cagliostro, so-called genuine magic died. Of the great pretenders to occultism he was the last to win any great fame. . . . Science has laughed away sorcery, witchcraft, and necromancy."[14] Carus issued the most dramatic celebration of this shift, describing the modern magic industry as a kind of apotheosis of Enlightenment thinking: "The new magic originated from the old magic when the belief in sorcery began to break down in the eighteenth century, which is the dawn of rationalism and marks the epoch since which mankind has been systematically working out a scientific world-conception."[15]

These sweeping claims of an epistemological break with the magical past (usually articulated through a blunt binary opposition of some sort: old versus new, genuine versus fake, Cagliostro versus Kellar) relied on a degree of historical revisionism. As Evans himself admitted, there were some magicians before Cagliostro who "practiced the art of sleight-of-hand" and "gave very amusing and interesting exhibitions. Very few of these conjurors laid claim to occult powers, but ascribed their *jeux*, or tricks, to manual dexterity, mechanical and scientific effects." The self-proclaimed modernists, in other words, were not the very first entertainers to admit their disenchanted status. And if one looks for the earliest published descriptions of magic as a form of eye-fooling dexterity (as opposed to supernatural power), the history of the epistemological shift celebrated by Carus, Burlingame, and Evans extends back much further. According to the *Oxford English Dictionary*, the first uses of the term "sleight of hand" to describe a clever performance date from the beginning of the seventeenth century—roughly the same period in which the first literary exposés of magic and witchcraft as "naturally" produced forms of earthly deception appeared (for example, Reginald Scot's 1584 *The Discoverie of Witchcraft*).[16]

Thus an important initial qualification seems to be in order. Although the champions of prestidigitatorial modernism clearly believed they were part of—even spearheading—a major historical redefinition of magic in Western culture, this transformation seems to have culminated, rather than originated, in the late nineteenth century (a qualification which applies to virtually every subspecies of aesthetic modernism).[17] Furthermore, when one examines the actual performances and reception patterns of the late eighteenth-century conjuring business, it becomes clear that the boundary separating the old and the new magic was still rather fuzzy as the Enlightenment was coming to a close. Consider the career of Etienne-Gaspard Robert (better known as Robertson), a Belgian optician often cited as the most important European progenitor of modern magic. Born in Liege in 1763, Robertson moved to Paris at the end of the century and soon announced his invention of a remarkable new form of entertainment: the marvelous phantasmagoria.[18]

The technology at the heart of Robertson's ghost show was itself an adaptation of much older ideas. Since the mid-seventeenth century at least (and probably much earlier than that), Europeans had known how to project an image onto a wall using light and mirrors.[19] Robertson added three new features to this basic idea. First, he developed glass slides that were completely opaque except for the translucent colored image to be projected. This eliminated the surrounding circle of white projector light common in magic lantern shows—a seemingly minor technical difference, but one which made it far less clear to viewers that the image before them was merely a representation. Second, Robertson placed his projector on rollers, which enabled him to enlarge or shrink his projected images in dramatic fashion. And finally, he removed his lantern apparatus from view by placing it behind the projecting surface (usually a lightly varnished, translucent sheet of white cloth). What Robertson's audiences saw before them, in other words, was not a popular entertainer in the act of creating an illusion, but the illusion itself.[20] It was this technique of rendering the means of production invisible—and projecting bogus images before crowds of urban consumers—that made the phantasmagoria such a powerful metaphor for capitalism among neo-Marxist critics like Walter Benjamin and Theodor Adorno over a century later.[21]

Robertson's stated purpose, however, was not to deceive his viewers but to demonstrate science's (and by extension, his own) ability to reproduce spectral visions using purely natural means. He first presented this sort of show in 1799 at the Pavillion de l'Echiquier in Paris and then moved to the Couvent des Capuchines. One contemporary writer described the latter setting as a "vast chapel, the floor of which consisted almost entirely of tombstones, the walls being hung with black drapery, while a funeral lamp shed a few pallid rays upon the expected audience."[22] Once seated—and with the room darkened almost completely—Robertson's voice greeted his Parisian audience: "What you are about to see, Citizens, is not merely a frivolous exhibition, but one which [is] intended for the instruction of men who think; for the philosopher, who . . . is fond of, now and then, wandering amongst the tombs."[23] Many of the phantoms in Robertson's shows represented morbid themes: a skeleton holding a spear, ghosts emerging from open tombs, even recently deceased political figures like the revolutionary Marat. But the illusionist interspersed these images of the dead "with jocular exhibitions of an amusing character."[24]

At the conclusion of his ghostly parade, Robertson offered "a long tirade against the folly of consulting magicians, sorcery, witchcraft, necromancy, palmistry, fortune-telling by cards, &c., &c.":

I have now shown you all the phenomena of the phantasmagoria and have revealed to you all the secrets of the priests of Memphis and of the more modern Illuminati. I have tried to show you the magic effects of natural philosophy—effects that only a few years ago would have been deemed supernatural. You philosophers have possibly smiled at my experiments, while the beauties at your side have possibly been terrified, but I will now show you the only really terrible spectacle, the only spectacle really to be feared by you all, whether you are strong or weak, rulers or subjects, believers or atheists, beautiful or ugly. Behold the destiny that is reserved for you all, and remember the phantasmagoria.[25]

And with this, Robertson bid *adieu* to his audiences by projecting an image "of a grinning skeleton . . . waving a scythe."[26]

Part of what made these philosophical exercises so compelling was their unprecedented level of verisimilitude in representing ghoulish objects on a screen—an innovation which has led some recent cinema scholars to cite Robertson's exhibitions as a forerunner of the modern horror film.[27] What needs to be emphasized here, however, are not simply the techniques and subjects of Robertson's phantasmagoria, but the ways in which he used them to fashion a new cultural identity for himself in post-revolutionary Paris. This Belgian optician was the very first performer in Western popular culture to disenchant his own magic tricks in public, to make self-directed exposé a central feature of magical entertainment. By presenting his simulations of the supernatural as a tool of Enlightenment rather than an antirational threat, Robertson was beginning to carve out a more respectable, secularized mode of magical performance: a magic defined as scientifically produced experiment rather than esoteric occultism, a magic suitable for the enlightened citizens of the 1790s rather than the superstitious subjects of the Old Regime.

Yet if Robertson was clearly pushing magical entertainment in novel directions, he was still playing both sides of the old magic/new magic divide. Perhaps most dramatically, he blurred philosophy and necromancy at the level of aesthetic technique, making his simulations of phantoms as convincing and undetectable as possible (by eliminating the surrounding circle of white projector light). So while part of the novelty of this entertainment lay in its aggressive rhetoric of disenchantment, Robertson simultaneously offered his Parisian audiences a brief diversion from Enlightenment: a relatively safe moment of visual cultural wonder, in which ghosts and skeletons really did seem to appear before the viewers' eyes. A newspaper account from the same period suggests, too, that at least a few of Robertson's philosophical viewers were eager to use the phantasmagoria as a means of conversing earnestly with the dead: "a young fop asked to see the apparition of a woman he had tenderly loved, and showed her portrait in miniature to the phantasmagorian. . . . Soon a woman became visible, with breast uncovered and floating hair, gazing upon her young friend with a sad and melancholy smile. A grave man, seated next to me, cried out, raising his hand to his brow: 'Heavens! I think that's my wife.'"[28] Such audience requests for spiritual visitations point to a paradox at the heart of the optician's enterprise. While Enlightenment rhetoric and cultural values were central to Robertson's performances, the success of this entertainment form still depended on a momentary (and for some, it seems, quite enduring) suspension of disbelief.

Other magicians' attempts to steer a safe and profitable course between philosophical instruction and supernatural excitement proved more problematic. Giovanni Giuseppe Pinetti, one of the very first magicians to perform successfully in a fashionable theater, was nevertheless hounded throughout the 1780s by a Frenchman named Henri Decremps, who accused his Italian rival of occultism and fraud in a published exposé, *La Magie Blanche Dévoilée, ou Explication* (1784). Pinetti, naturally, did his very best to counter Decremps' accusations, even publishing an explanation of some of his own tricks as a kind of literary counteroffensive (*Amusements Physiques, et Différentes Expériences Divertissantes*, 1784). But ultimately, Pinneti's best defense against Decremps' accusations was to put some serious distance between himself and his accuser, a decision which took him first to London's theater district and, finally, to Russia, where he spent the final years of his conjuring career.[29]

Another, far less fortunate target of attack in the philosophical magic business was the German-American showman, Andrew Oehler, who badly misnavigated the old magic/new magic divide while staging a phantasmagoria in Mexico a few years later. No doubt aware of

Robertson's remarkable success in Paris, Oehler decided to purchase a lantern projector and began assembling his own traveling ghost show, which he presented to the Governor of Vera Cruz and his entourage in 1806.[30] This was far and away the most important performance of Oehler's fledgling career, and with the hope of impressing his venerable guests, he decided to pull out all the stops:

> I prepared three rooms in an inn for the exhibition, and lined the walls with black tapestry throughout; over the tapestry I hung skeletons of the dead; in the first room sat a candle, just sufficient, (by its glimmering light) to bring to remembrance the solemn mansions of the dead! The second room was prepared with additional gloominess, and was still more frightful! The third, and last, was increased in every solemn and frightful form, and seemed to the spectator as though he had entered the gloomy house of demons and departed ghosts, who with implacable malice stood fixed and ready to seize upon their prey. . . . On entering into this room, the spectator, on stepping on the floor, was unexpectedly shocked with a strong touch of electricity; stepping forth on an insulated platform, amongst his fellow spectators, he saw their countenances pale and frightful as death![31]

To Oehler's eyes, this elaborate series of supernatural simulations seemed like a promising blueprint for philosophical amusement, but the Governor quickly pronounced the entire enterprise a dangerous act of heresy and put the traveling showman in jail for almost a year.[32]

It is not entirely clear what triggered Oehler's problems in Mexico. His solemn staging followed Robertson's decorating scheme for the Capuchin convent in Paris quite closely. And if there were any marked differences between the quality of their phantoms, one suspects that the projector technology employed in Oehler's roadshow was more primitive than that utilized by the Belgian optician (a distinction that would have translated into less convincing spectral visions in Vera Cruz). One suspects, too, that the contrast in reception patterns between these ghost shows was not simply a function of each group's exposure to philosophical ideas. This, after all, was Oehler's most sophisticated early nineteenth-century audience. And Robertson's audiences at the Couvent des Capuchines contained plenty of French "philosophers" who still retained at least some visceral faith in the possibility of real phantoms flying around the exhibition hall.

But whereas Robertson seems to have struck an acceptable balance between simulated hauntings and antioccultist indignation, Oehler (a social outsider in Vera Cruz, as well as a neophyte in the business) simply piled on the spectral visions—apparently, with little understanding of how his venerable patrons might perceive this novel performance. His crucial mistake, in fact, may have been that he did not talk to his Vera Cruz audience much at all, at least not in the proper, post-Enlightenment ways. In contrast to Robertson, who delivered lengthy tirades against the folly of superstition, Oehler offered few philosophical words, opting instead for a quick audience disclaimer that "the spirit . . . should not hurt them."[33] A few years later, living in the more comfortable surroundings of Trenton, New Jersey, Oehler confessed to being "weary of the whole business." With little to show from his career as a magician, Oehler sold his phantasmagoria equipment and (much like the Vera Cruz authorities who had thrown him in jail) denounced his former exhibitions as "nothing but a perfect imposition on the public."[34]

Professional magicians operating in the United States faced a number of pitfalls during these years, too. One was the lingering prejudice against theatricals of any kind—a prejudice which many early American magicians attempted to circumvent by promoting their shows as nothing more than demonstrations of "manual dexterity."[35] The early results of this promotional strategy were mixed. Throughout the eighteenth century, the few magicians who attempted to forge a career in the British American colonies often found themselves (much like their dramatic counterparts) targeted for censorship by religious groups. When Miles Burroughs began performing feats of "Legerdemain and Subtle Craft" in Massachusetts, for example, the town council quickly forced his departure. John Woolman, a devout Quaker, similarly wrote in his journal about chasing would-be patrons away from a 1763 sleight-of-hand performance in a New Jersey tavern, even though sleight of hand was officially legal in New Jersey by that time. And as late as 1808, a French magician by the name of Mr. Martin got into trouble while offering a phantasmagoria in lower Manhattan when it was discovered that the building had been used for religious services in the past. An anonymous letter to the *Commercial Advertiser* protested that it was a disgrace for "the devil" to dance "on stilts to the tune of a hand organ" in such sacred surroundings.[36]

Unlike Oehler, however, Martin fought back, issuing a letter of his own to the *Commercial Advertiser* a few days later. Public interest in his "devils," Martin reported, had increased dramatically in response to his accuser's charges—so much so that Martin now planned to extend his run, showing as "many devils as [the public] may desire to see, and in doing this he hopes to keep the devil from his pocket." As George Odell has noted, this skirmish represented one of the earliest American examples of the "truism that nothing so advertises filth as a crusade of a purity league" (a truism that Barnum would soon apply with gusto!).[37] Martin's apparent victory also seems to suggest that Americans were becoming more accustomed to—and tolerant of— the philosophical magic pioneered by Robertson and Pinetti. A year later, significantly, the thoroughly respectable Rubens Peale introduced just such an "experiment in natural philosophy" at the Philadelphia Museum, assuring readers of the *Aurora* that his new phantasmagoria demonstrations were designed solely as a means of proving the nonexistence of supernatural phenomena: "They are intended to enlighten and guard people against certain superstitious ideas they may have imbibed respecting witches and wizards, which, in past ages, have kept the human mind in fetters. . . . That such things never had existence, will be made fully manifest to those who will attend."[38] Much like the Peales' perpetual motion machine and Japanese mermaid, the phantasmagoria was perfectly welcome in the Philadelphia Museum, provided that it was clearly and publicly identified as a deception and properly rationalized as a tool for increasing "useful knowledge."

Supernatural simulations staged according to Enlightenment principles were also taking place in Boston, as William Frederick Pinchbeck (from a well-known English family of automaton builders) engineered a broad range of philosophical experiments for public consumption:

an acoustic temple, in which viewers received audible messages from an empty box perched on a table; a writing automaton which scribbled answers on paper to Pinchbeck's publicly delivered questions; and, most famously, the learned pig ("my grunting professor," as Pinchbeck affectionately called it), which identified playing cards chosen at random by members of the audience. Pinchbeck, however, took the Robertsonian program a step further, publishing *Expositor; or Many Mysteries Unravelled,* the first book-length exposé of conjuring tricks by a professional magician in this country. In contrast to Robertson and Peale, whose audiences were at least forced to speculate about how the supernatural simulations were achieved, Pinchbeck eliminated any need for guessing. Starting in 1805, the grunting professor's marvels came with printed instructions.[39]

As Barbara Maria Stafford has recently demonstrated, such literary explications of "the visible invisible" were a major component of Enlightenment entertainment, serving as a form of visual education among the rising bourgeoisie as well as a novel means of demonstrating a cultivated sensibility to friends and family.[40] What needs to be added here is that these entertaining how-to manuals also marked a turning point in the conventions of Western magical practice—especially when the publication in question was authored by a magician such as Pinchbeck. While exposés of magic and witchcraft had been common in Western literature for over two hundred years, their use as a promotional tool by the stage conjurer was largely unprecedented. For the first time, explaining the behind-the-scenes workings of one's magical performance was becoming almost as important and as central to the professional magician's craft as the more conventional work of designing and performing tricks.

Magical modernism, then, required not only the erosion of faith in supernatural agency achieved by two centuries of Enlightenment, but also the adoption of Enlightenment rhetoric, ideals, and personas by the leading simulators of the supernatural. It seems equally clear, however, that this particular Enlightenment project was far from complete at the dawn of the nineteenth century. Robertson routinely issued public tirades against superstition and necromancy in Paris, but also took requests for showing phantoms dear to his viewers' hearts. Oehler made no public claims to supernatural powers in Vera Cruz, but spent a year in a dungeon possibly for not disclaiming such powers vigorously enough. Martin fared somewhat better with his phantasmagoria shows in Manhattan, but also provoked moral attacks for raising ghosts in a former church.

The old magic, in other words, did not just die out. Rather, it is far more accurate to say that the larger category of sleight-of-hand entertainment—a category which had existed in one form or another for centuries—was changing in two dramatic ways. On the one hand, starting in the 1780s and 1790s, growing numbers of professional conjurers on both sides of the Atlantic began to reverse the aesthetic and ideological aims of their performances—transforming them from a somewhat shady and morally suspect form of realism to a more self-conscious and respectable mode of illusionism. Professional magicians, in short, began to claim disenchantment as their *raison d'être* in the post-Enlightenment world. On the other hand, these collective efforts to redefine the basic forms and functions of magical entertainment seem to have paved the way for stage magic's movement into a novel cultural location: the rapidly proliferating urban entertainment venues dominated by the rising middle class.[41]

Evidence of this trend appears in a number of places. One is George Odell's seemingly inconsequential observation in his history of the New York stage, that "magic and legerdemain were assuredly features of the mid-'30's in amusement halls. . . . Will the reader glance backward and forward in the record, to prove what I say?" Odell's real point here was not to underscore the novelty of legerdemain as such. As he documents in earlier volumes of his encyclopedic history, sleight-of-hand artists had appeared with some consistency in taverns, hotels, assembly rooms, and circuses of the late eighteenth century. Nor was this the moment when American magicians first appeared on theater stages; according to Odell's painstaking, year-by-year records, this transition began earlier, too. Rather, what seems to have caught his attention in the newspapers and handbills of the mid-1830s was the beginning of a more subtle and far-reaching shift taking place in the social status and conventional locations of American magic. Whereas sleight of hand had previously existed as a somewhat marginal presence in New York, by the mid-1830s it was becoming a prominent "feature" of the stage—accepted, patronized, and even celebrated in the city's most fashionable entertainment sites around lower Broadway. Also noteworthy is the very first performer Odell mentions in his lengthy catalog of magicians from the mid-1830s: Eugene Robertson (the Belgian optician's son), who brought his own phantasmagoria show to Euterpean Hall in 1834. Like his more famous father, Eugene made simulation and exposé his stocks in trade, promising that his shows would not "produce fright even with the youngest person; on the contrary, they excite the curiosity of the Philosopher." By this time, though, such philosophical promises had become the promotional rule rather than the exception. In fact it was now difficult to find any performer working on a New York sage who did not explicitly claim disenchantment as the goal and function of magical entertainment.[42]

The most dramatic evidence of these changes can be found in the very first memoir published by a professional conjuror in this country, Signor Antonio Blitz's *Fifty Years in the Magic Circle* (1872). Touring the English countryside during the 1820s, Blitz was repeatedly harassed by religious councils on the one hand, and peasants looking for supernatural favors, on the other.[43] In Exeter, charges were filed against him by a Bishop, and he was forced to appear before a council. In Cornwall, he was harassed by the local magistrate and solicited for supernatural assistance by miners. And in Manchester, his early attempts at philosophical magic became a point of heated debate with a clergyman who urged him to "renounce the devil and magic," to which Blitz responded "that I was no evil spirit in form or principle; and furthermore, my exhibitions were of a nature calculated to remove the long-prevailing impressions attached to the history of magic." In 1835 Manhattan, by contrast, Blitz found himself patronized solely for his ability to "please and astonish," as he offered philosophical wonders to "large and fashionable audiences" between orchestra concerts. Better still, Blitz observed, "there was, with a very slight exception, a total absence of an approach to the superstitious character which had constantly marked my progress through the 'Old Country'. . . . The great improvements in mechanical inventions, the elaborate perfection with which feats were presented to audiences, produced much sensation, and established the superiority of the modern performers, so that in a brief time professors of magic arose in abundance."[44]

One suspects that the ideological chasm Blitz claims to have crossed between 1820s Manchester and 1830s Manhattan was not quite as wide as he would have us believe. As the clever Signor no doubt understood, there was much to be gained by promoting the new magic to Americans as a mark of social advancement and cultural sophistication vis-à-vis the Old Country. Yet there is no disputing Blitz's central contention about the rapid growth and diffusion of the popular cultural form he brought with him in 1835. Within a year Blitz found steady employment as the house magician at Niblo's Gardens, before moving on to regular engagements at virtually every fashionable venue in antebellum America: the Peales' Philadelphia Museum, Barnum's American Museum, even a command performance for ex-President Van Buren at New York's Society Library (the same cultural site where the National Academy of Design's annual art exhibitions were held). And Blitz was hardly alone. By the 1850s and 1860s, magicians were beginning to appear not merely as entracte entertainers for Niblo's concerts or as one of hundreds of curiosities to be seen at Barnum's Museum, but as full-fledged theatrical headliners.

One recent chronicler of American magic has described these changes as "the dawning of a Golden Age."[45] What this does not explain, however, are the larger historical developments that led to Signor Blitz's "great improvements" and "the elaborate perfection" of "modern performers." Of particular importance here is the historical relation between the rising status of magic and the social constituency that seems to have driven its ascension. If Robertsonian gestures of disenchantment served as magic's springboard into the cultural confines of the new middle class, how, in turn, did this new constituency of consumers shape the conventional techniques employed by the leading performers? And what did Signor Blitz really mean in 1872 when he described his own magic as distinctly modern—a term that he never used in his earlier promotional materials?

Modern Miracles

Adding to the complexity of these questions is one of the most famous accusations in the history of stage magic. It came from Harry Houdini, who in 1906 issued a series of magazine articles arguing that the most widely celebrated modernist of all, Jean-Eugene Robert-Houdin, was a complete fraud.[46] Collectively published as *The Unmasking of Robert-Houdin* in 1908, Houdini's book and its accusations are not easily dismissed. The author was, after all, someone who knew a great deal—perhaps more than anyone alive at the time—about the long and complex history of post-Enlightenment magic. And by the first decade of the twentieth century, Houdini had collected an enormous library of books and documents on the subject (now housed in the Library of Congress' Rare Books Division) with which to substantiate his accusations. This was a young man, furthermore, who during the 1880s and 1890s had so deeply admired Robert-Houdin that he had taken the elder magician's name as his own and traveled to his French gravesite in 1902 to lay a wreath with the inscription: "Honor and Respect to Robert Houdin from the Magicians of America."[47] As Houdini emphasized in his introduction, attacking his modernist role model in print had been the furthest thing from his mind when he began the project:

> My interest in conjuring and magic and my enthusiasm for Robert-Houdin came into existence simultaneously. From the moment that I began to study the art, he became my guide and hero. I accepted his writings as my textbook and gospel. What Blackstone is to the struggling lawyer, Hardee's "Tactics" to the would-be officer, or Bismarck's life and writings to the coming statesman, Robert-Houdin's books were to me. To my unsophisticated mind, his "Memoirs" gave to the profession a dignity worth attaining at the cost of earnest, life-long effort. . . . I had re-read his works until I could recite passage after passage from memory.[48]

It is unclear exactly when and how these intense feelings of professional admiration gave way to literary exposé and condemnation.[49] But by 1908, as he was becoming an international celebrity in his own right, Houdini's thinking about the nineteenth-century patriarch of modern magic took a dramatic turn: "Alas for my golden dreams! My investigations brought forth only bitterest disappointment. Stripped of his self-woven veil of romance, Robert-Houdin stood forth, in the uncompromising light of cold historical facts, a mere pretender, a man who waxed great on the brainwork of others, a mechanician who had boldly filched the inventions of the master craftsmen among his predecessors."[50]

The central argument of *Unmasking* is easily summarized: virtually every one of the Frenchman's celebrated tricks had been invented by someone else—often decades or even centuries earlier. Houdini's key piece of evidence was the famous orange-tree trick, promoted in the handbills from the Frenchman's 1845 theatrical debut as "an entirely novel experiment." A brief description of the trick appeared in Robert-Houdin's memoir: "The next was a mysterious orange-tree, on which flowers and fruit burst into life at the request of the ladies. As the finale, a handkerchief I borrowed was conveyed into an orange purposefully left on the tree. This opened and displayed the handkerchief, which two butterflies took by the corners and unfolded before the spectators."[51] Houdini never actually saw the orange-tree performed this way. The most famous magician of the nineteenth century died in France in 1871, three years before the most famous magician of the twentieth century was born in Budapest. Nevertheless, based on what he described as cold hard facts, Houdini boldly asserted in 1908 that Robert-Houdin's famous claims of novelty and innovation were untrue.

An English clockmaker named Christopher Pinchbeck, Houdini charged, had invented the mechanism for the fruit tree sometime before 1730. Soon thereafter, Pinchbeck contracted with Isaac Fawkes, the leading cup-and-ball magician from the early eighteenth-century carnival circuit, and together they produced a fruit tree for public consumption at the Haymarket in London. By the middle

Jean-Eugène Robert-Houdin's "Fantastic Orange Tree," the trick that Harry Houdini denounced in 1908 as a form of prestigitatorial plagiarism. This illustration appeared in Robert-Houdin's *Programme Général*.

of the century, Pinchbeck's and Fawkes' children were producing their own trees. On a Pinetti handbill from 1784, Houdini discovered "Le Bouquet Philosophique" performed in London. And in 1822, the French magician Cornillot brought out an Enchanted Garden, which according to Houdini included multiple trees, each one blooming and producing different kinds of fruit simultaneously.[52] The rest of Houdini's chapters follow this same basic pattern. One by one, each of the French modernist's most celebrated tricks and techniques is unmasked by Houdini with a long paper trail of seventeenth and eighteenth-century books, handbills, and engravings. After 300 pages of this sort of brutal revisionism, Houdini concludes with a flourish:

> So ends the true history of Robert-Houdin. The master-magician, unmasked, stands forth in all the hideous nakedness of historical proof, the prince of pilferers. That he might bask for a few hours in public adulation, he purloined the ideas of magicians long dead and buried, and proclaimed these as the fruits of his own inventive genius. That he might be known to posterity as the king of conjurers, he sold his birthright of manhood and honor for a mere mess of pottage. . . . But the day of reckoning is come. Upon the history of magic as promulgated by Robert-Houdin the searchlight of modern investigation has been turned.[53]

For anyone interested in the technical evolution of sleight of hand, *Unmasking* is an essential document. Yet as a broader history of post-Enlightenment magic and its social significance, this is a problematic book on a number of counts. One is the larger historical pattern of generational revisionism that seems to be virtually endemic to post-Enlightenment magic. Etienne-Gaspard Robertson, it is important to remember, also began his magic career by denouncing those who had come before him as members of a wholly separate and backward tradition—as agents of superstition, mysticism, and occultism—taking no account of nonmystics such as Fawkes and Pinchbeck. Robert-Houdin, similarly, made his debut in Paris by defining his novel experiments as a clean break with the past, one designed to finally eradicate charlatanism in the magic profession. Thus, while Houdini's technical charges deserve careful consideration, they also need to be understood as part of a broader cycle in which each new generation of post-Enlightenment magicians attempts to stake its own turf by presenting the magical past as illegitimate, as a dangerous form of imposture whose eradication demonstrates the social value and progressive qualities of the present.

Moreover, if one reads *The Unmasking of Robert-Houdin* for what it really was—not only a technical history but also a deeply subjective reception document written by one of the late nineteenth-century's biggest fans of modern magic—then the evidence cuts two ways. By 1908 Houdini seems to have been genuinely convinced that many of

Robert-Houdin's mechanical devices and sleight-of-hand maneuvers were unoriginal. Yet this very same testimony suggests that originality made little difference in shaping Houdini's youthful impressions of them. Indeed, Houdini was so completely captivated by the image of Robert-Houdin—by the Frenchman's persona, values, and style— that modern magic quickly became his life's work. Houdini committed entire passages of Robert-Houdin's autobiography to memory and even changed his name to demonstrate his admiration. And the more carefully one looks into *Unmasking*, the more it becomes clear that Houdini himself was aware of the crucial difference between the raw materials of Robert-Houdin's stage tricks and their public presentation. Describing the Frenchman's debut, for example, Houdini made a key distinction: "Robert-Houdin went about decorating and furnishing this theater with a view to securing the most dramatic and brilliant effects, surrounding his simple tricks with a setting that made them vastly different than the same offerings by his predecessors. He was what is called today an original producer of old ideas."[54]

Here, a more nuanced approach to the cultural history of post-Enlightenment magic begins to emerge. It was precisely this "vast difference" that made all the difference for Andrew Oehler in Vera Cruz. And in many ways, this is the same sort of distinction that explains the novelty of nineteenth-century artful deception as a larger cultural current. It is the difference between Maelzel's and Kempelen's automaton chess-players; between Barnum's Mermaid and the copies exhibited by the Peale family in Philadelphia; and between What Is It? and the many wild men that pervaded Western popular culture prior to 1860. In the business of artful deception, innovation almost always involves original productions of old ideas. It is this distinction which defines and differentiates the entire aesthetic category.

How, then, did Robert-Houdin make magic seem modern during the 1850s and 1860s? The best place to begin is with his *Confidences d'un Prestidigitateur* of 1858—an autobiography that has been almost completely forgotten in our time, but which was translated and published in numerous languages (including English, Dutch, and Spanish) and had at least four different American editions during the second half of the nineteenth century.[55] It was also a relative novelty as a category of literature, being the first book that can be described as a full-fledged magical autobiography.[56]

Like Barnum's memoir from the same decade, *Confidences* begins with a discussion of the family business in a rural early nineteenth-century setting—in this case, watchmaking in the French town of Blois. "I am inclined to believe," the Frenchman explains, "that I came into the world with a file or hammer in my hand, for, from my earliest youth, those implements were my toys and delight. I learned to use them as other children learn to walk and talk. . . . It is certain that I have always felt an irresistible inclination for mechanism."[57] Yet, like Barnum, Robert-Houdin used his youthful training for something else, something grander, something that would take him far away from Blois: "although my father liked his trade, experience had taught him that a watchmaker rarely makes a fortune in a country town: in his practical ambition he, therefore, dreamed a more brilliant destiny for me, and he formed the determination of giving me a liberal education."[58]

Spurred by this dream of upward mobility, Robert-Houdin proceeds to the College in Orleans, where he studies diligently, receives good marks, and builds mechanical devices after classes. His most important professional lessons begin after graduation, as he moves in the direction of a full-time magical career through a series of chance encounters. The first takes place during an evening promenade next to the Loire River, where he meets a small-time sleight-of-hand artist known as Dr. Carlosbach, Conjurer and Professor of Mystics, who performs cup-and-ball tricks in the street. Following the performance, Robert-Houdin eagerly purchases a volume from Dr. Carlosbach, who professes to expose the frauds of medical charlatans. Yet this gesture of exposé proves as bogus as the street magician's jewels: having allied himself publicly with Enlightenment and fair business, Carlosbach proceeds to bilk the local innkeeper, fleeing town without paying his bill.[59]

Over the next few months, Robert-Houdin moves through a series of low-level, white-collar office jobs, which produce only boredom, frustration, and a deep longing for something else. Luckily, in 1828 he meets Torrini, another traveling magician, who rescues Robert-Houdin from delirium brought on by food poisoning.[60] This leads to an impromptu apprenticeship: in exchange for repairing Torrini's broken automaton, Robert-Houdin receives a series of sleight-of-hand lessons. He learns something, too, about public relations: how to win over an audience volunteer with verbal patter; how a good stage name can enhance one's public image (Torrini, according to Robert-Houdin, was a Frenchman named Edmond de Grisy; the Italian alias was just for show); and how important it is to practice effective advertising, a lesson Torrini demonstrates with some of the exaggerated promises and promotional puns regularly employed on the carnival circuit. Robert-Houdin even receives a kind of oral history of sleight of hand from his mentor, who claims to have started his conjuring career in 1796, after witnessing one of Pinetti's philosophical performances in Naples.[61]

At first glance, the larger significance of this apprenticeship story seems relatively obvious: covering over eighty pages in Robert-Houdin's memoir, it details the professional education which leads a small-town, watchmaker's son into a career as the most celebrated stage magician of the century. What makes these episodes with Torrini especially interesting, however, is that they seem to have been entirely fictional. Indeed, as far as anyone has been able to determine over the past century and a half, there simply was no magician named Torrini working the European carnival circuit. All of the lessons and intricately transcribed conversations seem to have been feats of literary *legerdemain* conjured directly from Robert-Houdin's imagination.[62] Yet precisely because Torrini plays such a prominent role in *Confidences*, it seems worth asking what Robert-Houdin sought to accomplish with this mode of self-representation. An answer begins to emerge in the specific ways that Robert-Houdin describes Torrini's complex social status. At the time of their initial encounter, Torrini had fallen into a somewhat disreputable grade of popular entertainment—he was an itinerant "carnival juggler"—a term with old, quasi-criminal associations in Western culture.[63] Torrini himself admits that Robert-Houdin's initial wariness about their partnership was probably justified: "You are surprised that a mountebank, a man belonging to a class not generally erring on the side of sensibility, should have evinced such compassion for your suffering."[64] A bit later in the story we learn that Torrini's carnival connection is a relatively recent development. In fact, he was actually the son of nobility, a Count de Grisy, who died defending Louis XVI at the Tuilleries! But even as Robert-Houdin points to Torrini's venerable lineage, he also expresses pity for the current state of his mentor, wondering how such a decent man "could have thus sunk to the lowest stage of his profession."[65]

True or not, then, Torrini is a remarkably flexible character. On one level, he represents Robert-Houdin's teacher, the carnivalesque virtuoso who shows a young provincial the ropes of the early nineteenth-century magic profession. But he is also Robert-Houdin's socioeconomic and professional other, a down-and-out figure working in a debased cultural setting, someone who (like Dr. Carlosbach) demonstrates what level within the profession to avoid. Torrini simultaneously serves as Robert-Houdin's bohemian fantasy and professional catalyst: he is the role model who provides a romantic alternative to the tedious world of low-level white-collar office work, as well as the kindly surrogate father who finally pushes Robert-Houdin into professional accomplishment. And because of his uniquely ambiguous social status (a traveling mountebank with philosophical magic credentials and noble parentage), Torrini is the perfect tour guide for exploring carnival culture. He opens up this morally suspect world for his middle-class apprentice—reveals its mysteries, pleasures, and eccentric characters—without actually making the young office clerk a permanent part of carnival.[66]

The specific timing of this mentorship is significant, too. Indeed, it was at this very moment—as Robert-Houdin was inventing himself as a middle-class professional—that Western carnival culture was entering into a period of dramatic transformation. The most prominent evidence of these changes can be seen in England's Bartholomew Fair, which for about five hundred years represented one of the major epicenters of the European carnivalesque. On numerous previous occasions during its long history, Bartholomew Fair had functioned as a kind of lightning rod for official scorn and sanction: it was routinely attacked by mayors, noblemen, and clerical leaders as seditious; and in some instances, its plebeian revelers were violently suppressed with military force. But through all of these conflicts, England's leading carnival institution managed to endure. In 1855, however, Bartholomew Fair was finally banned—a historical milestone some scholars have interpreted as the death knell of carnival culture in Europe.[67]

It is perhaps more accurate to say that the carnivalesque was reinvented to suit the values and economic concerns of the new middle class (for example, in industrial displays such as the Crystal Palace Exposition of 1851).[68] Or it was regulated by new cultural industries with somewhat stricter, family-oriented consumption codes (for example, Barnum's traveling circuses of the 1870s and 1880s). Or the old fair evolved into a new kind of cultural hybrid (for example, the 1893 Columbian Exposition, which juxtaposed self-congratulatory demonstrations of Western socioeconomic progress with caricatured exhibitions of non-Western exoticism and playfully vulgar amusements).

Robert-Houdin's fictional relationship with Torrini needs to be understood as part of these broader historical patterns. Immediately following their "painful separation," Robert-Houdin announces a new sense of conviction and determination: "It may be thought, perhaps, that I have dwelt too long on the events that followed my poisoning; but I was compelled to do so, for the experience I acquired from Torrini, his history, and our conversations, had a considerable influence on my future life. Before that period my inclination for conjuring was very vague: from that time it gained a complete mastery over me."[69] In the process of becoming a conjurer, however, virtually everything Robert-Houdin does involves a deliberate social and cultural distancing from Torrini and the world he represents. First, Robert-Houdin returns to his "native town" and is quickly married off to the daughter of a wealthy Parisian clock merchant—a turn of events which not only secures Robert-Houdin a solid domestic foundation (something Torrini and his carnivalesque colleagues had notably lacked), but also provides a fortuitous, Algeresque means of rapid upward mobility. With his domestic life and career plans now clear, Robert-Houdin moves to Paris.[70]

Over the next decade and a half, Robert-Houdin continues to develop and refine the sleight-of-hand techniques he first acquired under Torrini's tutelage. But most of his time and energy is spent on a mode of illusionism in which Torrini possessed very little expertise: the "science, or rather art, of making automata."[71] This expertise soon provides Robert-Houdin with an entrée into an entirely new type of fair, the industrial exhibition in Paris, where his mechanical marvels are applauded by some impressive visitors:

> The Exhibition of 1844 was about to open, so I asked and obtained leave to exhibit some specimens of my skill. The site granted me, opposite the door of honor, was undoubtedly one of the best in the hall, and I erected a circular stand, on which I placed a specimen of all the mechanical pieces I had as yet made. Among these my *Writer* took first place. . . . Louis Philippe paid daily visits to the Palace of Industry, and as my automata had been pointed out as deserving attention, he evinced a wish to see them. . . . [T]he crowd, kept back by the keepers of the palace and the police agents, left an open space round my exhibition. The king was in a charming humor, and seemed to take a pleasure in all I showed him.[72]

What this event inaugurated in Robert-Houdin's career was a kind of merger: one forged between a more respectable class of urban spectator and a more explicitly scientific brand of illusionism.[73] Louis Philippe's presence at the Palace of Industry was thus entirely appropriate. How fitting for the bourgeois monarch to preside over Robert-Houdin's first performance before the middle-class masses in Paris!

Immediately following the exhibition Robert-Houdin began "a complete regeneration in the art of conjuring." "The grand blow" came in 1845, when he opened a small theater in the Palais Royal, an elegant complex of arcades where French middle-class entertainment was essentially born.[74] The particular choices Robert-Houdin made inside were also innovative. He called them "reforms," the first of which involved a new stage design and approach to magical apparatus:

> I intended to have an elegant and simple stage, unencumbered by all the paraphernalia of the ordinary conjurer, which looks more like a toyshop than a serious performance. I would have none of those enormous metal shades usually placed over objects that are to disappear, and whose secret duties cannot escape the notice of the simplest spectator. Apparatus of transparent or opaque glass, according to circumstances, would suffice for all my operations. In the performance of my tricks I also intended to abolish those double-bottomed boxes of which some conjurers made such an abuse, as well as all instruments designed to make up for the performer's want of skill. Real sleight-of-hand must not be the tinman's work but the artist's, and people do not visit the latter to see instruments perform.[75]

Robert-Houdin continued this assault on carnival jugglery in a number of other ways. "Accomplices," he noted, would be "done away with" because they were "unworthy of a real artist." And to light his stage, he chose "jets of gas, covered by opaque globes," rather than "the thousands of candles, whose brilliancy is only intended to dazzle the spectators and thus injure the effect of the experiments." At the same time, he reformed the look of the performer, starting with his own: "Of course I abstained from any eccentric costume, and I never thought of making any change in the attire civilized society has agreed to accept for evening dress, for I was always of the opinion that bizarre accoutrements, far from giving the wearer any consideration, on the contrary cast disfavor upon him." He even regulated his manner of speaking on stage: "I . . . traced out for my performances a line of conduct from which I never diverged; that was to make no puns or play upon words, and never to permit myself to be guilty of a mystification, even were I sure of gaining the greatest success." All of these changes, Robert-Houdin concludes, were designed with one simple goal in mind: "I wished to offer new experiments divested of all charlatanism, and possessing no other resources than those offered by skillful manipulation, and the influence of illusions."[76]

At this point, it is easy to hear Houdini's charges of intellectual pilfering ringing in one's ears. As early as 1799, Etienne-Gaspard Robertson had also stood upon a Parisian stage and railed against magical charlatanism as part of his routine. And during the 1830s, Robertsonian disciples such as Signor Blitz had brought this explicitly disenchanted, post-Enlightenment mode of entertainment into new urban venues specifically catering to the middle class. Yet Robertson and Blitz never articulated their post-Enlightenment innovations as a set of professional principles—as carefully codified, published rules that might be disseminated as part of a larger movement and emulated by other magicians. They also understood the concept of charlatanism in very different terms. For Robert-Houdin, the mid-nineteenth-century charlatan was defined less by ties to older traditions of superstition and mysticism than garish clothing, gaudy stage design, unsophisticated lighting techniques, and offensive puns. The distinction between the old magic and the new magic, in other words, was beginning to shift once again. Whereas earlier generations of magicians had waged public battle against those claiming supernatural agency, Robert-Houdin's primary adversary was the conjurer afflicted with bad taste.[77]

The impact of this reform program was as swift, commercially successful, and far-reaching as those engineered a few years earlier by Maelzel and Barnum. Within the first months of Robert-Houdin's run at the Palais Royal, for example, French cultural journals such as *Charivari* and *Illustration* weighed in with energetic critical acclaim and commissioned sketches of his innovative theater design.[78] Robert-Houdin also began to show up in publications usually unconcerned with show business trends, such as Didot's *Nouvelle Biographie Générale,* which devoted an entire page to the new star of the French stage and his reformed magical persona.[79] Even the tumultuous events of 1848 failed to diminish the impact of the show, which Robert-Houdin now began to advertise as his "modern miracles."[80] Forced to close his theater in Paris during "the revolution of February," he quickly relocated to London and the "elegant assembly" of the

St. James Theater, where he received hearty applause from "gentlemen unafraid of bursting their gloves" and "ladies" who made "as much noise with their tiny hands as their strength allowed."[81]

Such bourgeois triumphs, one suspects, had much to do with Houdini's impression that Robert-Houdin gave to the magic profession "a dignity worth attaining at the cost of earnest, life-long effort." And Houdini was not the only admirer from afar. One of the more remarkable features of Robert-Houdin's international celebrity, in fact, was his surprisingly energetic and broad support from Americans, even though he never performed on an American stage. During the 1890s, for example, H. J. Burlingame hailed Robert-Houdin as the true "father of modern magic," the first to "elevate" sleight of hand "from vulgar jugglery to an art."[82] Henry Ridgely Evans made a similar claim in the first of his many histories of magic, *Conjuring and Its Professors:* "To Robert-Houdin we are indebted for a complete revolution in the art of conjuring. Prior to his time magicians draped their tables to the floor, thereby making them little more than huge confederate boxes. . . . Since his time, no first-class Prestidigitateur has dared to offend good taste by presenting his illusions in any other costume than that of a gentleman habited a la mode, nor has he dared to give a performance with draped tables."[83]

Of course, what these opinions documented most of all was Robert-Houdin's virtuosity as a maker of powerful new literary images. To get a sense of how the Frenchman's reforms were actually experienced by American theater audiences, then, it is necessary to turn our attention to one of his leading European rivals, Compars Herrmann, or Carl as he was known in this country, who did make the trip across the Atlantic in 1861. Over the previous three decades, his career had followed a trajectory very similar to that of the Frenchman. Born eleven years after Robert-Houdin in Hanover, Germany, Herrmann initially resisted a magical career in deference to his father, studied in France, charmed an impressive collection of European royalty (including Louis-Philippe), adopted the practice of performing in evening dress, and eliminated excess clutter and apparatus from his stage during the 1840s.[84] Many of Herrmann's most famous tricks

The illustration depicts one of Robert-Houdin's best-known modernist tricks, "Second Sight." The magician's son, blindfolded, guessed objects chosen by audience volunteers.

closely paralleled Robert-Houdin's, too: both men performed versions of an "inexhaustible bottle" (in which an endless supply of wine appeared to flow at the magician's command); both performed "second sight" routines (in which the blindfolded magician or an assistant guessed objects chosen by audience volunteers); and both performed some sort of "suspension" (in which an assistant seemed to levitate before the audience's eyes).[85]

But whereas Robert-Houdin was content to quit the stage during the late 1850s and work quietly on his memoirs in Saint-Gervais, Herrmann sailed for New Orleans, where he made his American debut at the St. Charles Theater, drawing explicit critical comparisons with Robert-Houdin. "The readers of the great Houdin's book upon thaumaturgy," the *Daily Picayune* noted, "will find several of that wonderful adept's experiments most beautifully executed by Herrmann."[86] Following the outbreak of the Civil War, Herrmann made his way north by train and found work in one of New York's most venerable cultural locations: the recently built Academy of Music. This was not the first performance by a stage magician before a fashionable American audience. Yet the very idea of a sleight-of-hand artist performing as the featured attraction in what was perhaps Manhattan's most elite cultural venue in 1861 (especially in the more stratified cultural landscape that began to emerge after the 1849 Astor Place Riot) provoked some initial resistance.[87] Prior to Herrmann's debut, the *Daily Tribune* explained, New York's social elite debated the wisdom of even allowing such a performance to take place: "The Muses of Irving Place had a meeting on Saturday evening, to consider the propriety of admitting him into their sacred temple."[88]

In the face of such bourgeois grumbling, the Academy's director, Mr. Ullman, quickly issued a series of personal testimonials. "Mr. Herrmann," Ullman argued in one *Daily Tribune* notice, "is not only a great artist, but unquestionably the greatest living in his peculiar art. The undersigned, during his yearly travels in Europe, has seen the performance of Mr. Herrmann at some of the first and most exclusive Opera Houses, drawing immense crowds at opera prices."[89] Herrmann took action, too, putting the material "spoils" of his magical career on display the day before the Academy's curtain went up. "A novel exhibition," the *Times* reported,

is now open to the Public at the establishment of Tiffany & Co., the Broadway jewelers. Closely adjoining the well-known center showcase, which encloses the richest and rarest gems and *articles de luxe* in the way of ornament, on the continent, is now placed another and larger case, containing the *optima spolia* of a ten year campaign in the field of magic. Herrmann, *the* Prestidigitateur, fills this case, and it might, in legal parlance, be denominated the great case of "Herrmann vs. a large party of crowned heads, nobles, artists, and less notorious *dilettanti.*" By the little cards attached to each piece, the Public can see that if Herrmann be indeed Devil, as the honest Hamburghers once thought him, nevertheless Christian and Jew, Emperors, Kings, Dukes, Duchesses, Marquises, Counts, Generals, Dons, Vons, Monsieurs, Scientific Academies, Benevolent Associations, and even—Editors, have paid him substantial tributes of admiration.[90]

This was something like Barnum's Jenny Lind tour of the previous decade: a clever advance promotional campaign based on Continental endorsements and published stories of aristocratic contacts, all designed to facilitate the entry of a major celebrity into an unconventional American venue—sight unseen. Except that this time the social and cultural polarities were reversed: rather than bring an august European artist before a diverse American audience, as Barnum had done with Lind, Ullman was bringing a European popular entertainment with a somewhat déclassé reputation into one of the leading artistic "temples" of the American bourgeoisie.

And just as in 1850, these 1861 promotional efforts worked to perfection. New York's theater-going elite swarmed into the Academy of Music on September 16; it was "an immense attendance—the largest ever congregated at any performance since the Academy was built."[91] "The soirees of the Prestidigitateur, Herrmann," reported the *Herald* a week later, "have created quite a furore. The opening night was a perfect jam, and the audiences since have continued so inconveniently crowded that it has been found necessary to resort to the plan of reserving seats. The success that has attended these performances is unexampled. No professor of the black art that has exhibited here has contrived so to awaken and keep alive public curiosity."[92] The *Times* also took note of this sudden surge of bourgeois passion for sleight of hand:

> Herrmann, the wizard, seems to have more power of attraction in his little magic *baton* than any of our conductors of the late lamented Italian opera. He performed last night and Tuesday before over-crowded houses, and neither rain nor mud prevented the gathering of a fashionable audience in the Temple of the Muses. At 7½ o'clock every seat in front was taken, and we are glad to announce to the public that from

to-day reserved seats will be sold at an extra charge of 25 cents; and also private boxes will be for sale, so as to accommodate people who are accustomed to come later than the *"profanum vulgus."*[93]

The exceptionality of this debut stemmed in part from its odd combination of art form, venue, and audience: a wizard of the black art, performing for those in the Academy's private boxes. What the commentators did not fully realize, however, was that the specific aesthetic choices driving this cultural realignment had been emerging in the major metropolises of Europe since the mid-1840s. Consider, for example, the New York *Times*'s very first review of Herrmann's Academy shows: "Mr. Herrmann [is] unlike any other conjurer in a great many respects. His talent is superior to anything we have ever witnessed here, and his manner is very different to the vulgar pretentiousness and stupid volubility of most wizards. Not the least remarkable thing about this entertainment is that all the tricks are performed without apparatus."[94] Their next review went into greater detail, applauding Herrmann for much the same kinds of reforms that had made Robert-Houdin famous in 1845:

> Conjuring has become one of the fine arts. A certain number of tricks constitute its classics. These have been studied devoutly by Mr. Herrmann, and his illuminations of old passages are in some instances very remarkable and beautiful. Like Goldsmith, he touches to improve. Even the ring business, which one has seen at every fair and booth in the country, becomes a respectable demonstration in his hands. The gun trick, too, assumes a more deadly interest, and, indeed, all the pieces seem different simply because they are done with neatness and without apparently exhausting the theme . . . he is by far the best Wizard we have seen in this country.[95]

Significantly, no New York reporter even mentioned superstition or necromancy in connection to these shows. Instead, what seems to have marked Herrmann's prestidigitation as new at the Academy of Music was its perceived difference from a very different sort of threat—the "vulgar pretentiousness" of most wizards, the old tricks "seen at every fair and booth in the country."

Modern Magic

Like any other fine art, the *Times* noted, Herrmann's Academy routines included a number of classics. Yet these re-presentations of carnival tricks did not elicit charges of pilfering. On the contrary, by refashioning "the ring business from the fair" into something *else*—something more artistic and respectable, something with a new French name—Herrmann seems to have exorcised the specter of carnival jugglery on a leading American stage. And by the end of Herrmann's first week, one reporter even suggested that the Muses of Irving Place were ready to try a little bit of the ring business at home:

> Herrmann, the great Prestidigitator, made his prestidigitatorial debut in New York on Monday evening last . . . and prestidigitated with such dexterity, and with so many prestidigitatorial graces, that we all fell in love with prestidigitation, and went home in the most prestidigitatic state of mind, prepared to make all kinds of prestidigital experiments, and prestidigitate ourselves, if possible, into so many prestidigitators and prestidigitatresses, as if the one end and aim of life was prestidigitatism, and the only science worth studying prestidigitatismatics.[96]

Some Confidence Men You Can Trust

Not surprisingly, each of the leading modernists operating on late nineteenth-century American stages added a few personalized twists to the mix. During the mid-1860s, for example, Robert Heller combined his second-sight routines with virtuoso piano recitals at the former French Theater (585 Broadway, across from Niblo's Gardens), a combination that produced one of the longest solo runs in New York theater history (over 365 shows).[97] Following 1,000 shows at London's Egyptian Hall, Alexander Herrmann carried on his older brother's legacy of American theatrical conquest with a program of impromptu sleight-of-hand feats performed directly in the midst of the audience, an innovative form of *diablerie* that he, too, debuted at the Academy of Music in New York (May 11, 1874). And during the mid-1880s, Harry Kellar became the darling of fashionable theatergoers in Philadelphia (including John L. Sullivan, Edwin Booth, and Mark Twain) for his on-stage exposés of spiritualist séance tricks, performing for

323 consecutive nights at the old Masonic Hall before moving on to set attendance records in New York, Cincinnati, and Chicago.[98]

Underlying these personalized touches, however, was a relatively consistent and cohesive program of reform. Following Robert-Houdin's lead, every major conjuring star performed in evening clothes, engaged in polite stage patter, bragged about his fashionable sets, and published at least one memoir attesting to all of these things.[99] In tandem with the larger project of bourgeois professionalism, the performers referred to themselves by new, more rarified terms (prestidigitator), explicated their craft with abstract principles and scientific frameworks (Robert-Houdin's published blueprint for regeneration), and founded a national professional organization (the Society of American Magicians).[100] And each and every conjuring star from these years exposed something or someone on stage, whether his own trickery, a demonized carnival mountebank of the past, or a spiritualist medium of the present. One might even say that modern magic was ultimately nothing but a collection of reforms, the qualifying adjective serving as a multivalent indicator that the man on stage was now operating on the right side of the aesthetic, social, and historical thresholds that Robert-Houdin had begun to put in place in 1845.

Yet there was always something a little bit slippery about this reform program. These reformers, after all, were not the usual Gilded Age suspects (Protestant clergymen, temperance leaders, or highbrow art critics), but a cadre of professional tricksters who, even in their most refined moments, were still described by the contemporary press as practitioners of a "black art." And their artistry was never purely a matter of elegant clothes, Tiffany's showcases, and uncluttered stage sets. Indeed, at the very core of this reform program was much the same project that had guided the sleight-of-hand business for centuries: a desire to trick the Muses of Irving Place blind—and to be applauded heartily for doing so. All in all, this was one of the more paradoxical enterprises in late nineteenth-century American popular culture: a reform movement which simultaneously traded in respectability and fraud, scientific principles and overt deception, ritualized exposé and aesthetic cover-ups. This modern magic was so thoroughly divested of charlatanism that it had earned the right to enter the Academy of Music and teach its fashionable audiences how to become prestidigitators and prestidigitatresses themselves.

What makes this cultural phenomenon even more paradoxical are the larger events that were transpiring outside America's urban theaters during the very same years. Just when Robert-Houdin was first receiving widespread attention for his conjuring reforms, a second type of modern illusionist began to capture the attention of the urban press—the so-called confidence man. The historical parallels here are striking. The specific term "confidence man" first appeared in 1849 (one year after Robert-Houdin's published claims of modern miracles in London) to describe the criminal activities of William Thomson, a New York swindler of genteel appearance who talked his victims out of their pocket watches. But much like the modern magician, this novel figure from the late 1840s quickly evolved into a far broader cultural categorization, one used to reference a variety of urban deviants whose feats of deception involved some combination of false appearances and verbal manipulations.[101]

The confidence man appeared frequently in advice manuals and etiquette books as a corrupter of character, a distinctly new middle-class species of urban criminal who threatened to steer the large numbers of unsupervised young men then moving to America's industrial centers away from traditional republican values.[102] The confidence man also routinely appeared in city guidebooks, often serving as a troubling literary personification of urban confusion. Much like the metropolis itself, in fact, what made confidence criminals particularly unsettling was their ability to defy visual interpretation, to maintain an impenetrable facade which gave no clue about the actual person or criminal agenda behind the misleading appearances.[103] These concerns about the opacity of urban things were themselves historically specific, a product of both the most rapid period of urbanization in American history and the radical restructuring of the older socio-economic orders that such rapid urbanization provoked.[104] As one popular guidebook explained, simply knowing the patterns and techniques of criminal deception in the new metropolis hardly guaranteed one's safety:

> There are scores of men and women whose appearance in the streets give no hint of their real character. Deception is their business, and they study its arts carefully. . . . Nearly all criminals lead double lives. Strange as it may appear, it is a fact that some of the most unscrupulous rascals who ever cracked a safe or turned out a counterfeit were at home model husbands and fathers. In a great many cases wives have aided their guilty partners in their villainy, and the children, too, have taken a hand in it.[105]

Like our own drive-by shootings and car-jackings, this was a type of crime that seemed to have reached such epidemic proportions that it required a completely new name, one designed to distinguish it from the countless forms of criminal fraud that had been a part of urban life for centuries. Similar to our world, too, was the relentless frequency with which the mid-century press reported confidence crimes. During the first week of Carl Herrmann's triumphant debut, for example, New York readers were bombarded almost daily with newspaper stories about urban swindlers: two young counterfeiters who passed bogus three-dollar notes on the Hampton Bank; a confidence man who cashed a $100 check from the payroll of a nonexistent company; a Bowery forger who used fabricated business records to purchase hardware for a store where he no longer worked; a card sharp whose partner removed the pocket watch of a Grand Street resident while the latter was absorbed in the game—the list went on and on.[106] New York police records suggest, moreover, that there was nothing especially unusual about these particular crimes, or this particular week of newspaper reporting. Although the scams went by a wide variety of names, the general pattern of imposture was clear: one out of every ten professional criminals prosecuted in New York City during the 1860s was some kind of confidence man.[107]

The challenge to Herrmann and his colleagues was how to position themselves as honest, upstanding illusionists rather than criminal impostors, to capitalize upon this intense public concern about urban deception without being condemned as part of the problem. To some extent, it was similar to the challenge of removing the stigma of the carnival juggler, but in this case the stakes were a bit higher, the risks of failure a bit more serious. Whereas perceptions of vulgar jugglery might produce empty seats in the boxes, suspicion of complicity with the confidence criminals working outside of the theater could make the magician himself a target, rather than an agent, of bourgeois reform.

It makes a great deal of sense, therefore, that criminal detection and exposé were central themes in the literary productions of the modern magician. Once again, Robert-Houdin was the major innovator here, generating a wide range of behind-the-scenes tales of his crime-fighting efforts during the late 1850s and 1860s. In *Confidences,* he tells the story of a promenade through the cafés of Paris in search of amateur sleight-of-hand talents. Soon he comes upon D——, a "young man of prepossessing appearance and very elegantly dressed, while his manners evidenced the thorough gentleman." But this image was misleading. After a "great many glasses of Bordeaux," D—— confesses quite openly to working as a professional card sharp in the bourgeois resorts of Paris: "When I am in society I am a young man of good family, and, like all young men, play. The only difference is, I have my own way of playing, which is not that of all the world, but it seems it is not bad, because it often renders chances favorable."[108]

Robert-Houdin was no doubt aware that such a story would provoke a tremor of moral anxiety among his bourgeois readers.[109] And in the very next sentences he seeks to allay these concerns, dutifully recording his own feelings of guilt about what he had just witnessed: "At length my Greek left me, and as soon as he was gone the remembrance of his confession sent the blood to my cheeks. I was as ashamed of myself as if I had been his accomplice." Nevertheless, Robert-Houdin confesses to being deeply impressed by the "finesse and perfection" of the young man's swindling: "I . . . reproached myself severely for the admiration I could not restrain, and the compliments it exhorted from me."[110] Over time, a complex pattern of ambivalence emerges: as a magician Robert-Houdin acknowledges the similarity between his own brand of illusionism and that of his criminal tutor's, and even allows for a momentary rush of admiration, yet for precisely those reasons he feels the need to engage in gestures of contrition and containment.

The opportunity for just such a gesture comes in 1849, when "a magistrate belonging to the police office of the Seine" asks Robert-Houdin "to examine and verify one hundred and fifty packs of cards, seized in the possession of a man whose antecedents were far from being as unblemished as his cards. The latter, indeed, were perfectly white, and this peculiarity had hitherto foiled the most minute investigation."[111] Over the next fortnight Robert-Houdin works diligently at detection, until finally:

> I fancied I noticed a pale spot on the glistening back of these cards, and near one of the corners. I stepped forward, and it disappeared, but, strangely enough, it reappeared as I fell back. "What a magnificent dodge!" I exclaimed, in my enthusiasm. "I have it: that is a distinguishing mark." And following a certain principle which D—— had explained to me, I assured myself that all the cards possessed a mark, which, according to its position, indicated the value and color.[112]

This story does not square easily with our conventional portrait of the nineteenth-century bourgeoisie and its moral relationship to urban crime.[113] To be sure, Robert-Houdin ultimately comes down on the right side of the law here, but only after taking his bourgeois readers through lengthy tales of social intimacy with the other side: tales which include hours of jovial conversation and wine drinking with a man he describes as a professional swindler; more than a few compliments directed at the swindler's skills ("What a magnificent dodge!"); and even a friendly footnote crediting the object of bourgeois reform with helping to solve the crime ("and following a certain principle which D—— had explained to me"). The separation of reform and deviance becomes even narrower in the next few pages, as Robert-Houdin eagerly demonstrates a variety of card-marking schemes, complete with diagrams to illustrate the precise techniques. Not surprisingly, these lessons are filled with moral qualifications, such as

Robert-Houdin's confession that "for the last quarter of an hour I have been burning with a desire to explain to my readers a most interesting process, but I am restrained by the fear that this ingenious swindling may facilitate false play." In the end, though, he goes ahead and explains the process anyway, on the grounds "that to avoid a danger, it must be known. Hence, if every player were initiated into the stratagems of the card swindlers, the latter would find it impossible to employ them."[114]

Over the next decade, this somewhat improbable program of reform through assimilation, detection, and exposé expanded into one of the major themes of modern magic. Five years later, for example, Robert-Houdin published *The Sharper Detected and Exposed,* an entire volume of tricks and impostures from the urban underworld—which, he carefully assured his readers, "are not the invention of my own brain."[115] Carl Herrmann got into this literary line, too, publishing a *Prestidigitatorial Collection of Humorous and Practical Tricks* for distribution at his Academy of Music shows, one of which detailed the magician's public victory against (and exposure of) an infamous French swindler at the gaming table.[116] As the pamphlet proudly concluded, the "spoils" went directly to a local hospital, "donated" by Herrmann in the name of the foiled card sharper.

The most ingenious practitioners of this sort of cultural reversal, however, were Alexander Herrmann and Harry Kellar, the acknowledged American leaders of modern magic during the 1880s and 1890s. Herrmann the Younger, as he was sometimes called, began his training in *les arts magiques* at an early age. Born February 11, 1843, in Paris, this self-described prestidigitatorial prodigy was doing tricks by the age of eight.[117] A decade later he entered the University of Vienna and completed much of his coursework, but before finishing his degree decided to devote himself to a magical career, with his first full-time job as Carl's assistant during the world tour which stopped at the Academy of Music in 1861. In 1869, when Carl returned to New York on his farewell campaign, he introduced Alexander to American audiences as his successor, the rightful heir to the Herrmann family conjuring dynasty.[118] Over the next quarter century,

An autographed publicity photo for the second "Herrmann the Great," Alexander, from the 1880s or early 1890s.

Alexander Herrmann and his wife Adelaide (who often served as his on-stage assistant) executed the most successful run in American magic prior to Houdini, achieving bookings at the Metropolitan Opera; publishing articles in high-toned journals such as the *North American Review, Scientific American,* and *Cosmopolitan;* and gaining a vast collection of material rewards, such as the Herrmann family mansion and yacht on Long Island.[119]

Harry Kellar's rise to prestidigitatorial stardom took a bit longer and lacked much of the glamour of his European rival. Born in 1849 to

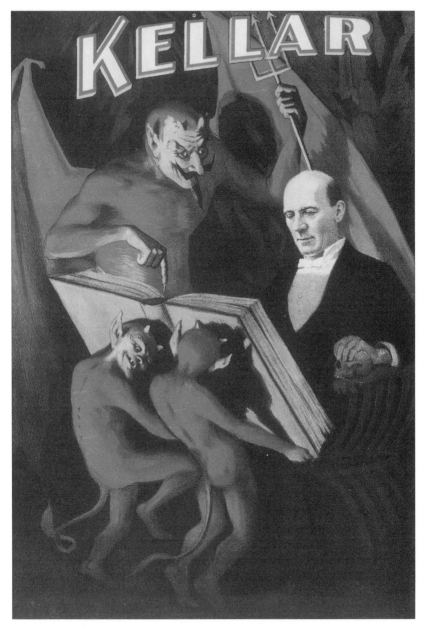

Harry Kellar training in the "black art," as shown in this 1894 poster by the
Strobridge Lithograph Company.

German immigrants, Harry (or Heinrich, as he was then known) quickly grew tired of life in Erie, Pennsylvania, and ran away on a freight train. As a teenager, he worked a series of odd jobs, first at a Cleveland dry-goods store and then selling newspapers on the streets of New York City. After being supported briefly by a British clergyman, Kellar ran off again, this time to pursue a career in show business. His training during these years included short stints with two well-known, mid-century magic performers, the Fakir of Eva and John Henry Anderson, Jr., as well as a longer apprenticeship with the Davenport Brothers, a highly successful pair of spiritualist mediums from Buffalo, famous for their "cabinet manifestations" on stage. By the early 1870s, Kellar had acquired enough capital and expertise to break into stage magic as a theatrical headliner and began a series of almost continuous world tours which eventually made him an international celebrity. When his star finally rose in this country during the mid-1880s, many observers (including a young Houdini) pronounced Kellar the most talented stage magician of his time.[120]

In almost every way, these two performers exemplified the persona of the modern magician first crafted by Robert-Houdin: well-dressed, well-mannered, and well-skilled in the arts of exposé.[121] Yet Herrmann and Kellar also pushed these conventions in new directions. During the 1880s, for example, both magicians created public furors by slipping into crowded urban areas—city squares, open-air markets, and elevated trains—and doing improvisations with unsuspecting strangers. In one particularly successful version of this performance strategy, Kellar ventured into New York's Washington Market and began palming some of the small items on display. A New York *Evening Sun* reporter described the scene in wonderful detail:

> Suddenly the magician turned to a tall young man with a red mustache who stood in the crowd, and, seizing him by the coat exclaimed "Look here, my man; you shouldn't do a thing like that." Before he had time to answer Kellar had pulled from the young man's pocket a large carrot. "You're a pretty fellow to be taking the old lady's carrots," exclaimed Kellar, addressing the crowd. "He says he didn't take it, and his pockets are full of vegetables now." And without more ado the conjurer grabbed him

again and proceeded to relieve him of a large bunch of turnips, which were in the man's inside pocket. This made the young man more angry than ever, and he was just about to hit Kellar when the latter grabbed the man's hat and lifted it from his head. Then the crowd hooted and yelled with delight, for as soon as the young man's hat was lifted there rolled from the inside of it some fifteen or twenty large white potatoes. This was too much for the young man. He gave Kellar one look of horrified wonder and fled in dismay. "It's Kellar, the magician!" some one shouted, and the news spread with lightning rapidity. The crowd increased until several hundred people had gathered.[122]

With this public identification, the moral status of Kellar's performance started to come more clearly into focus, shifting from an unsettling scene of apparent criminality to a more self-conscious, open-air demonstration of noncriminal conjuring skills. But Kellar's "circus," as the *Evening Sun* article described it, was far from finished. After "having fun" with a number of other vendors and patrons at the market, he turned to a policeman in the vicinity:

> "Officer," cried Kellar . . . "this place is full of thieves. They are stealing right and left." "Oh, I guess it's all right, Mr. Kellar," said the policeman with a grin. "What!" exclaimed Kellar. "Are you in league with them, too?" and he grabbed the policeman's coat, quickly unbuttoned it, and before the officer could interfere had pulled a live, cackling, fluttering chicken from the policeman's breast. . . . The officer jumped about four feet, got red, looked foolish, and backed away. . . . At the Washington and Vesey street entrance the crowd was so great that they broke the doors from their hinges and hurled them to the pavement. It resembled a riot. During the struggle to get out Kellar neatly picked a man's pocket and secured an old-fashioned silver watch and chain. A minute later he pulled the watch from a young woman's bosom and held it aloft.

At this point, the audience at Washington Market was becoming so frenzied that Kellar and his party were forced to use ventriloquist impressions of "a crying child and a squealing pig" to clear a path towards the exit. Once through the doors, they "hurried away with several hundred of the crowd at their heels. It wasn't until they boarded an uptown elevated train that they were left alone."[123]

Herrmann chose a busy corner of Union Square for a similar performance, provoking his own arrest by lifting pocket watches in the clear view of a pair of bystanders, who promptly called for the aid of a nearby police officer. After proceeding to police headquarters with a curious pack of onlookers in tow, the still unidentified magician confronted his accusers:

> "I will show the officer that these men are not what they pretend to be. Where is your badge officer?" The policeman looked down at his coat, and sure enough his badge was gone. He turned pale, for it is a serious thing for a policeman to lose his badge. "I will tell you, officer," went on Herrmann. "This man who accuses me stole your badge. I saw him take it." "You're a liar!" promptly exclaimed the complainant, but Herrmann only smiled and said, "Search him and see." The policeman didn't have to search the youth. He began rummaging his own pockets and pretty soon, with a look of absolute amazement on his face, he hauled out the badge. "You see," said Herrmann; "I told you so. And now, officer, see what else is gone. A man who would steal a badge would take anything." Holding on to the young man with one hand, the policeman began searching his pockets with the other. Suddenly he hit himself over the hip and exclaimed: "My pistol's gone!" "I suspected it," said Herrmann; "the other fellow's got that I'll bet."

Herrmann, it almost goes without saying, had already planted the pistol on this "other fellow," who by now was looking for the quickest way out of the station house. The prestidigitator saved his most remarkable tricks for the unsuspecting police officer in charge: "'Now search yourself,' said Herrmann, and when he insisted the officer did so, and found the watch in his inside coat pocket. 'You see, sir,' exclaimed Herrmann, 'I am the only honest man among them all'."[124]

On a very basic level, these dazzling performances served as clever (and entirely free) forms of urban advertising. And both Herrmann and Kellar seem to have repeated them on numerous occasions. The New York *Sun*, in fact, described the events at Union Square as "a favorite game with Herrmann," one which he "has time and again played . . . on the bluecoats in this city."[125] Beyond their obvious utility as clever publicity stunts, though, these sorties outside the theater also seem to have been designed with a more fundamental, self-representational goal in mind. By assimilating the criminal practices of urban thieves and turning them into a series of practical jokes, Herrmann and Kellar were constructing an alternative narrative to the stories of confidence men, in which "honest" tricksters emerged as the masters rather than the victims of deception in the streets. While sleight-of-hand artists had performed similar palming tricks for centuries, these late nineteenth-century representations took on powerfully new meanings amidst the sensory chaos of Washington Market or Union Square. In precisely the sorts of places where one expected to find pickpockets, swindlers, and confidence men at work, Herrmann and Kellar seemed to surpass the skills of the urban criminals whom they impersonated. They could outsmart their accusers and even baffle the cops. And unlike the criminal impostors who populated the Rogues' Gallery, Herrmann and Kellar always got away with it.

Of course, to speak of "getting away with something" here is also to acknowledge the considerable extent to which Herrmann and Kellar were engaging in deliberate acts of cultural transgression. In fact, one might argue that we have long since moved beyond anything even vaguely resembling criminal exposé or bourgeois reform. Certainly, the proud new owner of the carrots, turnips, and potatoes at Washington Market or the young man with the policeman's pistol in his pocket would have found it difficult to conceive of Herrmann and Kellar as "honest men." The very suggestion of honesty in this context was now nothing more than parody—a parody which actively undermined any lingering hopes that semiotic stability and urban social order might be maintained. The magicians' transgressive acts, moreover, seem to have produced their fair share of nonimaginary, volatile reactions. The crowd which broke down the doors of Washington Market and hurled them to the pavement, for example, was not simply engaging in an act of playful simulation. This was a form of performance art so close to the criminal source that it threatened to spill across the boundary separating signifier and signified. The scene, as the *Evening Sun* reporter noted, "resembled a riot."

In the end, though, the distinction between resemblance and the real thing made all the difference. The larger point of this *Evening Sun* article, after all, was not so much to tell the story of a real criminal or a full-fledged riot, but to record the remarkable performance of a magician who had so skillfully impersonated a swindler that his urban audience approached (but did not quite cross) the very threshold of riotous behavior. At Union Square, too, the newspaper reporter made it clear that the magician had flirted with but had not actually performed a criminal act. At the conclusion of the story, the policeman in charge sorts out the semiotic confusion:

> "I see," said the sergeant, who had witnessed the searching without comment, "and I'd like your name."
> "Herrmann, Alexander Herrmann," said the magician. I'm an honest performer, and . . ."
> "Yes, I know," interrupted the sergeant. "You did this pretty well, Mr. Herrmann, but in the future you'd better not joke with policemen. You can go."

With this bottom-line statement on the moral limits of practical joking we have come full circle from Robert-Houdin's efforts to cast the illusionist in the role of urban crime fighter. This is just about as far as the modern magician could venture in the direction of the confidence man without ending up in a jail cell himself! But that also seems to have been much the point of the entire exercise: to demonstrate in an amusing, almost allegorical way what particular forms of deception were—and were not—morally tenable in the larger society. Like the symbolic inversions of so many trickster figures before them, Kellar's and Herrmann's sleight-of-hand performances in the streets of New York City were intentionally ambiguous in their social meanings, serving both as dazzling imitations of the confidence man's mastery ("You did this pretty well, Mr. Herrmann") and as a powerful warning about the threshold of deviance ("but in the future you'd better not joke with policemen").

We are left, then, with a style of sleight of hand just as complex and ambiguous in its broader historical legacies as the supernatural forms of magic that persisted in the face of Enlightenment. While the modern magician assumed the unprecedented position of upwardly mobile, fully respectable reformer, this reform program ultimately collapsed back into itself, placing middle-class magic fans in the odd position of applauding the tricks of pickpockets and laughing at the police. That was the uneasy balance struck by modern magic: a cultural form which made the carnival juggler's tricks respectable, safe, and scientific enough for an enlightened bourgeoisie, but which also got the bourgeoisie in on the confidence game.

5

Queer Art Illusions

⊷⊨◉ ◉⊨⊷

In a footnote to one of his most familiar essays, Walter Benjamin makes an intriguing point about the relation between nineteenth-century cities, paintings, and viewers:

> The daily sight of a lively crowd may once have constituted a spectacle to which one's eyes had to adapt first. On the basis of this supposition, one may assume that once the eyes had mastered this task they welcomed opportunities to test their newly acquired faculties. This would mean that the technique of Impressionist painting, whereby the picture is garnered in a riot of dabs of color, would be a reflection of experiences with which the eyes of a big-city dweller have become familiar.[1]

This passage contains a number of ideas that have become conventional wisdom in recent studies of modern visual culture: the notion that vision itself—both as lived experience and as a theoretical construct—changed dramatically over the course of the nineteenth century; that these changes in the conventional techniques, models, and theories of vision were directly related to the disorienting upheaval of urbanization; and that Impressionism, the style of painting most frequently associated with modern urban life, reflected this process of visual adaptation in a variety of ways. The most interesting feature of Benjamin's footnote, however, is not so much its constituent parts, but the fascinating way he puts them all together. At the heart of the passage is the notion of testing one's eyes, something that Benjamin suggests took place as nineteenth-century urbanites slowly mastered the rush of the crowd and applied their newly acquired faculties to other similar tasks in the exhibition hall.

Benjamin rarely dwelled on his own provocative ideas. In the next line, he describes this one as a "hypothesis" that might be applied to the works of Monet—and then moves on to other artifacts and interpretations.[2] Yet this line of analysis seems ripe for broader historical exploration, particularly in a study of artful deception covering the very same years. Did certain late nineteenth-century exhibitions serve as "welcome opportunities" to test urban visual faculties already acquired? Or was the exhibition room itself an arduous task, one which exposed viewers to the same sorts of perceptual "shocks and collisions" that Benjamin defined as fundamental to modern urban experience?[3] These questions diverge somewhat from the recent groundbreaking scholarship on the history of visuality, in that they make the lived experiences of the observer their focal point, rather than the theories of visual experience developed by leading intellectuals and artists.[4] They also lead directly to an American form of artful deception that has received little attention in this scholarly discourse: the *trompe l'oeil* still life paintings produced by William M. Harnett and his followers between 1870 and 1900—a commercially successful, but critically ridiculed aesthetic phenomenon whose reception remains somewhat mixed even today.

Initially, at least, these paintings seem an improbable vehicle for exploring Benjamin's hypothesis. Unlike the French Impressionists, Harnett and his followers held no independent group exhibitions to challenge the authority of a powerful academy system and left behind no programmatic statements about innovative perceptual theories they were attempting to represent in their work. On the contrary, the rapid proliferation of *trompe l'oeil* painting that took place during the Gilded Age seems almost haphazard. As far as we know, William Harnett simply made a decision at some point during the early 1870s—entirely on his own, and against the advice of his teachers at the fine arts academies—to adopt *trompe l'oeil* painting as his primary mode of artistic expression. And within about a decade, the illusionism practiced by Harnett and his followers began to spark popular furors around the country, a spontaneous uproar by anonymous urban crowds in upscale barrooms, industrial expositions, and retail stores. In retrospect, these popular furors appear to have emerged so haphazardly and spontaneously that they seem almost coincidental to the artists' professional development, an amusing diversion from their largely unsuccessful attempts to rise within the contemporary academic establishment.

Unlike the works of Monet and the Impressionists, too, the *trompe l'oeil* paintings produced by Harnett and his colleagues demonstrate no self-conscious rupture with aesthetic precedent in the Western tradition. Indeed, the very idea of describing *trompe l'oeil* as a late nineteenth-century style is complicated, for this category of painting has a lineage that stretches back for centuries—back to the classical contest of artistic skill in verisimilitude described by Pliny. With this long illusionistic tradition in mind, many early studies of Harnett's work emphasized its resemblance to the well-known *trompe l'oeil* current running through seventeenth-century Dutch still life painting, for example, or the handful of *trompe l'oeil* canvases produced by Charles Willson Peale and his son Raphaelle in Philadelphia during the Early National Period.[5]

Such efforts to connect late nineteenth-century *trompe l'oeil* painting to more familiar, canonical precedents contributed to the rising status of Harnett and his followers during the 1990s and paved the way for a series of major museum retrospectives (for example, the 1992 retrospective of Harnett's work at the Metropolitan Museum of Art in New York). Yet by insisting on a theory of aesthetic "retrogression," these early studies also created a somewhat anachronistic historical identity for late nineteenth-century *trompe l'oeil* painting, as well as the impression that Harnett and his followers were always a little out of synch with the larger momentum of modernization.[6] As practitioners of an "old style" during a period of modernist rupture, Harnett and his colleagues have often appeared to represent the last gasp of the Renaissance tradition, a final attempt to resist modernism's epochal movement towards abstraction by intensifying the experience of mimesis.[7]

This chapter offers a very different picture of the historical development and ideological functions of late nineteenth-century *trompe l'oeil* painting.[8] First, it suggests that the illusionistic canvases produced by Harnett and his followers were part of a well-established tradition of (and market for) artful deception in the realm of popular culture; or, at the very least, that many of the artists and their viewers thought of *trompe l'oeil* painting in this way. It also suggests that the public furors surrounding these paintings can only be understood in relation to their disorienting urban contexts: a cycle of visual confusion, adaptation, and mastery similar to the testing scenario first imagined by Benjamin. Ultimately, though, it suggests that any sense of mastery provided by this painterly illusionism was tenuous and ephemeral at best. Indeed, if there was a larger visual cultural lesson of these "tests" for their American audiences, it was much the same lesson that the Impressionists were teaching in Paris: in the dizzying world of the new metropolis, perceptual certainty itself was an illusion.

Harnett's Painting and
Its Popular Cultural Context

As art historians have often noted, one of the distinctive characteristics of *trompe l'oeil* painting—one of the things that sets it apart from the much larger category of still life—is that its eye-fooling images aggressively deny the presence of the artist's hand.[9] Jean Baudrillard makes this point more emphatically, describing *trompe l'oeil* as a kind of anti-painting.[10] For him, *trompe l'oeil* is characterized by its absences: an absence of horizon, an absence of nature, an absence of natural light, an absence of a conventional vanishing point, and an absence of narrative—in short, an absence of almost all of the basic conventions of artistic representation. "Pure *trompe l'oeil* art," he argues, eliminates the discourse of painting. It is an art that largely forgets the grand themes and works against the "whole representative space elaborated by the Renaissance."[11]

In the case of late nineteenth-century American *trompe l'oeil* painting, these figurative absences are accompanied by a more literal absence of historical information about the artists' careers. "The truth," Nicolai Cikovsky, Jr. notes, "is, quite simply, that we do not know exactly what inspired William Michael Harnett to become a still-life painter or what artistic issues and experiences determined the particular type of painter he became."[12] Much the same can be said about Harnett's followers—John Haberle, J. D. Chalfant, Richard LaBarre Goodwin, N. A. Brooks, Victor Dubreuil, and George Platt—who enjoyed brief but intense moments of artistic celebrity before fading into historical obscurity.[13] Because most of their personal papers and studio effects were lost long ago, we have very few extra-pictorial records of where these artists first encountered *trompe l'oeil* as an aesthetic idea, why they found it worth pursuing, or how they responded to rejection by the leading academic critics of their day.

What remains is a void of artistic intention on arguably the most perplexing question in the entire history of this phenomenon: why, at a time when illusionistic still life painting was relegated to the lowest rung in the academy system's hierarchy of styles, did these academically trained oil painters nevertheless pursue *trompe l'oeil* as the central enterprise of their careers? What sort of professional motivation or logic was driving this explosion of image-making—a visual cultural phenomenon which involved well over a dozen different oil painters, a wide variety of American cities, and hundreds of eye-fooling canvases, all seemingly engaged in an exercise in collective professional suicide?[14]

Puzzling here, too, is that, unlike many of their more affluent academically trained peers, none of the painters who pursued *trompe l'oeil* as their professional calling card could afford to flout the academy's aesthetic mandates.[15] Consider, for example, Harnett's only recorded press interview, a conversation which seems to have taken place some time in the late 1880s and appeared in the short-lived New York *News*. At the time of the interview, Harnett had established himself as an artist of considerable public renown, and his *trompe l'oeil* marvels routinely captivated the urban middle-class crowds in the venues where they appeared. Yet he sounds almost apologetic about his aesthetic choices and subsequent commercial success, pointing to indigence as the driving force behind his career:

> My father died in Philadelphia when I was a little boy, and I was obliged to do something to help support my mother and the children. My first work was selling newspapers. After that I was an errand boy. I did not have much time to practice art, and consequently sometimes used the time in school that belonged to other duties. In telling you how I paint pictures from still life models, it would be well for me to give you in brief a sketch of my early career in art, for the trials and hardships that I underwent were the sole reasons for my taking up that line of art work.[16]

Harnett is unequivocal here about the cause-and-effect relationship between his early poverty and his decision to take up *trompe l'oeil* still life painting. Yet he never really explains why it looked like a way out of poverty. Institutional records show that he studied at three of the leading artistic academies in the United States—the Pennsylvania Academy of the Fine Arts, the National Academy of Design, and the Cooper Union—always in the night program. And this pattern of evening study grew out of his need to maintain a series of day jobs (for example, as an engraver). As he attempted to spend more time painting during the mid-1870s, the financial pressures became increasingly severe: "I devoted more than half my days and evenings to my art studies, only working at my trade enough to supply me with money for clothes, food, shelter, paint, and canvas. Consequently, I had not money to spare. This very poverty led to my taking up the line of painting that I have followed for the past 15 years."[17]

While Harnett's early poverty was most likely real, some aspects of this rags-to-riches story do not quite add up. Certainly, Harnett's comment about pursuing still life painting because he could not "afford to hire models as the other students did" seems a bit strange as an explanation of his long-term aesthetic choices. By the time of the *News* interview, Harnett was one of America's more prosperous and well-known oil painters. And his client list included a number of wealthy businessmen, including Thomas Walker (a Minneapolis lumber magnate), George Hulings (a leading Philadelphia retailer), Theodore Stewart (who owned businessmen's saloons in lower Manhattan), and most of the upper management ranks of the dry-goods industry.[18] But fame and prosperity did not alter Harnett's aesthetic direction—except perhaps to convince him of the wisdom of his original choice. From his very first postgraduate efforts of the mid-1870s right up until his death from rheumatism in 1892, he painted virtually nothing but *trompe l'oeil* still life pictures.

Another issue that needs to be reckoned with is the somewhat puzzling link the *News* interview implies between *trompe l'oeil* painting and market success. Regardless of whether indigence dictated his initial choice of models, Harnett must have been aware that continuing to work in this particular artistic mode made for a perilous career decision, especially for an up-and-coming oil painter who lacked both money and friends in high places. Precisely because he had trained at the leading programs, Harnett knew exactly what the academy thought of *trompe l'oeil* still life painting: that it was a low genre suitable for occasional training exercises in the studio, but not worthy of academic artists in a public forum. And if Harnett had not fully absorbed this message in his evening classes, one of the leading academic critics of the day, Clarence Cook, was all too happy to deliver it in the first major newspaper review of the young artist's work at the National Academy of Design.

This 1879 review from the New York *Daily Tribune* expressed the indignation (very much like the overheated journalistic attacks against the Impressionists' Parisian Salon entries around the same time) of a high cultural gatekeeper coming into contact with an artistic work he perceived as so obviously vulgar and threatening that it must be repressed immediately.[19] The work in question—Harnett's *The Social*

William M. Harnett, *The Social Club* (1879), the painting that horrified critic Clarence Cook at the National Academy of Design.

Club—was a small still life study (13 by 20 inches) of some pipes and matches, with relatively little overt illusionism. Yet it caught Clarence Cook's attention almost immediately among hundreds of entries at the National Academy. Following a brief note of praise directed towards John Singer Sargent, the venerable critic berated, in a four-paragraph outburst, "the many who stop and look with delight" at Harnett's canvas.[20]

"Last year," Cook begins, "Mr. William M. Harnett had several pictures in the exhibition of the same general character as this *Social Club,* and they attracted the attention that is always given to curiosities, to works in which the skill of the human hand is ostentatiously displayed working in deceptive imitation of Nature." Cook's phrase "general character" here is instructive. In addition to characterizing Harnett's poor choice of aesthetic mode and subject matter (*trompe l'oeil* still life), it seems to refer to a certain type of undistinguished urban middle-class viewer and a particularly unrefined mode of viewership ("the attention that is always given to curiosities"). To correct these offenses, Cook proceeds to offer a short "essay on this subject of imitative art":

> it could be shown by a score of examples culled from old books, from Pliny down to Vasari, that even in the ages we call the best this attempt to deceive the senses has been reckoned one of the legitimate aims of art. But it is equally true that all the greatest artists—even Duerer and Holbein—have known how to keep this imitative skill in its true place, as servant not as master, as a means or adjunct, not as an end, while the very greatest names of all in the list of men of genius never attempted imitation at all . . . there still remains a little dignity of purpose attaching to flower-pieces, fruit-pieces, game-pieces, and the like, and great painters, among them Vollon in our own time, have occasionally wreaked their superfluous strength and sportive leisure on painting pots and pans so sublimely as almost to make us ashamed of our principles. But we must remember that this is the play of good painters, never their serious employment; and the exquisite works of a Blaise Desgoffe, a Steinheil or a Benedictus ought not to make us forget that their pictures are to true art what a catch or glee is to true music.[21]

"Imitative work," Cook concluded, "is not really so difficult as it seems to the layman, and though there are degrees of it, yet when we come down to works like this of Mr. Harnett, it is evident that only time and industry are necessary to the indefinite multiplication of them. There are sign-painters in this city of ours—and in all great cities today—who have only to be discontented with their honest calling to aim at the name of artist, to rival Mr. Harnett."[22]

Harnett's interview with the New York *News* and Cook's New York *Daily Tribune* review have become familiar documents in the historical scholarship—almost too much so. Yet there is a hint of an untold story here—another way of thinking about the emergence of late nineteenth-century *trompe l'oeil* painting—that only becomes fully apparent when we read these two documents in tandem, and with a broader conception of the aesthetic choices and career paths open to academic painters during these years. It is a story, moreover, that helps to explain the odd tone of embarrassment and backward economic logic that dominates Harnett's lone public statement on his career.

Perhaps Harnett's improbable claim that poverty drove him to become a *trompe l'oeil* painter came from precisely the same ideological place as Cook's critical disgust at witnessing the delighted crowd standing before *The Social Club*. That is to say, perhaps both Harnett and Cook were fully aware that *The Social Club* represented a violation: not merely of the National Academy's stated aesthetic preferences, but also of the Academy's entire system of exhibitions, critical evaluation, and possibilities for patronage. Harnett, after all, must have known that a potentially lucrative market for illusionism existed somewhere in American culture during the mid-1870s. Otherwise, his decision to pursue *trompe l'oeil* painting at this critical juncture in his career would have led only in one sad direction, to more (and more desperate) levels of poverty. But Harnett also must have known what Cook knew, as the latter walked through the halls of the National Academy in 1879: namely, that the conventional place to experience *trompe l'oeil* was outside of the National Academy's hallowed halls, in the less rarified world of curiosities.

It is useful here to return to the particular form of curiosity viewership that Barnum had developed a few years earlier. Until very recently, Barnum has functioned as a somewhat shadowy presence in studies of Harnett: he lurks in the background as the century's best-known trickster, but the actual mechanics of his trickery (and their specific relationship to *trompe l'oeil* painting) are rarely explained. Paul Staiti has offered the richest analysis of this relationship, arguing that Harnett benefited from the popular cultural market built by Barnum (urban middle-class amusement centers) as well as the showman's distinctive recipe for middle-class trickery, which "depended upon getting people to think, and talk, and become curious and excited over and about the 'rare spectacle.' "[23] Staiti, in short, acknowledges precisely what Cook acknowledged (at least metaphorically) in his review: that Harnett's paintings shared both an aesthetic resemblance and a particular audience with curiosity viewership.

This argument represents a significant advance on earlier studies, which simply described Harnett as the P. T. Barnum of American painting. But Staiti's provocative analysis can be pushed even further.

As art historians have long noted, the overriding visual theme which drove Harnett's *trompe l'oeil*—well-worn hunting gear, scratched musical instruments, rusted horseshoes, weathered books, faded paper currency, torn letters, and so forth—was the mark of age.[24] Harnett himself explained to the New York *News* that this recurring pattern of battered and bruised still life subjects was not accidental: "To find a subject that paints well is not an easy task. As a rule, new things do not paint well. . . . I want my models to have the mellowing effect of age."[25]

Barnum employed a similar "effect" for his most successful exhibitory humbugs. In fact, it was a series of promotional claims about old things—wrinkled skin and shriveled hands, distant memories about raising little George in Virginia, a visibly worn bill of sale signed by Augustine Washington—that launched his show business career in 1835. Similarly, much of the appeal the Feejee Mermaid had for the young showman resided in its instantly recognizable marks of wear-and-tear. Barnum liked the fact that the Mermaid was a gnarled and somewhat scruffy object that might have actually spent some extended time in the Pacific before being transported thousands of miles by anonymous sea captains and roughly handled by a wide assortment of naturalists and showmen. In Barnum's brand of deception, the length of the accession record and the fascination of the curiosity went hand in hand—the longer the trail to the exhibition room, the more plausible the humbug.

Both of these forms of visual trickery adhered, at least in part, to what Roland Barthes has described as the "reality effect": a pervasive mode of contemporary literary representation in which verisimilitude emerged from seemingly useless details, redundant words, and insignificant objects. The most intriguing feature of the reality effect for Barthes is that its purpose is unavowed—a pattern he uncovers in the lengthy, almost soporific descriptions of household interiors in the novels of Flaubert, which seemed to serve no particular narrative purpose. But these useless details conveyed a very clear representational message to their reader. Collectively, they whispered, "we are the real."[26]

For Barnum and Harnett, unavowed verisimilitude played an important role, too, especially early on. The hidden brushstrokes, hard polished surfaces, and seemingly random dents and scratches, the surplus of advertised information about the Mermaid's round-about route to New York City and the straight-faced dodges executed by Lyman in the exhibition room: all of these subtle tricks were quite deliberately designed to make the viewer forget—at least momentarily—that what she or he was witnessing was nothing more than a representation. But as is always the case with *trompe l'oeil* images, this dynamic of indeterminacy and forgetting was momentary, and deliberately so. Indeed, quite unlike the literary realism described by Barthes, the suppression of the artist's hand in Barnum's humbuggery and Harnett's *trompe l'oeil* ultimately pushed in the opposite direction, towards a heightened suspiciousness. Or at the very least, the precise distinction between representation and object remained largely unresolved and actively debated among viewers. One viewer claimed that Harnett's hunting horn was painted, while another insisted that the wooden background was real. One viewer claimed to see a seam separating the body and tail of Barnum's Mermaid, while another insisted that the fusion was fully natural. For both Barnum and Harnett, the ultimate goal was to produce a highly unstable, perpetually contested brand of verisimilitude.

It was just this sort of self-conscious representational play—this attention that is always given to curiosities—that especially angered Clarence Cook as he glared at the delighted crowd surrounding Harnett's illusionistic canvas in 1879. And with good reason. For this was not simply a modest still life painting that shared a vague resemblance to Barnum's exhibitory tricks. Rather, *The Social Club* represented a more fundamental kind of encroachment of Barnumesque entertainment's dominant aesthetic principles, concerns, and patterns of viewership into the high cultural territory of the National Academy of Design. Yet Barnum's brand of humbug was merely one of many popular cultural curiosities that shared a kinship with Harnett's *trompe l'oeil* artistry.

William M. Harnett's most celebrated *trompe l'oeil* painting, the 1885 version of *After the Hunt*.

As Douglas Nickel has demonstrated, Harnett's most famous *trompe l'oeil* paintings—the four versions of *After the Hunt* produced between 1883 and 1885—were painted variations of the game pieces produced by the photographer Adolphe Braun in the late 1860s (which were themselves photographic variations on a common lithographic subject produced for middle-class dining rooms). Records from Harnett's estate sale, Nickel notes, "included many of the items employed as models in the *After the Hunt* series, so it is clear he did not paint directly from Braun's photographs." But Nickel also suggests that Braun's work was so widely distributed to "middle-class art lovers throughout Europe and the United States" during these years, and so close to the motifs Harnett employed in *After the Hunt* ("game bag, circular horn, dead rabbit and duck, diagonally slung rifle, nails"), that Harnett's indebtedness to Braun's photography "seems undeniable." Braun's large format work, moreover, was routinely celebrated in contemporary photographic journals for its ability to trick the eye and was often reproduced for the stereoscope, a popular entertainment device in the late nineteenth century that added the illusion of three-dimensional depth to the photographic image. In Nickel's view, the stereoscopic images of game pieces produced by various photographic firms during the 1870s represent the most striking popular cultural "alignment" with *After the Hunt,* for they seem to anticipate the artist's best-known *trompe l'oeil* painting in terms of both subject matter and visual style.[27]

These observations apply also to another contemporary visual entertainment: the panorama. As Stephan Oettermann has demonstrated, panoramas (as well as the numerous variations on the basic theme of large-scale *trompe l'oeil* painting such as moving panoramas, dioramas, cycloramas) were an almost continuous popular cultural presence in the United States.[28] The very first panorama, a sweeping view of London and Westminster, arrived in New York City in 1795, while the first permanent panorama building, a rotunda at the corner of Broadway and Reade Street, opened less than a decade later.[29] By the mid-1850s the panorama boom was beginning to taper off, but even during the leaner mid-century years the largest moving panoramas remained popular and commercially viable. And by the time Harnett began his academic training as an oil painter, a new wave of panorama popularity was taking shape in the United States, as French and Belgian stock companies capable of absorbing the considerable overhead costs necessary to produce these massive visual entertainments came to dominate the American cultural marketplace.[30]

Besides the obvious difference in scale, there are clear aesthetic differences between these two forms of *trompe l'oeil* painting. Whereas panorama painters preferred sweeping landscape studies that followed a horizon line (Versailles Palace, urban observation points, battlefields, and so on), Harnett and his followers often employed vertical compositions of relatively flat objects in shallow depth (letter racks full of envelopes and newspaper clippings, hunting gear or musical instruments hanging on a door, a banknote pasted to a textured surface). Yet one can argue that these seemingly disparate choices of subject matter and composition grew out of the same basic impulse: to achieve the most dramatic levels of verisimilitude possible, to present the viewer with a representational image that looks just like the real thing—at first glance. For panorama artists, this meant choosing exterior views that would appear completely natural and true to scale from the observation platform, as if the viewer were actually transported to and situated within the outdoor site represented on canvas. For Harnett and his followers, the goal was to find similarly plausible interior subjects that appeared to lie flush in the vertical plane of the canvas, so that the viewer might actually mistake the canvas for a wall or a cupboard door strewn with hanging objects.

The viewing sites for these two forms of *trompe l'oeil* artistry also seem to have been designed with the same entertainment principle in mind: to navigate a kind of middle course between complete illusion and self-conscious illusionism. As Oettermann reminds us, the panorama canvas is all of a piece with its exhibition space and techniques of display. The convex design of the exhibition building, the well-disguised skylights in the roof, the darkened tunnel through which patrons mounted the viewing platform, the physical barriers separating the platform and the canvas, the conventional wrap-around format from which the term "panorama" derives—all of these structural elements combined to produce an unprecedented level of verisimilitude by making it largely impossible for the viewer's eye to shift outside the frame.[31] Heightening this experience were display innovations developed by panorama producers over the course of the century: the simulation of rail and steamship travel achieved by rolling the canvas slowly across the visual field (moving panoramas); the simulation of changing conditions of light and atmosphere with gas lamps, transparencies, and colored filters (a technique most successfully developed by Louis-Jacques Daguerre for his dioramas); and the simulation of vast three-dimensional depth achieved by placing false terrain and mannequins in front of the canvas (a technique used to great effect in the massive battlefield cycloramas).[32]

Just how stunning these visual effects were for contemporary observers becomes clear in the wonderfully evocative *Daily Transcript* review of Paul Philippoteaux's "Cyclorama of the Battle of Gettysburg," a massive *trompe l'oeil* canvas of 400 by 50 feet, which made its debut in lower Manhattan only a few short blocks from, and at about the same time as, Harnett's 1885 *After the Hunt.* "It is quite impossible," the *Daily Transcript* explained, "to describe the effect which is received on first coming up out of the little passage into the midst of the picture. It is something as it would seem were one to become of a sudden a part of a picture. . . . In short, one feels quite helpless and wondering in the midst of this new and extraordinary nature." To remind oneself that Philippoteaux's cyclorama was merely a form of representation did not ease the perceptual vertigo:

> It would seem as though all these queer impressions might be at once met and settled by the simple consideration of the fact that it was only a picture. But that is just it: it is impossible to accept the thing as a picture. Not because it is absolutely natural, but because there is nothing by which to gauge the thing, one has no idea whether the canvas is ten feet distant or a thousand. And so, all means of rational judgment being removed, the spectator must remain, dazed and helpless, feeling much like the little girl in "Alice in Wonderland," when told that she was but a thing in the dream of the sleeping king.[33]

As we have seen, such unresolved representational play was thoroughly conventional during the Age of Barnum. From Maelzel's first American performances with the automaton chess-player to Herrmann's sleight-of-hand routines in Union Square, this was one of the century's most enduring popular cultural projects. By the mid-1880s, though, the project itself was no longer restricted to cultural forms understood as exclusively popular. Or at the very least, Harnett's paintings began to complicate and confuse the established boundaries between academic art and popular entertainment.

Consider Theodore Stewart's Warren Street Saloon, an upscale watering hole catering to New York businessmen, where the 1885 version of Harnett's *After the Hunt* first appeared in the United States. Quite unlike the National Academy's directors, the Saloon's proprietors carefully distanced viewers from *After the Hunt* by means of a brass railing anchored to the barroom's floor—a setup which dramatically enhanced the intended effect of the painting. So, too, did the velvet curtain proscenium visible in contemporary photographs of the Saloon's interior, as well as the gas sidelights which illuminated Harnett's 71.5 by 48.5-inch canvas.[34] In each case, these exhibition devices served to heighten the illusionistic impact of *After the Hunt,* encouraging saloon patrons to engage in a kind of guessing game about the painting's imagery. It is also clear that *After the Hunt* was not meant to be viewed in the same way as the dozens of other paintings in Stewart's extensive art collection. Harnett's canvas was set apart as a unique attraction, with the surrounding space physically regulated in a manner quite unlike the rest of the long room. What this particular corner of Stewart's Saloon most closely resembled, in fact, was not so much a conventional art gallery as a kind of panorama venue in miniature.

It was just this sort of arrangement, too, that the proprietors of Churchill's Saloon in Detroit encouraged for John Haberle's 96 by 66-inch *trompe l'oeil* canvas of 1890, *Grandma's Hearthstone.* "The location of the picture," stressed one reporter from the *Tribune,* "adds to the realistic effect. It is arranged at a dark end of the room, with electric light turned upon it in such a manner that upon entering the place it seems as if there really were an old-fashioned fire place

John Haberle's *Grandma's Hearthstone* (1890), the massive *trompe l'oeil* canvas that "fooled the cat" at Churchill's Saloon in Detroit.

there and the light was the reflection of the fire."[35] Following the well-established conventions of the panorama, the proprietors of Churchill's Saloon used theatrical lighting and clever positioning within the physical space of the barroom to embellish Haberle's *trompe l'oeil* artistry. And much like Philippoteaux's panorama audiences, visitors to Churchill's embraced this self-conscious perceptual play as a fascinating end in itself. In the words of the *Tribune's* writer: "The best critic upon the picture was the house cat. When the picture was first placed in position the cat came up from the cellar and started across the room. . . . The cat noticed the light of the blazing fire and went over to examine it. After critically scrutinizing the new affair she curled herself up before it and began to snooze completely illusionized."[36] This was Pliny's classic *trompe l'oeil* fable all over again. But now Zeuxis' grapes and the mythical birds were replaced by an "illusionized cat" in Detroit and an electrically enhanced middle-class bar game.

In many different ways, then, late nineteenth-century *trompe l'oeil* painting was becoming the stuff of modern popular culture. But it is important to be clear about the artists' specific roles in this process. None of the academically trained painters who engaged in *trompe l'oeil* after 1875 simply attempted to replicate contemporary forms of popular amusement. Harnett did not paint directly from stereographs of game pieces. Nor did he ever mention Barnum's humbugs or the cycloramas of Philippoteaux. Yet this pervasive contemporary landscape of artful deception offered two key things for Harnett and his followers. Most important early on, it provided a lucrative marketplace for pictorial illusionism, which in turn created unusual opportunities to carve out viable artistic careers somewhere between the more extreme professional choices of "true art" and "sign painting." At the same time, it raised aesthetic questions very different from those taught and enforced by the academies—questions about visual perception, authenticity, and representational truth that were being widely discussed in nonacademic exhibition rooms throughout the 1860s and 1870s.

Harnett's connection to this popular cultural landscape is subtle and indirect: it comes out in the strangely apologetic tone of the New York *News* interview; his behind-the-scenes commissions to paint *trompe l'oeil* pictures for Stewart's barroom galleries; and the particular metaphors chosen by contemporary critics to describe his *trompe l'oeil* work (a style of painting, as Cook put it, that relates to true art as a "catch or glee" relates to "true music").

Some of Harnett's followers were less circumspect about expressing these connections. Haberle, especially, had few qualms about admitting the market-driven logic behind his aesthetic choices. His lone contemporary press interview, published in *The Illustrated American*, began very much like Harnett's New York *News* interview, with the reporter noting that "Mr. Haberle was not born with a silver spoon in his mouth, and his early life was a succession of ups and down in which the downs predominated." A few lines later, however, the reporter explained how the young New Haven artist endeavored to pull himself out of poverty: "Mr. Haberle . . . determined to toil along the lines of close brush work, believing that in that field there was a ready market, and he has succeeded beyond his wildest expectations."[37] In some of his *trompe l'oeil* canvases from the 1880s and 1890s, too, the aesthetic resemblance between close brush work and contemporary forms of popular illusionism was often made explicit and even celebrated. Haberle's *Reproduction* of 1886, for instance, juxtaposes *trompe l'oeil* images of a photographic self-portrait, a ten-dollar bill, and a pair of newspaper clippings, one of which gleefully extols his "remarkable skills as an artistic counterfeit." These artistic tricks are so good, the fake newspaper text tells us, that Haberle's work "would humbug Barnum."

Such self-referential boasting articulated what Harnett could not quite bring himself to admit to the New York *News:* that any artist who "took up this line of painting" must have been conscious of working within a genre linked commercially, aesthetically, and ideologically to contemporary popular culture. But *Reproduction* also reminds us of a critical distinction: that Haberle's larger goal was to make a pictorial

A painting that "would humbug Barnum": John Haberle's *Reproduction* (1886).

statement about his own relation to Barnumesque culture, rather than simply replicate one of its existing forms. His pointed references to Barnum and humbug serve a number of specific painterly functions. First, they function as part of a pictorial narrative, one which begins at the center of the canvas with a standard *trompe l'oeil* image (a ten-dollar bill), proceeds clockwise to an image of Haberle in the process of creating the painting, and concludes with a newspaper story about the successful results of his illusionistic efforts. The references to Barnum and humbug also focus the viewer's attention on Haberle's specific methods of representation, encouraging us to engage the work self-consciously as a form of illusionism (rather than as an unacknowledged, realistic window into the painting). And finally, these references serve as a public means for Haberle to gloat—very much like the Prince of Humbug of the 1840s and 1850s—about his commercial success in making *trompe l'oeil* painting pay off.

All in all, this was Clarence Cook's worst fear fully realized: the return of the popular cultural other seven years later, except that now Cook's damning analogies had become the unabashed and explicit subject of the painting. As the large banknote in the middle of the canvas suggested, there really was not much academic critics could do to make it stop. By this time a growing number of academically trained American artists were actively engaged in bringing *trompe l'oeil* painting to the urban middle class masses. In open defiance of Cook's attacks, they continued to submit such paintings to the leading academic exhibitions—something which academic critics could at least discourage by withholding prizes and public praise. But these painters also submitted their illusionistic canvases to a variety of nonacademic venues: big-city barrooms, the galleries at the annual industrial expositions, even the display windows of urban retail stores. And it is in these less carefully regulated and less refined urban spaces where we can begin to hear the public "delight" that Clarence Cook had attempted to quell in 1879.

The Rumpus in the Exhibition Room

One of the more striking features of the early historical work on Harnett and his followers is its cursory treatment of the painters' popular reception. While these studies routinely acknowledge that *trompe l'oeil* was far better received by the urban middle class than the critical elites, it is the elite critics' voices which routinely dominate. In effect, the popular furors surrounding the works of Harnett and his followers serve as little more than a collection of amusing anecdotes (anecdotes whose historical meanings are usually summarized in a sentence or two). Even Alfred Frankenstein, American *trompe l'oeil* painting's most devoted and exhaustive chronicler, has little to say about the broader historical significance of the popular reception. "The esthetically unwashed," he simply concludes, "were more perspicacious than the professionals" in recognizing the virtues of Harnett's artistry.[38]

Again and again, the same basic pattern emerges in Frankenstein's work. He writes that a certain painting achieved great success in an urban, nonacademic venue of some kind. Then he tells amusing stories about its reception: assorted expressions of middle-class wonder and bewilderment, occasional arguments about particular objects in the painting, a wager or two between stubborn gentlemen who refuse to give way on their opinions, and finally, an energetic round of public applause for the artist's skill in achieving such a remarkably realistic effect. Over time, there is a numbing redundancy to these furors. Yet it is precisely the redundancy that begs further examination and explanation.

It seems worth asking, for example, why most of the popular triumphs for Harnett's *trompe l'oeil* occurred in exhibition sites containing large urban crowds—crowds which often received as much press treatment as the paintings themselves. The settings included Stewart's barroom picture gallery in lower Manhattan, through which "hundreds" of eager "art worshipers" reportedly passed each day; the gallery space at the Black, Starr, and Frost retail store on Fifth Avenue, which, according to *The Epoch*, attracted "numerous" enthusiastic visitors eager to witness the "realistic fidelity" of Harnett's *Faithful Colt;* the 1886 Cincinnati Industrial Exposition, where Harnett's *The Old Violin* was "hung in the north end of the gallery," with "a crowd of bewildered gazers continually about it"; and at the 1887 Minneapolis Industrial Exposition, where *The Old Violin* once again became an overnight sensation among thousands of objects on display, arousing "quite a furore."[39] As a reporter from the *Saint Paul and Minneapolis Pioneer Press* noted: "It was almost impossible to get within gunshot of the old violin in the art gallery at any time yesterday afternoon."[40]

Perhaps there were large urban crowds assembled around these paintings simply because there were large urban crowds passing through the saloons, expositions, and retail stores where the paintings were shown. Yet there is something vaguely unsatisfying (not to mention tautological) about explaining the furors by their presence in crowded urban sites. There were, after all, dozens—even hundreds—of other paintings hanging in all of these exhibition sites. And none of the other paintings in New York, Cincinnati, or Minneapolis elicited the same sort of middle-class frenzy aroused by Harnett's illusionism.

A century earlier, moreover, Charles Willson Peale and his son Raphaelle had exhibited quite a few *trompe l'oeil* canvases in Philadelphia, but never with the same outbursts of collective public excitement later provoked by Harnett and his followers.

When the Peales exhibited *trompe l'oeil* paintings, these works generally provoked proud critical comparisons to the "works of the Flemish school," or a polite press notice about "the correct manner" in which "each individual object" was "represented."[41] But there is no mention of excited urban crowds assembled around the paintings, not a word about expressions of collective bewilderment or noisy exhibition room debates.[42] When Harnett debuted *After the Hunt* at Stewart's Saloon during the mid-1880s, by contrast, it was greeted by "hundreds of prominent citizens—artists, journalists, judges, lawyers, men about town and actors," who "visit this wonderful work of art daily, and wildly wager and express opinions as to its being an optical illusion or a real painting." In Cincinnati, the pattern of intense and often volatile excitement was similar. Visitors to the Exposition, the newspapers explained in tones of wonder, "need no guidepost to Harnett's 'The Old Violin'. They will find it by following the crowd."[43]

What they also found were viewers in various states of energetic and even violent perceptual confusion: an "old man" in Cincinnati declared, "By Jove, I would like to play on that violin" and charged at the canvas; one "western man" at Stewart's Saloon "wickedly" attacked *After the Hunt* with his "cane"; his barroom colleague "from Chicago made a dash" towards the canvas and groped at Harnett's illusionistic images in search of answers. Such visceral expressions of excitement and confusion became so frequent at the Cincinnati Exposition that the managers were forced to hire a professional security guard. "It may seem like a strain upon the truth," a local reporter explained, "but it is a fact that an officer had to be placed on duty behind the rail, to keep inquisitive spectators from attempting the removal of the newspaper scrap with their finger-nails." "So real it is," explained another, "that one of Captain Wise's specials has been detailed to stand beside the picture to suppress any attempts to take down the fiddle and the bow."[44]

These marked variations in the reception patterns cannot be explained away by the sheer size of the crowd or the bad exhibition room manners of Harnett's viewers. Rather, they force us to consider what kinds of larger, historically specific concerns might have been at stake for those charging the canvases. The most detailed account of Harnett's popular audiences comes to us from a rather bemused foreign correspondent for the London *Commercial Gazette*, writing on Stewart's Warren Street Saloon and its artistic showpiece, *After the Hunt*, in 1885.

> Men come and stand before this picture for fifteen minutes at a time, and the remarks passed upon it are curious indeed. As a rule, city men are enraptured with it, and go into ecstasies over the feathery plumage of the birds and the furry coat of the rabbit, over the wonderful representation of the butt-end of an old snap-lock gun, over the extraordinary imitation of the brass work of the horn. But gentlemen from the country, and especially from Chicago, declare that nobody can take them in, and that the objects are real objects, hung up with an intent to deceive people. A drummer from the city of sin [Chicago] was very angry over the obvious imposition, and wagered $5 that the thing was not a painting. "Feel it," said his friend. He felt it and found it was a flat panel. "Well," he said, "I admit that the rabbit and the birds are painted. I ought to have seen that from the first, because, although they are wonderfully lifelike, there is a sort of yielding of the muscles in a dead thing which you don't see in this. But what got me was the hanging up of that bottle, because I could see in a moment that the string was real." The crowd behind them burst into a roar of laughter, and the drummer made a mad dash for the bottle; but his hands met only the flat surface of a panel. He was dumbfounded. "Gee whitakers!" at last broke from his lips; "that beats Chicago. It's all painted, frame and all, and that's what makes the illusion so perfect." There was another roar from the crowd that was taking in the scene with huge delight.[45]

These dumbfounded cries represent some of the more entertaining moments in the entire lore cycle of late nineteenth-century *trompe l'oeil* viewership. What makes them especially fascinating as historical evidence, though, is their striking resemblance to another, roughly contemporary cycle of urban-industrial folklore: the conventional tales of deception and misreading which routinely appeared in urban sketches and guidebooks (for instance, George G. Foster's best-selling *New York by Gas-Light* of 1850). The Chicago drummer above was in many ways the archetypal nineteenth-century greenhorn, an out-of-town visitor to Gotham supremely confident that "nobody can take him in," but ultimately exposed as an unsophisticated, gullible provincial. The amused New Yorkers assembled around him, by contrast, act as the *flaneurs* of the barroom picture gallery—sophisticated experts at reading the city, who treat the perceptual challenges of Harnett's painting as their urban sport and amusement.[46] Having sharpened their eyes on numerous previous occasions, they know the score and wait, with cosmopolitan composure, for another gentleman from the country to provide their afternoon's entertainment.

Harnett's *trompe l'oeil* painting functions here as both an emblem of and a catalyst for the perceptual confusion conventionally associated with the nineteenth-century metropolis. For the uninitiated, *After the Hunt* merely confirms suspicions about Gotham's propensity for deception. It is seen as a source of perceptual wonder greater even than the city of sin itself (a wonder which both literally and figuratively "beats Chicago"). For the Stewart's regulars, however, the unsettling moment provoked by Harnett' artistic tricks has long since ceased to inspire urban dread. These viewers now pronounce themselves "enraptured" with Harnett's "extraordinary imitation" and use it to mark their own urban sophistication.

In terms of Benjamin's hypothesis, these two categories of viewers represent a kind of "before and after" picture. Whereas the befuddled drummer still seems to be in an early state of visual acculturation (both in relation to *After the Hunt* and the larger urban environment), the Stewart's regulars treat Harnett's canvas in much the fashion Benjamin imagined: as a welcome opportunity to test visual faculties already developed in other urban contexts. Yet it is also clear that we are trading in caricatures here. The Chicago drummer and his New York hosts are literary composites—loaded with meaning, to be sure, but somewhat narrow in terms of the range of viewing experiences. It is worth looking at a larger picture.

Consider, for example, the six weeks of artistic fame enjoyed by George W. Platt, a *trompe l'oeil* painter about whom relatively little is known, and whose most famous painting, *Vanishing Glories,* seems to be permanently lost.[47] Platt was born in Rochester, New York (in 1839, about nine years before Harnett), and lived there until, as a young man, he decided to become a professional oil painter. The road he traveled to his goal paralleled Harnett's career path in a number of ways: five years at the Pennsylvania Academy of Fine Arts during the 1870s; some time in Europe (including the Academy in Munich) to enhance his artistic training; a subsequent day job as a commercial artist (a draftsman for a geological survey); and a period of struggle in New York City, where he briefly set up his own studio.[48] For the most part, Platt's artistic subjects closely paralleled Harnett's, too: some table-top fruit compositions, an occasional money picture, a very rare human portrait, and a number of larger, vertical *trompe l'oeil* compositions of "game pieces."[49]

In contrast to Harnett's game choices, Platt's paintings featured larger, more exotic hunting trophies (mountain sheep or buffalo), a decision which probably reflected Platt's more westerly choices of exhibition sites during the 1880s and 1890s (Chicago, St. Louis, Kansas City, Omaha, and Denver, where he eventually settled). Like Harnett, however, Platt gained his success in distinctly urban contexts, especially the annual industrial expositions. And by the early 1890s, Platt's fame was significant enough for him to be described in local newspapers as a "well known" artist.[50]

In almost every way, then, Platt resembled Harnett: he was a relatively talented painter who worked his way through a leading academic training program, added to his artistic knowledge in Europe, experienced temporary frustration in New York City, and eventually found enough success as a *trompe l'oeil* painter in nonacademic venues to achieve a modicum of artistic celebrity. The first known exhibition record for Platt's work is a brief listing of two paintings in the 1888 St. Louis Exposition Catalog: *Vanishing Glories* (#70) and *Peaches* (#71).[51] Thereafter, we hear nothing at all about *Peaches* in the extensive press coverage for the fair between September 5 and October 20. *Vanishing Glories*, by contrast, appears almost daily in the press notices, spurred by a spontaneous crescendo of public excitement. By early October, in fact, the St. Louis press had even given the nickname "Vanishing Glories" to the Exposition as a whole, a pun that testified to how much this six-week event had become linked with the painting in the minds of fairgoers.[52] All in all, it is one of the more intriguing episodes in late nineteenth-century American art history: how in the space of six weeks a mostly conventional *trompe l'oeil* painting by a minor artist emerged from the clutter of thousands of objects on display at the 1888 Exposition to become one of St. Louis's most talked about cultural attractions.

The first notice of exceptional public interest was the article of September 18 in the St. Louis *Post-Dispatch*, almost two weeks after the Exposition's opening ceremonies.

> A lot was made at the Exposition last night over a picture that has kept every one guessing since the galleries were opened. Just outside the east gallery is a picture which was painted by Platt. It is called "Vanishing Glories." Fastened to an old barn door, which is closed with an old-fashioned clasp, is a buffalo's skull, and on it hang the lariat, pistols, a Winchester, the sombrero, and all that was once the necessary outfit of a Western cowboy. The subject is a "catchy" one, and the work is excellently done— so well done, in fact, that there is a good deal of doubt about the material on which it is painted. There is no frame, but it sits against the wall, and its edges are concealed by a border of maroon cloth. A great many people think that the picture is painted on an old barn door, and others think that the artist has simply painted well the old weather beaten pine. It is a very puzzling question whether he has used wood or canvas, and every night there is a discussion over it between people of different opinions.

This description suggests that Platt probably had Harnett's *After the Hunt* in mind when he produced *Vanishing Glories*. Once again, hunting gear and animal trophies are arranged in a very shallow, vertical composition, one which juxtaposed bulky and obviously painted still life subjects with much flatter, hard-to-detect objects. And once again, there is a strong emphasis on well-worn materials—materials still appealing to urban eyes, but also clearly representative of a bygone pre-industrial era in the region's history.

It also seems that the St. Louis Exposition organizers collaborated with Platt in an attempt to create the same sort of public excitement provoked by Harnett in New York, Cincinnati, and Minneapolis a few years earlier. One clue is the maroon cloth that concealed the edges of *Vanishing Glories,* which suggests that the Exposition's art director, Mr. George Mills, was in on the *trompe l'oeil* fun with Platt. An even stronger indication of that appeared in the *Post-Dispatch* two days later:

> There is another bit of work in the picture that surpasses everything else. By a pre-arrangement Mr. Platt had his picture numbered 70 in the catalogue, and instead of having a cardboard stuck on it he has painted an imitation of the numbered cards, representing it as stuck in the crack of the door just by the clasp. It looks exactly like the little numbered cards that are on all the other pictures, and the visitors all think it is one until someone calls their attention to it. But there is a difference of opinion over it, too. Some say it is real and some that it is not. The question is often referred to Mr. Mills, but he will decide none of the disputed points because he says he has promised not to tell anything about the picture until the Exposition is over.[53]

The silence that Mills promised to uphold on Platt's behalf was one of the signal gestures of the nineteenth-century trickster—a silence which echoed from Johann Maelzel in 1826, Levi Lyman in 1835, P. T. Barnum in 1842 and 1860, and Harry Kellar in 1889. What makes this particular exercise in trickery especially interesting, however, is that it was taking place in an art gallery, a cultural venue not generally associated with such things. Just as Clarence Cook had feared in 1879, a *trompe l'oeil* still life painting was now transforming art viewership into curiosity viewership. And this time, the director of the art exhibition had given the *trompe l'oeil* artist his official blessing, even offered to serve as a co-conspirator. The St. Louis art establishment was in on the confidence game.

The plan worked well beyond anything Mills and Platt might have imagined. The day after the disclosure about the exhibition label, in fact, the *Post-Dispatch* sounded a somewhat alarmed note which suggested that Mr. Mill's control over the expanding controversy was becoming rather tenuous:

> *Vanishing Glories* is likely to cause trouble before the season is over. Two gentlemen got into such a warm discussion over whether the "70" was real or painted last night that their friends thought there was going to be a rumpus, but they calmed down and discussed very quietly whether the picture was painted on canvas or wood. It is amusing to see how Mr. Mills avoids the picture. So many people ask him to solve the picture that he grows tired of refusing, so he keeps away from it and from the discussion that is constantly going on around it.[54]

The day after this near-rumpus, the *Post-Dispatch* offered an article entitled "They Can't Stay Away":

> All night long there is a crowd about the curious painting guessing what it is. "What do you think it is?" asked a gentleman of his wife as they stood before it last night. "I think it is wood," was the answer. "Oh no!" replied the husband, "it's canvas." "Well, that is the best representation of wood I ever saw in my life, then," she said. . . . Some think that the border is of wood and that the center is of canvas, for they cannot understand how the artist can have painted the grains in the wood so well. "I'll bet a dollar and a half that border is wood," exclaimed a young man, but his companion ridiculed him, saying that anyone could see it was painted. "No it isn't. The grains stick out from the plank." "Well, you gilly, can't you see that they're painted that way. The pistol hangs out from the door, too, but you don't mean to say that it is real."[55]

These members of the St. Louis crowd were quickly becoming the co-stars of Platt's *trompe l'oeil* show. Yet it is worth noting that no single individual or social group (except perhaps, Platt himself) emerged as completely masterful: while the men certainly had the loudest public voices in these crowds, they frequently appeared as dupes. Some even appeared entirely helpless, a scenario well-documented in a conversation overheard between a father and his child:

> A gentleman who looked as if he hadn't the greatest confidence in his eyes was showing his little son *Vanishing Glories* last night, and the boy asked: "Is that hinge real or painted, papa?" "It's real son—no, I believe it's painted." "Is the revolver real?" "No, I think it's painted. I don't know." "Is the door real?" "I can't say, my son." "What is it painted on?" "I give it up, my boy. I can't tell a thing about it."[56]

In all this excitement nothing was more thrilling, however, than the opportunity to look at someone famous looking at Platt's canvas. Two figures, in particular, stood out: the well-known orchestra conductor, Patrick Gilmore, who was hired by the Exposition organizers to serve as master of ceremonies; and the so-called Lady in Black, who reportedly visited the art gallery every night by herself after Gilmore's concerts. In 1888, such visits were fascinating enough to make the Lady in Black a St. Louis celebrity. The *Post-Dispatch* recorded her presence in the art gallery over a half dozen times and devoted entire paragraphs to the rumors about her opinions (she asserted, quite correctly, that *Vanishing Glories* was painted on canvas).[57] And when, by sheer coincidence, Gilmore and the Lady in Black appeared before Platt's painting together one night, it was almost more excitement than the crowd could bear. "*Vanishing Glories* has deceived Pat Gilmore, the great conductor," exclaimed the *Post-Dispatch*. "He examined it critically, a few nights ago, and after studying it for a long time said he would not venture an opinion. . . . Merely by chance, Gilmore and the Lady in Black were looking at the picture at the same time, and the great leader, the picture, and the mysterious lady proved a trio that drew an immense crowd."[58]

Such immense crowds naturally required some kind of satisfying *dénouement* to the six-week furor in the art gallery. Mr. Mills therefore decided to bring Platt in all the way from Chicago to answer the single question most on the minds of St. Louis residents during the fall of 1888. Public word of his arrival came on October 12, exactly five weeks after the start of the Exposition and a solid month into the controversy that he and Mills had helped to create.[59] And not surprisingly, during the first days of his visit to the Exposition, Platt gracefully declined to "decide" the public discussions, opting instead to merely smile and comment on the clever means by which Mills had illuminated *Vanishing Glories* with "artificial light." But on October 20, closing day, St. Louis finally got its answer, in retrospect almost anticlimactic. The picture proper, Platt announced before returning to Chicago, was painted entirely on canvas. The border was entirely made of wood.[60]

Suckers? Dilettantes? Modernists?

Platt's brief moment of artistic fame merits reconsideration. First, because it included many of the standard features of the popular furor that so frequently surrounded late nineteenth-century *trompe l'oeil* painting: an illusionistic image of hunting gear and animal trophies; an urban exhibition venue through which thousands of anonymous, mostly middle-class spectators passed each day; a level of spontaneously generated public excitement that often bordered on mass hysteria; and an assortment of viewing rituals (noisy debates and public arguments, improvised wagers and practical jokes) far more typical of contemporary popular entertainment than of an art exhibition. This in turn produced dozens of long and astonished press reports, each one offering detailed play-by-play stories of viewership for the folks at home. No other exhibition of this genre of painting provoked as much public comment as the one sparked by this relatively obscure Chicago artist and his rather shameless knock-off of *After the Hunt*.

There is no simple or singular historical explanation for these popular furors. And the often narrow terms of the public discourse—comment after comment about wood and canvas, feathers and fur—push more in the direction of careful speculation than hard and fast conclusions. It may be, as David Lubin has recently suggested, that late nineteenth-century *trompe l'oeil* painting encouraged a particularly masculine sort of artistic experience, defined as such not merely by its conventional subject matter (rough-hewn, pre-commodity artifacts), but also by the particular mode of viewership encouraged by its illusionism (a perceptual competition).[61] Lubin suggests further that the professional men who "drank, dined, and conducted business" in the saloons where Harnett's *trompe l'oeil* paintings hung used them as a kind of therapeutic aid, both to repair masculine identities injured by the world of white-collar office work and to express nostalgia for the pre-industrial world they were leaving behind.[62]

Even a quick consideration of some of the titles attached to Harnett's *trompe l'oeil* paintings—*After the Hunt, The Bachelor's Friends, The Broker's Table*—reinforces Lubin's notion of a specific resonance of these paintings for the affluent businessmen who generally purchased them. Yet the further one digs into the reception evidence, the more it becomes clear that this argument about endangered white-collar masculinity and pre-industrial nostalgia does not suffice as a general explanation for the intense nonacademic popularity of *trompe l'oeil* painting.[63]

Consider once again the London *Commercial Gazette* reporter's account of Stewart's Saloon. On one level, it overflows with gendered symbolism, rituals, and implications, from the macho reveling in Harnett's bloody animal corpses and snap-lock gun, to the hearty roars from the crowd at the Chicago drummer's mistakes. The real point of the London reporter's story, however, was to identify a select group of "city men" whose grasp of Harnett's *trompe l'oeil* painting separated them from their more provincial counterparts. It is this process of urban differentiation that drives the entire article. And at the end of the article, the London reporter comes back to the distinction again, noting that it was a Westerner who, in a fit of perceptual frustration, wickedly stuck his cane into the painting (before being "shown out the door" by his New York hosts). Wide-eyed provincials, the reporter concludes with obvious amusement, would be well-advised to steer clear of this cosmopolitan art scene.

Much the same point was made in the other nonacademic venues where *trompe l'oeil* painting flourished—albeit usually in less specifically gendered ways (a difference which makes perfect sense given the more heterosocial audiences surrounding *trompe l'oeil* painting everywhere except the barroom picture galleries). In the press coverage surrounding *Vanishing Glories,* local reporters were careful to record the differences in reception patterns between visitors to the Exposition from St. Louis itself and those visiting from more far-flung locations. "It is interesting," began one article, "to stand by visitors from the far West while they examine *Vanishing Glories* and it is flattering to the artist that they find no fault with it. They think it is 'great' and seldom stop to quarrel over whether it is painted on canvas or wood, because they are firmly convinced that no artist could paint an old barn door so perfectly on canvas. The general opinion among them is that the picture is on wood, but in that they differ from the people here, who incline to the other opinion."[64]

In this case, there are no mad dashes or wicked attacks against the canvas because the caricatured provincials in the audience seem to be completely unaware that it is a canvas (and therefore seldom stop to quarrel). Nevertheless, the moral of this St. Louis reception story is much the same as the one in New York: those from the far West might know an authentic picture of cowboy gear when they see one (it is flattering to the artist they find no fault), but they lack the perceptual *savoir-faire* of the local urbanites. That late nineteenth-century *trompe l'oeil* viewers told these kinds of stories about each other is not surprising. As W. J. T. Mitchell has noted, the larger discourse of aesthetic illusion has always been "deeply interwoven with structures of power and social otherness." Hierarchies of viewership, he suggests, are what these stories of reading and misreading most reliably produce.[65]

But why was such social differentiation necessary or appealing at this particular historical moment and in these particular contexts? A more specific answer begins to emerge when we consider some of the other press reports on the 1888 Exposition. On the very first day, the *Post-Dispatch* issued a somewhat anxious warning entitled, "Bewildering Displays":

> It is as if instead of one stage and one company at the theater, the playgoer should find himself confronted with a dozen of each, and should lose his head in an impossible effort to drink in simultaneously

panorama, comedy, and the spectacular, with an infinite number of attractions staring at him from the lobbies and claiming his attention from the wings. When one finds himself in a predicament such as this, and he surely will if he visits the Exposition, he must make his mind up at once to see one thing at a time.[66]

Four days later, the *Post-Dispatch* returned to the problem of bewildered fairgoers again, offering a story about yet another out-of-town patron in the throes of perceptual confusion, this time on her way out of the automaton exhibit:

> "Is that real," asked an innocent-looking country girl, pointing at a man who sat by one of the displays at the Exposition. "Yes, he's real," said the big policeman: "Why do you ask?" "Why, I saw some dummies carryin' on just like they was real. I'm getting' so now I can't tell a dummy from a live man in this here place." The big policeman looked incredulous and walked away. But stranger things than that happen and questions as odd as that are asked every day under the big roof.[67]

These articles serve as useful illustrations of Benjamin's notion that nineteenth-century eyes had to adapt to new, more disorienting forms of urban spectacle.[68] And read against the reception evidence for *Vanishing Glories*, they seem to confirm the second key idea in Benjamin's hypothesis: his suggestion that having gone through such visual adaptation, one's eyes might welcome the opportunity to test their newly acquired faculties in the exhibition room. Precisely because the Exposition as a whole was so bewildering, the public debates surrounding Platt's painting were just as much about semiotic control and social differentiation as about the aesthetic distinction between wood and canvas. To be sure, the evidence cuts two ways here. Depending on which audience member's voice we focus on, Platt's trickery can be read as either a source of disorientation or a means of one-upmanship—that, in a sense, is what the public wagers were all about. Yet, for those victimized the first time around, there was always another country gentleman or Western visitor to serve as scapegoat. That was the beauty of looking at *trompe l'oeil* paintings in this particular context: one simply needed to wait around long enough in the

urban crowd for an unsuspecting greenhorn to walk in and steal away
the title of resident dupe.

Following the six-week furor in St. Louis, the scrapbooks from
Platt's career suggest a modest but steady pattern of professional
advancement. Between 1888 and his death in 1899, he moved to Denver and won a professorship at the local university's School of Art; he
received invitations to serve as superintendent of the art departments
at various Chautauqua meetings; he gained membership in the Denver and Colorado Art clubs; and he enjoyed occasional sojourns to the
mountains, where he "whiled away the summer days sketching the
surrounding scenery." What really sticks out in these scrapbooks,
though, is a sideline he seems to have developed to capitalize on his St.
Louis celebrity: a second career as a traveling public lecturer. Platt's
lectures, the clippings suggest, included magic lantern slides to illustrate his points, as well as a fairly broad Midwestern touring circuit
(the Chicago Society of Artists, the Photographic Society of Chicago,
the Lininger Gallery in Omaha, and a Chautauqua meeting in Colorado). And in each case, the format of the performance seems to
have been roughly the same. Platt stood before his audiences and
spoke in a "clear and able manner" on the topic most commonly associated with his name after 1888: "Illusions in Art."[69]

The lectures did not survive, but the reviews provide useful clues
about their content. Some merely pointed to Platt's mixture of scientific principles and entertaining visual aids, suggesting that Platt may
have brought along a few of his *trompe l'oeil* canvases out on the lecture circuit. Other reviews went into greater detail, describing the talk
as "a consideration of some of those properties of vision which tend
most to deceive when viewing or producing works of art. The art of
painting is but a continuation of the art of seeing, to which all must
attend from the time their eyes are first born."[70] The most extensive
contemporary review appeared in an 1889 volume of *The Beacon:*

> Mr. G. W. Platt then delivered an exceedingly interesting and instructive
> lecture on "Illusions in Art," and enforced his statement by a series of
> beautiful illustrations, especially those in connection with the difference

between objective and subjective vision, which unmistakably showed that "seeing is not always believing." The lantern was brought into play to show the effects of fatigue on the various bundles of nerve rods in the retina, when black became gray, and each color, on its being withdrawn, left in its place the appearance of a similar image in its complimentary color.[71]

Following so many descriptions of warm discussions and wagers at the St. Louis Exposition, these rather erudite references to visual subjectivity and retinal fatigue come as something of a surprise. And perhaps that was precisely what Platt was trying to accomplish here: a dramatic reinvention of his public persona, from a second-tier artist working in a low genre to a more thoroughly respectable artistic expert on the subtleties of human perception. Significantly, many of the most important breakthroughs in nineteenth-century perceptual science seem to have influenced Platt's lectures: Johann Wolfgang von Goethe's experiments on retinal afterimages, for example, which served as one of the earliest scientific challenges to the long-held Enlightenment assumption that the eye works as a nonmediating, physiological gateway between sensation and consciousness. The *Beacon* review also suggests Platt's familiarity with the somewhat later studies of Herrmann von Helmholtz, James Sully, and William James, which demonstrated the eye's potential to misread and even deceive consciousness—findings that led them to redefine sight as a thoroughly subjective mode of human perception.[72] How much of these scientific studies Platt read is impossible to determine. But he seems to have both absorbed and transmitted their revolutionary central thesis: seeing might be believing, but it does not necessarily correspond to reality.

It is hard to generalize from Platt to other artists and their audiences. Admittedly, no other evidence suggests that Platt's colleagues made similarly self-conscious theoretical statements through their illusionistic canvases (nor, for that matter, is there any evidence to suggest that they were aware of the scientific theories which informed Platt's lectures). And in general, the running criticism of *trompe l'oeil* painting was that it promoted empty-headed exhibition-room nonsense. This perceived dearth of serious intellectual engagement surrounding Harnett's work is what fueled Clarence Cook's metaphorical comparisons to curiosities. An 1887 reviewer from *The Studio* likewise employed this line of comparison, scolding artists who simply cheat "the untrained eye." "Only children and half-taught people," the reviewer insisted, "take pleasure in such tricks of the brush as Mr. Harnett has lately made the fashion."[73]

These accusations echo the most common stereotype about the nineteenth-century arts of deception as a whole: that they were, in the end, nothing more than popular cultural tricks played on unsophisticated suckers. And in this particular case, it is tempting to side with the highbrow critics. Perhaps, that is to say, there simply was not much *serious* aesthetic analysis taking place at Stewart's Saloon, Black, Starr, and Frost, and the various Midwestern industrial expositions. Perhaps Platt's subsequent efforts to make *trompe l'oeil* painting the center of a public discussion about subjective vision was the exception rather than the rule. Perhaps the rumpus in the art gallery really was nothing more than a rumpus.

This argument, though, ignores one very basic and easy-to-miss lesson in the reception evidence: namely, that those excitable St. Louis fairgoers seem to have reached much the same sort of conclusion about perception that Platt later presented in his scientific lectures. Indeed, the consensus that emerged from the dozens of recorded voices in the fall of 1888 was that they simply did not know what to make of Platt's puzzle; that their eyes were not perfectly reliable in this endeavor. One "young man bet a dollar and a half that border is wood," but another ridiculed him as a gilly for not recognizing that it was "painted that way." A great many people ventured that "the picture was painted on an old barn door," but others suggested that the artist simply "painted well the old weather beaten pine." Patrick Gilmore examined the painting for hours, but in the end he, too, admitted that he could not make up his mind. Even the mysterious Lady in Black, who was entirely correct in her "suspicions," never came out and pronounced the puzzle solved.

Can such collective doubts be described as a self-conscious aesthetic principle or program? Maybe not. Clearly, this sort of collective uncertainty was very different from the more celebrated (and contemporaneous) doubts about vision that historians have long celebrated as one of the central features of French Impressionism.[74] The most obvious difference has to do with how these doubts were defined and articulated. Whereas Impressionism grew out of a collective artistic enterprise—achieved through published statements of aesthetic principles and independent exhibitions mounted in open defiance of academic convention—American *trompe l'oeil* lacked a collectively engineered movement. Harnett, as best we can tell, was simply trying to find a successful artistic niche somewhere between the academy system and Barnumesque entertainment. And while Platt seems to have followed Harnett in this enterprise, it was not an act of collusion in a planned, antiacademic rebellion. Platt, it seems, was simply doing his best to replicate Harnett's recipe for commercial success on the Exposition circuit.

The specific aesthetic techniques that grew out of and expressed these doubts diverged in important ways as well.[75] The key distinction has to do with the specific relationship between seeing and representing that each aesthetic mode fostered. Tirelessly moving back and forth from the canvas, the Impressionists operated in multiple perceptual positions in the act of painting: patches of pigment that appeared to be unrelated at close viewing coalesced into recognizable images and figures only when seen from a distance. The larger effect of this practice was to undermine what T. J. Clark has described as the dominant "logic" of "equivalence," which for hundreds of years had governed the larger Western project of representing an object with paint. With the advent of Impressionism, the material process of brush strokes substituting for something in the real world became shockingly explicit.[76] *Trompe l'oeil* artists undermined this logic in shocking ways, too, but by moving in the opposite direction (towards the canvas rather than away from it). Harnett's virtuoso *trompe l'oeil* signatures, for example, which upon casual viewing appear to be engraved or carved in the wooden backgrounds of his famous paintings, were a kind of inversion of the basic Impressionist technique. Harnett, in other words, must have spent countless hours alternating between one perceptual position—mere inches from the canvas for the intricate application of his microscopic brushstrokes—and another position much farther away, to refocus his eyes on the fully formed representation of a signature seemingly carved in wood.

This difference in techniques is one of the key distinctions that has dominated our conventional understanding of what constitutes aesthetic modernism. Whereas *trompe l'oeil* painting has often been described as a form of hyper-realism—and thus the last gasp of a long tradition of Renaissance perspectivalism—Impressionism has conventionally been celebrated as a radical break with this tradition, one which led directly to abstraction and the twentieth century. Yet, as Jonathan Crary has argued recently, there is a fundamental flaw with this binary model and the core narrative it supports. Simply put, the visual doubts fueling both of these modes seem to have grown out of a common historical source: the "modernization of vision" that first found expression in early nineteenth-century perceptual science.[77] Crary's point is not to make a case for a particular lineage of ideas or influences, as if the Impressionists sat down to read Goethe or Helmholtz and began to paint in new ways. Rather, he claims that these scientific and artistic expressions were part of an ongoing epistemological shift which redefined the typical observer in all corners of Western culture. The result was a new, post-Enlightenment conception of vision, understood as prone to error and often in need of correction through other sensory mechanisms—in short, a *subjective* vision very much like that explicated by George Platt on the Midwestern lecture circuit.

Here we can begin to understand the popular success of Harnett and his followers in a more historically convincing way—perhaps not as part of aesthetic modernism in the canonical sense, but at least engaged with the same nineteenth-century processes of visual adaptation and modernization described by Crary and Benjamin. As an illustration of this engagement, consider one final piece of evidence from Harnett's career, a remarkable review article from the late 1880s, entitled "Queer Art Illusions."[78] The anonymous reviewer, it seems clear, was very well-read and educated, referring to the writings of Fechner,

Helmholtz, and Sully to substantiate the discussion of how illusions emerge in human visual experience. But the final proof is experimental rather than scientific: the author recommends a trip to Theodore Stewart's saloons, where "art illusion" is "wonderfully exemplified" in the works of "Mr. W. M. Harnett."[79]

"The spectator," the author notes,

> may place himself at any point of observation, remote or near, and he will find it difficult, if not impossible, to convince himself that he is not looking at real objects. He will remark to a bystander, perhaps, that he can see that this or that *other* object is not and *cannot* be other than real, being adroitly suspended or placed in front of the painted parts for the purposes of deception. He will be positive of this—*very* positive, and when, by some means, as by getting close to the wall on which the picture is fastened on the side opposite the light, he obtains a strong reflection of light which covers and neutralizes the tone of portions of the picture, he convinces himself that what he thought was a real thing was only a flat surface, he is then ready to avow that the parts that he thought *"might be painted"* are real, and by a trick of grouping, are made to enhance the effect of the artist's proper work. By dint of long study of the picture he at length admits that it is *"all painting,"* but the illusion even then persists, and he at last turns away, generally with the exclamation, "Marvelous! The most remarkable thing I ever saw!"

All of the common *trompe l'oeil* reception patterns are at work here: the spectator's initial confidence, which eventually erodes in the face of Harnett's aesthetic trickery; the somewhat frantic movements around the canvas in search of some stable point of perceptual control; the uneasy wavering between various claims of authenticity and artifice; and finally, the exhibition room concession speech, in which the viewer admits that the image is all painting, only to succumb to lingering doubts about that solution. In this case, though, the author suggests that perceptual fallibility might serve as the moral of the story itself. We hear nothing, significantly, of this confused spectator's travels to Stewart's Saloon from some provincial locality. Nor does the author anxiously invite Harnett to visit the saloon to settle the matter once and for all. Indeed, this time Harnett's tricks serve primarily to illustrate how human perception itself is often dead wrong:

> From the first dawn of intellect we struggle through life in an effort (often in vain) to learn how accurately to perceive the things which environ us. We commit errors in the use of each of our senses, and only correct them even partially in checking one sense against another. . . . To think we see what does not exist, and therefore, cannot really be seen, is one of the commonest of illusions, and Sully has proved that the human imagination is one of the most important factors in causing this fallacious seeing.[80]

To define such fallaciousness as entirely human, common, and inevitable was the final nineteenth-century form of visual adaptation. And it was this new, more subjective understanding of vision that connected *trompe l'oeil* painting not merely to Barnum's brand of popular amusement, but also to the very origins of Western modernism.

Epilogue
Barnum's Ghosts

⋯▷═▷ ◁═◁⋯

By the dawn of the new century, all of the leading arts of deception from the Age of Barnum were either gone or in decline. In 1869 the automaton chess-player was revived in a new version—Ajeeb, the Oriental Wonder—and spent almost forty years entertaining audiences at New York's Eden Musée and Coney Island. But like the Kempelen original, Ajeeb perished by fire in 1929. Similarly, the Feejee Mermaid seems to have perished in one of the devastating fires that eventually pushed Barnum out of the museum business during the late 1860s. A What Is It? exhibition made the transition with Barnum into the circus industry and had a strong second career as Zip, the most famous and enduring of Barnum's racialized sideshow curiosities. But this too finally came to an end in 1926, when the last man to wear the fur suit, William Henry Johnson, passed away.

In 1908 Harry Kellar began a quiet semi-retirement in southern California, appearing now and again at a Society of American Magicians banquet to the applause of his youthful admirers. By this time, though, it was already clear that a new form of magical modernism

Harry Kellar (seated) passes the torch of modern magic to his friend, Harry Houdini (early twentieth century).

was taking shape. Its most famous avatar was Harry Houdini, who performed his very first "jail break" in 1900. Whereas Kellar had presented himself as a confidence man whom the new middle class could trust, Houdini actually broke out of prison cells, straitjackets, and handcuffs in a symbolic inversion of criminality which traded Enlightenment rhetoric and bourgeois refinement for raw physical power and dramas of self-liberation. A similar transition marked the decline of *trompe l'oeil* painting. By the time of the landmark Armory Show of 1913, Harnett's "queer art illusions" were largely forgotten in American art circles, pushed out of favor not by the polemics of conservative critics like Clarence Cook, but through the ascendancy of another sort of modernist impulse—abstraction. With pictorial realism now serving as the passé principle against which much of the avant-garde defined itself, the *trompe l'oeil* canvases of Harnett and his followers slowly found their way to antique shops, flea markets, and family attics, where they often languished for decades.

Yet this story of nineteenth-century artful deception's movement into the dustbin of history is somewhat misleading, for it confuses specific artists and exhibitions with their much larger and older popular cultural categories. Artful deception never disappears for very long: it keeps coming back, producing new historical cycles, aesthetic variations, and social inflections. And this is true in our own age as well as Barnum's, a pattern which becomes clear as soon as we turn our attention to some of the most widely discussed cultural developments of the past decade.

One good example is the recent wave of "uncensored" television talk shows, most of whose freakish stars (and carefully choreographed controversies) are just about as "real" as Barnum's living curiosity exhibitions. A little further down the dial we come to an almost perpetual cycle of professional wrestling, whose sellout crowds engage in a collective suspension of disbelief larger and more enthusiastic than anything seen in American popular culture since the heyday of modern magic. And then there are the virtual wonders which appear now in almost every corner of American visual culture, a digitized form of *trompe l'oeil* at once as uncanny and as difficult to confuse with non-virtual reality as the painted hunting gear which used to hang on the wall at Stewart's Saloon.

Even some of the specific names, rituals, and raw materials of Bar-

Epilogue

numesque deception have returned recently in new guises. In 1995, for instance, a Feejee Mermaid made a guest appearance on (where else?) the *X-Files*, this time playing the role of a serial killer! Or think of the recent wave of "Masked Magician" television specials, which once again present the stage conjuror as an enlightened expositor, laying his tricks bare for a curious public at home. One can point also to the ongoing, critical rehabilitation of late nineteenth-century *trompe l'oeil* painting, a process which reached its high water mark in 1992, with the retrospective Harnett exhibition at the Metropolitan Museum of Art in New York. Even the automaton chess-player seems to be back again. Except that this time its stage name is Deep Blue, its costume consists of a sleek plastic cabinet, and its managers are a team of computer programmers from IBM, whose goal is to befuddle Gary Kasparov, the world chess champion.

My point here is not to champion a reductive argument about the cyclical nature of history, nor even to suggest that there is something straightforwardly repetitive about the late twentieth-century history of artful deception. Rather, all of these recent cultural phenomena (even the Harnett retrospective at the Met, which included the very same paintings) seem to have as much in common with their nineteenth-century predecessors as Kempelen's automaton chess-player show had with Maelzel's. In each case, that is to say, these contemporary artifacts and performances are best understood as historically specific inflections of artful deceptions that have been returning in one guise or another for centuries. Each era reinvents its own cultural tricks for its own particular reasons. And the values and concerns expressed through these tricks are always unique. What they document is not the cyclical nature of history (or our own perpetually unenlightened condition), but the remarkable durability, plasticity, and utility of artful deception as a mechanism for individual and social differentiation.

This is what tricksters provide in any era: the indeterminate object, the uncertain image, the morally suspect act—an engaging assortment of cultural deceits with which an eager public gauges its moral and aesthetic thresholds, defines itself. But if the tricks keep coming back in new forms, what can we conclude about the broader historical legacies of trickster culture in the Age of Barnum?

Perhaps the best way to answer this question is to compare the shifting conceptions of representational truth which have defined the arts of deception over the past two centuries. For Kempelen and Peale, the primary concern was to maintain clear epistemological distinctions between playful illusionism and the more truthful, morally productive work of Enlightenment. To exhibit a bogus automaton, perpetual motion machine, or Japanese mermaid was all well and good, but these things needed to be defined and differentiated as illusionism. Or, at the very least, they needed to be marked as a subordinate form of intellectual play in an unambiguous hierarchy of curiosities, so that the business of *bagatelles* did not eclipse their more honest enterprises. This was the threshold of tricksterism that Barnum's predecessors would bend but not break. Even as a thriving market for overt popular cultural fraud began to emerge at the end of the eighteenth century, Kempelen and Peale responded with enlightened clarity. They simply would not become purveyors of trickery as an end in itself.

Maelzel and Barnum, by contrast, had no such scruples. Indeed, it was precisely the undifferentiated cultural object and the mass-circulated equivocation which served as the foundation of their show business success. Yet it might also be argued that Maelzel and Barnum were ultimately a bit *too* successful in their efforts to tease, distort, and provoke. During the final decades of Barnum's career, one of his standard public complaints was directed at patrons who suspected that all of his exhibitory wonders, even the real ones, were probably fakes. As early as 1865, Barnum wrote about this problem in *Humbugs of the World,* a text which includes some of the showman's most revealing statements about the ongoing challenges of "managing" a mass audience raised on a steady diet of Barnumesque hoaxing.

An early chapter entitled "The Whale, the Angel Fish, and the Golden Pigeon" addresses the problem head on. It begins with a brief anecdote about a "sharp Yankee lady" and her daughter, who arrive at

Epilogue

the American Museum eager to see the showman's heavily promoted Labrador Whale. This whale, Barnum explains, was kept in a large, top-lit tank in the American Museum's basement and rarely surfaced, a pattern which led some patrons to dispute its very existence. The Yankee lady, however, had a different explanation:

> "Mr B., it's astonishing to what a number of purposes the ingenuity of us Yankees has applied india-rubber." I asked her meaning, and was soon informed that she was perfectly convinced that it was an india-rubber whale, worked by steam and machinery. . . . From her earnest, confident manner, I saw it would be useless to attempt to disabuse her mind on the subject. I therefore very candidly acknowledged that she was quite too sharp for me, and I must plead guilty to the imposition; but I begged her not to expose me, for I assured her that she was the only person who had discovered the trick.

In the end Barnum concludes that this lady "evidently received double her money's worth in the happy reflection that she could not be humbugged, and that I was terribly humiliated in being detected through her marvelous powers of discrimination."[1]
Barnum then relates an anecdote about a Connecticut neighbor, "Mrs. H.," who confronts him after viewing the Golden Angel Fish in the American Museum aquarium:

> "You can't humbug me, Mr. Barnum; that fish is painted!" "Nonsense!", said I, with a laugh; "the thing is impossible!" "I don't care, I know it is painted; it is as plain as can be." "But, my dear Mrs. H., paint would not adhere to a fish while in the water; and if it would, it would kill him. Besides," I added, with an extra serious air, "we never allow humbugging here!" "Oh, here is just the place to look for such things," she replied with a smile.[2]

In many ways, of course, this was everything Barnum had worked for during the first thirty years of his show business career: a thoroughly respectable "family audience" playfully engaged with his newest American Museum curiosities. These spirited curiosity-seekers, more-over, were quite willing to indulge Barnum's penchant for "puffery," adhering to much the same conception of promotional license that

Barnum defined as "modern" in his opening chapters. They under-stood his fibbing, that is to say, not so much as a morally troubling "imposition," but as the clever teases of an "honest" impresario, one who "arrests public attention" with "glittering appearances, outside show, and novel expedients"—and then delivers a quota of amuse-ment "fully equivalent" to the admission price.[3]

Yet this cash-value conception of truth came with one great, unin-tended consequence: sometimes the showman's audiences looked for artful deception in the exhibition room even when none was involved. Initially at least, Barnum tried to laugh the problem away, describing his female accusers as quasi-delusional. These were precisely the sorts of viewers, he insisted, who have "such a horror of being taken in, or such an elevated view of their acuteness, that they believe everything to be a sham, and in this way are continually humbugging them-selves."[4] One gets the sense, though, that Barnum was fully aware of the larger dilemma that the Yankee Lady and Mrs. H. represented. At the very moment when the American public was becoming fully acculturated to the built-in fuzziness of Barnum's representations, the representations themselves began to defy his control. Deconstructing the literal truth produced a new kind of promotional problem during the 1860s—for once deconstructed, it was not especially easy to put back together again.

Other tricksters found themselves trapped in similar kinds of self-made dilemmas. Harnett, for example, was unceremoniously arrested for counterfeiting by a team of New York treasury agents in 1886. At issue were his *trompe l'oeil* paintings of banknotes, two of which hung on the walls in Stewart's saloons, only a few short blocks from City Hall and Wall Street. The arrest did not last very long. As Harnett later told the *New York News:* "I was let go with a warning not to paint any more life-like representations of the national currency—a warning it is almost needless to say that I conscientiously heeded."[5] The arrest reports left behind by the agent in charge, A. L. Drummond, explain why Harnett was let go. While these money pictures had "come within the spirit" of the contemporary counterfeiting law, prosecution was deemed unnecessary because "no fraud was intended."[6]

Epilogue

This was only half true. With each painstaking, microscopic brush-stroke, Harnett had quite deliberately intended the most convincing fraud he could possibly muster, one which would leave the bankers and downtown businessmen in Stewart's Saloon thoroughly uncertain. Yet these efforts at ambiguity were never designed to cross the threshold of criminality. As Harnett nervously explained to the treasury agents, the "nature" of his pictorial trickery was entirely "harmless." The legal remedy devised by Drummond and his treasury men was similarly paradoxical, and spoke volumes about the morally ambiguous status of artful deception during these years. In the future, Harnett's banknote pictures were to be confined to Stewart's private gallery of art, so as not to give the bar patrons any bright ideas.[7]

In the modern magic business, the most pressing concern was almost the opposite of the one facing the *trompe l'oeil* painter—how to avoid too much exposé (rather than too much deception). During an 1886 show in Chicago, for example, Kellar found himself under fire from an English magic fan who claimed to have read about the prestidigitator's tricks as a young man. Although most of this particular Kellar show was new to Chicago, the Englishman's charges were correct. Kellar had in fact purchased some of his tricks during the early 1880s from another magician working on the other side of the Atlantic, John Nevil Maskelyne. And in true modernist fashion, Maskelyne had explained some of the tricks in print, part of his own efforts to carve out a public identity as a literary expositor. When the English magic fan saw recycled wonders on Kellar's stage, he made a beeline for a *Chicago Daily News* reporter at the first intermission:

> "The posters and announcements of this man makes one smile," he said during a pause in the refreshments. "From them one would think [Kellar] was going to prove a mixture of the devil and Dr. Faustus, while, on the contrary, the tricks he performs were old when I was a boy. . . . Take this levitation act for instance. The posters represent him sailing all over the auditorium. That, of course, is mere theatrical advertising. He does not even leave the stage. The theater is darkened and a stuffed dummy with a phosphorescent mask is swung about the theater by a wire."[8]

Kellar, naturally, could not let these public accusations go unchallenged and denounced the *Daily News* on stage the following night, offering a $500 reward if anyone could actually prove the charges. The English magic fan, however, remained undeterred and went right back to the *Daily News* with another exposé, this time involving Keller's second sight trick: "No, Kellar didn't explain that, but I will, at the risk of having him denounce the *Daily News* again from the stage. I take a fiendish delight in doing so, because he seemed to make a mystery of it, whereas the explanation of that and every other trick he does can be found in any cheap book on parlor magic."[9]

Kellar's difficulties illustrate the central dilemma of post-Enlightenment conjuring: with each cheap book on parlor magic—each new round of self-exposé—modern magicians never knew quite what to expect from their enlightened audiences, or where exactly they stood in relation to the larger culture of decipherment they had already created. While the tricksters on stage usually remained one step ahead of their exposers, the very fact that magicians now routinely traded in exposé created the need for almost constant reform, continuous novelty. As the circle of prestidigitatorial knowledge widened, so too did the required pace of innovation.

This was the brave new world that the tricksters had made. It was a world in which playful forms of exhibitory fraud routinely skirted across the mimetic threshold separating art and life, producing their own unexpected realities. It was also a world in which the slippery behavior of the tricksters became a central subject of commercial entertainment—one of its built-in, defining characteristics—and the growing cynicism of mass audiences became increasingly reflexive.[10] Neither the producers nor the consumers of this culture maintained complete control. While the tricksters often found themselves caught in illusionistic webs of their own spinning, the audiences entered into an almost perpetual meta-discourse about their own consumption behavior. As the Age of Barnum came to a close, what most viewers debated was not merely the manipulations of the tricksters (is this curiosity real?), but also how they were being manipulated by the debates (is this larger exercise moral, entertaining, worth the money, and so forth).[11]

Is this our world, too? Let me conclude with one last example of modern humbug in action, a humbug which inadvertently became perhaps the most dramatic—and troubling—popular cultural event of 1999. It all began in Kansas City, Missouri, before 16,300 screaming fans at a World Wrestling Federation championship. Like most of these events, the evening's entertainment included a series of wildly theatrical promotional stunts—stunts which, as most regular wrestling fans know, are routinely embellished or faked for maximum excitement. In this case, though, the unthinkable happened. As one of the show's stars, Owen Hart, was rappeling down from the rafters of Kemper Arena, the mechanism supporting his suspension cable broke, and Hart fell 90 feet to the ring below.[12]

For the next few minutes paramedics attempted unsuccessfully to revive the fallen wrestler, while the resident WWF emcee tried his best to explain what was happening over the public address system. "Folks," he nervously announced to the crowd, "we've got a problem here." Yet, as Kemper Arena's general manager later confessed to a reporter from *Newsweek*, the difference between entertaining illusionism and gruesome tragedy remained unclear for many of those watching from the stands. "Since this was the WWF," he concluded, "a lot of people thought it was a stunt." And the wrestling matches simply continued, as if Hart's descent from the rafters really had been a publicity stunt.[13]

I leave it to others to explain what this remarkable event might tell us about the aesthetic and moral conventions of illusionism at the close of the twentieth century. But one larger conclusion seems clear. As Owen Hart's WWF handlers scrambled to find their way out of the tragic debacle they had created in Kansas City, the ghosts of 1835 were still haunting American popular culture.

Notes

Index

Notes

→⊨◉ ◉⊨←

Introduction

1. P. T. Barnum, *The Life of P. T. Barnum, Written by Himself* (New York: Redfield, 1855), p. 148; *Pennsylvania Inquirer,* July 15, 1835.
2. Barnum, *Life of Barnum,* pp. 143–146.
3. For a useful discussion of the differences between traditional and modern popular culture, see Michael Kammen, *American Culture, American Tastes: Social Change and the 20th Century* (New York: Knopf, 1999), pp. 3–26.
4. Barnum, *Life of Barnum,* pp. 150–151. For details see the original contract, pp. 150–152. See also Neil Harris, *Humbug: The Art of P. T. Barnum* (Chicago: University of Chicago Press, 1973), pp. 20–26; A. H. Saxon, *P. T. Barnum: the Legend and the Man* (New York: Columbia University Press, 1989), pp. 21, 66–67; Bluford Adams, *E Pluribus Barnum: The Great Showman & The Making of U.S. Popular Culture* (Minneapolis: University of Minnesota Press, 1997), pp. 2–10; and Benjamin Riess, "P. T. Barnum, Joice Heth, and Antebellum Spectacles of Race," *American Quarterly,* 51/1 (March 1999), pp. 78–107.
5. On Broadway as a popular cultural epicenter, see Peter Buckley, "Culture, Class, and Place in Antebellum New York," in John Hull Mollenkopf, ed., *Power, Culture, and Place: Essays on New York City* (New York: Russell Sage Foundation, 1988); Stuart Blumin, "George Foster and the Emerging Metropolis," in *New York by Gas-Light* (Berkeley: University of California Press, 1990); and Edwin G. Burrows and Mike Wallace, *Gotham: A History of New York City to 1898* (New York: Oxford University Press, 1999).

6. Barnum, *Life of Barnum*, p. 152; George C. D. Odell, *Annals of the New York Stage* (New York: Columbia University Press, 1928–1949), vol. 4, pp. 43–47, 105–108.

7. Quoted in Barnum, *Life of Barnum*, p. 154.

8. On the historical contours of the black mammy stereotype, see Deborah White, *Ar'n't I a Woman: Female Slaves in the Plantation South* (New York: Norton, 1985); and Nell Irvin Painter, *Sojourner Truth: A Life, A Symbol* (New York: Norton, 1996).

9. Barnum, *Life of Barnum*, pp. 153–155.

10. Ibid.

11. Undated handbill (c. September, 1835) for a show in Hingham, Massachusetts, in the Fred D. Pfening III Collection, Columbus, Ohio.

12. Quoted in Barnum, *Life of Barnum*, p. 154.

13. Ibid.

14. Undated advertisement from the Providence *Daily Journal*, reprinted in the Hingham handbill. The Fred D. Pfening III Collection. According to Bluford Adams, this "fraudulent promise" appeared in the *Daily Journal* on August 31, 1835, the *Lowell Courier* on September 12, 1835, and an anonymous promotional pamphlet, "The Life of Joice Heth."

15. Barnum, *Life of Barnum*, p. 156.

16. Ibid., p. 157. Although the evidence points to Barnum as the author here, it is not entirely clear whether the showman himself planted this initial accusation of fraud. The ad was merely signed "A Visitor." But in any case, Barnum aggressively encouraged this way of thinking during the exhibition's remaining weeks; and there is no question that he traded in self-directed, public accusations in his later exhibitory frauds.

17. Ibid., pp. 157–159.

18. Ibid., pp. 171–176.

19. New York *Sun*, February 25, 1836.

20. New York *Herald*, February 27, 1836.

21. Barnum, *Life of Barnum*, pp. 155–156. Barnum's italics.

22. The evidence here is often contradictory. As A. H. Saxon notes, Barnum claimed in a letter from the early 1850s that he was an unwitting victim of false representations by Heth and her previous manager, R. W. Lindsey (*P. T. Barnum*, p. 73). But Barnum also claimed in the semi-autobiographical "Adventures of an Adventurer" series in the 1841 New York *Atlas*, and in a British magazine article by Alfred Smith, "A Go-A-Head Day with Barnum," *Bentley's Miscellany*, vol. 21, 1847, that he had known about the hoax and did everything he could to perpetuate it. Saxon seems to favor the Barnum-as-victim hypothesis, attributing the showman's public claims of agency to "youthful bravado." But as Saxon himself documents, Barnum's denials of agency during the 1850s may have been part of a larger effort to refashion his image as a respectable impresario.

23. Robert Bogdan, *Freak Show: Presenting Human Oddities for Amusement and Profit* (Chicago: University of Chicago Press, 1988). See also David Gerber, "The 'Careers' of People Exhibited in Freak Shows: The Problem of Volition and Valorization," in Rosemarie Thomson, ed., *Freakery: Cultural Spectacles of the Extraordinary Body* (New York: New York University Press, 1996).

24. One good source for measuring the pervasiveness of artful deception in nineteenth-century America is Odell's year-by-year *Annals of the New York Stage*, which contain hundreds—even thousands—of listings for automata, dubious curiosities, sleight-of-hand artists, panoramas, etc. Odell's listings also document that this popular cultural

current does not conform to any particular category of venue. Exhibitions of stage magic, for example, sometimes appear in Odell's listings for particular theaters. But on other occasions, one finds stage magic in his listings for assembly rooms, museums, pleasure gardens, industrial fairs, and circuses.

25. Harris has described this as Barnum's "operational aesthetic," *Humbug*, pp. 59–89. I return to this issue and offer further qualifications in Chapter Two.

26. On the long history of this famous phrase, see Saxon, "Appendix: Barnum Apocrypha," in *P. T. Barnum*, pp. 334–337.

27. Barnum, *Life of Barnum*, p. 171.

28. W. J. T. Mitchell, *Picture Theory: Essays on Verbal and Visual Representation* (Chicago: University of Chicago Press, 1994), pp. 323–344. Mitchell playfully acknowledges this "slipperiness" in a set of nine "theses" which preface his discussion. Whereas Thesis 3 states that "illusion must be sharply distinguished from illusionism," Thesis 5 admits that "illusionism cannot be sharply distinguished from illusion." Thesis 8 concludes that "the notion of a theory of illusion is the last illusion of theory" (p. 329).

29. Ibid., p. 325.

30. Ibid.

31. George M. Frederickson, *The Black Image in the White Mind: The Debate on Afro-American Character and Destiny, 1817–1914* (Hanover, Conn.: Wesleyan University Press, 1971); Robert Toll, *Blacking Up: The Minstrel Show in Nineteenth-Century America* (New York: Oxford University Press, 1978); Reginald Horsman, *Race and Manifest Destiny: The Origins of American Racial Anglo-Saxonism* (Cambridge, Mass.: Harvard University Press, 1981); White, *Ar'n't I a Woman;* Alexander Saxton, *The Rise and Fall of the White Republic: Class Politics and Mass Culture in Nineteenth-Century America* (New York: Verso, 1990); Ronald Takaki, *Iron Cages: Race and Culture in 19th-Century America* (New York: Oxford University Press, 1990); David Roediger, *The Wages of Whiteness: Race and the Making of the American Working Class* (New York: Verso, 1991); Eric Lott, *Love and Theft: Blackface Minstrelsy and the American Working Class* (New York: Oxford University Press, 1993); Painter, *Sojourner Truth;* W. T. Lhamon, *Raising Cain: Blackface Performance from Jim Crow to Hip Hop* (Cambridge, Mass.: Harvard University Press, 1998).

32. Mitchell hints at such a dialectical relationship between illusionism and realism, calling them "intertwined traditions" in Western culture. *Picture Theory*, p. 325.

33. In this respect, Barnum's brand of artful deception was similar to the blackface minstrel show, whose representations were understood as both "authentically Negro" and as white "delineations" of African-American cultural forms. But it is important not to push this line of comparison too far: while blackface minstrelsy involved a degree of *trompe l'oeil* performance on stage, it was never understood as an exhibitory guessing game. In other words, few if any minstrel show viewers debated the question of whether T. D. Rice was, literally, a black man.

34. *The Natural History of Pliny* (London: Henry G. Bohn, 1890), p. 251.

35. Norman Bryson, *Looking at the Overlooked: Four Essays on Still Life Painting* (Cambridge, Mass.: Harvard University Press, 1990), pp. 10–13.

36. Ibid., p. 13.

37. On the durability of popular culture and the problems of historical interpretation this durability sometimes creates, see Robert Darnton, "Peasants Tell Tales: The Meaning of Mother Goose," in his *The Great Cat Massacre* (New York: Vintage Books, 1984).

38. Mitchell, *Picture Theory*, p. 329.

39. Barnum, *Life of Barnum*, p. 242; Saxon, *P. T. Barnum*, pp. 202, 287.
40. Philadelphia *Public Ledger*, December 4, 1840.
41. A good contemporary example of this pattern can be found in David Meredith Reese's *Humbugs of New York* (1838), which employed "humbug" as a pejorative term to condemn ultraism, phrenology, and abolitionism as outrageous swindles.
42. It is important to acknowledge that these were, in fact, mass audiences. As Barnum himself emphasized, the viewers who witnessed his curiosities in the exhibition room were part of a much broader public—one which included thousands of urban newspaper readers. And this readership often multiplied quickly, as local stories were reprinted nationwide. P. T. Barnum, *Struggles and Triumphs* (Buffalo: Warren, Johnson, 1872), pp. 130–131.
43. For more on Barnum's audience see my essay, "Mass Marketing and Cultural History: The Case of P. T. Barnum," *American Quarterly*, 51/1 (March 1999), pp. 175–186.
44. Relative to population size, Barnum's audiences may have been larger than the late twentieth-century audiences for Disneyland. As Saxon has noted, Barnum's two American Museums (1841–1868) generated approximately 42 million admission tickets—a remarkable number when we consider the fact that the total population of the United States was only about 35 million in 1865. *P. T. Barnum*, pp. 107–108.
45. On these issues, see Burton J. Bledstein, *The Culture of Professionalism: The Middle Class and the Development of Higher Education in* America (New York: Norton, 1976); Mary P. Ryan, *The Cradle of the Middle Class: The Family in Oneida County* (Cambridge: Cambridge University Press, 1983); Stuart Blumin, *The Emergence of the Middle Class: Social Experience in the American City, 1760–1900* (Cambridge: Cambridge University Press, 1989); Robert Allen, *Horrible Prettiness: Burlesque and American Culture* (Chapel Hill: University of North Carolina Press, 1991); and Anne C. Rose, *Voices of the Marketplace: American Thought and Culture, 1830–1860* (New York: Twayne Publishers, 1995).
46. The best analysis of this issue can be found in Adams, *E Pluribus Barnum*, pp. xi–xiv, 75–76.
47. George Allen, "History of the Automaton Chess-Player in America," Daniel Willard Fiske, ed., *The Book of the First American Chess Congress* (New York: Rudd & Carleton, 1859), p. 432.
48. Alfred Frankenstein, *After the Hunt: William Harnett and Other American Still Life Painters 1870–1900* (Berkeley: University of California Press, 1969), p. 79.
49. Robert Laurence Moore, *In Search of White Crows* (New York: Oxford University Press, 1976); Karen Halttunen, *Confidence Men and Painted Women: A Study of Middle-Class Culture in America, 1830–1870* (New Haven: Yale University Press, 1982); Elaine Abelson, *When Ladies Go A-Thieving: Middle-Class Shoplifters in the Victorian Department Store* (New York: Oxford University Press, 1989); John Kasson, *Rudeness and Civility: Manners in Nineteenth-Century America* (New York: Hill and Wang, 1990); Alan Trachtenberg, *Reading American Photographs: Pictures as History* (New York: Hill and Wang, 1990) and Trachtenberg, "Introduction," in Horatio Alger, Jr., *Ragged Dick, Or, Street Life in New York with the Boot Blacks* (New York: Signet Classic, 1990); Ann Fabian, *Card Sharps, Dream Books, & Bucket Shops: Gambling in 19th-Century America* (Ithaca: Cornell University Press, 1990); and Jackson Lears, *Fables of Abundance: A Cultural History of Advertising in America* (New York: Basic Books, 1994).

50. Halttunen, *Confidence Men and Painted Women;* Kasson, *Rudeness and Civility;* Stuart Blumin, "Explaining the New Metropolis: Perception, Depiction, and Analysis in Mid-Nineteenth-Century New York City," *Journal of Urban History,* 11/1 (November 1984), pp. 9–38, and his "George G. Foster and the Emerging Metropolis"; David S. Reynolds, *Beneath the American Renaissance: The Subversive Imagination in the Age of Emerson and Melville* (New York: Knopf, 1988); and Dana Brand, *The Spectator and the City in Nineteenth-Century American Literature* (Cambridge: Cambridge University Press, 1991).

51. The classic texts on the semiotic challenges of nineteenth-century modernization are Walter Benjamin, "On Some Motifs in Baudelaire," in Hannah Arendt, ed., *Illuminations* (New York: Schocken Books, 1968), pp. 155–200; and Georg Simmel, "The Metropolis and Mental Life," in Donald N. Levine, ed., *On Individuality and Social Forms* (Chicago: University of Chicago Press, 1971), pp. 324–339. See also Marshall Berman, *All That Is Solid Melts Into Air: The Experience of Modernity* (New York: Penguin Books, 1988); Susan Buck-Morse, *The Dialectics of Seeing: Walter Benjamin and the Arcades Project* (Cambridge, Mass.: MIT Press, 1991); and Ross Posnock, *The Trial of Curiosity: Henry James, William James, and the Challenge of Modernity* (New York: Oxford University Press, 1991).

52. On play as a broader cultural practice, see Brian Sutton-Smith, *The Ambiguity of Play* (Cambridge, Mass.: Harvard University Press, 1997), and Jay Mechling, "Performing Imaginary Rhetoric," *American Quarterly,* 52/2 (June 2000), pp. 364-370.

53. Harris, *Humbug,* pp. 61–89.

54. My larger goal here is to explain what was culturally and historically distinctive about tricksterism in the nineteenth-century show trade. That said, it is important to acknowledge the rich body of literary, anthropological, and historical studies that have explored the concept of the trickster figure in other forms and contexts. See especially Roger D. Abrahams, "Trickster, the Outrageous Hero," in *Our Living Traditions: An Introduction to American Folklore,* ed. Tristan Peter Coffin (New York: Basic Books, 1968), pp. 170–178; Victor Turner, *The Ritual Process* (Chicago: Aldine Publishing, 1969); Barbara A. Babcock, ed., *The Reversible World: Symbolic Inversion in Art and Society* (Ithaca: Cornell University Press, 1978); Mary Douglas, *Purity and Danger* (London: Routledge, 1991); Lawrence W. Levine, *Black Culture and Black Consciousness: Afro-American Folk Thought from Slavery to Freedom* (New York: Oxford University Press, 1977); Halttunen, *Confidence Men and Painted Women;* Carroll Smith-Rosenberg, *Disorderly Conduct* (New York: Oxford University Press, 1985); Henry Louis Gates, Jr., *The Signifying Monkey: A Theory of African-American Literary Criticism* (New York: Oxford University Press, 1988); William M. Hynes and William G. Doty, eds., *Mythical Trickster Figures* (Tuscaloosa: University of Alabama Press, 1997); Lewis Hyde, *Trickster Makes This World* (New York: North Point Press, 1998); and Lori Landay, *Madcaps, Screwballs, and Con Women: The Female Trickster in American Culture* (Philadelphia: University of Pennsylvania Press, 1998).

55. On trickster tales as pre-industrial oral culture, see Levine, *Black Culture and Black Consciousness;* Darnton, "Peasants Tell Tales: The Meaning of Mother Goose," in *The Great Cat Massacre;* and Charles Joyner, *Down by the Riverside: A South Carolina Slave Community* (Urbana: University of Illinois Press, 1984). On tricksters in nineteenth-century American fiction, see Warwick Wadlington, *The Confidence Game in American Literature* (Princeton: Princeton University Press, 1975); and Gary

Lindbergh, *The Confidence Man in American Literature* (New York: Oxford University Press, 1982).

56. On the vexed issue of audience manipulation in the context of modern popular culture, see the "AHR Forum" in the *American Historical Review,* 97/5 (December 1992), pp. 1369–1430 with essays by Lawrence Levine, "The Folklore of Industrial Society: Popular Culture and Its Audiences"; Robin D. G. Kelley, "Notes on Deconstructing 'The Folk'"; Natalie Zemon Davis, "Towards Mixtures and Margins"; and Jackson Lears, "Making Fun of Popular Culture." See also Stuart Hall, "Notes on Deconstructing 'the Popular'," in Ralph Samuel, ed., *People's History and Socialist Theory* (London, 1980), and George Lipsitz, *Time Passages: Collective Memory and American Popular Culture* (Minneapolis: University of Minnesota Press, 1990). It is worth noting that none of these excellent essays and books mentions Barnum at all (despite the fact that he virtually invented promotional manipulation in its modern forms). This may be because Barnum's self-directed accusations of deceit do not fit easily within the long-running scholarly debates between "bottom-up" audience choice and "top-down" culture industry control. What his career seems to demonstrate, in fact, is that modern commercial entertainment has always included a degree of meta-discourse about the promotional process. While some viewers simply debated the authenticity of Barnum's curiosities, others discussed how they were being manipulated *by the debate,* treating the showman's promotional tricks as a second, equally fascinating topic of moral and economic evaluation.

1. The Automaton Chess Player

1. John Kearsley Mitchell, "The Last of a Veteran Chess Player," *The Chess Monthly,* 1 (February 1857), pp. 3–4.
2. "It is supposed that in the course of his various exhibitions he has been seen by more eyes than any terrestrial object ever exhibited . . ." Philadelphia *Public Ledger,* December 4, 1840, p. 2. See also Edgar Allan Poe, "Maelzel's Chess-Player," *Southern Literary Messenger,* 2 (April 1836): "Perhaps no exhibition of the kind has ever elicited so general attention. Wherever seen it has been an object of intense curiosity to all persons who think."
3. Heinrich Christian Beck's play, *Die Schachmaschine,* was first published in 1797 and went through numerous translations and reprintings. Sir David Brewster, *Letters on Natural Magic* (London, 1833), pp. 269–282. E. T. A. Hoffmann's "Die Automate" was first published in *Zeitung fuer die elegante Welt,* 1814. The story is translated as "Automata" and reprinted in *The Best Tales of Hoffmann* (New York: Dover Books, 1967).
4. Poe, "Maelzel's Chess-Player," reprinted in *Complete Tales & Poems of Edgar Allan Poe* (New York: Vintage, 1975), pp. 421–439.
5. Joseph Earle Arrington, "John Maelzel, Master Showman of Automata and Panoramas," *Pennsylvania Museum of History and Biography,* 84 (1960), pp. 56–92; Ernest Wittenberg, "*Echec!* The Bizarre Career of the Turk," *American Heritage,* 11/2 (February 1860), pp. 34–37, 82–85; Charles Michael Carroll, *The Great Chess Automaton* (New York: Dover Books, 1975); Milbourne and Maurine Christopher, "The Automaton Chess Player," in *The Illustrated History of Magic* (Portsmouth: Heinemann, 1996), pp. 30–47. For a literary critical angle, see W. K. Wimsatt, "Poe and the Chess Automaton," *American Literature,* 11/2 (May 1939), pp. 138–159; and John T. Irwin, *The Mys-*

tery to a Solution: Poe, Borges, and the Analytic Detective Story (Baltimore: Johns Hopkins University Press, 1994). Stephen P. Rice has examined the automaton in relation to industrialization in a recent conference paper, "Maelzel's Automaton Chess-Player: Marking the Boundary between Humans and Machines in Antebellum America," American Studies Association Annual Meeting, Nashville, Tenn., October 1994.

6. One finds these categorical distinctions at work in numerous scholarly works on the history of cabinets, museums, and exhibitions. On the European side, see Richard Altick, *The Shows of London* (Cambridge, Mass.: Harvard University Press, 1978); Oliver Impey and Arthur MacGregor, eds., *The Cabinet of Curiosities in Sixteenth-and Seventeenth-Century Europe* (Oxford: Clarendon Press, 1985); Krzystof Pomian, *Collectors and Curiosities, Paris and Venice, 1500–1800* (Cambridge: Polity Press, 1990); Joy Kenseth, ed., *The Age of the Marvelous* (Hanover, N.H.: Hood Museum of Art, 1991); and Barbara Maria Stafford, *Artful Science, Enlightenment Education and the Eclipse of Visual Education* (Cambridge, Mass.: MIT Press, 1994). On the American history see Neil Harris, *Humbug, The Art of P. T. Barnum* (Chicago: University of Chicago Press, 1973); Charles Coleman Sellars, *Mr. Peale's Museum* (New York: Norton, 1980); Sidney Hart and David C. Ward, "The Waning of an Enlightenment Ideal: Charles Willson Peale's Philadelphia Museum, 1790–1820," in Lillian B. Miller and David C. Ward, eds., *New Perspectives on Charles Willson Peale* (Pittsburgh: University of Pittsburgh Press, 1991), pp. 219–235; and William T. Alderson, ed., *Mermaids, Mummies, and Mastodons: The Emergence of the American Museum* (Washington, D.C.: The American Association of Museums, 1992).

7. Information on Kempelen—especially his life away from the automaton—is hard to come by. In addition to the late eighteenth-century sources listed below, I have used Carroll, *The Great Chess Automaton;* Christopher and Christopher, *The Illustrated History of Magic;* and *Neue deutsche Biographie* (Berlin: Duncker and Humblot, 1977), vol. 11, p. 484.

8. Karl Gottlieb von Windisch, *Inanimate Reason; Or a Circumstantial Account of That Astonishing Piece of Mechanism, M. de Kempelen's Chess Player. . . .* (London: S. Blandon, 1784), p. 20. This is the first English translation of *Briefe ueber den Schachspieler des Herrn von Kempelen* (Basel: Mechel'schen Kunstverlage, 1783).

9. Michael Hunter, *Science and Society in Restoration England* (Cambridge: Cambridge University Press, 1981). See also Walter Houghton, "The English Virtuoso in the Seventeenth Century," *Journal of the History of Ideas*, 3 (1942), pp. 51–73, 190–219; Robert Darnton, *Mesmerism and the End of the Enlightenment in France* (Cambridge, Mass.: Harvard University Press, 1968); Mark A. Schneider, *Culture and Enchantment* (Chicago: University of Chicago Press, 1993); and Paula Findlen, *Possessing Nature: Museums, Collecting and Scientific Culture in Early Modern Italy* (Berkeley: University of California Press, 1996).

10. Hunter, *Science and Society*, esp. chap. 3.

11. Houghton claims that the virtuoso as a social type had largely ceased to exist by the 1720s; Schneider argues that both the concerns of the virtuoso and their implementation as a kind of profession survived until at least the end of the Old Regime.

12. Charles Hutton, *A Mathematical and Philosophical Dictionary*, vol. I (London: J. Johnson, 1795). Thomas Collinson added in the Appendix that Kempelen's real mechanical genius lay in creating the appearance of a thinking machine, p. 730.

13. See Jacques de Vaucanson's own pamphlet, *Le Mécanisme du flûteur automate, présenté à messieurs de l'Académie Royale des Sciences. . . .* (Paris: Jacques Guérin,

1738); Altick, *The Shows of London;* Christopher and Christopher, *The Illustrated History of Magic;* and Stafford, *Artful Science.*

14. *Observations on the Automaton Chess Player. . . . by an Oxford Graduate* (London: J. Hatchard, 1819), pp. 12–13.

15. Windisch, *Inanimate Reason,* p. 41.

16. Ibid., p. v.

17. This may have been the "room of moderate size" in E. T. A. Hoffmann's *Die Automate,* where the automaton is seen by "a continual stream of visitors, of all sorts and conditions, from morning to night." *The Best Tales of Hoffmann,* p. 78.

18. Windisch, *Inanimate Reason,* p. 31.

19. In addition to the places listed here, the automaton played in London, Amsterdam, and Dresden. Carroll discusses these appearances in *The Great Chess Automaton.* His sources include Friedrich Melchior Grimm, *Correspondance littéraire, philosophique et critique de Grimm et de Diderot depuis 1753 jusqu'en 1790* (Paris: 1829), entry for September 1783; Jules Lardin, *Philidor peint par lui-même* (Paris: 1847), extracted in *Le Palamède, revue mensuelle des échecs,* 7 (January 1847); and Johann Jacob Ebert, *Nachricht von dem berühmten Schachspieler und der Sprachmaschine des k. k. Hofkammerraths Herrn von Kempelen* (Leipzig: 1785). The Kempelen-Franklin correspondence is in the "Chess Collection of George A. Allen," at the Library Company of Philadelphia. Kempelen's letter to Franklin inviting him to play the automaton in Paris is dated May 28, 1783.

20. Ebert, *Nachricht von dem berühmten Schachspieler . . . ,* quoted in Carroll, *The Great Chess Automaton,* p. 27.

21. A roughly contemporary dictionary entry (Noah Webster, *An American Dictionary of the English Language,* New York: S. Converse, 1828) defines the term "curiosity" as "that which excites a desire of seeing." Other subentries suggest the more concrete context of the curiosity cabinet: "a nice experiment," "wrought with care and art," "rare," "singular."

22. Altick, *The Shows of London,* esp. chaps. 1 and 2; Pomian, *Collectors and Curiosities;* Kenseth, ed., *The Age of the Marvelous;* Stafford, *Artful Science,* esp. chap. 4; and Katie Whitaker, "The Culture of Curiosity," in N. Jardine, J. A. Secord, and E. C. Spary, eds., *Cultures of Natural History* (New York: Cambridge University Press, 1996), pp. 75–90.

23. Rotraud Bauer and Herbert Haupt, "Das Kunstkammerinventar Kaiser Rudolfs II, 1607–11," in *Jahrbuch der kunsthistorischen Sammlungen in Wien,* vol. 72, 1976. On collecting practices in Vienna, see Thomas DaCosta Kaufman, "From Treasury to Museum: The Collections of the Austrian Habsburgs," in John Elsner and Roger Cardinal, eds., *The Cultures of Collecting* (Cambridge, Mass.: Harvard University Press, 1994), pp. 137–154.

24. On the larger historical contexts for this transition, see Peter Burke, *Popular Culture in Early Modern Europe* (New York: Harper and Row, 1978), and Robert Isherwood, *Farce and Fantasy, Popular Entertainment in Eighteenth-Century Paris* (New York: Oxford University Press, 1986). For curiosity exhibitions and itinerant shows on this side of the Atlantic, see Sellers, *Mr. Peale's Museum;* Peter Benes, ed., *Itinerancy in New England and New York* (Boston: Boston University, 1986); and David R. Brigham, *Public Culture in the Early Republic: Peale's Museum and Its Audience* (Washington, D.C.: Smithsonian Institution Press, 1995).

25. *Observations on the Automaton Chess Player, by an Oxford Graduate,* p. 12; Windisch, *Inanimate Reason,* pp. 14–15.
26. Windisch, *Inanimate Reason,* p. 11. Jacques Ozanam and Edmé Guyot were leading literary experts on mathematical recreations and philosophical amusements during the Age of Reason.
27. Hans Blumenberg, *The Legitimacy of the Modern Age* (Cambridge: MIT Press, 1983), esp. part 3.
28. "Augustine's world," Blumenberg explains, "is not fulfilling but seductive, and *curiositas* is a 'temptation' *(forma tentationis)* in the double sense that to test oneself on and with what is resistant and uncommon *(tentandi causa)* is at the same time to be tempted *(tentatio)*." Ibid., p. 312.
29. *Oxford English Dictionary,* 2nd ed., pp. 143–145.
30. Ibid. Consider, for example, the use of the word in J. Hayward, *Biondi's Eronema,* 12, 1632: "A noble and solid curiosity of knowing things in their beginnings."
31. Windisch, *Inanimate Reason,* p. v.
32. Ibid., pp. 12 and 17.
33. Hoffmann, *The Best Tales of Hoffmann,* pp. 79–80.
34. As Stafford has demonstrated in *Artful Science,* much of the popular visual entertainment of the late eighteenth-century—automata, phantasmagoria, electrical demonstrations, etc.—offered this sort of opportunity. Alternatively described as "mathematical recreations" and "philosophical amusements," these entertainments served as an important means of visual education.
35. Windisch, *Inanimate Reason,* p. 12.
36. Historians usually describe chess as a descendant of the much older Indian board game Shatranj, which was brought to Persia around A. D. 600. See, for example, R. C. Bell, *Board and Table Games from Many Civilizations* (New York: Dover Books, 1979), pp. 58–59.
37. Joseph Friedrich Freiherr zu Racknitz, *Ueber den Schachspieler des Herrn von Kempelen . . .* (Leipzig: Joh. Gottl. Immanuel Breitkopf, 1789). The connection to "magical powers" is quoted in translation in Carroll, *The Great Chess Automaton,* p. 37.
38. Edward Said, *Orientalism* (New York: Vintage Books, 1979). Quotations are on pp. 51, 103.
39. Paul Hofmann, *The Viennese* (New York: Anchor Book, 1988), and Lonnie R. Johnson, *Central Europe: Enemies, Neighbors, Friends* (New York: Oxford University Press, 1996).
40. Hoffmann, *Best Tales of Hoffmann,* p. 82.
41. Ibid., p. 81.
42. Mary Shelley's *Frankenstein, or, the Modern Prometheus* appeared in 1818.
43. These reports appeared in Lardin's "Philidor peint par lui-même," *Le Palamède,* 7 (January 1847).
44. The automaton may have suffered one other defeat. Carl Friederich Hindenburg claimed that Kempelen's prodigy lost to one of the challengers ("as good as Philidor") at the Michaelmas Fair in Leipzig (1784): *Ueber den Schachspieler des Herrn von Kempelen Nebst einer Abbildung und Beschreibung seiner Sprachmaschine* (Leipzig: Johann Gottfried Muellerschen Buchhandlung, 1784).
45. According to Carroll, Kempelen spent the rest of his life as a Viennese civil servant. *Neue deutsche Biographie* notes only that he was promoted to "court official" in 1786 and retired in 1798. He died in Vienna on March 26, 1804.

46. Of Racknitz's published exposé, Thomas Collinson wrote in 1795: "This discovery at Dresden accounts for the silence about [the automaton] in Vienna." *A Mathematical and Philosophical Dictionary . . . ,* p. 730.

47. Vaucanson, *Le Mecanisme du flûteur automate,* p. 18. This claim is translated and quoted in Stafford, *Artful Science,* p. 193.

48. Windisch, *Inanimate Reason,* p. 55.

49. Arrington, quoting Kempelen in his article for the *Pennsylvania Museum of History and Biography,* p. 58. Other versions are cited in virtually every contemporary document on the automaton without any mention of where or when the words were spoken. The original source is probably Windisch, who wrote in 1783: "The inventor was far from coveting such celebrity, nor did he wish his machine to be considered as a prodigy. He passed it for no more than it was, a machine not void of mechanical merit, and whose effects seem the more wonderful, for the boldness of the thought, and the happy choice of means employed in the deception." *Inanimate Reason,* pp. 41–42. Later on, Windisch adds: "Of all his inventions, the Automaton chess-player is that which he prides himself least on; he frequently speaks of it as mere bagatelle; and though considering it merely as a machine, whatever be the mode of putting it in motion, it certainly has great mechanical merit" (pp. 55–56).

50. Windisch explains: "I must not forget to mention the little case which M. de Kempelen places on a small table near the machine . . . It has been generally supposed, that this case is a totally detached piece, merely calculated to distract the attention: the inventor, notwithstanding, has given me the most positive assurances, that it is so indispensably necessary, that the Automaton could not play without it." *Inanimate Reason,* p. 28. On the issue of the small case, see also Hindenburg, *Ueber den Schachspieler des Herrn von Kempelen,* p. 24.

51. Windisch mentions the fountain system in *Inanimate Reason,* p. 55. Collinson claims that "the baron (for I think he is such) shewed me some working models which he had lately made—among them, an improvement on Arkwright's cotton-mill, and also one which he thought an improvement on Boulton and Watt's last steam-engine." *A Mathematical and Philosophical Dictionary,* p. 730.

52. Windisch, *Inanimate Reason,* p. 48.

53. Ibid., p. 42.

54. Ibid., p. 43.

55. Stafford discusses this social and moral threshold at some length in *Artful Science,* pp. 73–130.

56. On Maelzel's early life see the notes, letters, and interviews compiled by George A. Allen during the 1850s for his address to the First American Chess Congress in Philadelphia, 1857. Allen's "History of the Automaton Chess-Player in America" appears in Daniel Willard Fiske, ed., *The Book of the First American Chess Congress* (New York: Rudd & Carleton, 1859). This volume as well as the manuscript materials that went into it are in the "Chess Collection of George A. Allen" [hereafter cited as CCGA] at the Library Company of Philadelphia. See also Henrike Leonhardt, *Der Taktmesser: Johann Nepomuk Maelzel—Ein lückenhafter Lebenslauf* (Hamburg: Kellner, 1990).

57. Arrington describes the Panharmonicon as a kind of poly-instrument—including all the pieces of a military band plus clarinets, violins, violas, and violin-cello—enclosed in a large cabinet case. "John Maelzel, Master Showman of Automata and Panoramas," in *Pennsylvania Museum of History and Biography,* p. 56.

58. This is the date and sum Allen gives in *Book of the First American Chess Congress*, p. 425. Arrington puts the date of purchase at 1809.

59. Duke Bernhard of Saxe-Weimar-Eisenach claimed to have seen it "in 1812, in Milan, in the palace of the vice-king of Italy." *Travels Through North America* (Philadelphia: 1828), pp. 197–198. The "vice-king" described here was Beauharnais. George Walker, an early nineteenth-century English writer, describes Beauharnais' declining interest: "True, he could amuse himself with it, by suffering it to march in his suite; but it appeared that a good player, a real living man, was a necessary accompaniment to produce the desired degree of éclat. The prince found himself in a most unkingly description of a dilemma. He had got the lamp, but found he must also retain the genius of the lamp, or else throw away his toy, like a child when it has broken the works of its three-penny watch to see what made it tick." "The Anatomy of the Chess Automaton," *Fraser's Magazine*, June 1839, p. 726.

60. Allen, *Book of the First American Chess Congress*, pp. 425–427. This second European tour lasted from late 1818 until late 1825 and included stops in Paris, London, and Amsterdam. For the London exhibitions see W. Hunneman, *Chess. A Selection of Fifty Games, from Those Played by the Automaton Chess-Player During Its Exhibition in London, in 1820* (London: W. Pople, 1820); *Observations on the Automaton Chess Player . . . by an Oxford Graduate;* and Robert Willis, *An Attempt to Analyse the Automaton Chess Player of Mr. De Kempelen* (London: J. Booth, 1821).

61. Philadelphia *Public Ledger,* December 4, 1840.

62. According to Maelzel's advertisement (June 7, 1819) in the London *Times*, "the Conflagration of Moscow, [is] a moving panorama: the view is taken from the Kremlin, and represents the gradual progress of the Fire, the entrance of the French Army, the Flight of its Inhabitants, &c. tending to impress the spectator with a true idea of a scene which baffles all powers of description."

63. Letter from William Lewis to George Allen, London, March 5, 1850. CCGA, Library Company of Philadelphia.

64. Ibid. These items appear as hearsay in published materials on the automaton before Lewis's correspondence with George Allen. "An old valued friend of mine who played frequently," writes Lewis, "told me he was sure he could beat the Aut. though he somehow or other always lost; when he afterward learned that I was the Director said, if he had known that he should have saved many half crowns."

65. Significantly, when George Allen set out to write the first comprehensive history of the automaton chess-player during the 1850s, he went straight to Lewis and Mouret for information.

66. London *Times*, December 25, 1818 and January 5, 1819.

67. Ibid., May 12, 1819, p. 1.

68. Why Maelzel decided to leave Europe remains unclear. The chess journal, *Le Palamède,* attributed his departure to a court battle with the Beauharnais family, in which the operations of the automaton were subpoenaed as public evidence. Yet, as George Allen notes, the family already had the secret in 1812. Moreover, public disclosure was hardly in the Beauharnais' interests as long as part of the automaton's profits went into their bank accounts.

69. New York *Evening Post*, April 12, 1826, p. 2.

70. On the consumption practices that dominated other corners of New York popular culture during the 1820s and 1830s, see David Grimsted, *Melodrama Unveiled* (Berkeley: University of California Press, 1987); Sean Wilentz, *Chants Democratic* (New York:

Oxford University Press, 1984); Peter G. Buckley, "To the Opera House: Culture and Society in New York City, 1820–1860," Ph.D. diss., State University of New York at Stony Brook, 1984; and Luc Santé, *Low Life* (New York: Vintage Books, 1991).

71. As David R. Brigham has observed, fifty cents for a ticket was more than the average manual worker could afford. *Public Culture in the Early Republic*, pp. 26–27. On worker budgets, see also Billy G. Smith, *The "Lower Sort": Philadelphia's Laboring People, 1750–1800* (Ithaca: Cornell University Press, 1990), and Richard B. Stott, *Workers in the Metropolis: Class, Ethnicity, and Youth in Antebellum New York City* (Ithaca: Cornell University Press, 1990).

72. In addition to the automata featured in these two collections, Maelzel competed with an exhibition of a "military Automaton or Mechanical Trumpeter," which had arrived in New York in January of 1826. See George C. D. Odell, *Annals of the New York Stage*, vol. 3, p. 214.

73. Allen, *The Book of the First American Chess Congress*, p. 432.

74. Poe, *Complete Tales and Poems*, p. 434.

75. Ibid.

76. Ibid., p. 435.

77. New York *Evening Post*, April 14, 1826, p. 2.

78. Ibid., April 21, 1826, p. 2.

79. Ibid., April 24, 1826, p. 2. Quoted in Allen, *The Book of the First American Chess Congress*, p. 430.

80. Ibid., April 14, 1826, p. 2. "The doors of this chest," noted the reporter, "consisting of three in front and two behind and also a drawer were then opened, and a lighted candle was introduced among the machinery, to shew it, and to prove that no person was concealed within; although such has been ingeniously demonstrated, by a great mathematician, in the Edinburgh *Journal of Arts and Sciences*, to be the fact."

81. New York *Evening Post*, April 21, 1826, p. 2.

82. Ibid., April 27, 1826, p. 2.

83. Ibid., April 28, 1826, p. 2.

84. Boston *Sentinel*, October 14, 1826; and Boston *Gazette*, October 15, 1826. A transcription of Maelzel's letter to the editor also appears in a note from Joseph A. Potter to George Allen, Salem, Mass., August 12, 1858, CCGA, Library Company of Philadelphia.

85. These regional conflicts seem to have been mostly played out in a single publication, the New York *American*. See, especially, the letters to the editor on November 7 and 11, 1826 (the source of these quotations). Allen discusses the Boston–New York rivalry in *Book of the First American Chess Congress*, pp. 441–443.

86. Numerous references to these plays appear in Odell, *Annals of the New York Stage*, vol. 3. See also Grimsted's appendixes in *Melodrama Unveiled*, pp. 249–256, which tabulate antebellum plays by title and category for certain cities.

87. Luther S. Luedtke, *Nathaniel Hawthorne and the Romance of the Orient* (Bloomington: Indiana University Press, 1989); Timothy Worthington Marr, "Imagining Ishmael: Studies of Islamic Orientalism in America from the Puritans to Melville," Ph. D. diss., Yale University, 1997; and Malini Johar Schueller, *U.S. Orientalism: Race, Nation, and Gender in Literature, 1790–1890* (Ann Arbor: University of Michigan Press, 1998).

88. This is the sum total of what Poe had to say about the mannequin's appearance: "A figure is seen, habited as a Turk, and seated, with its legs crossed. . . . The left arm of the

figure is bent at the elbow, and in the left hand is a pipe." Poe, in another words, treated the automaton almost exclusively as a form of illusionism (rather than realism).

89. New York *Evening Post,* May 27, 1826, p. 2. This article noted two losses and a number of "draws."

90. Letter from Joshua I. Cohen to John Spilman and George Allen, Baltimore, September 5, 1858. CCGA, Library Company of Philadelphia.

91. Undated clipping from the Philadelphia *Gazette,* CCGA, Library Company of Philadelphia.

92. New York *Evening Post,* May 9, 1826, p. 2.

93. Ibid.

94. By now, Maelzel had made Philadelphia his home base and had purchased the Masonic Hall for all of his shows in the city. He also now employed a small workshop of Philadelphia mechanics and artists to construct spare parts and scenery for his American tours and booked other respectable entertainments to fill the venue when he and the automata were away. The artisans included Joseph A. Mickley, a maker of pianofortes. According to Mickley, Maelzel was always careful to divide his work orders into small units, so that none of the artisans knew much about the larger picture of the automaton's workings. Transcribed interviews with Mickley appear in Allen's *Chess Commonplace Book,* pp. 5–13. CCGA, Library Company of Philadelphia. Allen discusses the scope of Maelzel's Philadelphia operations in *Book of the First American Chess Congress,* pp. 443–446.

95. Allen, *Book of the First American Chess Congress,* p. 466.

96. Once again, George Allen is the best source of information here. Schlumberger was born in Alsace around 1800 and moved to Paris to escape work in his father's business. There he played and taught chess at Philidor's old stomping grounds, the Café de la Régence, before being recruited by Maelzel to work as the automaton's leading American director. *Book of the First American Chess Congress,* pp. 436–441. According to Allen, Schlumberger played as himself (i.e. not inside the automaton) against the top club players in both Boston and Philadelphia and won every match. Allen also claims, without a source, that Schlumberger "had peremptory orders" to lose to Mrs. Fisher. Ibid., pp. 436–446.

97. Herbet G. Gutman, *Work, Culture, and Society in Industrializing America, 1815–1919* (New York: Vintage Books, 1976); Alan Dawley, *Class and Community* (Cambridge, Mass.: Harvard University Press, 1976); Bruce G. Laurie, *Working People of Philadelphia, 1800–1850* (Philadelphia: Temple University Press, 1980); Wilentz, *Chants Democratic;* and Charles Sellers, *The Market Revolution: Jacksonian America, 1815–1846* (New York: Oxford University Press, 1991).

98. On the gender roles conventionally associated with trickster cultures, see Lori Landay, *Madcaps, Screwballs, and Con Women: The Female Trickster in American Culture* (Philadelphia: University of Pennsylvania Press, 1998). Maelzel, it is worth noting, did include one other role for women in his productions. On some occasions, "half-grown girls" passed out treats to the children in the audience.

99. New York *American,* April 22, 1826, p. 2.

100. New York *Evening Post,* May 27, 1826, p. 2.

101. These events are reconstructed through a number of sources in the CCGA: a letter from Baltimore resident Joshua Cohen to George Allen during the late 1850s; Allen's interviews in his *Chess Commonplace Book;* and clippings from the Baltimore and Washington, D.C. newspapers.

102. Baltimore *Gazette,* June 1, 1827.
103. Allen, *Book of the First American Chess Congress,* p. 452.
104. Washington, D.C. *Daily National Intelligencer,* June 4, 1827, p. 3.
105. Allen, *Book of the First American Chess Congress,* pp. 452–53.
106. P. T. Barnum, *The Life of P. T. Barnum, Written by Himself* (New York: Redfield, 1855), p. 156.
107. Philadelphia *National Gazette Literary Register,* February 6, 1837, p. 1.
108. Confirmation of this explanation can be found in a personal letter to George Allen from Lloyd P. Smith, dated July 7, 1858. CCGA. In a wonderful bit of historical coincidence, Smith worked as "the soul of the automaton" during the early 1840s, before becoming the Director of the Library Company!
109. According to Allen, Mouret gave his information to a man named De Tourney, whose story first appeared in the French *Magasin Pittoresque* in 1834. The *National Gazette* claimed that its article was a translation of an article from the *Journal de la Garde Nationale.* Whatever the exact order of transmission, there is no question that Mouret's information appeared in a number of publications in Europe and the United States between 1834 and 1840.
110. We do know that Maelzel was aware of the story. The copy of the *National Gazette* article which still exists in the CCGA originally belonged to Maelzel and was found in his personal papers after his death.
111. Allen, *Book of the First American Chess Congress,* pp. 478–479.
112. "The Automaton Chess Player," The Philadelphia *North American and Daily Advertiser,* October 12, 1840, p. 1. The Philadelphia *Public Ledger* drew a similar conclusion: "Though public curiosity has been partially gratified as to its *modus operandi,* there was still an undefined conviction that the *truth, the whole truth and nothing but the whole truth* had never been told." December 4, 1840, p. 2.
113. Blumenberg, *The Legitimacy of the Modern Age,* pp. 438–439.
114. Mitchell, *The Chess Monthly,* 1, February 1857, p. 4. Ricky Jay attributes this passage to Silas Weir Mitchell (the doctor's more famous son) in "The Turkish Automaton's Final Act," Kenneth Finkel, ed., *Philadelphia Almanac and Citizen's Guide* (Philadelphia: Library Company of Philadelphia, 1994), p. 161.

2. The Feejee Mermaid

1. New York *Times,* March 18, 1868, p. 4.
2. Lawrence Levine, *Highbrow/Lowbrow, The Emergence of Cultural Hierarchy in America* (Cambridge, Mass.: Harvard University Press, 1988). See also Neil Harris, "The Gilded Age Revisited: Boston and the Museum Movement," in *American Quarterly,* 14 (Winter 1962), and "Four Stages of Cultural Growth: The American City," in his *Cultural Excursions* (Chicago: University of Chicago Press, 1990); and Paul DiMaggio, "Cultural Entrepreneurship in Nineteenth-Century Boston: The Creation of an Organizational Base for High Culture in America," in Chandra Mukerji and Michael Schudson, eds., *Rethinking Popular Culture* (Berkeley: University of California Press, 1991).
3. Neil Harris, *Humbug, The Art of P. T. Barnum* (Chicago: University of Chicago Press, 1973), p. 79.
4. Ibid., p. 4.

5. Ibid., pp. 67–89. The most insightful study of Barnum prior to Harris is Constance Rourke's wonderful chapter on the showman in *Trumpets of Jubilee* (New York: Harcourt, Brace, 1927). See also Morris Werner, *Barnum* (New York: Harcourt, Brace, 1923); and Irving Wallace, *The Fabulous Showman: The Life and Times of P. T. Barnum* (New York: Signet, 1959).

6. Recent books that make use of Harris's "operational aesthetic" include Robert Bogdan, *Freak Show: Presenting Human Oddities for Amusement and Profit* (Chicago: University of Chicago Press, 1988); Miles Orvell, *The Real Thing: Imitation and Authenticity in American Culture, 1880–1940* (Chapel Hill: University of North Carolina Press, 1989), p. 58; Eric Lott, *Love and Theft: Blackface Minstrelsy and the American Working Class* (New York: Oxford University Press, 1993); and Andie Tucher, *Froth & Scum: Truth, Beauty, Goodness, and the Ax Murder in America's First Mass Medium* (Chapel Hill: University of North Carolina Press, 1994).

7. Charles Coleman Sellers, for example, describes the two museums as intellectual and moral opposites in *Mr. Peale's Museum: Charles Willson Peale and the First Popular Museum of Natural Science and Art* (New York: Norton, 1980), p. 308. This view is reinforced by the recent exhibition catalog, *Mermaids, Mummies, and Mastodons: The Emergence of the American Museum* (Washington, D.C.: American Association of Museums, 1992).

8. Barnum purchased Rubens Peale's New York Museum in 1843 and part of Charles Willson Peale's Philadelphia Museum in 1848 (the other half went to Moses Kimball). See Sellers, *Mr. Peale's Museum*, chap. 9.

9. Harris, *Humbug*, pp. 74–75, 79.

10. Tucher, *Froth & Scum*, p. 57.

11. Karen Halttunen, *Confidence Men and Painted Women: A Study of Middle-Class Culture in America, 1830–1870* (New Haven: Yale University Press, 1982), pp. 1–55; Charles Sellers, *The Market Revolution: Jacksonian America, 1815–1846* (New York: Oxford University Press, 1991); Jackson Lears, *Fables of Abundance: A Cultural History of Advertising in America* (New York: Basic Books, 1994); and David M. Henkin, *City Reading: Written Words and Public Spaces in Antebellum New York* (New York: Columbia University Press, 1998).

12. P. T. Barnum, *Humbugs of the World* (New York: Carleton, 1865), p. 13.

13. My discussion here builds on a number of recent studies of "market culture." See Jean-Christophe Agnew, *Worlds Apart: The Market and the Theater in Anglo-American Thought, 1550–1750* (Cambridge: Cambridge University Press, 1986); Thomas Haskell and Richard F. Teichgraeber III, eds., *The Culture of the Market* (Cambridge: Cambridge University Press, 1993); and Lears, *Fables of Abundance*, esp. part 1.

14. For useful assessments of the current scholarship on the American market revolution and its impacts, see Sean Wilentz, "Society, Politics, and the Market Revolution, 1815–1848," in Eric Foner, ed., *The New American History* (Philadelphia: Temple University Press, 1990); and Melvin Stokes and Stephen Conway, eds., *The Market Revolution: Social, Political, and Religious Expressions, 1800–1880* (Charlottesville: University Press of Virginia, 1996).

15. The best place to begin exploring the Feejee Mermaid's career is the first edition of Barnum's autobiography, *The Life of P. T. Barnum, Written by Himself* (New York: Redfield, 1855). Scholarly works that discuss Barnum's Mermaid include Harris, *Humbug*; A. H. Saxon, *P. T. Barnum, the Legend and the Man* (New York: Columbia

University Press, 1989); and Kenneth Greenberg, *Honor and Slavery* (Princeton: Princeton University Press, 1996).

16. Barnum, *Life of Barnum*, pp. 234–35.

17. "The said Kimball and Barnum shall equally share and divide the profits of said traveling exhibition, after paying all the expenses of said exhibition including the expenses and salary of a man whom the said Kimball will furnish to travel with it and whose salary will not be more than eight dollars per week also one fourth of the net profits which will be given to Mr. Levi Lyman or some equally capable person for attending the same. . . ." Barnum-Kimball Mermaid Agreement, dated June 18, 1842. The Fred D. Pfening III Collection, Columbus, Ohio.

18. Barnum, *Life of Barnum*, p. 237.

19. Ibid.

20. "The receipts of the American Museum for the four weeks immediately preceding the exhibition of the mermaid, amounted to $1,272. During the first four weeks of the mermaid's exhibition, the receipts amounted to $3,341.93." Ibid., p. 242.

21. On the Western history of mermaids, see Henry Lee, *Sea Monsters Unmasked* (London: William Clowes and Sons, 1883); Richard Carrington, *Mermaids and Mastodons, A Book of Natural and Unnatural History* (London: Chatto and Windus, 1957); Gwen Benwell and Arthur Waugh, *Sea Enchantress, The Tale of the Mermaid and her Kin* (New York: Citadel Press, 1965); Cynthia Behrman, *Victorian Myths of the Sea* (Athens, Ohio: Ohio University Press, 1977); and Lee Ellen Griffith, *The Tale of the Mermaid,* Exhibition Catalog (Philadelphia: Philadelphia Maritime Museum, 1986).

22. See Barnum's letter to Kimball, from Bridgeport, dated June 25, 1859: "I have returned [from Europe] bringing the mermaid in good order & for which I give you many thanks & owe you heaps of gratitude . . . I found in the London Mirror of Nov 1822 an account of this very animal exhibited at that time by an American sea captain named Eades. I also copied following adnt. *'The mermaid. The wonder of the world—* the theme of the Philosopher, the Historian, and the Poet. The above surprising natural production may be seen at Watson's Turf Coffee House 39 St. James Street. . . .'" Shelbourne Museum Collection, Shelbourne, VT. Raymund Fitzsimmons, *Barnum in London* (New York: St. Martin's Press, 1970), and Richard Altick, *The Shows of London* (Cambridge, Mass.: Harvard University Press, 1978), p. 303, briefly mention the St. James connection. On the earlier history of the St. James Mermaid, see Harriet Ritvo, *The Platypus and the Mermaid: And Other Figments of the Classifying Imagination* (Cambridge, Mass.: Harvard University Press, 1997), pp. 178–183.

23. "The Mermaid," London *Mirror,* November 9, 1822, pp. 7–9, and 35–37; "The Mermaid," London *Times,* November 21, 1822. (Batavia is now called Bandung.)

24. "Mermaids and Mermen," London *Literary Gazette,* 1823, p. 13.

25. Saxon makes a similar point: "The Feejee Mermaid is another example of Barnum's ability to take a mildly interesting object that had been around for some time and to puff it almost overnight into an earthshaking 'event'." *P. T. Barnum, The Legend and the Man,* p. 119. On eighteenth-century exhibitions, see Altick, *The Shows of London,* esp. chaps. 1 and 2.

26. For engravings of late eighteenth- and early nineteenth-century mermaids, see Griffith, *The Tale of the Mermaid,* fig. 5.

27. Quoted in Thomas Frost, *The Old Showmen and The Old London Fairs* (London: Tinsley Brothers, 1874), p. 162.

28. P. T. Barnum to Moses Kimball, September 4, 1843. Boston Athenaeum. This ad later ran in numerous newspapers.
29. Frost, *The Old Showmen and the Old London Fairs,* pp. 22–60.
30. Ibid., pp. 62–63. Altick draws a similar conclusion about early modern exhibitionism: "Seldom do we find reports of particular deceptions being exposed—of showmen treated as, for example, Swift dealt with the astrologer John Partridge. Nonsense was more acceptable in the exhibition field than elsewhere, or at least less fuss was made about it." *The Shows of London,* p. 49.
31. Ibid., p. 23. According to Altick, this trade emerged in Paris and Amsterdam in the seventeenth century (p. 13), a dating consistent with the conventional historical wisdom about the rise of market capitalism in Europe.
32. Barnum, *Life of Barnum,* p. 143.
33. Ibid., p. 144.
34. Ibid., pp. 207–208.
35. Ibid., p. 209.
36. On the causes and multiple impacts of the market revolution in America, see Sean Wilentz, *Chants Democratic: New York City & the Rise of the American Working Class, 1788–1850* (New York: Oxford University Press, 1984); Christopher Clark, *The Roots of Rural Capitalism: Western Massachusetts, 1780–1860* (Ithaca: Cornell University Press, 1990); Sellers, *The Market Revolution;* Winifred Barr Rothenberg, *From Market Places to a Market Economy* (Chicago: University of Chicago Press, 1992); and Stokes and Conway, eds., *The Market Revolution in America.*
37. Harris makes this point in *Humbug,* pp. 12–13.
38. Pennsylvania *Packet,* July 7–November 12, 1786. Both the admission ticket and the ad are reproduced in Sellers, *Mr. Peale's Museum,* pp. 23 and 37.
39. Frost, *The Old Showmen and The Old London Fairs,* pp. 205–206.
40. Charles Willson Peale to Thomas Jefferson, February 26, 1804. Quoted by Sellers, *Mr. Peale's Museum,* p. 159.
41. *Philadelphia Museum Company Minutes and Records, 1808–1842.* Smithsonian Institution Archives, Washington, D.C.
42. Jonathan Crary, *Techniques of the Observer, On Vision and Modernity in the Nineteenth Century* (Cambridge, Mass.: MIT Press, 1990), p. 29.
43. *Records. Philadelphia Museum.* Collection of the Historical Society of Pennsylvania, Philadelphia.
44. Philip Slater Fall to Rubens Peale, June 5, 1818. *Philadelphia Museum Company Papers,* Smithsonian Institution Archives.
45. *Records. Philadelphia Museum,* entry for May 6, 1806. Collection of the Historical Society of Pennsylvania, Philadelphia.
46. Rubens Peale, *Memorandum and Events of His Life,* p. 15. American Philosophical Society, Philadelphia. My emphasis.
47. Sellers, *Mr. Peale's Museum,* p. 225.
48. The mermaid "copy" is discussed in the Philadelphia Museum *Curator's Report for June, July, and August, 1842.* Smithsonian Institution Archives, Washington, D.C.
49. Sellers, *Mr. Peale's Museum,* p. 304.
50. Ibid.
51. The Fred D. Pfening III collection, Columbus, Ohio.
52. See, for example, the New York *Herald* and *Tribune,* July 28, 1842.
53. Philadelphia *Spirit of the Times,* August 2, 1842.

54. Philadelphia *Public Ledger and Daily Transcript,* August 8, 1842, p. 1.
55. Harris, *Humbug,* pp. 211–212. On the history of this character, see also William R. Taylor, *Cavalier and Yankee: The Old South and American National Character* (New York: George Braziller, 1961).
56. The first installment appeared on April 11, 1841. Barnum may have worked with a collaborator or ghostwriter on these articles. Yet, as A. H. Saxon notes, Barnum was a frequent contributor to the *Atlas;* furthermore, many specific details from the novella are so close to the actual events in Barnum's early career as to make it virtually inconceivable that anyone else could have created them. *P. T. Barnum: the Legend and the Man,* p. 88.
57. New York *Atlas,* April 11, 1841.
58. Ibid., May 2, 1841.
59. Ibid., May 16 and 30, October 10, 1841.
60. Ibid., April 25, 1841, p. 1.
61. On the moral ambiguity of trickster tales, see Lawrence W. Levine, *Black Culture and Black Consciousness: Afro-American Folk Thought from Slavery to Freedom* (New York Oxford University Press, 1977); Halttunen, *Confidence Men and Painted Women;* Carroll Smith-Rosenberg, "Davy Crockett as Trickster: Pornography, Liminality, and Symbolic Inversion in Victorian America," in *Disorderly Conduct* (New York: Oxford University Press, 1985); and Lewis Hyde, *Trickster Makes This World* (New York: North Point Press, 1998).
62. New York *Herald,* August 9, 1852, p. 3.
63. Ibid., August 14, 1842, p. 3.
64. Barnum, *Life of Barnum,* p. 237. Anonymous, *A Short History of Mermaids, Containing Many Very Interesting Particulars Concerning Them. Also, a Description of the One Now Exhibiting at the Boston Museum* (Boston: Marden, 1842). This pamphlet is in the Library Company of Philadelphia.
65. Anonymous, *A Short History of Mermaids,* p. 15.
66. New York *Herald,* August 12, 1842, p. 3.
67. On the retirement of Rubens Peale and Barnum's purchase of the New York Museum's collections, see Sellers, *Mr. Peale's Museum,* p. 305.
68. New York *Tribune* of November 14, 1842. An ad for the Feejee Mermaid appeared directly above this, in the very same column.
69. Ibid., November 16, 1842.
70. Philadelphia *North American and Daily Advertiser,* August 13, 1842. The Peales, according to this article, had acquired their mermaid quite some time ago: "It has been considered, however, of so little amount as to have been laid aside for several years, but as mermaids are coming into fashion again, the judicious superintendent is about to restore it to the showcase."
71. New York *Tribune,* November 14, 1842.
72. Ibid., November 10, 1842.
73. Agnew, *Worlds Apart.*
74. New York *Herald,* August 11, 1842, p. 2. It should be acknowledged that some of the negativity in this review may have stemmed from James Gordon Bennett's lingering animosity towards Barnum after the Joice Heth hoax.
75. New York *Tribune,* August 4, 1842, p. 2.
76. Chandos Michael Brown, "A Natural History of the Gloucester Sea Serpent: Knowledge, Power, and the Culture of Science in Antebellum America," *American Quar-*

terly, 42/3 (September 1990). Brown's evidence points in much the same direction that I am demonstrating here. He ends his article by recounting the skeptical mid-century reaction of paleontologist Gideon Mantell to a whaler's sighting of yet another "sea serpent": "possibly an Enaliosaurian!—still more probable—a hoax—in other words a Yankee lie" (p. 431). By the middle of the nineteenth century, in other words, unequivocal faith in newly discovered "sea monsters" was as hard to find as the monsters themselves.

77. Philadelphia *Spirit of the Times,* August 6, 1842.
78. Ibid., August 9, 1842.
79. Charleston *Mercury,* January 21, 1843.
80. Bachman's attacks appear in the Charleston *Mercury,* January 20 and 21, 1843. See also Harris, *Humbug,* pp. 65–67; Saxon, *P. T. Barnum,* pp. 121–123; and Greenberg, *Honor and Slavery,* pp. 3–16.
81. Greenberg, *Honor and Slavery,* chap. 1.
82. Charleston *Courier,* February 6, 1843.
83. Ibid.
84. Greenberg, *Honor and Slavery,* p. 6.
85. Augusta *Chronicle and Sentinel,* February 8, 1843.
86. Charleston *Mercury,* January 20, 1843.
87. Charleston *Courier,* February 6, 1843.
88. Barnum to Kimball, February 21, 1843. Boston Athenaeum.
89. Greenberg, *Honor and Slavery,* pp. 3–15.
90. Ibid., pp. 11, 51.
91. Ibid., pp. 9–16.
92. On this issue see ibid., chap. 2.
93. As Peter Sloterdijk has noted, "an essential aspect of power is that it only likes to laugh at its own jokes," *Critique of Cynical Reason* (Minneapolis: University of Minnesota Press, 1987), p. 103.
94. Here I would strongly disagree with Greenberg's suggestion that neither Bachman nor Yeadon "devoted much of their newspaper discussion" to the topic of "whether or not this was a natural mermaid" (*Honor and Slavery,* p. 6). Yeadon was *deeply* interested in this question, as his lengthy February 6, 1843, article in the *Courier* makes clear: "The only point, on which we have authoritatively joined issue with our opponents, is as to the existence of a 'seam' or 'seams', perceptible to sight or touch, establishing the point of junction between the supposed Monkey and the supposed Fish. . . . They saw it through a glass darkly, and neither touched nor handled the unclean thing; we saw it laid bare to our vision, without glass case or intervening obstruction, and handled it too, with the express view of looking for and detecting seams, and could find none." True, at another point in the same issue, Yeadon asserts: "Now we care not a whit, not a stiver, whether the Mermaid is real or not—*the Courier never asserted it was.*" But this statement seems to have been designed not to express a lack of interest in the Mermaid's authenticity, but to differentiate between two methods of judging the creature. Whereas Bachman simply looked at the Mermaid and declared it a biological impossibility, Yeadon insisted on treating the Mermaid's authenticity as plausible—and continued to investigate and defend this plausibility for the next couple of weeks.
95. Charleston *Courier,* February 8, 1843.
96. Barnum to Kimball, February 21 and March 27, 1843. Boston Athenaeum.
97. Ibid., March 27, 1843.

98. Ibid.
99. Sellers, *The Market Revolution*, p. 47.
100. Ibid., p. 54. The case described by Sellers here was *McFarland v. Newman*. See also Walton H. Hamilton, "The Ancient Maxim Caveat Emptor," *Yale Law Journal*, 40/8 (June 1931); Lawrence M. Friedman, *A History of American Law* (New York: Simon and Schuster, 1973).
101. Morton Horowitz, *The Transformation of American Law, 1780–1860* (Cambridge: Harvard University Press, 1977), p. 263.
102. Quoted in Fowler V. Harper and Mary Coate McNeely, "A Synthesis of the Law of Misrepresentation," *Minnesota Law Review*, 22/7 (June 1938), p. 956. The case was *Medbury v. Watson*.
103. Friedman, *A History of American Law*, p. 234. The case in question was *Barnard v. Yates*.
104. Barnum to Kimball, April 4, 1843.
105. Charleston *Mercury*, March 29, 1843.
106. On the background and tastes of Charity Barnum, see Saxon, *P. T. Barnum*, pp. 35–38, 125–26.
107. Adams, *E Pluribus Barnum*, p. 21.
108. Barnum, *Life of Barnum*, p. 297.
109. Barnum, *Humbugs of the World*, p. 2.

3. Describing the Nondescript

1. These terms come from Robert Bogdan, *Freak Show: Presenting Human Oddities for Amusement and Profit* (Chicago: University of Chicago Press, 1988). Following his lead, scholarly attention to Barnum's "living curiosities" has increased in recent years. See, for example, John Kuo-Wei Tchen, "New York Before Chinatown," Ph.D. diss., New York University, 1992; Rosemarie Garland Thomson, ed., *Freakery: Cultural Spectacles of the Extraordinary Body* (New York: New York University Press, 1996); and Bluford Adams, *E Pluribus Barnum* (Minneapolis: University of Minnesota Press, 1997). The classic study of "freakishness" in Western culture is Leslie Fiedler, *Freaks: Myths and Images of the Secret Self* (New York: Simon and Schuster, 1978).
2. The seminal critique in this area is Barbara Jeanne Fields, "Ideology and Race in American History," in *Region, Race, and Reconstruction*, J. Morgan Kousser and James M. McPherson, eds. (New York: Oxford University Press, 1982), p. 155. See also Fields, "Slavery, Race and Ideology in the United States of America," *New Left Review*, 181 (May-June, 1990). Over the past decade, the most sophisticated work on stereotyping has focused on another nineteenth-century entertainment, the blackface minstrel show. See David R. Roediger, *The Wages of Whiteness: Race and the Making of the American Working Class* (London: Verso, 1990); Eric Lott, *Love and Theft: Blackface Minstrelsy and the Working Class* (New York: Oxford University Press, 1993); Dale Cockrell, *Demons of Disorder: Early Blackface Minstrels and Their World* (Cambridge: Cambridge University Press, 1997); and W. T. Lhamon, *Raising Cain* (Cambridge, Mass.: Harvard University Press, 1998).
3. On liminality and performance, see Victor Turner, *From Ritual to Theatre: The Human Seriousness of Play* (New York: Performing Arts Journal Publications, 1982); and *Blazing the Trail: Way Marks in the Exploration of Symbols* (Tucson: University of Arizona Press, 1992).

4. Philip B. Kunhardt, Jr., Philip B. Kunhardt III, and Peter W. Kunhardt, *P. T. Barnum, America's Greatest Showman* (New York: Knopf, 1995), p. 149.

5. My discussion of race and racial definition has been influenced by a number of recent studies. In addition to the work by Fields, Roediger, and Lott cited above, I have found the following especially helpful: Henry Louis Gates, Jr., "Writing 'Race' and the Difference It Makes," in Gates, ed., *Race, Writing, and Difference* (Chicago: University of Chicago Press, 1986), pp. 1–20; Michael O'Malley, "Specie and Species: Race and the Money Question in Nineteenth-Century America," in *The American Historical Review*, 99/2 (April 1994); and David Hollinger, *Postethnic America* (New York: Basic Books, 1995).

6. Quoted in the London *Times*, April 27, 1847.

7. George C. D. Odell, *Annals of the New York Stage*, vol. 4 (New York: Columbia University Press, 1928–1949), p. 368.

8. Years later, Barnum claimed that Leech approached him and *asked* to be exhibited in London. *The Life of P. T. Barnum, Written by Himself* (New York: Redfield, 1855), p. 346.

9. *Wemyss' Chronology of the American Stage From 1752 to 1852* (New York: Taylor, 1852), p. 92. Barnum, *Life of Barnum*, p. 346.

10. Barnum letter to Boston Museum manager, Moses Kimball, August 18, 1846. New York Public Library; reprinted in A. H. Saxon, ed., *Selected Letters of P. T. Barnum* (New York: Columbia University Press, 1983), pp. 35–36.

11. See, for example, the London *Times*, Saturday, August 29, 1846.

12. "Before half an hour had elapsed, one of the visitors, who knew 'Hervio Nano,' recognized him through his disguise and exposed the imposition. The money was refunded to visitors." *Life of Barnum*, p. 346. More recently, Richard Altick discovered an undated clipping in the Egyptian Hall file at London's Guidhall Library, according to which Leech's exposer was an American showman named Carter who had become angry with Barnum for refusing to loan out Tom Thumb; *The Shows of London* (Cambridge, Mass.: Harvard University Press, 1978), pp. 266–267.

13. Leech, he falsely claimed, "made immediate arrangements with two Americans, who took him to London. They stained his face and hands, and covered him with a dress made of hair, and resembling the skin of an animal. They then advertised him as a curious nondescript, called 'What is It?'. . . . I was let into the secret, on condition of 'keeping dark.'" P. T. Barnum, *Life of Barnum*, p. 346.

14. Robert Bogdan has written that Johnson's "large, long nose connected with the top of his small head without the interruption of a forehead. His head thus appeared to come to a point. This effect was a result in part of his physiology and in part of the fact that, for the purpose of exhibition, his head was shaved except for a patch about two inches in diameter at the top" (*Freak Show*, p. 134). But a New York *World* reporter at Johnson's funeral wrote: "The form in the coffin was that of a man in evening dress. The head may have been a trifle longer than ordinary, but there was no queer tuft of hair on the top. There was nothing unusual about the nose. And most of all there was no woolly hair 'like a giant gorilla.'" "Zip Grins in Death, Mask Off at Last," New York *World*, April 29, 1926, p. 17.

15. For descriptions of Johnson by Barnum employees see: "Zip, Barnum's Famous 'What is It?' Freak Dies of Bronchitis in Bellevue; his Age Put at 84," New York *Times*, April 25, 1926, p. 1.

16. Information on Johnson's sister (her name was alternatively spelled "Van Duyne" and "Vanduinne") appears in the New York *World*, April 29, 1926, p. 8. See also "Many Circus

Folk at Zip's Funeral," New York *Times*, April 29, 1926, p. 48; and Bogdan, *Freak Show*, p. 293. These sources identify a brother (named Theo) and locate the grave for William Henry Johnson in Bound Brook, New Jersey. The 1860 U.S. Federal Census Records for Bound Brook, New Jersey (where Johnson's sister claimed he was born), list only one African-American family named Johnson (p. 581). Family members listed in the census include: William (age 35), Mahala (24), Theodore (8), and William (3). On the basis of these ages, it seems unlikely that either William was the man on Barnum's stage in 1860.

17. P. T. Barnum to Sol Smith, American Museum, April 4, 1860. This letter is in the Sol Smith Collection, Missouri Historical Society, St. Louis, and is reprinted in Saxon, ed., *Selected Letters of P. T. Barnum*, p. 104.

18. There are no dates on the Brady photographs, but the fact that they are in the carte-de-visite format virtually assures that they were taken during the early 1860s, around the time of the exhibition's New York debut. In addition, a magazine article—which includes commentary from the family which originally collected the photos—dates them in the "middle 1860s." "Barnum and Brady, Pictures from the Collection of Frederick Hill Meserve," *Colliers*, April 29, 1944, p. 21.

19. On Stratton's entry into show business, see Saxon, *P. T. Barnum: The Legend and the Man*, chaps. 1 and 6.

20. On the precarious legal and economic situation faced by African Americans in the antebellum North, see Graham Russell Hodges, *Root and Branch: African Americans in New York and East Jersey, 1613–1862* (Chapel Hill: University of North Carolina Press, 1999).

21. David Hevey, *The Creatures That Time Forgot: Photography and Disability Imagery* (New York: Routledge, 1992). For a more specific discussion see Rosemarie Garland Thomson, "Introduction: From Wonder to Error—A Genealogy of Freak Discourse in Modernity," in *Freakery*, pp. 1–19.

22. New York *Clipper*, March 31, 1860. Bluford Adams suggests in *E Pluribus Barnum* that many viewers of What Is It? thought of the exhibition as "Barnum's latest fraud" (pp. 159–160). My sense is that in 1860 perceptions of *complete* fraud were few and did not lead to the same kind of blanket accusations of inauthenticity that we encounter in the earlier reception for the Feejee Mermaid. Adams points to this distinction when he observes that "the public . . . seems not to have cared."

23. New York *Herald*, March 19, 1860, p. 1.

24. Altick, *Shows of London*, p. 265. On early modern European and European-American attitudes towards Africans and "wildness," see Winthrop Jordan, *White Over Black* (New York: Norton, 1968); and Hayden White, "The Forms of Wildness: Archaeology of an Idea," in *Tropics of Discourse: Essays in Cultural Criticism* (Baltimore: Johns Hopkins Press, 1978).

25. An ad for Peale's anthropoid ape appears in David Rodney Brigham, *Public Culture in the Early Republic: Peale's Museum and Its Audience* (Washington, D.C.: Smithsonian Institution Press, 1995), p. 131.

26. Barnum to Kimball, Brighton, England, August 18, 1846. Reprinted in Saxon, *Selected Letters of P. T. Barnum*, pp. 37–38.

27. This is the second definition of "nondescript" as noun in the *Oxford English Dictionary*, 2nd ed., p. 490.

28. The *OED*'s earliest reference for this second sense of "nondescript" is from 1811: "The House contains about 250 country gentlemen, 120 courtiers [etc.]. The rest are nondescripts."

29. Philadelphia *Public Ledger,* December 22, 1849, p. 3. The guidebook was published in New York by J. S. Redfield (1849).

30. For a discussion of early modern ideas about biological intermixture, see Fielder, *Freaks;* and Ramona and Desmond Morris, *Men and Apes* (New York: McGraw-Hill, 1966).

31. Philadelphia *Public Ledger,* December 21, 1849, p. 2.

32. Barnum, *Life of Barnum,* p. 350.

33. New York *Herald,* March 8, 1860, p. 1.

34. Ibid., March 15, 1860, p. 1.

35. This program is reprinted in Bernth Lindfors, "P. T. Barnum and Africa," *Studies in Popular Culture,* 7 (1984), pp. 21–22. Barnum also frequently used this text in ads. See, for example, the New York *Herald,* March 19, 1860, p. 1.

36. Claude Lévi-Strauss, *The Raw and the Cooked: Introduction to a Science of Mythology,* trans. John and Doreen Weightmann (New York: Harper and Row, 1969).

37. New York *Herald,* March 19, 1860, p. 1. My emphasis.

38. Philadelphia *Public Ledger,* April 30, 1850.

39. Robert Toll, *Blacking Up: The Minstrel Show in Nineteenth-Century America* (New York: Oxford University Press, 1974); Alexander Saxton, *The Rise and Fall of the White Republic: Class Politics and Mass Culture in Nineteenth-Century America* (London: Verso, 1990); and Lott, *Love and Theft.*

40. Allan Nevins and Milton Halsey Thomas, eds., *The Diary of George Templeton Strong, 1860–1865* (New York: Macmillan, 1952), p. 12. This is the diary entry for March 2, 1860.

41. "The Prince's Third Day," New York *Tribune,* October 14, 1860, p. 1.

42. On this process as a larger pattern in late nineteenth-century American culture, see Lawrence W. Levine, *Highbrow/Lowbrow: The Emergence of Cultural Hierarchy in America* (Cambridge, Mass.: Harvard University Press, 1988). For its more specific trajectory in the American circus and amusement park, see Bogdan, *Freak Show,* chap. 2.

43. Fields, "Ideology and Race in American History," in *Region, Race, and Reconstruction.*

44. Ibid., p. 155.

45. Lott, *Love and Theft,* chap. 8.

46. David Potter, *The Impending Crisis* (New York: Harper and Row, 1976); Michael Holt, *The Political Crisis of the 1850s* (New York: Wiley, 1978); and Kenneth Stampp, *America in 1857, A Nation on the Brink* (New York: Oxford University Press, 1990). See also Thomas F. Gossett, *Uncle Tom's Cabin in American Culture* (Dallas: Southern Methodist University Press, 1985).

47. Lott, *Love and Theft,* pp. 213–233.

48. *The Liberator,* December 16, 1853. Quoted in Lott, *Love and Theft,* pp. 218–219.

49. Lott, *Love and Theft,* p. 223

50. On the John Brown materials, see the New York *Times* for January 2, 1860: "Wax Figure of Ossawatomie Brown. Two Spears From Harper's Ferry. Link of the Shackles That Were Cut by Coppic and Cook. Autograph Letter from John Brown." Dion Boucicault, *Plays by Dion Boucicault,* Peter Thompson, ed. (New York: Cambridge University Press, 1984).

51. Joseph Jefferson, *The Autobiography of Joseph Jefferson,* Alan S. Downer, ed. (Cambridge, Mass.: Harvard University Press, 1964), pp. 162–163.

52. Adams, *E Pluribus Barnum,* pp. 147–163.

53. See Don E. Fehrenbacher, *Slavery, Law, and Politics: The Dred Scott Case in Historical Perspective* (New York: Oxford University Press, 1981); and Stampp, *America in 1857,* esp. chap. 4.

54. As Fehrenbacher notes, "Only one thing was absolutely certain. Dred Scott had lost his eleven-year battle for freedom." *Slavery, Law, and Politics,* p. 173.

55. Quoted in the New York *Herald,* March 1, p. 7.

56. These quotations appear in various 1860 New York newspaper reviews: *Times,* March 5 and April 7; *Sunday Times,* February 25; *Herald,* February 28; *Evening Post, Sun Express,* (no dates) reprinted in *Herald,* March 1 and 2; *Commercial Advertiser, Courier and Inquirer* (no dates) reprinted in *Herald,* March 16; *Tribune,* February 27, 29, and March 12; *Frank Leslie's Illustrated Newspaper,* March 3, 10, and 24.

57. See Ronald Takaki, *Iron Cages* (New York: Oxford University Press, 1990), esp. chap. 6.

58. W. E. B. Du Bois, *The Souls of Black Folk: Essays and Sketches* (1903; rpt. New York: Fawcett, 1961), p. 17.

59. Jordan, *White Over Black,* pp. 29–32.

60. Quoted in the *Herald,* March 16, 1860, p. 7.

61. New York *Tribune,* February 29, p. 7.

62. New York *Express,* quoted in the New York *Herald,* March 1, 1860, p. 7.

63. On this topic, see George Fitzhugh, *Sociology for the South; or, the Failure of Free Society* (New York: Burt Franklin, n.d.); Takaki, *Iron Cages,* p. 124; Stampp, *America in 1857,* p. 116.

64. New York *Times,* March 5, 1860, p. 5.

65. My argument here draws on Saxton's influential study of nineteenth-century racial and class politics, *The Rise and Fall of the White Republic,* esp. parts I and II. The terms "hard" and "soft" racism are his.

66. On "ventriloquism" in nineteenth-century popular culture, see Michael Denning, *Mechanic Accents: Dime Novels and Working-class Culture in America* (London: Verso, 1987). I am thinking here of Denning's "first" form of ventriloquism, which involves "throwing one's voice into the form of another: the reformer who writes dime novels—Horatio Alger, for example," p. 83.

67. Saxton provides numerous examples of such practices among antebellum Whigs and Democrats in *The Rise and Fall of the White Republic,* pp. 67–72. See also George Frederickson, *The Black Image in the White Mind* (Middletown: Wesleyan University Press, 1987), esp. chap. 4.

68. New York *Tribune,* February 29, 1860, p. 7; March 12, 1860, p. 7. On the various political leanings of the antebellum "penny press," see Alexander Saxton, "Problems of Class and Race in the Origins of the Mass Circulation Press," *American Quarterly,* 36/2, 1984, pp. 211–234; Michael Schudson, *Discovering the News: A Social History of American Newspapers* (New York: Basic Books, 1978); and James L. Crouthamel, *Bennett's New York Herald and the Rise of the Popular Press* (Syracuse: Syracuse University Press, 1989).

69. Quoted in New York *Herald,* March 1, 1860, p. 7.

70. New York *Tribune,* January 28, 1864, p. 8.

71. In "The Emancipation of the Negro Abolitionist," Leon Litwack notes: "Equally annoying to Negroes was the patronizing attitude of some white abolitionists and the application of a double standard which strongly suggested the Negro's basic inferiority. After exiling himself to England . . . Negro abolitionist William G. Allen wrote to Garri-

son that the English treated him warmly, in contrast to the 'patronizing (and, of course, insulting) spirit, even of hundreds of the American abolitionists,' who had always seemed so overly conscious of color differences." In Martin Duberman, ed., *The Antislavery Vanguard: New Essays on the Abolitionists* (Princeton: Princeton University Press, 1965). See also Frederickson, *The Black Image in the White Mind,* pp. 107, 127, 140–144; and Stephen Jay Gould, *The Mismeasure of Man* (New York: Norton, 1981), pp. 32–35.

72. All in all, we might say this was a popular entertainment program that operated much in the same way that Slavoj Zizek has defined "successful" ideology more generally—a success defined by the moment when "even the facts which at first sight contradict it start to function as arguments in its favour." *The Sublime Object of Ideology* (London: Verso, 1989), p. 49.

73. Saxon, *P. T. Barnum,* p. 220.

74. New York *Herald,* March 9, 1867. My emphasis. See also Saxon, *P. T. Barnum,* pp. 82–85.

75. On this point, see Fields, "Ideology and Race in American History," pp. 151–152, and "Slavery, Race and Ideology in the United States of America," pp. 95–118. See also Christopher Lasch, *The World of Nations* (New York: Knopf, 1973), and David Brion Davis, *The Problem of Slavery in the Age of Revolution, 1770–1823* (Ithaca: Cornell University Press, 1975). Nathan Huggins has pointed to this pattern, too: "The oppression and exploitation of blacks would not end with emancipation. As freedmen, however, their oppression and exploitation could be rationalized as natural, given their backwardness." "The Deforming Mirror of Truth," in *Black Odyssey,* rev. ed. (New York: Vintage Books, 1990), p. iii.

76. All the quotations are from Barnum's American Museum guidebook. They are reproduced in the New York *Herald,* March 19, 1860, p. 1.

77. The phrase "scientific first principles" comes from Fields, "Ideology and Race in American History," p. 152.

78. *The Diary of George Templeton Strong,* vol. 3, entry for March 6, 1860, p. 13.

79. Ibid.

80. On his return visit on March 3, Strong described What Is It? as "palpably a little nigger." Ibid., pp. 12–13. Strong mentioned the exhibition briefly in two additional diary entries: June 6, 1860, and February 17, 1862.

81. As Loren Eiseley explains, Darwin offered but "one solitary and wary sentence upon the evolution of man" in the first edition of the *Origin of Species:* " 'Light,' he cryptically intimated in the conclusion . . . 'will be thrown on the origins of man and his history.' " *Darwin's Century: Evolution and the Men Who Discovered It* (New York: Doubleday, 1958), p. 255. See also Cynthia Eagle Russett, *Sexual Science: The Victorian Construction of Womanhood* (Cambridge, Mass.: Harvard University Press, 1989).

82. The *Origin of Species* received little attention in this country during the first months of 1860; see Richard Hofstadter, *Social Darwinism in American Thought,* rev. ed. (Boston: Beacon Press, 1955), pp. 13–14. On evolutionary science's late nineteenth-century social applications, see also Russett, *Sexual Science;* Gould, *The Mismeasure of Man;* and Peter Bowler, *Evolution: The History of an Idea,* 2nd ed. (Berkeley: University of California Press, 1989).

83. Eisley, *Darwin's Century,* pp. 6–10; A. O. Lovejoy, *The Great Chain of Being* (Cambridge, Mass.: Harvard University Press, 1942); Milton Millhauser, *Just Before Darwin* (Middletown: Wesleyan University Press, 1959); William Stanton, *The Leopard's*

Spots, Scientific Attitudes Towards Race in America 1815–1859 (Chicago: University of Chicago Press, 1960); and Jordan, *White Over Black.*

84. Quoted in the New York *Herald,* February 28, 1860, p. 1.
85. According to Eiseley, "The scholars of the eighteenth century recognized quite well that the ape stood next to man on the Scale of Nature, but they did not find this spectacle as appalling as a nineteenth-century audience listening to Thomas Huxley. There was a very simple reason for this: The *Scala Naturae* in its pure form asserts the immutability of species." *Darwin's Century,* p. 8.
86. Quoted in the New York *Herald,* February 28, 1860, p. 1.
87. New York *Times,* March 5, 1860, p. 5.
88. Quoted in the New York *Herald,* March 1, 1860, p. 7. On Fowler and American phrenology, see Russett, *Sexual Science,* pp. 19–22; Reginald Horsman, *Race and Manifest Destiny* (Cambridge, Mass.: Harvard University Press, 1981), esp. chap. 8; Madeleine Stern, *Heads and Headliners: The Phrenological Fowlers* (Norman: The University of Oklahoma Press, 1971); and John D. Davies, *Phrenology: Fad and Science, A 19th-Century American Crusade* (New Haven: Yale University Press, 1955).
89. Horsman, *Race and Manifest Destiny,* p. 143.
90. O. S. and L. N. Fowler, *New Illustrated Self-Instructor in Phrenology and Physiology* (New York: Fowler and Wells, 1859), pp. 92–95, 131–133, 138–141.
91. This reviewer may have been William Cullen Bryant, the *Evening Post's* editor. On Bryant's support for Fowler and phrenology, see Davies, *Phrenology: Fad and Science,* p. 62. On etiquette books, see John F. Kasson, *Rudeness and Civility: Manners in Nineteenth-Century Urban America* (New York: Hill and Wang, 1990).
92. On "freak" photographs, see Bogdan, *Freak Show,* pp. 11–16; Michael Mitchell, *Monsters of the Gilded Age* (Toronto: Gage Books, 1979); and William C. Darrah, *Cartes de Visite in Nineteenth Century Photography* (Gettysburg: W. C. Darrah, 1981). On Brady, see Alan Trachtenberg, *Reading American Photographs: Images as History, Mathew Brady to Walker Evans* (New York: Hill and Wang, 1989).
93. New York *Times,* February 25, 1860, p. 7.
94. Pierre Bourdieu, *Distinction: A Social Critique of the Judgment of Taste* (London: Routledge and Kegan Paul, 1984), p. 4. The quotation here—a paraphrase of Bourdieu's definition—comes from Peter Stallybrass and Allon White, *The Politics and Poetics of Transgression* (Ithaca: Cornell University Press, 1986), p. 42.
95. Leon Litwack, *North of Slavery: The Negro in the Free States, 1790–1860* (Chicago: University of Chicago Press, 1961); Litwack and August Meier, eds., *Black Leaders of the Nineteenth Century* (Urbana: University of Illinois Press, 1988); Shane White, *Somewhat More Independent: The End of Slavery in New York* (Athens: University of Georgia Press, 1991); Henry Louis Gates, Jr., "The Trope of the New Negro and the Reconstruction of the Image of the Black," in Philip Fisher, ed., *The New American Studies* (Berkeley: University of California Press, 1991); Nell Irvin Painter, *Sojourner Truth: A Life, A Symbol* (New York: Norton, 1996); Shane and Graham White, *Stylin': African-American Expressive Culture From Its Beginnings to the Zoot Suit* (Ithaca: Cornell University Press, 1998).
96. Painter, *Sojourner Truth,* pp. 185–199.
97. Frederickson, *The Black Image in the White Mind,* esp. chap. 4. Orville Dewey, *A Discourse on Slavery and the Annexation of Texas* (New York: 1844), p. 10.
98. See, for example, Karen Halttunen, *Confidence Men and Painted Women: A Study of Middle-Class Culture in America, 1830–1870* (New Haven: Yale University Press,

1982); Elaine Abelson, *When Ladies Go A-Thieving: Middle-Class Shoplifters in the Victorian Department Store* (New York: Oxford University Press, 1989); Kasson, *Rudeness and Civility;* and Tom Gunning, "Tracing the Individual Body: Photographs, Detectives, and Early Cinema," in Leo Charney and Vanessa Schwartz, eds., *Cinema and the Invention of Modern Life* (Berkeley: University of California Press, 1995).

99. Halttunen, *Confidence Men and Painted Women*, pp. 33–123.

100. Ibid, pp. 153–190.

101. Stallybrass and White, *The Politics and Poetics of Transgression*, pp. 5–6. Robert Rydell has pointed to a similar mixture: "The White City and the Midway Plaisance, were truly symbolic, but not antithetical, constructs. Rather, the vision of the future and the depiction of the nonwhite world as savage were two sides of the same coin—a coin minted in the tradition of American racism, in which the forbidden desires of whites were projected onto dark-skinned peoples, who consequently had to be degraded so white purity could be maintained." *All the World's a Fair* (Chicago: University of Chicago Press, 1984), p. 67. To this I would only add that such cultural efforts at "degradation" did not always produce images of *pure* (that is to say, unequivocal) "savagery." Indeed, as Rydell implies here, for the "projection" process to work, the viewer needed to be able to see something of him/herself in the object of desire/degradation.

4. Modern Magic

1. *Webster's Ninth New Collegiate Dictionary* (Springfield: Merriam-Webster, 1988), p. 715.

2. Keith Thomas, *Religion and the Decline of Magic* (New York: Charles Scribner's Sons, 1971), pp. 636–668.

3. Ibid., p. 660.

4. Ibid.

5. Ibid., p. 668.

6. On pre-industrial magic see also Lynn Thorndike, *A History of Magic and Experimental Science* (New York: Columbia University Press, 1923–58); Francis A. Yates, *Giordano Bruno and the Hermetic Tradition* (Chicago: University of Chicago Press, 1979); and Richard Kieckhefer, *Magic in the Middle Ages* (Cambridge: Cambridge University Press, 1989).

7. There are some important exceptions to this rule. On eighteenth and early nineteenth-century European magic in the form of "rational amusement," see Richard Altick, *The Shows of London* (Cambridge, Mass.: Harvard University Press, 1978); Barbara Maria Stafford, *Artful Science, Enlightenment Entertainment and the Eclipse of Visual Education* (Cambridge, Mass.: MIT Press, 1994); and Terry Castle, *The Female Thermometer: 18th-Century Culture and the Invention of the Uncanny* (New York: Oxford University Press, 1995). On the American side, two scholars have recently explored the career of the best-known magician of the early twentieth century: Kenneth Silverman, *Houdini!!!: The Career of Ehrich Weiss* (New York: Harper Collins, 1996); and John Kasson, *Houdini, Tarzan, and the Perfect Man: The White Male Body and the Challenge of Modernity in America* (forthcoming). Finally, there is a vast and useful literature on the history of magic written by magicians. See, for example, Milbourne Christopher, *The Illustrated History of Magic* (New York: Thomas Y. Crowell, 1973); Charles Joseph Pecor, *The Magician on the American Stage, 1752–1874* (Washington,

D.C.: Emerson and West, 1977); and Ricky Jay, *Learned Pigs & Fireproof Women* (New York: Warner Books, 1986).

8. Max Weber, *Economy and Society*, vol. 1 (Berkeley: University of California Press, 1978), esp. chap. 6.

9. Dr. Paul Carus, "Introduction," in Henry Ridgely Evans, *The Old and the New Magic* (Chicago: Open Court, 1906), pp. xviii–xix.

10. On technical innovations see Christopher, *Illustrated History of Magic*, chaps. 7–13.

11. H. J. Burlingame, *Herrmann the Magician, His Life; His Secrets* (Chicago: Laird and Lee, 1897), pp. 48–49.

12. This was perhaps the most frequently quoted statement in late nineteenth-century magic. It seems to have originated with Robert-Houdin, *Comment on Devient Sorcier: Les Secrets de la Prestidigitation et de la Magie* (1878; rpt. Paris: Ressources, 1980), p. 29.

13. H. J. Burlingame, *History of Magic and Magicians* (Chicago: Charles L. Burlingame, 1895), p. 5. In the *Houdini Pamphlets: Magic and Tricks*, 13/1. Harry Houdini Collection, Library of Congress (hereafter cited as HHC).

14. This essay served as the introduction to Albert A. Hopkins, ed., *Magic: Stage Illusions and Scientific Diversions including Trick Photography* (New York: Munn, 1898), p. 6.

15. Carus, "Introduction," in Evans, *The Old and the New Magic*, pp. xvi–xviii.

16. *The Compact Oxford English Dictionary*, 2nd ed. (Oxford: Oxford University Press, 1991), p. 1791. Scot's *Discoverie* of 1584 is generally described as the first English how-to manual on conjuring, although its more specific goal was to refute an epidemic of late sixteenth-century witch-hunters by demonstrating that many magic tricks could be achieved through natural means. It is now available in a reprint edition (New York: Dover, 1972). See also Arthur F. Kinney, ed., *Rogues, Vagabonds & Sturdy Beggars: A New Gallery of Tudor and Early Stuart Rogue Literature* (Amherst: University of Massachusetts Press, 1990). This anthology contains a reprint of Samuel Rid's *The Art of Juggling* (1612).

17. On this issue, see Matei Calinescu, *Five Faces of Modernity* (Durham: Duke University Press, 1987).

18. For a more complete history of Robertson's career, see his autobiography, *Mémoires récréatifes, scientifiques et anecdotiques d'un physicien-aéronaute*, 2 vols. (Paris: 1831–33); David Robinson, "Robinson on Robertson," *New Magic Lantern Journal*, 4/1, 2, 3 (April 1986); Terry Castle, "Phantasmagoria," *Critical Inquiry*, 15/1 (Autumn 1988); and X. Theodore Barber, "Phantasmagorical Wonders: The Ghost Show in Nineteenth-Century America," *Film History*, 3 (1989), pp. 73–86.

19. Most scholars attribute the invention of the magic lantern to one of two seventeenth-century figures, Christiaen Huygens or Athanasius Kircher.

20. On the technology of the phantasmagoria see John Allen, *The Magic Lantern; Its Invention and History: With Full Directions for Its Use* (London: Dean and Son, n.d.); R. Child Bayley, *Modern Magic Lanterns, A Guide to the Management of the Optical Lantern, for the Use of Entertainers, Lecturers, Photographers, Teachers, and Others* (London: L. Upcott Gill, 1896); *The Magic Lantern, How to Buy and How to Use It, Also How to Raise a Ghost, by a "Mere Phantom"* (London: Houlston and Sons, 1880).

21. On phantasmagoria as metaphor, see Castle, "Phantasmagoria"; Susan Buck-Morss, *The Dialectics of Seeing: Walter Benjamin and the Arcades Project* (Cambridge, Mass.: MIT Press, 1989); and Martin Jay, *Downcast Eyes* (Berkeley: University of California Press, 1993).

22. Fulgence Marion, *L' Optique* (C. W. Quin, trans.), quoted in *The Magic Lantern, Its Principles and How to Use It* (New York: De Witt Publisher, c. 1890).

23. Ibid., p. 7.

24. Ibid.

25. Ibid., pp. 7–8.

26. Hopkins, ed., *Magic: Stage Illusions and Scientific Diversions including Trick Photography*, p. 7.

27. See, for example, Barber, "Phantasmagorical Wonders," pp. 84–85; and Erik Barnouw, *The Magician and the Cinema* (New York: Oxford University Press, 1981).

28. Quoted in Castle, "Phantasmagoria," p. 35. According to Castle, the author of this review was Armand Poultier and first appeared in *L'Ami des Lois*, 8, Germinal, Year VI (March 28, 1798).

29. Christopher, *Illustrated History of Magic*, pp. 82–96.

30. Andrew Oehler, *The Life, Adventures, and Unparalleled Sufferings of Andrew Oehler* (Trenton: 1811). HHC. See also Erik Barnouw, "The Fantasms of Andrew Oehler," in *Quarterly Review of Film Studies*, 9 (Winter 1984), pp. 40–44.

31. Andrew Oehler, *The Life, Adventures, and Unparalleled Sufferings*, pp. 128–129.

32. Ibid., p. 131.

33. Ibid., p. 129.

34. Ibid., pp. 222–223.

35. Pecor, *The Magician on the American Stage*, pp. 13–123. On antitheatrical prejudice, see David Grimstead, *Melodrama Unveiled, American Theater and Culture 1800–1850* (Chicago: University of Chicago Press, 1968); David R. Brigham, *Public Culture in the Early Republic: Peale's Museum and Its Audience* (Washington, D.C.: Smithsonian Institution Press, 1995); and Bruce C. Daniels, *Puritans at Play: Leisure and Recreation in Colonial New England* (New York: St. Martin's Griffin, 1995).

36. Christopher, *The Illustrated History of Magic*, pp. 48–68.

37. George C. Odell, *Annals of the New York Stage* (New York: Columbia University Press, 1928–1949), vol. 2, pp. 304–305.

38. Charles Coleman Sellers, *Charles Willson Peale* (New York: Charles Scribner's Sons, 1969), p. 336.

39. William Frederick Pinchbeck, *Expositor; or Many Mysteries Unravelled* (Boston: 1805).

40. Stafford, *Artful Science*, pp. 72–130.

41. As Jackson Lears has noted, it was not until 1831 that magic was used as a synonym for sleight of hand—a linguistic shift which probably grew out of the changes I am describing here. *Fables of Abundance: A Cultural History of Advertising in America* (New York: Basic Books, 1994), p. 421.

42. Odell, *Annals of the New York Stage*, vol. 4, pp. 43–44.

43. Signor (Antonio) Blitz, *Fifty Years in the Magic Circle; Being an Account of the Author's Professional Life; His Wonderful Tricks and Feats; With Laughable Incidents, and Adventures as a Magician, Necromancer, and Ventriloquist* (Hartford: Belknap and Bliss, 1872), esp. pp. 34–112.

44. Ibid., p. 114.

45. Pecor, *The Magician on the American Stage*, dates the dawning of this Golden Age between 1850 and 1874.

46. These articles appeared in Houdini's journal, *The Conjurers' Monthly Magazine*, between September 1906 and 1908.

47. Silverman, *Houdini!*, pp. 93–95, 125–134.

48. Harry Houdini, *The Unmasking of Robert-Houdin* (New York: The Publishers' Printing Co., 1908), p. 7.
49. In his introduction to the Dover reprint of Robert-Houdin's autobiography, Milbourne Christopher suggests that Houdini's change of heart may have been the result of a snub by the French magician's son, Emile. *Memoirs of Robert-Houdin* (New York: Dover Publications, 1964), p. viii.
50. Houdini, *The Unmasking of Robert-Houdin*, pp. 8–9.
51. Ibid., p. 51. These quotations are from Houdini. The Library of Congress contains two American editions of Robert-Houdin's autobiography from 1859: *Memoirs of Robert-Houdin: Ambassador, Author, and Conjurer* (Philadelphia: G. G. Evans); and *Life of Robert Houdin; The King of the Conjurers* (Philadelphia: Porter and Coates). Hereafter, I will cite the G. G. Evans edition. There is also a modern facsimile edition: Lascelles Wraxal, transl., *Memoirs of Robert-Houdin* (New York: Dover Publications, 1964).
52. Houdini, *The Unmasking of Robert-Houdin*, pp. 51–82.
53. Ibid., pp. 318–319.
54. Ibid., p. 43.
55. For a discussion of this publishing history, see Milbourne Christopher's introduction to the Dover edition of *Memoirs of Robert-Houdin*.
56. Predecessors such as William Pinchbeck's *Expositor* (1805), Andrew Oehler's *Life* (1811), and Etienne-Gaspard Robertson's *Memoires* (1834) did not explicitly discuss magic as a career choice and were not considered foundational texts by subsequent generations of magicians.
57. Robert-Houdin, *Memoirs of Robert-Houdin*, p. 18.
58. Ibid., p. 20.
59. Ibid., pp. 27–34.
60. Ibid., pp. 52–58.
61. Ibid., pp. 36–56.
62. Milbourne Christopher makes this point in the *Memoirs of Robert-Houdin* (p. 326). Some French biographers of Robert-Houdin have concluded that Torrini was simply an invention designed to "spice up" the early years of the *Confidences*. See, for example, Jean Chavigny, *Robert-Houdin, Rénovateur de la Magie Blanche* (Blois, 1969).
63. The 1806 edition of Noah Webster's *Compendious Dictionary of the English Language*, for example, defined a "juggler" as "one who juggles, a cheat, a deceiver." On early modern usage, see Stephen Greenblatt, *Shakespearean Negotiations* (Berkeley: University of California Press, 1988), pp. 40–65; and Alfred F. Kinney, ed., *Rogues, Vagabonds, & Sturdy Beggars: A New Gallery of Tudor and Early Stuart Rogue Literature* (Amherst: University of Massachusetts Press, 1990), pp. 1–8, 11–57, 315.
64. Robert-Houdin, *Memoirs of Robert-Houdin*, p. 32.
65. Ibid., p. 33.
66. In many of these respects, Robert-Houdin's story of Torrini resembles another cultural fable from the very same time period: T. D. Rice's oft-repeated tale of encountering a poor African-American man "jumping Jim Crow" on the Cincinnati levee in 1831.
67. See, for example, R. W. Malcolmson, *Popular Recreations in English Society 1700–1850* (Cambridge: Cambridge University Press, 1973); and Altick, *The Shows of London*. Peter Burke marks the decline of carnival around 1800, in *Popular Culture in Early Modern Europe* (New York: Harper and Row, 1978).

68. Peter Stallybrass and Allon White, *The Politics and Poetics of Transgression* (Ithaca: Cornell University Press, 1986), pp. 32–35.
69. Robert-Houdin, *Memoirs of Robert-Houdin*, p. 137.
70. Ibid., pp. 140–141.
71. Ibid., p. 155.
72. Ibid., p. 231.
73. On this model of bourgeois exhibitions and commodity display, see Rosalind Williams, *Dream Worlds: Mass Consumption in Late 19th-Century France* (Berkeley: University of California Press, 1982); Thomas Richards, *The Commodity Culture of Victorian England* (Stanford: Stanford University Press, 1990); and Robert W. Rydell, *All the World's a Fair* (Chicago: University of Chicago Press, 1984).
74. Robert-Houdin, *Memoirs of Robert-Houdin*, p. 236. On the Palais Royal, see Robert Isherwood, *Farce and Fantasy: Popular Entertainment in Eighteenth-Century Paris* (New York: Oxford University Press, 1986), pp. 217–255.
75. Robert-Houdin, *Memoirs of Robert-Houdin,* pp. 234–235.
76. Ibid., pp. 235–236.
77. The trick here is that Robert-Houdin often pointed to the bad fashion sense of previous magicians as *evidence* of their unenlightened condition (the "carnival juggler" who wears "wizard's robes," for example). It is also important to note that this modernist persona was routinely figured as white, European, and male—a pattern which becomes much clearer in a subsequent chapter of *Confidences,* in which Robert-Houdin describes a government-sponsored trip to Algeria to put down an anticolonial uprising using magic tricks. American magicians seem to have been less immediately concerned with non-Western threats/subtexts during the antebellum decades. But that changed dramatically at the turn of the twentieth century, as denunciations of "Oriental jugglery" and staged contests with a wide variety of Asian magicians became standard features of American magic—right on the heels of the Open Door policy, the Spanish-American War, and the Boxer Rebellion. See Christopher, *Illustrated History of Magic,* pp. 241–258.
78. Robert-Houdin, *Memoirs of Robert-Houdin,* pp. 251–252.
79. Ibid., p. 1.
80. This first use of the term "modern" in relation to magic appeared in playbills for Robert-Houdin's 1848 run at the St. James Theater. See Christopher, *The Illustrated History of Magic,* p. 147.
81. Robert-Houdin, *Memoirs of Robert-Houdin,* pp. 319–322, 330–334.
82. H. J. Burlingame, *Leaves from the Conjurer's Scrap Books* (Chicago: Donohue, Henneberry, 1891), p. 11; and *Herrmann the Magician,* p. 55
83. Evans, *Magic and Its Professors,* pp. 18–19. Many Americans outside the conjuring industry were impressed, too. Brander Mathews, a professor of literature at Columbia University, described *Confidences* as "worthy of comparison with all but the very best autobiographies—if not with Cellini's and Franklin's, at least with Cibber's and Gibbon's." Quoted in Evans, *The Old and the New Magic,* p. 124.
84. See Carl Herrmann, *Prestidigitatorial Collection of Humorous and Practical Tricks, Played by the Great Prestidigitateur Herrmann, During His Travels in Europe and America* (New York: Wynkoop, Hallenbeck & Thomas, 1861); Burlingame, *Leaves from the Conjurer's Scrap Books,* pp. 64–69; "Carl Herrmann in America," *The Sphinx,* 3/2 (April 1904), p. 19; Christopher, *Illustrated History of Magic,* pp. 181–190; and Pecor, *The Magician on the American Stage,* pp. 255–277.

85. A French workman had been selling "replicas" of Robert-Houdin's equipment to rival magicians, which could account for the similarity of the show. Christopher, *Illustrated History of Magic*, p. 182.

86. New Orleans *Daily Picayune*, April 10, 1861.

87. On the Astor Place Riot and stratification, see Peter Buckley, "To the Opera House: Culture and Society in New York City, 1820–1860," Ph.D. diss., State University of New York at Stony Brook, 1984; and Lawrence W. Levine, *Highbrow/Lowbrow: The Emergence of Cultural Hierarchy in America* (Cambridge, Mass.: Harvard University Press, 1988).

88. New York *Daily Tribune*, September 16, 1861.

89. Ibid., September 11, 1861.

90. Ibid., September 15, 1861.

91. Ibid., September 17, 1861.

92. New York *Herald*, September 22, 1861.

93. New York *Times*, September 19, 1861.

94. Ibid., September 16, 1861.

95. Ibid., September 17, 1861.

96. New York *Leader*, September 21, 1861.

97. Robert Heller's real name was William Henry Palmer. He was born in England in 1826 and decided to become a stage magician after witnessing one of Robert-Houdin's shows. *Illustrated History of Magic*, pp. 211–212.

98. Pecor, *The Magician on the American Stage*, pp. 234–240, 283; Christopher, *Illustrated History of Magic*, pp. 192, 217; Harry Kellar, *A Magician's Tour, Up and Down and Around the Earth, Being the Life and Adventures of the American Nostradamus* (Chicago: Donohue, Henneberry, 1886), pp. 200–207.

99. Between Robert-Houdin's 1858 *Confidences* and Houdini's 1908 *Unmasking*, virtually all major stage magicians—John Henry Anderson, Carl Herrmann, Robert Heller, Antonio Blitz, John Neville Maskelyne, Harry Kellar, and Alexander Herrmann—published autobiographies, travel anecdotes, histories of magic, and how-to books for their most famous tricks. See, for example: John Henry Anderson, *Twenty-Five Cent's Worth of Magic and Mystery* (New York: Wynkoop, Hallenbeck & Thomas, 1860); Carl Herrmann, *Prestidigitatorial Collection of Humorous and Practical Tricks;* Signor (Antonio) Blitz, *Fifty Years in the Magic Circle;* John Nevil Maskelyne, *The History of a Mystery* (Brighton: J. F. Eyles, 1873); Harry Kellar, *A Magician's Tour;* Alexander Herrmann, *Herrmann's Black Art: A Treatise on Magical Sciences, Witchcraft, Alchemy, Mesmerism, etc.* (New York: Street and Smith Publishers, 1890); and Robert Heller, *Heller's Hand-Book of Magic and Its Mysteries* (New York: Street and Smith Publishers, 1891).

100. Burton Bledstein, *The Culture of Professionalism* (New York: Norton, 1976), pp. 31–37.

101. The best known example of this pattern is Herman Melville's 1857 novel, *The Confidence Man*. For scholarly discussion, see Johannes Dietrich Bergmann, "The Original Confidence Man," *American Quarterly*, 21 (Fall 1969), pp. 560–577; Gary Lindbergh, *The Confidence Man in American Literature* (New York: Oxford University Press, 1982); Karen Halttunen, *Confidence Men and Painted Women: A Study of Middle-Class Culture in America, 1830–1870* (New Haven: Yale University Press, 1982); and the "Historical Note" in Herman Melville, *The Confidence Man* (Chicago: Northwestern University Press, 1984), pp. 276–285.

102. Halttunen, *Confidence Men and Painted Women*, pp. 1–6.

103. See ibid.; Alan Trachtenberg, *Reading American Photographs* (New York: Noonday Press, 1989); Elaine S. Abelson, *When Ladies Go A-Thieving: Middle-Class Shoplifters in the Victorian Department Store* (New York: Oxford University Press, 1990); John Kasson, *Rudeness & Civility: Manners in Nineteenth-Century Urban America* (New York: Hill and Wang, 1990); Stuart M. Blumin, "George Foster and the Emerging Metropolis," in *New York by Gas-Light* (Berkeley: University of California Press, 1990); Ann Fabian, *Card Sharps, Dream Books, & Bucket Shops: Gambling in 19th-Century America* (Ithaca: Cornell University Press, 1990); Lears, *Fables of Abundance;* and Tom Gunning, "Tracing the Individual Body: Photography, Detectives, and Early Cinema," in Leo Charney and Vanessa R. Schwartz, eds., *Cinema and the Invention of Modern Life* (Berkeley: University of California Press, 1995).

104. Kasson, *Rudeness & Civility,* pp. 70–71.

105. Helen Campbell, et al., *Darkness and Daylight; or, Light and Shadows of New York* (Hartford: Hartford Publishing Group, 1895), pp. 694–695.

106. "General City News" section of the New York *Times,* September 15–23, 1861.

107. Roger Lane, *Policing the City: Boston 1822–1885* (Cambridge, Mass.: Harvard University Press, 1967), pp. 143–144. Halttunen cites these numbers as well.

108. Robert-Houdin, *Memoirs of Robert-Houdin,* pp. 209–213.

109. On this issue, see Fabian, *Card Sharps, Dream Books, & Bucket Shops,* pp. 55–70.

110. Robert-Houdin, *Memoirs of Robert-Houdin,* p. 213.

111. Ibid., pp. 213–214.

112. Ibid., p. 214.

113. See, for example, Paul Boyer, *Urban Masses and Moral Order in America, 1820–1920* (Cambridge, Mass.: Harvard University Press, 1978). For an alternative approach, see David S. Reynold's discussion of "subversive reform" in *Beneath the American Renaissance: The Subversive Imagination in the Age of Emerson and Melville* (New York: Knopf, 1988).

114. Robert-Houdin, *Memoirs of Robert-Houdin,* p. 215.

115. "Whatever, dear reader, may be the value you attach to the knowledge of the knaveries I am about to reveal to you, you will assuredly never pay so dearly for them as I have. You will easily understand, that the tricks and impostures exposed in this work, are not the invention of my own brain." Robert-Houdin, *The Sharper Detected and Exposed* (London: Chapman & Hall, 1863), p. 1

116. Carl Herrmann, *Prestidigitatorial Collection of Humorous and Practical Tricks,* pp. 12–13.

117. William E. Robinson, "Alexander Herrmann Prestidigitateur," *Scientific American,* March 20, 1897; "Alexander Herrmann," *The Sphinx,* 2/3 (May 1903); "Two Great Magicians. Carl and Alexander Herrmann," *Mahatma,* June and July 1898; H. J. Burlingame, *Herrmann the Magician, His Life; His Secrets;* C. A. George Newmann, "Scrapbook on the Herrmanns," #52, McManus-Young Collection, Library of Congress; Henry Ridgely Evans, *The Old and the New Magic;* and the newspaper obituaries following his death on December, 17, 1896.

118. See, for example, the ads for Carl Herrmann in the New York *Times,* September, 1869. Alexander is listed here as a co-star.

119. Alexander Herrmann's published items include: "The Art of Magic," *North American Review,* July 1891; "Jugglery," *Scientific American Supplement,* September 5, 1891; "Some Adventures of the Necromancer," *North American Review,* October 1892; and "Light on the Black Art," *Cosmopolitan,* December 1892. For photographs of Alexan-

der Herrmann's yacht and mansion, see Christopher, *Illustrated History of Magic,* p. 191. Adelaide Herrmann went on to a long and successful vaudeville career following her husband's death in 1896.

120. In addition to Kellar's autobiography, see Harry Houdini Scrapbook #45, HHC; Harry Kellar Folder, McManus-Young Collection, Library of Congress Rare Books Division; Ridgely Evans, *The Old and the New Magic;* Burlingame, *Leaves from the Conjurer's Scrap Books;* "Harry Kellar," *Conjurers' Monthly Magazine,* 2/11 (July 15, 1908); and the newspaper obituaries following his death on March 10, 1922. Kellar never achieved quite the same level of literary celebrity as Alexander Herrmann, but he did have a few successes here, too: "How I Do My Tricks," *Ladies Home Journal,* November 1891.

121. Virtually everything published under the names of these two performers included at least a couple exposés of card-sharping or fraudulent medium tricks. In addition to the items cited above by Alexander Herrmann, see *Herrmann's Hand-Book of Parlor Magic* (New York: Dick & Fitzgerald, n.d.); *Herrmann's Little Jokes and Some Amusing Tricks* (New York: Excelsior Publishing House, 1897); and *Herrmann's Conjuring for Amateurs* (Chicago: Henneberry, 1901). Publications which list Kellar as author include *Kellar's Variety Entertainments* (Chicago: Henneberry, n.d.); and *Kellar's Wizard's Manual* (Philadelphia: Royal, n.d.).

122. "Kellar's Circus," New York *Evening Sun,* March 21, 1889. In Houdini Scrapbook, #45, HHC.

123. Ibid.

124. This is from a New York *Sun* article, "Turning the Tables on a Policeman" (no date), reprinted in *Herrmann's Little Jokes and Some Amusing Tricks,* pp. 16–18.

125. Ibid. For additional descriptions of this promotional technique, see Burlingame, *Herrmann the Magician,* pp. 80, 97–98; and *Herrmann's Little Jokes and Some Amusing Tricks,* pp. 24–25. During his 1861 run in New York City, Carl Herrmann performed impromptu sleight of hand at Washington Square Market, too: *Prestidigitatorial Collection of Humorous and Practical Tricks,* p. 9. The elder Herrmann, however, seems to have taken a somewhat different approach: whereas Alexander actually simulated various swindling activities—allowing his own identity to merge briefly with the swindler's—Carl simply used public markets as an alternative stage for his sleight of hand.

5. Queer Art Illusions

1. Walter Benjamin, "On Some Motifs in Baudelaire," in *Illuminations,* transl. Harry Zohn (New York: Schocken Books, 1968), p. 197.

2. "A picture like Monet's 'Cathedral at Chartres', which is like an ant heap of stone, would be an illustration of this hypothesis" (*Illuminations,* p. 197). As far as I have been able to determine, there is no such Chartres Cathedral painting. Benjamin probably meant Monet's famous Rouen Cathedral series of 1894. I am grateful to Margaretta Lovell, who first alerted me to this discrepancy, and to T. J. Clark, who confirmed the nonexistence of a Chartres Cathedral painting by Monet.

3. Benjamin, *Illuminations,* pp. 160–194.

4. Hal Foster, ed., *Vision and Visuality* (Seattle: Bay Press, 1988); Jonathan Crary, *Techniques of the Observer: On Vision and Modernity in the Nineteenth Century* (Cam-

bridge, Mass.: MIT Press, 1990); Martin Jay, *Downcast Eyes: The Denigration of Vision in Twentieth-Century French Thought* (Berkeley: University of California Press, 1993); and Nicholas Mirzoeff, ed., *The Visual Culture Reader* (New York: Routledge, 1998).

5. For examples of this view, see Alfred Frankenstein, *After the Hunt: William Harnett and Other Still Life Painters, 1870–1900,* rev. ed. (Berkeley: University of California Press, 1969); William H. Gerdts, *Painters of the Humble Truth: Masterpieces of American Still Life, 1801–1939* (Columbia: University of Missouri Press, 1981); and John Wilmerding, *Important Information Inside: The Art of John Peto and the Idea of Still Life Painting in Nineteenth-Century America* (New York: Harper and Row, 1983). Wilmerding is less insistent on this point, connecting Peto's choices of subject matter to late nineteenth-century contexts even as he argues for seventeenth-century Dutch still life and the Peales as the primary aesthetic influences.

6. The term "retrogression" comes from Frankenstein: "When he left the Academy, Harnett did not move forward, as Eakins did, but backward; he quickly made an astonishing, fruitful retrogression to a still life style that had flourished in Philadelphia three-quarters of a century earlier." *After the Hunt,* p. 31.

7. Robert Hughes, for example, has argued that Harnett's work represented "the end of an older tradition, that of the allegorical table piece, the *vanitas* paintings that were so popular in the Netherlands in the 17th century." "A Reliable Bag of Tricks," *Time,* May 11, 1992, p. 61.

8. A number of recent essays have argued against the retrogression thesis. Those especially helpful for this chapter include: Barry Maine, "Late Nineteen-Century Trompe L'Oeil and Other Performances of the Real," in *Prospects,* 16 (1991); Paul J. Staiti, "Illusionism, Trompe L'Oeil, and the Perils of Viewership," in Doreen Bolger, Marc Simpson, and John Wilmerding, eds., *William M. Harnett,* exhibition catalog (New York: Harry N. Abrams, 1992); Johanna Drucker, "Harnett, Haberle, and Peto: Visuality and Artifice among the Proto-Modern Americans," *The Art Bulletin,* 74/1 (March 1992), pp. 37–50; and David M. Lubin, *Picturing a Nation: Art and Social Change in Nineteenth-Century America* (New Haven: Yale University Press, 1994).

9. See, for example, Charles Sterling, *Still Life Painting: From Antiquity to the Twentieth Century* (New York: Harper and Row, 1981); Drucker, "Harnett, Haberle, and Peto," p. 38; and Lubin, *Picturing a Nation,* p. 273.

10. Jean Baudrillard, "The Trompe L'Oeil," in Norman Bryson, ed., *Calligram: Essays in New Art History From France* (Cambridge: Cambridge University Press, 1988), p. 53.

11. Ibid., pp. 53–54.

12. Nicolai Cikovsky, Jr., " 'Sordid Mechanics' and 'Monkey Talents': The Illusionistic Tradition," in Bolger, Simpson, and Wilmerding, eds., *William M. Harnett,* p. 19.

13. For information about the careers of these artists see Frankenstein, *After the Hunt.* On Haberle, see also Robert F. Chirico, "John Haberle and *Trompe-L'Oeil,*" *Marsyas,* 19 (1977–78), pp. 37–43; and Gertrude Grace Sill, *John Haberle: Master of Illusion,* exhibition catalog (Springfield, Mass.: Museum of Fine Arts, 1985). On the rediscovery of Harnett in 1935, see Elizabeth Johns, "Harnett Enters Art History," in *William M. Harnett,* pp. 101–112. I have quite deliberately chosen not to include John Peto in this list of followers, despite the fact that he and Harnett were personal acquaintances and have long been linked to one another in the art historical literature. The reason is straightforward: Peto's less illusionistic canvases rarely sparked the sorts of popular furors that constitute my primary subject in this chapter. For a discussion of this differ-

ence, see Frankenstein, *After the Hunt,* pp. 109–111; and Wilmerding, *Important Information Inside.*

14. On the broad scope and volume of late nineteenth-century *trompe l'oeil,* see Frankenstein, *After the Hunt,* esp. pp. 125–160.

15. On this issue see Henry Adams, "A Study in Contrasts," in *William M. Harnett,* pp. 62–64.

16. "Painted Like Real Things: The Man Whose Pictures Are a Wonder and a Puzzle," interview in the *New York News,* 1889 or 1890. This newspaper interview has proven remarkably resistant to years of archival searching by historians. For the 1992 retrospective exhibition of Harnett's career, in fact, a large group of scholars were unable to locate an original copy anywhere in the United States. Yet we know that this article did appear. It exists on film (without a specific date visible) in the Smithsonian Institution's Archives of American Art (Alfred Frankenstein Papers, reel 1374, 945). And it is quoted extensively in Frankenstein, *After the Hunt,* pp. 29, 54–56.

17. Ibid. James Edward Kelley—a sculptor and illustrator in New York during these years—described Harnett's apartment during the 1870s as a "rickety old two-story tenement" with "the smallest, coolest cook's stove in the city" (*After the Hunt,* p. 38).

18. Doreen Bolger, "The Patrons of the Artist: Emblems of Commerce and Culture," *William M. Harnett,* pp. 73–85.

19. For a discussion of the rhetoric unleashed against Manet and the French Impressionists, see T. J. Clark, *The Painting of Modern Life: Paris in the Art of Manet and his Followers* (Princeton: Princeton University Press, 1984).

20. Clarence Cook, "Academy of Design: Fifty-fourth Annual Exhibition, New York *Daily Tribune,* April 26, 1879, p. 5.

21. Ibid. For a discussion of imitation as a larger cultural concern during these years, see Miles Orvell, *The Real Thing: Imitation and Authenticity in American Culture* (Chapel Hill: University of North Carolina Press, 1989).

22. New York *Daily Tribune,* April 26, 1879, p. 5.

23. Staiti, "Illusionism, Trompe L'Oeil, and the Perils of Viewership," *William M. Harnett,* p. 43. Staiti is quoting here from Barnum's autobiography.

24. For discussions of Harnett's conventional subjects, see *William M. Harnett,* pp. 161–167. 211–307.

25. Quoted in Frankenstein, *After the Hunt,* p. 55.

26. Roland Barthes, "The Reality Effect," in *The Rustle of Language* (Berkeley: University of California Press, 1989), pp. 141–148.

27. David R. Nickel, "Harnett and Photography," in *William M. Harnett,* pp. 177–183.

28. Stephen Oettermann, *The Panorama: History of a Mass Medium,* transl. by Deborah Lucas Schneider (New York: Zone Books, 1997). For a more focused discussion of the panorama in the United States, see: John L. Marsh, "Drama and Spectacle by the Yard: The Panorama in America," in *Journal of Popular Culture,* 10 (Winter 1976), pp. 581–590; Hans Bergmann, "Panoramas of New York, 1845–1860," *Prospects,* 10 (1985), pp. 119–137; and Robert Wernick, "History From a Grandstand Seat," *Smithsonian,* 16/5 (August 1985), pp. 68–85.

29. Oettermann, *The Panorama,* pp. 313–314.

30. Ibid., pp. 314, 342–343.

31. Ibid., p. 51.

32. Ibid., pp. 49–83.

33. "Art Notes," *Daily Transcript,* December 30, 1884. This review is quoted in a souvenir program attached to the exhibition: *Cyclorama of the Battle of Gettysburg, by Paul Philippoteaux,* n.d.
34. This arrangement is visible, for example, in a photo entitled "World-renowned Café of Theodore Stewart," in the collections of the New York Historical Society.
35. Quoted in "It Fooled the Cat," New Haven *Evening Leader,* June 10, 1893.
36. Ibid.
37. Jane Marlin, "John Haberle: A Remarkable Contemporaneous Painter in Detail," *The Illustrated American,* December 30, 1898, pp. 517–518.
38. Frankenstein, *After the Hunt,* p. 95.
39. Untitled article from the London *Commercial Gazette,* quoted in Frankenstein, *After the Hunt,* p. 79; "Quotations from the Cincinnati Papers," reprinted on a trade card for "The Old Violin" published by the F. Tuchfaber Company, 1886; *Saint Paul and Minneapolis Pioneer Press,* September 16, 1887.
40. "Another Very Great Day," *Saint Paul and Minneapolis Pioneer Press,* September 16, 1887.
41. These comments come from George Murray's reviews of Raphaelle Peale's entries to the Pennsylvania Academy of the Fine Arts in *The Port Folio,* July 1812 and July 1814, quoted in Nicolai Cikovsky, Jr., *Raphaelle Peale Still Lifes* (New York: Henry Abrams, 1988), pp. 100–101. Cikovsky's essay in the same catalog, "Democratic Illusions," provides a useful overview of the Peales' *trompe l'oeil* painting.
42. One probably apocryphal story is told about an elderly George Washington standing silently before Charles Willson Peale's *Staircase Group* and bowing to the human figures in the painting before he left. See Charles Coleman Sellers, *Mr. Peale's Museum* (New York: Norton, 1980), pp. 93–94.
43. Untitled article from the London *Commercial Gazette,* quoted in Frankenstein, *After the Hunt,* p. 79; "Quotations from the Cincinnati Papers," reprinted on the Tuchfaber trade card for "The Old Violin."
44. Ibid.
45. Quoted in Frankenstein, *After the Hunt,* pp. 79–80. Large portions of this article also appeared in a New York *Star* article from December 30, 1885, entitled "Art's Counterfeiting." It is unclear which document appeared first. I have chosen to cite the *Commercial Gazette* as my source, as it includes a number of rich paragraphs not included in the New York *Star* text.
46. On the early challenges of city reading and their relationship to *flanerie,* see Benjamin, "On Some Motifs in Baudelaire," pp. 163–185. See also Dana Brand, *The Spectator and the City in Nineteenth-Century Literature* (Cambridge: Cambridge University Press, 1991); and Ross Posnock, *The Trial of Curiosity: Henry James, William James, and the Challenge of Modernity* (New York: Oxford University Press, 1991).
47. On Platt's estate see Frankenstein, *After the Hunt,* pp. 128–131. But Frankenstein never found *Vanishing Glories.* It is still listed as lost in the Inventory of American Art at the Smithsonian Institution.
48. These biographical details come primarily from Platt's 1899 obituaries. See, for example, the Denver *Tribune,* September 28, 1899.
49. For an inventory of the pictures in the estate of Platt's widow, Ella, see the Alfred Frankenstein Papers, Smithsonian Archives of American Art, roll 1377, no. 737.
50. *Rocky Mountain News,* September 17, 1899.

51. Alfred Frankenstein Papers, Smithsonian Archives of American Art, roll 1377, no. 685.
52. Denver *Times*, February 14, 1892. "Vanishing Glories" features prominently in St. Louis newspaper advertisements for the Exposition in mid-October, 1888.
53. St. Louis *Post-Dispatch,* September 20, 1888.
54. Ibid., September 22, 1888.
55. Ibid., September 23, 1888.
56. Ibid., September 30, 1888.
57. See, for example, the St. Louis *Post-Dispatch* articles from September 27, as well as October 1 and 6.
58. Ibid., October 1, 1888.
59. Ibid., October 12, 1888. The first mention in the *Post-Dispatch* that Platt might come to St. Louis appeared on September 24: "It is reported that Mr. Geo. Platt, who painted '*Vanishing Glories*', will be in the city soon and it is possible that he may be induced to decide the question that has caused so much discussion—whether the picture is painted on canvas or wood."
60. Ibid., October 20, 1888.
61. Lubin, *Picturing a Nation,* pp. 273–288.
62. Ibid., pp. 318–319.
63. My point here is not to disparage Lubin's argument (clearly one of the very best on the topic), but to push it further and add new wrinkles. The real issue, it seems to me, is how to explain the popular reception beyond the context of Stewart's Saloon—a somewhat exceptional exhibition venue in the larger history of *trompe l'oeil*.
64. St. Louis *Post-Dispatch,* October 2, 1888.
65. W. J. T. Mitchell, *Picture Theory* (Chicago: University of Chicago Press, 1994), pp. 331–344.
66. St. Louis *Post-Dispatch,* September 6, 1888.
67. Ibid., September 10, 1888.
68. For a discussion of this sort of disorientation in relation to early motion pictures, see Ben Singer, "Modernity, Hyperstimulus, and the Rise of Popular Sensationalism," in Leo Charney and Vanessa R. Schwartz, eds., *Cinema and the Invention of Modern Life* (Berkeley: University of California Press, 1995), pp. 72–99. On the illusory qualities of late nineteenth-century commodity culture see Rosalind Williams, *Dream Worlds: Mass Consumption in Late 19th-Century France* (Berkeley: University of California Press, 1982) and Orvell, *The Real Thing*.
69. The clippings are in the Alfred Frankenstein Papers, at the Smithsonian Archives of American Art.
70. The Denver *Daily News,* July 17, 1891.
71. *The Beacon,* 1/6 (June 1889).
72. On the European scientific literature, see Crary, *Techniques of the Observer,* and Jay, *Downcast Eyes*. Staiti relates Harnett's aesthetic tricks to William James's discussions of perceptual fallibility. "Vocally participating in a world in which the perception of objects was corrigible instead of fixed," Staiti argues, "the viewing circle around Harnett's pictures was a populist outpost of the new phenomenological psychology." *William M. Harnett,* p. 32.
73. *Studio,* n.s. 2/12 (June 1887), p. 217.
74. The term "doubts about vision" comes from Clark, *The Painting of Modern Life,* p. 12. Other scholars of French Impressionism have employed similar phrases ("a crisis of seeing," "a determination to see in new ways," and so forth). See also John Rewald, *The*

History of Impressionism (New York: Doubleday and Company, 1961); *The New Painting: Impressionism 1874–1886* (San Francisco: Fine Arts Museums, 1986); and Robert L. Herbert, *Impressionism: Art, Leisure, & Parisian Society* (New Haven: Yale University Press, 1988).

75. Drucker reaches a similar conclusion via a different route by focusing on the "formal devices" and "thematics" of American *trompe l'oeil* painting rather than on the popular reception. My one quarrel with her sophisticated essay is its concluding suggestion that the work of Harnett and Haberle was "fundamentally anti-illusionistic" (p. 48). While it is true that American *trompe l'oeil* painting broke the conventional "contract of illusion" passed down from the Renaissance, this does not mean that the painted images were read "as the things themselves" in the exhibition hall. What drove the popular furors was the paintings' nagging representational indeterminacy. Almost every viewer recognized these works as paintings, yet many continued to argue about the status of particular objects/images.

76. Clark, *The Painting of Modern Life*, pp. 20–21.

77. Crary, *Techniques of the Observer*, pp. 1–11. See also Jay, *Downcast Eyes*, pp. 113–186.

78. This anonymous article is one of a number of undated, unidentified press clippings preserved in a scrapbook by a family friend, William A. Blemly, whose father had worked with Harnett earlier in the New York silver engraving shop of Wood and Hughes. The "Blemly Scrapbook" is in the Archives of American Art, Smithsonian Institution.

79. "Blemly Scrapbook," Archives of American Art, Smithsonian Institution, reel 1374, frame 327.

80. Ibid.

Epilogue

1. P. T. Barnum, *Humbugs of the World* (New York: Carleton, 1865), p. 55.

2. Ibid., p. 56.

3. Ibid., pp. 18–21.

4. Ibid., p. 53.

5. Alfred Frankenstein, *After the Hunt: William Harnett and other American Still Life Painters 1870–1900* (Berkeley: University of California Press), p. 56.

6. Ibid., p. 82.

7. Ibid., pp. 56, 82.

8. "A Magician Unmasked," *Chicago Daily News*, June 19, 1886. The date is handwritten in the margin of the article, probably by Houdini himself, in Scrapbook #45, Harry Houdini Collection, Library of Congress.

9. "Kellar's Tricks," *Chicago Daily News*, June 23, 1886.

10. In his *Critique of Cynical Reason* (Minneapolis: University of Minnesota Press, 1987) Peter Sloterdijk has defined modern cynicism as the dominant ideological malaise of our time. Yet the skeptical consumers of the Age of Barnum seem to have lacked the darker features of current cynicism. The most obvious difference lies in the emotional tone. Whereas Sloterdijk characterizes the "cynical subject" of today as a "borderline melancholic" who "mourns for a lost innocence," Mrs. H and the Yankee Lady responded to Barnum's manipulations with a sense of gusto and agency, energy, smiles and laughs. Nineteenth-century consumers still believed it was possible to get to the bottom of things—or at least to have fun trying. On present cynicism, see also Slavoj Zizek, *The Sublime Object of Ideology* (London: Verso, 1989), pp. 1–53; Timothy

Bewes, *Cynicism and Postmodernity* (London: Verso, 1997); and Chase Madar, "Dog Days," *Lingua Franca,* October 1999, pp. 25–28.

11. This reception pattern (well-illustrated by late nineteenth-century consumers such as the Yankee Lady, Mrs. H., and Kellar's Chicago antagonist) is perhaps the most distinctly modern ideological legacy of the Age of Barnum. Long before the late twentieth-century insights of critical theory and postmodernism, in other words, many American consumers thought about, discussed, and resisted the ways that they were manipulated by the culture industry. It may just be the case, in fact, that the culture industry has *always* provoked this kind of meta-discourse. The classic scholarly critique of culture industry manipulation (first published in 1944) is Max Horkheimer and Theodor Adorno, *Dialectic of Enlightenment* (New York: Continuum, 1991), esp. pp. 120–167.

12. T. Trent Gegax and Jerry Adler, "Death in the Ring," *Newsweek,* 133/23, June 7, 1999, pp. 64–65.

13. Ibid., p. 64. See also Sharon Mazar, *Professional Wrestling: Sport and Spectacle* (Jackson: University of Mississippi Press, 1998).

Index

Index

Index

Index

Humbug: contemporary understandings of, 7, 23, 73–74, 78, 272n41; Barnum's model of, 19, 77–81, 84–104; defined by Barnum as modern, 262. *See also* Artful deception

Humbugs of the World, 78, 118, 260–262

Illusionism: Barnum's model of, 10, 19; definitions, 17–18, 23, 179, 271n28. *See also* Artful deception

Impressionism, 215–217, 220, 252, 306n74

Industrialization, 62

James, William, 250

Jefferson, Joseph, 142

Jefferson, Thomas, 91

Johnson, William Henry, 128–129, 256

Kasparov, Gary, 259

Kellar, Harry: as leading figure of modern magic, 166, 199–200; early history of, 206–208; Washington Market performance, 208–209, 211–212; retirement of, 256–257; problems of representational control, 263–264

Kempelen, Wolfgang von: early history of, 34; Pressburg workshop, 35, 37; anxieties about fraud, 47–48, 69; inventions, 48; retirement of, 49. *See also* Automaton chess-player; Trickster figure(s)

Kimball, Moses, 81, 94, 115–116, 133

Lady in Black, 284

Learned Pig, 178

Leech, Hervey, 126–128, 133

Legerdemain. *See* Magic: defined as sleight of hand

Lewis, William, 51

Lind, Jenny, 107, 117, 120, 197

Linnaeus, C., 91

Living curiosities, 18–19, 119–121

Locke, Richard Adams, 10

Lott, Eric, 141–142

Louis Philippe, 191, 194

Lubin, David, 245–246, 306n63

Lyman, Levi, 5, 81–82

Maelzel, Johann: as mentor for Barnum, 8, 66, 71; early history of, 49; inventions, 50, 53; public personas, 54–55, 62, 69, 70, 80. *See also* Automaton chess-player; Trickster figure(s)

Magic: defined as modern, 26, 166–170, 178, 181–182, 189, 191, 193–194, 198–201, 205, 205, 211, 213, 299n80; reception of, 160, 169, 180–181, 185, 193–194, 197–199; types of, 163–164; problems of periodization, 164; decline of, as supernatural phenomenon, 164–165; leading figures of, 166; defined as sleight of hand, 170–171, 176; prejudices against, 176–177, 180–181; literary exposés of, 178, 263–264; social status of, 180–181, 191, 193–194, 196–199, 202, 204, 210–211, 213; symbolic relation to crime, 189, 202–205, 208–213; professionalization of, 200; Orientalism in, 299n77

Magicians: 165, 167–168, 173, 175–177, 180, 186, 189–191, 193, 196–198, 201–204, 208–213

Market revolution, 78, 80–81, 88–89, 103, 106, 111–112, 114–116, 118, 160

Masked Magician (television show), 259

Maskelyne, John Nevil, 263, 300n99

Mermaids, 80, 83–85

Mills, George, 242–244

Missouri Compromise, 141–144

Mitchell, John Kearsley, 30, 59, 68, 72

Mitchell, W. J. T., 17, 247, 271n28

Monet, Claude, 215

Monsieur Adrien, 5

Mouret, 51, 67

Mozart, Wolfgang Amadeus, 36

Mr. Martin, 176–177

National Academy of Design, 181, 220–221, 223, 225

New middle class: definitions of, 25; tastes of, 25–26; scholarship on, 27–29; anxieties of, 26–28, 160–161, 201

New York Museum, 54, 101–102

Niblo's Gardens, 3, 181

Nickel, Douglas, 227

Index

Index

Stallybrass, Peter, 162
Stereoscope, 227
Stewart's Warren Street Saloon, 26, 230, 237–239, 246, 254–255, 262
Stowe, Harriet Beecher, 141
Strand Mermaid, 83
Stratton, Charles, 19, 119, 120, 121, 129
Strong, George Templeton, 139, 151–152
Sully, James, 250
Sultan Mohammed IV, 43
Sultan Suleiman I, 43

Taney, Roger, 122, 144
Taylor, Alanson, 82–83, 108–112, 115
Thomas, Keith, 164–165
Thomson, William, 201
Tiffany & Company, 196, 200
Tom Thumb. *See* Stratton, Charles
Trickster figure(s): Barnum as, 6, 66, 80, 99, 117–119, 223, 260; types of, 28–29, 63, 66, 70, 78, 80, 200, 259–260, 264; Kempelen as, 47–49, 260; Maelzel as, 63, 65–66, 69, 260
Trickster tales, 29, 99, 117
Trompe l'oeil painting: lineages, 20, 216; American development of, 215–217; recent scholarship on, 215–218, 235, 253; in relation to Impressionism, 215–217, 252–255; problems of periodization, 216–217, 303n6; popular cultural contexts of, 217, 223–225, 227–230, 232–234, 236, 242, 245–246; academic proscriptions against, 220–222; in relation to gender, 243–246

Truth, Sojourner, 159
Tucher, Andie, 76

Uncle Tom's Cabin, 141–142
Unmasking of Robert-Houdin, 182–186

Van Duyne, Sarah, 128–129, 133
Vaucanson, Jacques de, 35–36, 47
Virtual reality, 258
Virtuoso, 35, 87, 275n11
Visuality: scholarship on, 214–215, 253

Weber, Max, 166
Weiss, Ehrich, 167, 182–186, 257–258
What Is It?: 1860 exhibition, 121, 126, 129–133, 136–138, 143, 147–150, 156–159; reception for, during the early 1860s, 124–125, 129, 132, 139–140, 144–156, 158, 161–162; 1846 exhibition, 126–128, 133–134. *See also* Nondescript
White, Allon, 162
Wilmot Proviso, 143
Windisch, Karl G. von, 34, 41
Woolly Horse, 135–136
Woolman, John, 176

X-Files, 259

Yankee, 97–99
Yeadon, Richard, 109–110, 113–116

Zeuxis, 20, 232
Zizek, Slavoj, 293n72, 307n10